# Mondo Agnelli

# Mondo Agnelli

*Fiat, Chrysler, and the Power of a Dynasty*

Jennifer Clark

**WILEY**

John Wiley & Sons, Inc.

Published by John Wiley & Sons, Inc., Hoboken, New Jersey.
Published simultaneously in Canada.

For general information on our other products and services or for technical support, please contact our Customer Care Department within the United States at (800) 762–2974, outside the United States at (317) 572–3993 or fax (317) 572–4002.

Wiley also publishes its books in a variety of electronic formats. Some content that appears in print may not be available in electronic books. For more information about Wiley products, visit our Web site at www.wiley.com.

*Library of Congress Cataloging-in-Publication Data:*

Clark, Jennifer, 1972–
    Mondo Agnelli: Fiat, Chrysler, and the power of a dynasty / Jennifer Clark.—1
    p.  cm.
    Includes bibliographical references and index.
    ISBN 978–1–118–01852–1 (cloth); ISBN 978–1–118–22196–9 (ebk);
    ISBN 978–1–118–23611–6 (ebk); ISBN 978–1–118–24120–2 (ebk)
       1. Fiat (Firm)—History.   2. Agnelli family.   3. Businessmen—Italy.
       4. Automobile industry and trade—Italy.   I. Title.
    HD9710.I84F477 2011
    338.7'629222092245—dc23
    [B]

                                                                                    2011039738
Printed in the United States of America

10 9 8 7 6 5 4 3 2 1

*To Dino*

# Contents

"The men who have changed the universe have never gotten there by working on leaders, but rather by moving the masses. Working on leaders is the method of intrigue and only leads to secondary results. Working on the masses, however, is the stroke of genius that changes the face of the world."

—*Napoleon Bonaparte*

# Agnelli Family Tree

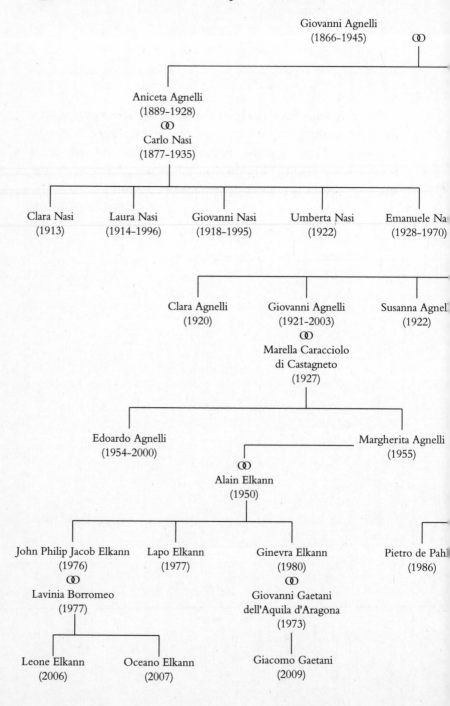

Giovanni Agnelli
(1866-1945)

Aniceta Agnelli
(1889-1928)
Carlo Nasi
(1877-1935)

Clara Nasi
(1913)

Laura Nasi
(1914-1996)

Giovanni Nasi
(1918-1995)

Umberta Nasi
(1922)

Emanuele Na
(1928-1970)

Clara Agnelli
(1920)

Giovanni Agnelli
(1921-2003)
Marella Caracciolo
di Castagneto
(1927)

Susanna Agnel
(1922)

Edoardo Agnelli
(1954-2000)

Alain Elkann
(1950)

Margherita Agnelli
(1955)

John Philip Jacob Elkann
(1976)
Lavinia Borromeo
(1977)

Lapo Elkann
(1977)

Ginevra Elkann
(1980)
Giovanni Gaetani
dell'Aquila d'Aragona
(1973)

Pietro de Pahl
(1986)

Leone Elkann
(2006)

Oceano Elkann
(2007)

Giacomo Gaetani
(2009)

Clara Boselli
(1869-1946)

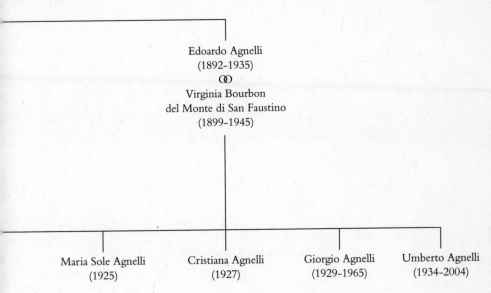

Edoardo Agnelli
(1892-1935)
∞
Virginia Bourbon
del Monte di San Faustino
(1899-1945)

Maria Sole Agnelli
(1925)

Cristiana Agnelli
(1927)

Giorgio Agnelli
(1929-1965)

Umberto Agnelli
(1934-2004)

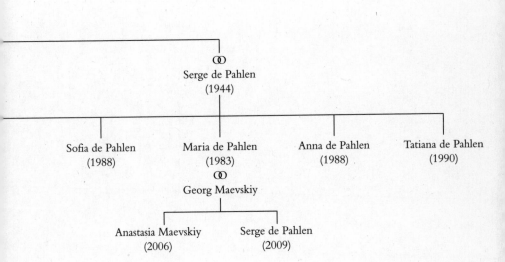

∞
Serge de Pahlen
(1944)

Sofia de Pahlen
(1988)

Maria de Pahlen
(1983)
∞
Georg Maevskiy

Anna de Pahlen
(1988)

Tatiana de Pahlen
(1990)

Anastasia Maevskiy
(2006)

Serge de Pahlen
(2009)

# Timeline

| | |
|---|---|
| **July 30, 1863** | Henry Ford is born in Dearborn, Michigan. |
| **August 13, 1866** | Giovanni Agnelli is born in Villar Perosa, near Turin. |
| **April 2, 1875** | Walter Percy Chrysler is born in Wamego, Kansas. |
| **August 5, 1882** | Italian engineer Enrico Bernardi, working in Padua, Italy, obtains patent number 14,460 for an internal combustion engine for use "in small machines." |
| **April–October 1884** | Enrico Bernardi presents motorized three-wheeled car at Turin International Exposition. |
| **January 29, 1886** | In Germany, Karl Benz patents a gasoline-powered engine, after having tested it on a three-wheeled vehicle. |
| **March 8, 1886** | Gottlieb Daimler installs an internal combustion engine of his own design on a stagecoach. |

| | |
|---|---|
| **January 2, 1892** | Edoardo Agnelli is born in Verona, Italy. |
| **May 18, 1895** | First Italian car race is held, from Turin to Asti. |
| **July 1, 1899** | Fabbrica Italiana Automobili Torino, or FIAT, is founded in Turin. |
| **November 30, 1901** | Henry Ford founds Henry Ford Company in Detroit. |
| **March 8, 1906** | Agnelli becomes largest shareholder of Fiat. |
| **April 1906** | Agnelli makes his first trip to the United States. |
| **June 23, 1908** | Agnelli and two partners are accused of market rigging in the 1906 market crash. |
| **August 12, 1908** | Ford Motor Company makes its first Model T. |
| **1912** | Agnelli visits Detroit again. |
| **July 5, 1913** | Court of Appeals confirms Agnelli's acquittal in market rigging trial. |
| **June 8, 1919** | Edoardo Agnelli marries Virginia Bourbon del Monte. |
| **September 1, 1920** | Fiat workers occupy Fiat factories. |
| **March 12, 1921** | Gianni Agnelli is born. |
| **October 28, 1922** | Benito Mussolini's March on Rome. |
| **March 1, 1923** | Giovanni Agnelli is named a senator by Benito Mussolini. |
| **July 24, 1923** | Edoardo Agnelli is named chairman of Juventus, the Agnelli family soccer team. |
| **October 25, 1923** | Fiat's Lingotto factory is inaugurated by Benito Mussolini. |
| **June 6, 1925** | Chrysler Corporation is founded. |
| **July 27, 1927** | *Senatore* Giovanni Agnelli creates family holding company IFI. |

| | |
|---|---|
| **April 12, 1932** | Fiat presents the Balilla, a successful small "people's car," at the Milan Fair. |
| **July 14, 1935** | Edoardo Agnelli, 42, dies in airplane accident. |
| **December 19, 1936** | Virginia Agnelli receives court order denying her custody of her seven children. |
| **May 15, 1939** | Mirafiori is inaugurated by visit of Benito Mussolini. |
| **June 10, 1940** | Italy enters World War II on Axis side. |
| **July 25, 1943** | Mussolini is ousted from power. |
| **September 8, 1943** | Italy announces its surrender to Allied powers, which had occupied southern half of the country. |
| **May 10, 1944** | Karl Wolff, Supreme Commander of Nazi SS forces in Italy, discusses German withdrawal with Pope Pius XII in meeting organized with help of Virginia Agnelli. |
| **November 26, 1944** | Fiat manager Vittorio Valletta is denounced by workers' committee as a traitor for collaboration with Fascist government in report made to the CLN, the de facto government of occupied Italy. |
| **January 12, 1945** | Benito Mussolini's Republic of Salò includes Fiat on a list of companies to be nationalized. |
| **April 28, 1945** | Turin is liberated by partisans; Valletta, Agnelli, and Camerana to be tried in "purge" of alleged Fascist-era collaborators. |
| **May 2, 1945** | German forces in Italy surrender. |
| **November 30, 1945** | Virginia Agnelli dies in a car accident. |
| **December 16, 1945** | *Senatore* Giovanni Agnelli dies of a heart attack. |
| **December 19, 1945** | Giovanni Agnelli and Vittorio Valletta are found not guilty of charges of Fascist collaboration. |

**December 1, 1948**     Valletta travels to Washington, D.C., to request $35 million in Marshall Plan aid to equip Fiat plants for mass production. Financing is approved on April 27, 1949.

**August 21, 1952**      Gianni Agnelli almost loses his leg in a car accident in the South of France.

**November 18, 1953**    Gianni Agnelli marries Marella Caracciolo, daughter of Prince Carlo Caracciolo.

**March 9, 1955**        Fiat 600 is presented in Geneva, eventually selling four million units.

**July 4, 1957**         Fiat Nuova 500 is launched, and will go on to sell 3.6 million cars.

**October 4, 1957**      Gianni Agnelli and David Rockefeller watch the Sputnik launch together, at a Bilderberg Group meeting in Fiuggi, Italy, starting a long friendship.

**August 7, 1962**       Jacqueline Kennedy flies to Italy for the start of a three-week vacation with Agnelli and other friends on the Amalfi coast.

**April 29, 1966**       Vittorio Valletta tells Fiat board he resigns, paving the way for Gianni Agnelli to become chairman.

**May 4, 1966**          Fiat chairman Vittorio Valetta signs protocol to build factory in the Soviet Union in Togliattigrad.

**March 30, 1969**       First of several strikes occurs, indicating a deep radicalization of Fiat's labor force.

**June 21, 1969**        Fiat buys 50 percent of Ferrari.

**October 16, 1973**     OPEC announces 70 percent increase in price of oil, leading to the first "oil shock" of the 1970s.

**May 30, 1974**         Agnelli is elected chairman of Confindustria, Italy's business lobby.

**October 18, 1974**     Cesare Romiti starts work as Fiat's finance director.

**June 20, 1975**     Umberto Agnelli is elected senator with Christian Democrat party.

**April 30, 1976**     Carlo de Benedetti joins Fiat as CEO; he leaves in August after "disagreement on company policy."

**December 1, 1976**     Agnelli announces that Libyan Arab Foreign Bank takes 9.7 percent stake in Fiat for $415 million.

**November 2, 1978**     Lee Iacocca becomes president and CEO of Chrysler.

**March 26, 1979**     OPEC announces 15 percent increase in price of oil in the wake of Iranian Revolution, touching off second oil shock.

**September 21, 1979**     Fiat's Carlo Ghiglieno is killed by Prima Linea terrorists.

**July 31, 1980**     Umberto Agnelli announces decision to step down as Fiat CEO, paving the way for massive layoffs as well as the ascent of Romiti to position of CEO.

**September 11, 1980**     Romiti announces 14,469 job cuts, touching off a strike that ends October 14 with the "March of 40,000" middle managers. Fiat abandons plan for job cuts, and instead lays off 23,000 people.

**January 20, 1983**     Fiat launches the best-selling Uno at Cape Canaveral. The car will go on to sell six million units.

**July 13, 1983**     Chrysler president and CEO Lee Iacocca pays back loan guarantee to U.S. Treasury.

**October 8, 1985**     Fiat and Ford release statement saying plans for a joint venture, which had started in the spring, were no longer on the table.

**September 23, 1986**  Agnelli family holding company IFI buys back stake from Libyan Arab Foreign Bank in order to pursue U.S. defense contracts.

**November 6, 1986**  Italian government holding company IRI SpA announces decision to sell Alfa Romeo to Fiat, which had elbowed aside Ford Motor Company at the last minute to grab the state-owned automaker.

**1989**  IFI-IFIL begins diversifying into food, tourism, and hotel businesses.

**May 10, 1990**  Chrysler chairman and CEO Lee Iacocca writes Fiat chairman Gianni Agnelli a letter outlining the benefits of a merger between Chrysler and Fiat.

**February 22, 1993**  Milan public prosecutors issue arrest warrant for Fiat finance director Paolo Mattioli; Fiat becomes one of the many companies probed for corruption in an investigation that would change the face of Italy and pave the way for Silvio Berlusconi's entry into politics.

**August 31, 1993**  Fiat Punto is unveiled, eventually becoming a top seller and symbol of Fiat's 1990s comeback.

**September 28, 1993**  Fiat is forced to ask shareholders for $3 billion capital increase; Gianni Agnelli is to stay in chairman's post until 1996, forcing Umberto—who had been in line to become chairman—to step aside a second time.

**November 15, 1993**  Fiat announces Giovanni Alberto Agnelli has been named to Fiat board. Umberto Agnelli resigns from the board.

**January 1994**  Fiat starts producing the Punto at its new high-tech, automated plant at Melfi in Basilicata, which opened in September 1993 with the help of government financing.

| | |
|---|---|
| **December 11, 1995** | Gianni Agnelli announces he is stepping down as chairman; Cesare Romiti is to take his place. |
| **April 10, 1996** | Gianni Agnelli creates Dicembre, an unlisted company holding his controlling stake in the family's limited partnership. The statutes say that administrative powers will be transferred to John Elkann in the event of Gianni's death. |
| **July 17, 1996** | Gianni Agnelli writes letter leaving Edoardo Agnelli's unwanted stake in Dicembre to John Elkann. |
| **December 13, 1997** | Giovanni Alberto Agnelli, Umberto's son, dies of a rare form of cancer. |
| **December 19, 1997** | John Elkann is named to Fiat board at age 21. |
| **May 7, 1998** | Daimler-Benz AG and Chrysler Corporation announce plans to merge in what is initially billed as a "merger of equals." |
| **March 13, 2000** | Fiat and General Motors announce partnership. |
| **November 15, 2000** | Edoardo Agnelli commits suicide. |
| **March 1, 2002** | Fiat announces 791 million euro loss for 2001, after having turned a profit in 2000,the last year it would earn a profit until 2005. |
| **May 9, 2002** | Gianni Agnelli flies to New York for prostate cancer treatment. |
| **May 27, 2002** | Fiat signs memorandum for three billion euro convertible loan with eight banks. The loan will be converted to equity in 2005 if Fiat is unable to pay it back. |
| **October 13, 2002** | Fiat top management visits Prime Minister Silvio Berlusconi at his villa to outline job cuts and recovery plan. |
| **January 24, 2003** | Gianni Agnelli dies of prostate cancer. |

| | |
|---|---|
| **February 24, 2003** | Margherita Agnelli refuses to sign papers regarding transfer of stakes in Dicembre, the company that holds Gianni Agnelli's controlling stake in Fiat. |
| **February 26, 2003** | IFIL announces appointment of Umberto Agnelli as chairman and Giuseppe Morchio as CEO. It names a new board, including Luca de Montezemolo and Sergio Marchionne. |
| **February 28, 2003** | Fiat announces a group loss of 4.3 billion euros for 2002. |
| **December 17, 2003** | Lapo Elkann, Fiat marketing executive, launches a sweatshirt with Fiat's vintage logo emblazoned across the front. |
| **February 18, 2004** | Margherita Agnelli and Marella Agnelli sign an accord agreeing on division of Gianni Agnelli's wealth. Margherita receives over one billion euros in the settlement. |
| **March 2, 2004** | The new Fiat 500 precursor, the Trepiuno, is presented at Geneva Auto Show. |
| **May 28, 2004** | Umberto Agnelli dies of cancer. |
| **June 1, 2004** | Fiat board names Sergio Marchionne as CEO, its fifth in two years. |
| **September 1, 2004** | Marchionne names new Fiat Auto management team. |
| **September 4, 2004** | John Elkann and Lavinia Borromeo marry on Lake Maggiore. |
| **February 14, 2005** | Fiat announces it has dissolved partnership with General Motors. |
| **April 23, 2005** | Fiat's creditor banks receive letter from a Lehman Brothers banker with offer from an unnamed buyer for a stake in the company. |
| **April 25, 2005** | Fiat's banks announce they will convert three billion euro loan to equity on September 20; on the same day, IFIL chairman Gianluigi |

Gabetti approves plans for unlisted finance arm Exor to enter an equity swap contract for Fiat shares.

**July 8, 2005**        Marchionne gives optimistic presentation about Fiat's turnaround to analysts at Mediobanca in Milan.

**September 15, 2005**  IFIL announces equity swap.

**January 30, 2006**    Fiat says Fiat Auto returned to profit (21 million euros) in the fourth quarter after 17 consecutive quarters of losses. Fiat Group ends 2005 with a net profit of 1.4 billion euros, compared to a loss of 1.6 billion euros the year before.

**February 13, 2007**   Italian stock market watchdog Consob fines Gianluigi Gabetti, Franzo Grande Stevens, and Virgilio Marrone a total of 16 million euros for equity swap.

**May 14, 2007**        Cerberus Capital Management announces plan to buy Chrysler brand from Daimler Chrysler.

**May 31, 2007**        Margherita Agnelli announces she is suing Franzo Grande Stevens, Gianluigi Gabetti, Siegfried Maron, and Marella Agnelli in order to gain full disclosure of her father's assets.

**July 4, 2007**        Fiat launches new 500 with big event in Turin.

**March 12, 2008**      Chrysler president and vice chairman Tom LaSorda visits Fiat CEO Sergio Marchionne in Turin for the signing of Fiat's purchase of a Chrysler engine plant, and they discuss making a small car model together.

**July 2, 2008**        Merrill Lynch issues an analyst report suggesting General Motors could go bankrupt, sending its shares into a tailspin.

| | |
|---|---|
| **September 15, 2008** | Lehman Brothers announces bankruptcy filing, credit markets shut down, and consumers are no longer able to borrow money to buy cars. |
| **November 4, 2008** | U.S. Senator Barack Obama is elected President of the United States. |
| **November 18, 2008** | Chrysler chairman and CEO Robert Nardelli, General Motors chairman and CEO Richard Wagoner, and Ford Motor Company chairman and CEO Alan Mulally attend hearing at U.S. Senate on their $25 billion federal aid request. The three executives have traveled to Washington on a corporate jet, sparking outrage. Another hearing will take place December 4. |
| **December 19, 2008** | U.S. President George Bush approves emergency financing for Chrysler and GM. |
| **December 29, 2008** | Chrysler and Fiat sign memorandum of understanding giving Fiat a 35 percent stake in Chrysler in exchange for engine and other technology. |
| **December 31, 2008** | Loan and Security Agreement awards $4 billion to Chrysler. |
| **February 17, 2009** | Chrysler and General Motors submit viability plans to Task Force. |
| **February 20, 2009** | U.S. President Barack Obama announces creation of his 10-member Presidential Task Force on the Auto Industry. |
| **March 25, 2009** | Marchionne and team reach outline of deal at meeting with Steve Rattner and Ron Bloom of Task Force. |
| **March 30, 2009** | Obama makes speech saying that Chrysler has 30 days to come to an agreement with Fiat or face liquidation. |

| | |
|---|---|
| **June 10, 2009** | Marchionne makes his first speech to Chrysler employees at the Auburn Hills headquarters. |
| **November 4, 2009** | Chrysler releases five-year plan. |
| **March 17, 2010** | Turin court rejects Margherita Agnelli's request for her father's advisers to provide a full accounting of his wealth. She later appeals; case is ongoing. |
| **May 21, 2010** | Marchionne unveils new Jeep Grand Cherokee at Jefferson North Assembly Plant. |
| **September 14, 2010** | Chrysler presents model refreshes to dealers at Orlando Dealer Announcement Show. |
| **February 6, 2011** | Eminem Super Bowl commercial airs. |
| **May 24, 2011** | Payback day. Chrysler repays loan from U.S. Treasury. |
| **July 28, 2011** | Marchionne creates a single management team for Fiat and Chrysler. |

# Prologue

At 10:13 A.M. on May 24, 2011, Chrysler CEO Sergio Marchionne received a phone call with confirmation from Citigroup that the smallest of the Big Three Detroit car companies had repaid the U.S. and Canadian taxpayers for $7.6 billion in loans made in 2009, when the two governments stepped in with funding to keep the near-dead automaker up and running.

Marchionne turned back to his Macintosh, finishing up the two speeches he would give in the next few hours: the first to employees at Chrysler's headquarters, and the second to factory workers at Sterling Heights. He combed through his palylist until he found what he was looking for: Bruce Springsteen's version of "Eyes on the Prize."

After the green light from Citi, Marchionne left his office and rode down the escalator in the glass-topped atrium of Chrysler's giant headquarters in Auburn Hills, Michigan, to give his first speech of the day to employees, who were gathered around the four floors of the open space cheering as he passed by on his trip down to the podium below. It was the same podium he had used to make his first speech to his new staff on June 10, 2009, the day Chrysler came out of bankruptcy and began the long, hard slog that had turned it from a money-losing company back into a profitable one.

Marchionne had spent the nearly two years that had elapsed since then shuttling back and forth on Fiat's rented jet between Turin and

Detroit, working to meld the two companies into one, often sleeping on the flight over the Atlantic and putting in a full working day when he arrived. Sometimes he had been so tired that he seemed hard-pressed to remember what he was saying. But he thrived in his high-profile role as the auto industry's new conqueror, albeit one who looked like a university professor and sounded at times like a late-night disc jockey.

Marchionne took the podium wearing his trademark black sweater, which today was decorated with a red, white, and blue button that proclaimed, "PAID, May 24, 2011." The button might as well have read "How the hell . . . ?" He thanked employees in his curiously accented English for their hard work in achieving their goal of releasing 16 new or reworked car models in just under two years. They had accomplished what almost everyone said would be impossible. At one point during the speech, his deep voice became emotional and he had to pause.

If someone had told Marchionne when he arrived at Fiat in 2004 that he would be at Chrysler headquarters today making this speech, or that he would be planning to build a Maserati SUV at Chrysler's Jefferson North Assembly Plant (JNAP) or launching the Fiat 500 in the United States, he would have laughed his head off. Ridiculous. After all, Fiat had been bleeding millions of euros each and every day back then. It didn't have the right cars and wasn't in the right markets. And, worst of all, the company that had once symbolized modern Italy's own postwar comeback had ceased to be loved by Italians themselves.

From the outside, Fiat's cashless offer for Chrysler, the bones of which had been hammered out in great haste with private equity fund Cerberus at the end of 2008, had looked every bit as laughable as a Fiat turnaround had in 2004. After all, if the hallowed German auto giant Daimler-Benz—the company founded by the inventors of the internal combustion engine—couldn't run Chrysler profitably, how could Fiat, a much smaller, mass-market carmaker? And Chrysler had already been saved by the government once back in 1979. But Marchionne knew in his gut he could do it. Each company had what the other one lacked. Fiat had small cars and was a player in Europe and Latin America, but was nowhere in the United States. Chrysler had some strong-selling trucks and minivans, but no international presence. As he delved into Chrysler's books in early 2009, or walked down its long corridors, or sat around the table at the U.S. Treasury Department in Washington, D.C., he had played out the turnaround movie in his head. The trick was to combine the two. He saw quite clearly how he could meld the two companies into one and make it work.

■ ■ ■

When Lee Iacocca repaid the $1.5 billion in loan guarantees Chrylser had received from the U.S. Congress in 1979, he chose to make his 1983 announcement at the historic National Press Club in Washington, D.C. "We at Chrysler borrow money the old-fashioned way," he said with a proud flourish, ever the showman. "We pay it back."[1] Chrysler's payback in 2011 was decidedly a more low-key affair. Marchionne was not standing in front of a large check. He was standing in front of his factory workers. For the public ceremony, Chrysler chose its Sterling Heights assembly plant.

The choice was an apt one. The old Chrysler had earmarked the plant, where 1,200 people produced the Dodge Avenger and its sibling the Chrysler Sebring, as one of five to be closed when the company entered bankruptcy. Both of these midsize cars had not sold well, competing with the better-selling Toyota Camry, Honda Accord, Chevy Malibu, and Ford Focus. *Consumer Reports* called the Sebring "one of the least competitive family sedans on the market."[2]

Soon after Chrysler emerged from bankruptcy, the plant—and the cars—got a second chance. Sterling Heights reopened in June 2009. The Sebring and the Avenger were among the first Chrysler models to benefit from the transfer of Fiat technology, both of them earmarked for a Fiat dual-clutch transmission, which delivers a boost in fuel economy that will help them compete with the more gas-efficient models from Honda, Ford, and Hyundai for the 2012 model year. More importantly, perhaps, the decision signaled to skeptical engineers inside Chrysler that Fiat planned to make good on its promise to share technology.

The Sebring's transformation went far beyond a new transmission. It kept the same motor and body, but got a new grille, front end, rear end, fenders, lights, interior, suspension, instrument panel, seats, and name—the Chrysler 200. The old Chrysler had been forced offload many of its poor-selling models like the Sebring onto rental and corporate fleets, and 2010 had been no exception, since the company lacked fresh product. But the Chrysler 200 was on track to pare its January-to-August 2011 fleet sales by half of what they had been for the same period the year before.

After rap star Eminem took a Chrysler 200 on a proud, defiant spin through a grim Detroit in the award-winning "Imported from Detroit" Super Bowl ad, the former ugly duckling became the top-selling Chrysler-brand car in May 2011.[3] It still had a hard time competing against leaders from Toyota and Honda, but it was no longer simply a joke.

Even though today's payback day was a low-key affair, that didn't mean it wasn't an important day for Chrysler. Repaying the government loan six years ahead of time, with money borrowed on Wall Street, was made possible by the recovery of the U.S. financial markets, as well as by Chrysler's own progress. It was an opportunity that Marchionne grabbed, and was important for several reasons. It let Chrysler cut its interest payment by about $300 million each year. It gave Fiat the chance to increase its stake to 46 percent from 30 percent, thus bolstering its management control. And above all, it was a symbolic milestone in Chrysler's long road to recovery. It had posted a $116 million profit in the first quarter, its first profit in five years.

Chrysler was still not out of the woods, but it had started to recover a lot more quickly than anyone had predicted.

At Sterling Heights later that day, Marchionne took a factory tour with veterans of the Presidential Task Force on the Automotive Industry: Ron Bloom, who was serving as President Obama's assistant for manufacturing policy at the time; Brian Deese, deputy director for the National Economic Council; and United Automobile Workers (UAW) vice president General Holiefield. UAW president Bob King was there, too. Hundreds of ecstatic workers were sporting "PAID" buttons. There were smiles, handshakes, backslaps, and bear hugs all around.

For Marchionne, the spring of 2011 was his "Houdini" moment. Detroit and Washington had watched transfixed as he was nailed into a metaphorical packing crate and lowered into water, in the car world's equivalent of the great escape artist's most popular act. *Time* magazine in April had included Marchionne on its list of the world's 100 most influential people.

If it was a big day for Marchionne, in a way it was even bigger for union leader General Holiefield, who stood half a head taller than Marchionne when he handed him his black UAW T-shirt onstage and, beaming, shook his hand. Holiefield's bargaining skills in 2008 had resulted in the union's health care trust becoming the second-biggest shareholder after Fiat. Holiefield had worked at Chrysler for 38 years, starting at the Jefferson assembly plant. His father had worked there before him.

He had witnessed Chrysler's annual revenue fall from $66.1 billion in 1998, when Daimler-Benz bought the company for $38 billion, to just $41.9 billion in 2010. He had seen employment wither to 51,623 from 123,180 during that same time.[4] And finally, he had ended up sitting at the U.S. Treasury around a table with Marchionne, Ron Bloom, former UAW chief Ron Gettelfinger, and a bunch of other people, hammering out a deal that would save Chrysler. The sooner Fiat paid back the government and turned the company around, the sooner the union's health care fund could cash in what was essentially an IOU for real money.

Sergio and General had launched some blistering exchanges at one another during the talks in Washington that led to Fiat's taking management control of Chrysler. Both liked to use highly colored language to make a point. The stakes for the union were high: the Task Force had rolled back historic salary and benefit gains made by the union in its 70 years of negotiations. And the unions had already made concessions with the creation of the health care trust a few years before. But Holiefield knew that if the union dug in its heels and refused, Chrysler workers would lose their jobs *and* their health care fund. The union's concessions on its generous labor contract gave Detroit's automakers the flexibility they needed to end decades of bad practices—like making too many cars in order to keep factories running and then shoving the unwanted metal onto dealer lots and into showrooms. As a result, inventory volumes had fallen in 2010, and so had rebates. So far, it was a happy ending—until the next economic slump.

Holiefield was realistic about the auto industry's problems and its prospects. He knew that Chrysler's heyday was long gone, and that the world as he'd known it had vanished. He knew the poor quality of Detroit's cars was partly to blame, and saw Fiat's technology and factory management systems as a way to remedy that. He and Marchionne had both recognized that they wanted to get the job of fixing Chrysler done, and to move on. If he couldn't get a whole loaf of bread, he would try to get three-quarters. And that's what he did.

Fiat's controlling shareholder, Fiat chairman John Elkann, was not at Sterling Heights that day, and most of the workers probably would not have recognized the tall, slim, and quiet young man if he had been. John had been sitting on Fiat's board since 1997, when he was 21 years old, and then inherited control of Fiat from his grandfather, Gianni Agnelli, when the elderly patriarch of the auto dynasty passed away in 2003. In a sense, he had been preparing Fiat for this partnership for his entire adult life. Where Agnelli had basked in the limelight afforded him by his powerful position as a leading industrialist, John preferred to appear in public much less. But he had been deeply involved with Marchionne since the CEO arrived in 2004 to turn Fiat around, and had totally backed Sergio in his audacious bid for Chrysler. The two spoke nearly every day, and communicated back and forth on private message via BlackBerry. Later on "PAID" day, Sergio would fly to Washington, D.C., to meet up with John, who was spending the day there, and the pair would fly back to Italy together.

The Fiat-Chrysler partnership had been a big decision for John and his family. Many of the world's car companies, including Toyota, Ford, Peugeot-Citroën, and Porsche, are still linked to the families that founded them. A mix of family ownership and government protectionism had often thrown up roadblocks to auto industry mergers in a business that sorely needed them, since too many carmakers were chasing too few buyers. By accepting a diluted stake in a bigger company with a stronger chance of surviving, John had positioned the family as an industry trailblazer.

Ron Bloom took the stage for the first speech of the day, his average Joe face looking uncharacteristically cheerful. His unflappable manner and quiet voice masked razor-sharp negotiating skills. Ron's background on Wall Street and in restructuring the steel industry as it downsized in the 1990s had made him uniquely suited for his task of shepherding Chrysler's squabbling stakeholders into an agreement in those frantic months as winter turned to spring in 2009.

His experience with the steel industry had made Bloom believe for many years that General Motors was heading for bankruptcy, and he had told former UAW chief Ron Gettelfinger as much five years before, when Ron still worked for the United Steelworkers union.

Bloom's role in the Chrysler talks had been key. First of all, he had banged Fiat and Chrysler's no-cash deal into a format that he felt would be more acceptable to U.S. taxpayers, working on milestones to mark Fiat's technology transfer and reduce the risk that it could simply loot the company. At the same time, he had helped convince President Obama that Chrysler had been worth saving, because letting it go under might push the U.S. economy from recession to depression. Last, he had done more than anyone to find the common ground between Fiat and the UAW that had led to them all being at Sterling Heights that day. Ron had taken a very carefully calculated risk for the benefit of workers and their families. And it had paid off.

The talks at the Treasury Department "had been neither simple nor easy," Bloom told the crowd of autoworkers, who frequently interrupted his speech with cheers.

President Obama "did what a government does in times of crisis: he lent the company a helping hand," he said.

Finally, it was Sergio's turn to speak. Someone yelled, "Thank you!" as Marchionne took the podium.

"Look, I already gave a speech in Auburn Hills this morning and I almost broke up, so don't *start* this!" he joked, pointing a finger out into the crowd.[5]

Marchionne deeply believed in the power of groups of people to change entire organizations if the right conditions are created by their leaders, and today that belief provided one of the main themes for his speech. That change, in turn, creates personal transformation that shapes future leaders and the people they lead, he told the crowd. He mentioned Lou Gerstner's resurrection of IBM, the Manhattan Project, and Bill Clinton's 1992 victory as examples of how leaders "have the power to refuse our consent."

He continued, "Survivors are different people, special people. You and I are survivors. We have collectively found the strength to fight against the death sentence. We are special people. I urge you never to forget the experience we've been through."

As he often does, before the end of his speech he told his listeners they still had a lot of work to do.

"Today is a major milestone for Chrysler Group, but our work is by no means finished," he warned, quoting Winston Churchill's famous statement after the British won an important World War II victory. "This is not the end. It is not even the beginning of the end. But it is, perhaps, the end of the beginning."

■ ■ ■

This is a tale about power, and unexpected outcomes. It is a Greek tragedy with a Hollywood ending, spanning two centuries and uniting two continents. It is about a family's power to shape a country, an individual's power to shape a company, and a government's power to shape an industry.

Fiat's purchase of a stake in Chrysler for sweat equity in 2009 was one of the most surprising results of the economic chaos unleashed by the bursting of the U.S. credit bubble and its subsequent devastation of the world's largest economy. Little known in the United States, Fiat was the only automaker willing to step up to the plate with a plan to partner with Chrysler, giving the scrappy American icon its last chance to live to fight another day.

The story starts on January 24, 2003, when Agnelli family patriarch Giovanni Agnelli (known as Gianni) died of cancer amid one of Fiat's worst crises in its 104-year history. Then it reaches back to the end of the nineteenth century to look at the passion that drove a group of auto industry pioneers to set up what became Fiat, and how the earlier Giovanni Agnelli (Gianni's grandfather) founded a dynasty powerful enough to dictate policy to governments, but scarred by private tragedy.

The story then jumps to the early twenty-first century, when Giovanni Agnelli's descendants were struggling to avert Fiat's collapse, which would have sent a tidal wave of unemployment across Italy's slow-growth, manufacturing-based economy. It documents how Fiat recovered under the leadership of an unlikely group of individuals thrown together by chance and necessity, who galvanized Fiat's workforce to help them rip apart the automaker and reinvent it for a new era.

The story ends in the United States, where bold—and controversial—moves by two presidents from two different parties lent taxpayers' money to support an industry that the government decided was too important to fail. Chrysler's lifeline was given on the condition that the carmaker come up with a viable survival plan, which, in turn, forced the company into a frantic search for a partner. Fiat was the only company that stepped up to the plate, because its past experience had given it the skills and the vision to attempt to execute a transatlantic auto merger where others in the past had been unsuccessful.

How Fiat CEO Sergio Marchionne, working with the Agnelli family, achieved the seemingly impossible turnaround of not one but two "left for dead" carmakers is the subject of this book.

# Part I

# THE POWER OF
# A FAMILY

# Chapter 1

# The Scattered Pieces

A short time before he died, Gianni Agnelli had asked his younger brother Umberto, who had come to visit him every day at Gianni's mansion on a hill overlooking Turin, to do something very difficult. Umberto said he needed to think about it. Now, at the end of January 2003, Umberto had come to give Gianni an answer.

Gianni was confined to a wheelchair, spending his final days at home. He had once found solace looking out of the window onto his wife Marella's flower gardens below, especially his favorites, the yellow ones. But now it was winter. Gianni looked out at the city of Turin, which was visible across the river through the bare trees. Street after street stretched out toward the horizon in the crisp January air, lined up like an army of troops marching to meet the Alps beyond. It was a clear day, and he could see Fiat's white Lingotto headquarters, as well as the vast bulk of Fiat's Mirafiori car factory on the far side of the city. The factories had been built by their grandfather, Giovanni Agnelli.

Gianni wouldn't admit to his family that he was dying, but they all knew.

Gianni had always thought he would die a violent death.[1] He had broken his two legs a total of five times. He had fought in World War II, and had lived through the terrorism of Italy's *anni di piombo*, or years of lead. He had pushed his body and mind to the limit repeatedly. And yet now here he sat, cocooned in the soothing beauty of Villa Frescot's flowered wallpaper, worried about Fiat.

Umberto was shown into the study by Bruno, Gianni's trusted butler. He walked across the antique rug, which had a threadbare patch in front of the chair, and sat down next to Gianni.

"I want you to accept the chairmanship of Fiat after I go, as I asked you a few days ago," Gianni said.[2]

In normal times, being chairman of Fiat would have been more of a privilege than a duty. It was Italy's largest industrial group, a big employer, and enjoyed huge political clout. As Fiat chairman, Umberto would find journalists hanging on his every word, and heads of state would be obliged to visit him when they came through Italy. But this was not a normal time. Fiat's car business was bleeding money. It looked unfixable. And, worse yet, both the company and the country seemed to have lost their pride in the Agnelli-owned group.

Umberto, who was 68, knew there was no way he could refuse, although part of him wanted to. He had been left fatherless as an infant when their father died in an accident, and Gianni, 13 years older than Umberto, had been more a parent than a brother to him. The two men were almost mirror opposites—Gianni a restless globe-trotter, Umberto a family man—but they shared a sense of duty toward the company that made it come above anything else, certainly above any personal considerations. If Fiat was going to go down in the storm, Gianni wanted an Agnelli on deck, and Fiat's current chairman, Paolo Fresco, was not a family member. It was the responsible, dutiful thing to do.

The pair fell silent, both lost in thought.

Gianni's request to Umberto was calculated. In just over two years' time, Fiat's creditor banks could call in a three-billion-euro loan made in 2002 and take a majority stake in Fiat if the Agnellis were unable to repay. Gianni had no illusions that Fiat could repay, but he refused to resign himself to the banks becoming the largest shareholder of the company founded by his grandfather. The family's chances of keeping the banks in line—or even keeping control of the company—were better if Umberto was chairman than if the company was run by a manager found from outside, Gianni figured.

In theory, Umberto was entitled to turn Gianni down. He certainly had more than enough reason. Gianni had promised him the chairmanship in 1987, when they had both worked at Fiat together. The idea was that Umberto would eventually step into the top spot. But in 1993, Umberto was forced out in a power struggle with Fiat managers and Mediobanca, Fiat's main bank, without Gianni lifting a finger to defend him. The memory of those days still smarted for Umberto.

Moreover, Umberto and Gianni disagreed about Fiat's car business. Gianni had passed up many chances to sell it, unable to part with his grandfather's creation. Umberto, who since leaving Fiat had managed the family's nonauto investment company, was more pragmatic and had made no secret about his view that the family needed to reduce its exposure to the money-losing car business.[3] He had also told Gianni many times he thought Fiat Auto, the car unit, was badly managed. But Gianni's views were the only ones that counted. The Agnelli family had operated on the principle that "only one person can rule at a time," adopting a favorite saying of the kings of the House of Savoy, Italy's royal family up until 1946, after the end of World War II. So the views of Umberto, who was named after the Savoy crown prince,[4] were brushed off.

Umberto did not possess Gianni's charisma or his love of the good life, preferring to eat dinner at home with his family rather than flitting about from one residence to another by helicopter, like Gianni did. He did not possess Gianni's swept-back hair, stunning smile, high forehead, or aquiline nose. Umberto's long, thin face would pass unnoticed in a crowd, and his smile was sweet rather than stunning. But both possessed a gritty sense of discipline. The aura of wealth and privilege that surrounded Gianni and the rest of the Agnellis belied the street-fighting spirit of the dynasty's founder, Giovanni Agnelli, a former military officer who won himself a place of honor as one of international capitalism's original robber barons.

Umberto could have told his dying brother that Fiat Auto was too small and too badly managed to survive. In the absence of the right conditions, which were lacking, he favored selling it to Fiat's U.S. partner, General Motors, which Fiat was entitled to do under the terms of a 2000 contract. In a few months, Fiat would announce its biggest-ever loss, 4.3 billion euros. Umberto could have told Gianni that he didn't want to be the one with his face in the papers that day. And he could have said he didn't want to have to tell the family that it would get no dividend for 2002.

Last but not least, Umberto could have pointed out that taking the helm at Fiat would mean he would need to find someone to replace himself at IFIL Group, the family investment company. He had no one. The month before, he had had a painful falling-out with his longtime lieutenant, Gabriele Galateri, a victim of Fiat's downward spiral. If he took over at Fiat, Umberto would be terribly alone.

But to say no to Gianni would have been the equivalent of betraying his brother, his family, his company, and all that they stood for. Both men idolized their grandfather, and each kept a picture of the old man in his office. Neither could turn their back on the family legacy.

"I've thought it over, and have decided it is my duty to honor your request. *Va bene*, Gianni," he said, his thin face looking even thinner.

Gianni was visibly moved.

"Thank you, Umberto," he said. "I am very happy."[5]

Umberto knew he had one last chance to fix the company. He had the three billion euros from the banks. He could convince the family to put up more money. And if he could cut costs and find a good manager, he might be able to make it work.

It was worth a shot.

■ ■ ■

On January 24, 2003, while it was still dark, Umberto called Italian President Carlo Azeglio Ciampi and told him that Gianni was dead. It was announced publicly at 8 A.M. In Fiat factories, loudspeakers relayed the news to workers on the floor, and at Mirafiori, once Europe's largest auto plant, the production lines halted. At Turin's city hall, flags were lowered to half-mast.

"He created work . . . he gave us jobs," a Fiat employee, Domenica Zaccuri, told a newspaper reporter as she wiped away tears, standing outside the Mirafiori gate shortly after Agnelli's death.[6]

Gianni Agnelli had lived many lives, and not one of them could be called ordinary. Born into one of Europe's most powerful industrial dynasties, he fought both for Mussolini and for the Allies during World War II before embarking on a career as one of Europe's wealthiest and most talked-about playboys in the 1950s. When it came time to choose a mate, he married an internationally acclaimed beauty, taste-maker, and princess, Marella Carraciolo. He grew elegantly old as an industrialist-cum-elder statesman, but never truly settled down.

Fiat's downward spiral in 2002 seemed to mirror Gianni Agnelli's physical decline as he shuttled back and forth between Turin and New York fighting off prostate cancer. "When my father died, it seemed as if the springs of a watch broke, and all of the pieces were scattered," Margherita said years later.[7]

As leader of the family, Umberto faced what seemed to be an impossible task: fix the family car business. Selling it to General Motors was against Prime Minister Silvio Berlusconi's wishes, Umberto knew, as well as against Gianni's. But he also knew he might not be capable of fixing the business.

The day Gianni died the sky was a deep, brilliant blue and the snow-covered Alpine peaks gleamed in a blaze of white on the horizon near Turin, lit up as if by spotlights, just a few minutes' drive from the city.[8]

Umberto drove up to Villa Frescot to say a final good-bye to his brother, and then to a family meeting at Fiat's history museum, housed in the very first factory where his grandfather and his partners had set up shop. Formerly on the outskirts of the city, now it was surrounded by buildings, such as the hideous modern construction that housed *La Stampa*, the Turin daily paper owned by the Agnellis, with its satel-lite dishes poking out from its roof. Umberto parked his car in a spot behind a row of other dark-colored cars belonging to the rest of the clan. Normally, Umberto would have been cheered by news that day that a new small car was rolling off the assembly line in Tychy, Poland, where Fiat had just revamped the factory that, a few years later, would produce the wildly popular new 500 that would become an icon of Fiat's recovery. But today was different.

The meeting of Giovanni Agnelli & C. (GA&C), the family's limited partnership, had been scheduled for some time. The limited partnership was one of the secrets of why the Agnelli dynasty had lasted over one hundred years. Gianni didn't share power with the rest of the family. Most family members belonged, but there was no group decision making. He could consult with others, but decisions were his to make. It kept the shareholders, which numbered over 80 people, from fighting. Fiat was a family-controlled company, but only one person held the family's controlling stake. That person, for nearly 60 years, had been Gianni, and GA&C had been his command center.

While other family business dynasties, like the Barings, the Guggenheims, the Rothschilds, and the Rockefellers, may have lost the prominence they once held in their industries, the Agnelli clan had stayed at center stage in theirs. Year after year, through wars, bombings, the oil crisis, and terrorism, through strikes and booms and busts, they had persevered. They were still leaders in their industry, and they continued to have their say in Italy and worldwide. Umberto was proud of his family, of Fiat, and of his brother.

The GA&C partnership was worth about 1.3 billion euros,[9] and its assets consisted of listed holding companies Istituto Finanziario Industriale (IFI) and Istituto Finanziaria di Partecipazioni (IFIL), through which the family controlled Fiat and IFIL's stakes in other companies.

This year's meeting had been scheduled before Gianni died, of course. But the company was doing so badly and pressure was so intense that the family had decided to go ahead with the meeting despite the fact that they were in mourning. On that January morning, as the family assembled hours after Gianni's death, it turned to Umberto to lead. Much of the 40-minute meeting was taken up by red tape and organizational details involving Gianni's passing. Then Umberto made a short speech.

"In order to reach the final amount of the capital increase planned for later this year, the family needs to put in 250 million euros," he said, aware that some members would have a hard time coming up with their part. "The family has to do its share. Remember that everything we own, we owe to Fiat. So we owe this to Fiat."

Umberto did not try to win the family over with a fancy speech; it wasn't his style. But he didn't need to. The family respected him.

Umberto had dedicated his life to running Fiat and, after he was pushed out, to managing the rest of the Agnelli family holdings at IFIL, and he knew the companies inside out. IFIL's fat investment portfolio included stakes in Club Méditerranée, French conglomerate Worms & Cie., and department store chain La Rinascente, and provided the family with a steady stream of reliable dividends that offset the wild fluctuations of profitability—and lately, loss—at Fiat. Up until 2000, IFIL's profits had grown every year for 15 years, and it had paid 82.7 million euros in dividends to IFI, its parent company, in 2000.[10] Umberto deeply loved Fiat. He delighted in visiting the Fiat design center and Fiat factories, and unveiling new cars at auto shows.

The family approved the plan to name Umberto as Fiat chairman, sending him back to an operating role at the company for the first time since he had been forced out years earlier. The family also confirmed Umberto as head of the limited partnership for the time being. Umberto proposed the capital increase, and the family approved it. The meeting broke up.

"It's a very sad moment . . . but the world must go on, and we must continue to manage well," said Fiat chairman Paolo Fresco, who tendered his resignation the day after the funeral, as he left.[11]

■ ■ ■

The line to say good-bye to Gianni Agnelli's coffin started forming at 9 A.M. the next day, and snaked through the belly of the former Lingotto factory, up the long, twisting spiral ramp that was built to drive cars from the factory floor directly up to the rooftop test track. Now, instead of cars, somber mourners shuffled slowly forward dressed in overcoats to shield themselves against the winter chill.

The Lingotto had long since ceased being a factory, and Gianni—working with architect Renzo Piano—had transformed it into a shopping mall complete with the Pinacoteca Giovanni e Marella Agnelli art galleries, a multiplex, a luxury hotel, and a conference center. Piano had added a helicopter landing pad with a futuristic glass bubble on top. Across from the glass bubble was an odd-looking metal box plunked on top of the Lingotto that Piano rather whimsically referred to as a "jewel box," which housed part of Gianni and Marella's art collection. In front of this former factory with its onion-shaped bubble on top stood another building with Fiat's executive headquarters, where Agnelli had his offices. The offices provided continuity with the company's past. If a company could have a spiritual home, the Lingotto was Fiat's.

At the time of Gianni's death, Fiat was definitely at low ebb. So were Europe's other automakers, and Detroit was suffering, too. The Big Three had lost more ground to foreign manufacturers in 2002, leaving General Motors, Ford, and Chrysler with their smallest market share in history. In March 2003, the United States would invade Iraq and oil prices would skyrocket.

While Detroit had the Big Three, Turin had just one, and the sense of worry hung like a cloud over the crowd that day. What would become of Fiat? Would the family sell it to General Motors? Fiat without an Agnelli was inconceivable, as was Turin without Fiat.

Gianni Agnelli lay in a closed coffin underneath a blanket of white roses, amid a flower-strewn room perched high atop the former factory. His body had been transported in a makeshift Fiat van— no ordinary funeral hearse would do, and Fiat didn't make hearses. Behind his coffin was a religious picture painted by his daughter Margherita that Gianni had kept over his bed. Classical music played in the background. Behind the coffin stood two *carabinieri* (military police officers) in full dress uniform, their gold helmets gleaming. As a backdrop, a glass wall revealed a stunning view across the city. At this height, from high above the rooftops, the Alps looked near enough to touch. Marella had chosen this location for mourners to pay their respects because the Pinacoteca was Gianni's pride and joy. Her choice was a fortunate one, because no one in the family or at Fiat expected the huge river of people that now washed over the bewildered family like a vast Ganges of human sentiment.

Gianni's grandson John Elkann and Umberto, standing near the coffin with Gianni's daughter Margherita and Gianni's widow Marella, got their second surprise of the day when the first people started coming through the door. The family thought they would stop at the coffin briefly and then be on their way. Instead, to their amazement, stranger after stranger came over to Umberto, Marella, John, and other family members to shake their hands and thank them personally.

"The *Avvocato* gave us a job, a house, a future for our family," said one worker to Umberto, referring to Gianni by his nickname (which meant "the lawyer").

Turin mayor Sergio Chiamparino and the governor of Piedmont, Enzo Ghigo, were also among the first to arrive, murmuring their condolences.

Left-wing labor leader Sergio Cofferati, who until six months earlier had led the mighty Italian General Confederation of Labour (CGIL) workers union, was among the earliest guests to pay his respects. Italy's largest company and Italy's largest union had locked horns often in Agnelli's time, and had been in conflict since virtually the day Fiat had been founded. Italy's Communist Party, which in the mid-1970s had been Europe's largest, usually had few good things to say about Agnelli.

Umberto was amazed by the huge crowd. He had expected to see people like Cesare Romiti, who had run Fiat for decades along with his brother, and people like Antonio D'Amato, the head of Italy's business lobby. Likewise, sports stars like world champion Formula One driver Michael Schumacher, who drove for Ferrari, had personal links to the family because Agnelli was an avid racing fan in addition to being the owner of the team. Fiat-owned Ferrari's chairman Luca di Montezemolo, a close family friend, stood by the coffin, wiping away the tears.

What surprised and impressed Umberto was the display of sympathy and feeling from the city and from Fiat's employees. In a vast, collective outpouring of grief, the normally reserved city of Turin showered its fallen patriarch with heartfelt affection and gratitude.

For decades, Agnelli had been criticized by politicians, unions, stock market investors, and some sections of the press for being too powerful, given Fiat's status as one of Italy's few multinational heavy-weights. Family-owned companies were blasted as a deadweight on Italy's economy, since family owners tend to favor control rather than growth, and can sometimes put their interests ahead of those of the collectivity. But in the days surrounding Gianni's death, those considerations were overshadowed by an awareness of his role in Italy's national history.

"I think Gianni Agnelli was a symbol of Turin, and his disappearance is mourned by all of us," one of the people standing in line told a television crew.

By seven o'clock in the evening, Umberto was exhausted after such an emotionally intense day. But the line showed no sign of thinning out. Italian papers would later report that some 100,000 people filed by the coffin. Agnelli's widow Marella, in consultation with the rest of the family, decided to keep the doors open all night. The family's youngest generation took turns keeping a vigil. John's brother Lapo and a cousin, Edoardo Teodorani, were drafted for the wee hours, from 2:00 A.M. to 4:00 A.M.

As the crowds filed past Agnelli's casket, preparations for the funeral over at Turin's cathedral, or *duomo*, the next day were becoming increasingly frenetic. They would continue all night. Umberto was not the only one who was surprised at the huge crowds drawn to say good-bye to the *Avvocato*; Turin prefect Achille Catalani and his staff were scrambling to beef up security and crowd control as they realized that there would be masses of people packed into the square outside the church the next day. Fiat had announced the previous October that it would seek temporary layoffs of 8,000 workers, more than a fifth of its domestic workforce. It planned to close a plant in Sicily. The news had set off protests across the country. What if some laid-off worker or left-wing extremist would decide to seek his 15 minutes of fame by getting even at the funeral of Italy's most famous citizen? Catalani had ordered all the streets around Turin's cathedral closed to traffic. The tram that usually clattered through the square in front of the Renaissance church had been rerouted.[12] But he needn't have worried.

The next day crowds started forming at 7 A.M. outside Turin's cathedral, San Giovanni Battista, the church where Agnelli's funeral would be held hours later. Some 50,000 people were expected to attend. They pressed against the barricades, where loudspeakers had been set up to broadcast the eulogy from Cardinal Severino Poletto, Turin's archbishop. The funeral would also be broadcast live on national television.

Unlike other Italian cities like Rome, Florence, or Venice, Turin does not have a long artistic or intellectual history to show off. It was not home to the Renaissance like Florence, or to one of Europe's first universities like Bologna. Turin was just a small town when the House of Savoy moved its seat from Chambéry in France across the Alps to the banks of the Po River in 1563 and set about making the city its capital. The Savoy dynasty brought with it to Turin a military tradition that shaped the city for centuries, and would later shape Fiat. Turin became the capital of Italy when it was united as a country in 1861 under the Savoy crown. Fiat's founder, Giovanni Agnelli, was a former military officer in the Savoy army. And the craftsmanship for a budding auto industry came from the workshops that supplied arms and carriages to the royal family.

When the House of Savoy was dethroned after World War II, a new dynasty stepped up onto the pedestal Italy's royal family had left vacant to be lionized, imitated, criticized, or loathed. That dynasty was also based in Turin. Its name was Agnelli. Instead of an army and its knights, it reigned over managers and machines. Instead of reviewing military parades on horseback, its sovereign's place of public honor was in the VIP box at the soccer games of its Juventus football team, or in the pits of Ferrari Formula One races. Now, the city was saying farewell.

By 10:30 A.M., when the funeral began, the square in front was completely full. Italians have centuries of experience in staging public spectacles, and Gianni Agnelli's funeral was no exception. An honor guard of three rows of brown-uniformed *lancieri*, a cavalry regiment that looks like a holdover from Napoleon's day, stood ramrod-straight front of the church, their gold-tipped lances raised to the sky. Cardinal Poletto, resplendent in purple robes, waited on the steps, which were stacked high with wreaths of flowers that had been brought over from the Lingotto that morning. Uniformed *carabinieri* stood guard next to the cathedral doors, horsetail plumes flowing from their helmets.

One after another, chauffeur-driven cars, some with police escorts, discharged their passengers while the crowd looked on, craning to see who they were. Italy's president, Carlo Azeglio Ciampi, whose leadership had been crucial in squeezing Italy into Europe's single currency, was the first to arrive, and was applauded by the crowd as he strode past. Ciampi shook hands with Umberto and greeted the rest of the family. When Prime Minister Silvio Berlusconi followed him a few minutes later, catcalls drowned out the applause. Turin traditionally voted center-left. Plus, the premier had committed an unpardonable error by arriving in a foreign car.

The bell in the red brick tower in front of the church began to toll, its deep sound reverberating through the crowd. Gianni's grandson

John heard it from a distance as he approached, penetrating the closed windows of the car where he sat as it motored along with the rest of the family behind the police car and two police motorcycles. As the car pulled closer, he could hear the crowd applauding over the sound of the police sirens, mixing with the organ music pouring from the church. The applause continued as family climbed out of the car and filed into the church, behind the coffin and a procession of priests holding a cross and candles.

The cathedral, which held 2,500 people, was full, with the 80 members of the Agnelli family taking the right-hand pews, along with Fiat managers like Paolo Fresco and Ferrari chief Luca di Montezemolo. The left-hand side was reserved for politicians, wrapped in dark overcoats and cashmere scarves to ward off the cold. The area around the altar was so crammed with cavalry in high uniform that it would have seemed they were saying farewell to a general rather than an auto baron. The front of the church was packed with a colorful confusion of choir singers, musicians, priests, flowers, and banners. A group of purple-robed priests filed in, shuffled up the steps, and took their places at the altar, which was crowded with priests from parishes with connections to the family, including Don Luigi Ciotti, who had tried unsuccessfully to help Gianni's son Edoardo deal with his heroin addiction.

Marella, sitting in the front row next to Margherita, wore a simple black coat, and looked pensively into the distance as a priest read a passage from St. Paul. Margherita's second husband, Serge de Pahlen, and their five children, sat next to her.

Cardinal Poletto stood in front of the altar, the same place where the Turin Shroud is exhibited in certain years for the faithful to file past and say a prayer in front of what many believe to be the cloth that covered Christ's body after the Crucifixion. The Cardinal had assisted Gianni Agnelli in his dying moments, giving him his last rites, and had no doubt been of great comfort to Gianni during the difficult months in November and December as his disease worsened. The Cardinal's stiff and formal eulogy offered few glimpses of the real man, except for one.

"On Friday our Lord called the *Avvocato* to his side," Poletto began. "I take the liberty of calling him *Avvocato*, because one day I asked him, 'Do you prefer I call you *Avvocato*, or Senator?'

"'*Avvocato*,' he replied, 'because it's a stage name!'"[13]

And indeed it was. Agnelli's proverbial wit did not desert him during his final days. He had created a marvelously exciting character, and seemed to greatly enjoy playing him. But for a man who obviously loved life, his funeral was a somber affair fit for a head of state.

The rest of the ceremony was rigorously religious, and a few times even touched on politics. Cardinal Poletto recounted how Agnelli had wanted to make his confession before he died, as well as celebrate Mass and take communion. "In this way, he prepared himself to consign himself into God's hands, which he did as he died, after having received the last rites. . . . I say this because I believe that this important and intimate event in his life be known for his own and for God's glory . . . a sign for us that such an important man on the world stage had decided to prepare for death as a good Christian."

In a moment of prayer, Margherita crossed her hands over her chest, as a Mozart concerto, K. 229, played, one of Gianni's favorites. There were no testaments from his famous friends, like Henry Kissinger or David Rockefeller, and no readings from family members. A visitor from outer space would have had no way of knowing that Agnelli was a bon vivant with a string of lovers, for none of them were visible to Fiat's television cameras among the crowd.

The family seemed detached, and the political guests self-conscious. Marella and the rest of the family sat composed and displayed little emotion, like true *Torinesi*, until a military salute was played by a lone trumpet player. Marella wiped away the tears.

During communion, as the sounds of Mozart poured through the church, the family let themselves go. Margherita was visibly moved. Lapo was crying. John's brother Lapo had inherited Gianni's flair and dress sense—as well as his voracious appetite for late-night partying. Always "on," Lapo had Gianni's gift of gab and his famous grandfather's talent for zinging one-liners. He even wore his hair combed back like his grandfather.

After the communion, Cardinal Poletto greeted the family, squeezing their hands in comfort. President Ciampi's wife, Franca, stepped across the aisle and embraced Marella, in one of the few displays of genuine emotion captured by Fiat's cameras. Cardinal Poletto moved over to greet Italy's political leaders in the other pews, stopped in front of Berlusconi to apologize for the unintentional snub of not welcoming him by name along with the other politicians. Berlusconi smiled and shook his head several times, looking slightly embarrassed.

The service ended and the cathedral's big bells erupted again, this time in a booming salute that reverberated deep within the bones. Gianni's coffin moved slowly down the aisle, people in the pews touching it as it went by. Applause from the crowd, as befitting an exit by a great actor, burst forward from the square to greet the coffin as it was carried out of the church.

The family filed out to their chauffeured cars waiting outside, to take Gianni's body to be buried at the family estate in the town of Villar Perosa outside of Turin.

■ ■ ■

A few days after the funeral, Gianluigi Gabetti stopped by Umberto's office at IFIL to say good-bye. Gabetti had walked these same parquet-paved corridors since 1971, when he had joined the group as director general of IFI, IFIL's parent company. The building on Turin's Corso Matteotti that housed both IFIL and IFI was built in the style of the austere Renaissance masterpiece Palazzo Strozzi, in Florence, and had at one time been the Agnelli family home. The parking lot visible from the small stone-paved lobby had been a courtyard where Gianni Agnelli and his brothers and sisters had once played.

A lawyer by training, the white-haired Gabetti was more than a manager at IFI. He was also something of a diplomat. He had been Gianni's closest financial adviser for over 30 years. His piercing gaze could be intimidating, yet his manner was courtly and never rude. He was fond of painting and of Mozart, and he could talk on any subject. At any important Fiat event over the past 30 years, Gabetti was probably standing near either Gianni or Umberto, wearing a gray suit during the day and a dark blue one in the evening, listening. He was now retired and living in Geneva, Switzerland, with his American wife Bettina.

"I want to say farewell, *Dottor* Agnelli," he said, entering the office he knew as well as his own closet. Paintings from Umberto's art collection hung on the walls.

Umberto motioned for him to sit down, surprised.

"You cannot leave me alone," Umberto told Gabetti. "I promised my brother I would become chairman of Fiat. And that means, of course, I have to leave IFIL."

IFIL was very important to the Agnelli family. Its investments had helped the family ride out the ups and downs of the auto industry. Gabetti was not surprised by Gianni's request that Umberto become Fiat chairman. He had expected it, though it was none of his business to ask.

Then Umberto told him something he hadn't known. Umberto's CEO at IFIL, Gabriele Galateri, had left at the family's request in the middle of 2002 to run Fiat, and then abruptly left Fiat in December for reasons that were not exactly clear.

Umberto's predicament, in part, was of his own making. Galateri, after all, had left IFIL to become Fiat CEO because the family asked him to. A good Turinese through and through—his father was a military officer—Galateri accepted. But it was a mistake all around. His financial expertise was not what Fiat needed.

"*Dottor* Umberto, I am eighty years old," Gabetti said, the unwavering gaze from his brilliant blue eyes never changing, as usual. His wife Bettina was very sick, and living in another country. "I need to think about it."

Gabetti started turning over the situation in his mind. He had met Gianni in New York in the 1970s at a Museum of Modern Art exhibition where Gabetti was a trustee. They had clicked, and Gabetti—along with his wife—moved to Turin. If he stayed on, Bettina would have to agree to come to Turin again. Perhaps she would, Gabetti thought. It was for the family, after all.

If Gianni and Umberto had dedicated their lives to Fiat, Gabetti had dedicated his to the Agnelli family. After Umberto, Gabetti was probably the person closest to Gianni. But unlike others among his associates, Gabetti never presumed he could be on a first-name basis with the two brothers. For over 30 years, he had always called Gianni "*Presidente*," and not even by his nickname "*Avvocato*," even though he was involved in every aspect of Agnelli's business affairs. Gabetti felt he could do his duty better if he stayed at arm's length. He was so reserved that Gianni had asked him once, years ago, if he enjoyed his job. "Sometimes you seem stiff," he had told Gabetti. Yet they had a very warm, disciplined relationship. That's the sort of thing Gabetti took pride in.

Like Umberto, Gabetti had been raised to do his duty. It was in his DNA.

Umberto seemed to sense the elderly man's moment of hesitation.

"It's only for a year," he promised. "Prepare yourself to be head of IFIL."

Gabetti would end up there for far longer, because Umberto did not keep his promise for reasons beyond his control.

■ ■ ■

Umberto had little time to stop and mourn the man that had both ruled and entertained their family for nearly 60 years.

Gianni Agnelli was Italy's leading businessman, its best-known citizen, and its unofficial ambassador. He owned Italy's largest company and believed his main task in life was to ferry it, intact, into the twenty-first century.[14] His various careers as a soldier, playboy, auto executive, art collector, publisher, senator, sailor, and soccer fan were linked by a common thread—a sense of stewardship, and an awareness of how he could use his image as a tool in a media-dominated world.

Agnelli inherited a company founded by his grandfather, who had modeled it after Ford Motor Company. Gianni's reign began during the heyday of Italy's economic boom, and he saw the company's car production swell from 250,000 to a million and then beyond. Fiat rode the economic boom and also drove it, its small cars symbolizing the country's transformation from a poor agricultural nation to a modern, motorized one. Fiat's leading role in the economy meant it was a driver in social change, too, as thousands of poor Italians streamed north from villages in the south. Some 300,000 southerners moved to Turin in 1968 alone.[15] But the hangover from the boom was vicious. In the 1970s, Agnelli faced down terrorism and labor unrest, eventually finding a compromise with unions even as he completely mechanized Fiat's factories.

Fiat's size in Italy's economy was lopsidedly big; imagine Boeing and General Motors combined. Agnelli carefully managed the company with this in mind. This power was the source of bitter and continual criticism. But after his death, Agnelli was seen by many as "a man who knew how to reconcile his own interests with that of the country," in the words of President Ciampi.

Gianni's death would set in motion two chains of events, both unexpected. The first one would save the company, and even make it a trailblazer during the collapse of the U.S. auto industry in 2009 when Fiat took control of a bankrupt Chrysler. The other would see Gianni's daughter Margherita turn against her family, splintering its unity for the first time ever.

Despite Umberto's worries, the Agnellis would succeed in resurrecting Fiat, which went from being a "laughingstock," in the words of Sergio Marchionne,[16] its future CEO, to making its stunning swoop on Chrysler almost six years to the day after Agnelli's death. Gianni's wish to keep Fiat in the family's hands set it on a new course. Had Umberto decided to turn the car business over to General Motors, or a new investor, Fiat's CEO would not have had the scope to make the risky decision to partner with Chrysler. When the crisis hit in 2008, Fiat needed to act fast. Family ownership, combined with a strong CEO, was a plus because John Elkann, as chief shareholder, was free to make his decision quickly.

Moreover, family owners manage their companies for the long term. Managers and financial investors are more focused on meeting their quarterly targets, whereas families like the Agnellis are asking themselves, "What will I be leaving for my children?"

As Umberto soldiered on in the months after Gianni's death, the limelight was searing. Italy and Detroit both watched, and observers made no secret of the fact they thought the family didn't have what it took to fix the company. As the clock ticked down to the day in 2004 when Fiat had the right to force General Motors to buy the remaining 80 percent of Fiat Auto, Umberto and his advisers knew that GM didn't want it.

"My grandfather's funeral was one of the hardest days of my life," John Elkann's brother Lapo would say later. "Fiat was doing terribly, and everyone was taking potshots at us because it was easy to hit a lame duck."[17]

During the next 18 months, Umberto and his management team dismantled the old Fiat and recapitalized the new, smaller, more car-focused company that started to emerge from the wreckage. The generational changeover took several years and resulted in two lawsuits that caused great vexation and pain. But when it was complete, the family discovered it had reserves of strength it hadn't dreamed of.

But while Umberto and later John were able to set Fiat on a new course, they were unable to steady the destabilizing effect Gianni's death had on his immediate family, laying bare the emotional dysfunction the charismatic leader would leave in his wake. The Agnellis were able to right Fiat, but the dynasty itself risked splintering for the first time. By the time Fiat took over Chrysler, John and his mother would no longer be on speaking terms. His mother Margherita would eventually sue *her* mother Marella over Gianni's will, in a lawsuit that shocked Italy and made the Agnellis tawdry gossip-page fodder, another first. As details of the lawsuit leaked out, fueled by speculation that Gianni had left cash stashed away hidden from tax authorities in offshore tax havens, his reputation was tarnished in a way that deeply hurt John and others close to Gianni. The lawsuit came at a time when the company was struggling to stay afloat, creating no small amount of ill will toward Margherita. She eventually gave up her stake in the company, and walked away with a reported 1.2 billion euros.

John, chosen by Gianni as his heir at Fiat, had little choice but to side with his grandfather's advisers, Gabetti and Grande Stevens, whom his mother later accused of hiding Gianni's wealth from her to the detriment of her other children.

John's brother Lapo was also distraught, but could not see the situation as dispassionately as John. In 2005, Lapo would nearly die of a drug overdose after a night of partying at the home of a transvestite, and would be forced to leave the company.[18] Gianni had been able to keep his image pristine because of Fiat's power and its control of two national newspapers. Not so for Lapo, whose flameout was covered in embarrassing detail by an Italian press that seemed to revel in seeing one of the Olympian Agnelli clan being dragged through the mud.

Margherita was right about one thing—for the family, Gianni's death was like the springs of a watch breaking, and as the pieces were scattered here and there, the family did what it could to collect them. For Fiat, on the other hand, Umberto started the company on a long road that would eventually transform it into something quite different.

# Chapter 2

# A Dynasty Is Born

The car company that would become Fiat was born in a coffee bar, a sort of late nineteenth-century Starbucks called Café Burello. Unlike Turin's surviving historic coffeehouses today, with their mirrored walls and marble tables, the now-vanished Café Burello was a run-down hole-in-the-wall with faded gilt, chipped paint, and a dirty yellow exterior.[1]

The roof that protected the outside café tables from the weather was long gone. But what it lacked in ambience it made up for in location. Sitting across the street from Turin's train station, the café was a convenient meeting point for businessmen coming to town, and for people looking to buy and sell horses and carriages.

Giovanni Agnelli, a gentleman farmer who had just abandoned a promising career in the military, and his group of upper-crust friends who gathered at the Burello at the turn of the century to talk politics found their attention turning more and more to the horseless carriage. When one of these new creatures came through Turin, the driver would stop in front of the Burello, where Agnelli—Tuscan cigar in hand—and the other café patrons would cluster around and bombard the brave motorist with questions.

The excitement of auto racing captured the imagination of crowds and élite alike, and Agnelli and his friends were soon swept up in an investment hysteria we now would call an "auto bubble." The mass-produced automobile was born of the wide-open spaces in the New World. But it was the Europeans who pioneered auto engineering when Gottlieb Daimler and Karl Benz almost simultaneously perfected the gasoline engine in 1886. After that, wealthy landowners and businessmen competed to find the most elegant cars to flaunt their status, impress their friends, and often risk their necks in dangerous races. In the first Italian auto race in 1895, a motley crew of five drivers showed up, piloting vehicles made by Daimler and Benz. Among them was a motorbike driven by Giovanni Battista Ceirano, a pioneer whose company would later become the backbone of the early Fiat.[2]

Those cars were luxury items, painstakingly hammered together piece by piece by groups of craftsmen in grimy, primitive workshops, or else oddball inventions overseen by engineers who were often more interested in making a unique creation than a quick fortune. The idea that the car could appeal to a wider public and be mass-produced was still in the future.

Giovanni Agnelli was not the wealthiest or most distinguished of his group. At the turn of the century, he was in his early 30s and casting around for a calling in life other than tending his huge family estate outside Turin in a town called Villar Perosa. He had left the military, partly out of boredom with the routine.[3] Italy's capital had moved from Turin to Rome, taking the House of Savoy's court with it. The life of an officer in the Savoyard army now that the Savoy king had to spend most of his time in Rome did not offer huge prospects for advancement.

"All of us were young, enthusiastic, and gripped by a sort of automotive euphoria," recalled Carlo Biscaretti di Ruffia, son of Count Roberto Biscaretti di Ruffia, one of Fiat's founders.[4] "We instinctively felt that Giovanni Agnelli was our leader."

The idea that Italy could make cars to rival the French and Germans—and, later, create an industry modeled after Ford—was preposterous. Italy was a poor agricultural country and had little industry to speak of. In the Belle Epoque years of the late 1800s, Italy was still a young nation—barely more than "a geographical expression," as Austrian Chancellor Prince Metternich had called it in 1847, when nationalist revolutions were disrupting Europe's old balance of power. "There is no country in the world where popular consumption is as burdened as in Italy, and no country where inequality afflicts the poor in such a jarring way," said Giovanni Giolitti in 1898; Giolitti was Italy's top political leader until the advent of Fascism.[5]

Unlike his future partners, Agnelli realized that the automobile should be produced in series, and not one by one, by hand, the way Michele Lanza, a Turin businessman, was doing.

"You should thank the good Lord that your factory makes candles instead of cars, because right now with cars like yours you'd be out of business," Agnelli yelled at Lanza one evening at Café Burello.[6]

Underneath the excitement, the patrons of Café Burello may have also been driven by fear. The gawky little automobiles they saw sputtering around the streets of Turin were made in France or Germany. Italy, already a latecomer to industrialization, risked falling even further behind if it didn't start producing its own cars. Landowners like Agnelli, along with Count Emanuele Cacherano di Bricherasio (who founded the Italian Automobile Club) and prominent lawyers like Cesare Goria Gatti (another Fiat backer), didn't waste any time.

■ ■ ■

On July 1, 1899—four years before Ford's incorporation as a company—the founding shareholders of the Fabbrica Italiana Automobili Torino (FIAT) met at the Palazzo Bricherasio, a stone's throw away from the royal palace, to sign papers in a parquet-floored room loaded floor to ceiling with gilt decoration. Count Bricherasio received the other shareholders wearing a black smoking gown with white lapels.[7]

"The colors of the house," Agnelli commented, alluding to the Bricherasio family crest. "If your ancestors could see you now, how happy they would be! How very democratic of you."

"Democracy should go hand in hand with a pinch of aristocracy," the Count replied. "If not, what becomes of tradition?"

It was Bricherasio, not Agnelli, who first had the idea of setting up a car company, based on the Welleyes model prototype built in 1898, developed by the Ceirano brothers—Matteo, Ernesto, Giovanni Battista, and Giovanni—and an engineer named Aristide Faccioli.[8] And Bricherasio was the one who recruited banker Gustavo Deslex, lawyer Cesare Goria-Gatti, and Biscaretti di Ruffia.

Biscaretti, the other driving force behind the deal, plopped into an armchair. Bricherasio went to sit down at a desk. He pulled out a piece of "Bricherasio Administration" letterhead paper from the drawer, and began the outline of Fiat's founding statutes.

"May I add your signature, Agnelli?" he said when he was done, turning to Giovanni.

"Here is my signature, but on one condition: that we take this seriously," he told the group.[9] "We can't waste any time. You should have seen what I saw the other day on my trip to Nice. Hannibal is at the gates. In France, even the public sector is starting to use the motorcar."

When it came time to name the first board of directors, Bricherasio wouldn't hear of being named chairman. That honor went to a gentleman named Ludovico Scarfiotti. Agnelli was secretary of the board, a marginal role.

Agnelli's fellow shareholders recognized his dynamism, single-mindedness, and organizational abilities, but it was far from clear he had the drive and substance to become a captain of industry.[10]

However Agnelli leaped out of the starting gate in a flurry of activity. He oversaw the building of the factory, which began in the second half of 1899.[11] It was his idea to buy Ceirano GB & C., Turin's first carmaker, outright, including workshop and patents, in exchange for Ceirano's exclusive rights for all sales in Italy.[12]

Of the few early partners, Agnelli, with his combination of technical experience and military background, was the one who was able to fuse the two into an industrial vision. In turn, the early Fiat partners dominated their competitors because they brought capital together with engineering know-how.

Surprisingly, neither Giovanni Battista Ceirano nor Michele Lanza—the two pioneers in Turin with hands-on experience in building automobiles—were among Fiat's founders. Fiat's official literature and historians skim this aspect of the company's birth. Was their exclusion due to snobbery, or were they elbowed aside? One assumes Lanza decided not to join the group because he wanted to pursue his own automaking vision; the Ceirano brothers continued making cars in factories that were eventually swallowed up by Fiat.

The new company got off to a rocky start. The investors couldn't decide whether they wanted to design, engineer, and produce their own models; import and assemble cars from France or Germany; or a mixture of both.[13] Once they settled that question by deciding to make their own cars, they disagreed about who their customer was: a wealthy motorist who wanted new technical solutions or a less sophisticated consumer who could be satisfied with products already available (like the one made in France by Panhard et Levassor).

Agnelli, unsurprisingly, was in the second camp. "A car is not a poem, it's a product for sale," he said.[14]

The issue came to a head after his trip to the Paris Auto Show in 1900, where Agnelli first saw the Benz air-cooled radiator, which he wanted to license for Fiat's start-up auto production.[15] Fiat's brand-new factory's technical director was Aristide Faccioli, the inventor of the Welleyes and one of the few men in Turin who knew how to build an automobile. When Agnelli got back from Paris, he told Faccioli to build a radiator based on the same idea.

Faccioli refused. As his endless tinkering had already made Agnelli impatient, at a meeting with other board members at the new factory on Corso Dante on April 18, 1901, Agnelli bitterly criticized Faccioli's methods.

The other directors defended the technician, telling Agnelli, in essence, "We'd like to see *you* try it." After all, Fiat was a start-up. The company was not even two years old. What sense did it make to fire the only guy in town who knew how to make a decent car?

Agnelli told the board: "If you give me the mandate and let me handle it, I believe I can solve the problem."[16]

He called Faccioli into his office and told the man who had crafted one of Italy's first motorcars that he was "too intelligent for us."

Agnelli told Faccioli, "My friends and I have put up the capital to create this factory; we know we can't get profits right away, but we can't tolerate our capital being used up waiting for you to design a car we can produce and sell; therefore, for the reasons mentioned above, we must deprive ourselves of your handiwork."[17]

Agnelli replaced Faccioli with Giovanni Enrico.

"We know you are an excellent engineer . . . let us give you some advice on how you design the next car. Europe's most popular car right now is the Mercedes-Benz," he told the young engineer. "I will get you an example, not for you to copy, but so that you can be inspired by it and follow the trend."[18]

Under Agnelli's methods and direction, the young company was quick to turn a profit. It started making money in 1902.[19] It quickly diversified from automobiles to ship engines and trucks. Airplane engines would soon follow. In 1903, the company listed on the stock exchange, and shares immediately shot from their par value of 25 lire each to 425 lire. At a shareholders' meeting in 1906, Agnelli announced a huge dividend and a surprise move: the old Fiat was liquidated and a new company created with more shares and that counted Agnelli and two other founders as the main shareholders.

Lifted by a frenzy of speculation and strong profits, the stock soared in the summer of 1906, only to plummet, wiping out small investors and founder Count Cacherano di Bricherasio.[20] The Turin prosecutor's office opened an investigation to see if Fiat's stock had been manipulated or its balance sheets falsified. The trial ended in 1913 with Agnelli and Scarfiotti being acquitted. In the meantime, Agnelli had scooped up Fiat's near-worthless stock at rock-bottom prices to emerge as the biggest shareholder.[21]

As his early moves show, Agnelli was an imposing man whose modus operandi was to simply bulldoze anyone who got in the way of his vision to create an automobile giant.

■ ■ ■

Giovanni Agnelli seemed to conjure Fiat like a genie, fully formed, from a lamp. Just 20 years separated the meeting of mustachioed men in an aristocrat's drawing room and the opening of Fiat's Lingotto factory, which was so huge it looked as if an ocean liner had somehow found its way up the Po River and run aground on the riverbanks at the foot of the Alps.

But Fiat's very size, paradoxically, would at times turn out to be an Achilles' heel. Italy had little manufacturing industry to speak of and Fiat was able to grab dominant positions in the nation's auto, air, ship, and train manufacturing industries, giving it an outsized importance in the nation's economy. Its towering position gave it huge influence with Italy's government in Rome, which could be useful in terms of shaping legislation to fit Fiat's needs. But the Turin-Rome embrace would also weaken the company over the decades to come, shielding it from the sort of market competition that it needed to remain in trim, fighting form. And its very size made it a sitting duck for the labor movement and, later, for terrorism.

Agnelli was very much a product of his age, and Fiat, in turn, was the offspring of the social, geographical, and historical forces swirling around Turin in the years that had forged modern Italy.

Tucked away in the northwest corner of Italy near France, protected—but also hedged in—by the natural barrier of the Alps, Turin had been passed over by the burst of creative energy that had animated the Renaissance and made Florence, Venice, and Rome into jewel boxes of Italy's artistic heritage. While Turin lacked a Michelangelo or a Raphael, it had an asset that other Italian cities didn't: centuries of political stability under the rulership of the House of Savoy, one of Europe's oldest dynasties, dating all the way back to the days of William the Conqueror.

By the late 1700s, long before Italy was a nation, "the Kingdom of Savoy became, in Italy, the most efficient and well organized bureaucratic-militaristic state, with a dynasty that enjoyed the full trust of its subjects," according to historian Gianni Oliva.[22]

Turin was different from other Italian cities. Gianni Agnelli, Giovanni's grandson, was fond of saying it was a "bit Prussian." For centuries leading up to its fall from power after World War II, the House of Savoy had slowly and methodically carved out a kingdom by dominating the Alpine passes connecting Italy and France, doggedly and at times ruthlessly shifting their alliances to exploit an advantage in diplomacy, marriage, and war.

When it came time to finally unite Italy into a single country in the 1860s, the House of Savoy was a natural rallying point for patriots seeking an Italian identity. The court of the House of Savoy did not stand out for wealth, style, or learning. Short Alpine summers did not produce enough hay or food to feed large numbers of people or animals through the frozen winters. Indeed, the House of Savoy's dynastic seat in Chambéry, France, with its three towers looking out across to the Alps, is clearly a military fortress and not a Renaissance palace. Chambéry castle was so small that the Duke of Savoy had a hard time finding room for royal guests.[23]

The Medici of Florence created a vast library; "constantly increased by Cosimo and his heirs, it was eventually to contain no less than ten thousand *codices* of Latin and Greek authors,"[24] and the Venetians threw their carnivals "celebrated with so many festivities, fireworks and masquerades that one might have imagined the city back in its golden age."[25] The dukes of Savoy instead passed their time jousting or doing military exercises. Chambéry was plain. The mansions of court aristocracy had spiral staircases, because they were cheaper and easier to make than the grand ramps of stairs in other palaces, and the cathedral had simple trompe l'oeil paintings instead of fine frescos.[26]

When the House of Savoy moved its capital to Turin at the end of the 1500s, the Piedmontese city was a backwater. But the House of Savoy's military sense of discipline, as well as the workshops creating armor and carriages, later provided the basis for an industrial capital.

When Fiat's founder, Giovanni Agnelli, was born in 1866, Italy had only recently become a unified nation under the Savoy flag. Agnelli may not have been an aristocrat, but he grew up in a splendid Baroque villa with a façade touched up by the Savoy family's royal architect, Filippo Juvarra, who modeled its arched-top windows on the garden façade of the Palace of Versailles.[27] Acquired by his father in 1853,[28] the villa is now the symbol of the Agnelli dynasty and was much beloved of Giovanni's grandson Gianni, who kept a painting of it behind his desk.[29] Gianni recalled fond memories of playing in Villar Perosa's huge grounds as a child with his band of brothers, sisters, and cousins, passing the time studying, riding a horse, or later driving his motorcycle up and down the surrounding hills.[30] His daughter Margherita was married there in the 1970s, and Agnelli family members would be later laid to rest—many of them prematurely, as tragedy struck again and again—in the family vault in the town's cemetery.

Giovanni's grandson Gianni was a shrewd exploiter of the villa's symbolic value.

"I remember a few times he called me and said 'Come to Villar,'" said a former Fiat executive. "It's not that he couldn't have come to Turin. It was the symbolism of having meetings here—a symbol of the dynasty. I was sure he wanted to show us that it was the Windsor Castle. Then he would offer to fly me back to Turin in the helicopter."

■ ■ ■

Giovanni Agnelli's father Edoardo had first come to Villar Perosa to invest in the nascent silk production industry and was wealthy enough to leave the land surrounding the villa to be cultivated by a family of sharecroppers when he became mayor. Agnelli's father died in 1871, and his mother, Aniceta Frisetti, decided that the young Giovanni should become a cavalry officer, "in order to mark the family's definitive entry to the circle of new social relationships that were gradually being formed between the old aristocracy and the more recent wealthy bourgeoisie from the provinces," says Fiat historian Valerio Castronovo.[31]

Giovanni's father grew rich enough from silk production and agriculture to buy an imposing villa from descendents of local aristocracy. But social customs of the day were a holdover from the eighteenth century. Giovanni would never be able to socialize with the best circles or the aristocracy unless he became a high-ranking military officer. "It was almost like taking revenge against those schoolmates of his who, since they were from the nobility, did not have permission from their parents to speak to someone from a different social class like him," wrote Castronovo.[32]

After a solitary adolescence in the gloomy baroque splendor of Villar Perosa, Giovanni was packed off to a military academy in Modena at 18 years of age in 1884, and in 1889 was named a lieutenant in the Savoy cavalry. A photograph of the young officer in 1891 in full dress uniform reeks of the formality of a bygone era, his left hand on a sword so long it touches the ground. A long sash with tassels crosses his chest, and a rigid helmet topped by a sort of metallic chicken's crest adorns his head.

Indeed, the cavalry was no longer in its heyday, as Agnelli discovered when he arrived in Verona for his posting with his young wife, Clara.[33] They lived on the Corso Cavour, a street lined with grand neoclassical palaces, in the Palazzo Balladoro—which was less famous than the neighboring piles but could still boast a *piano nobile* with colorful frescoes by a pupil of Tiepolo, the Venetian master.[34] More importantly, the palace was next to a large garage that doubled as a mechanical workshop.

Agnelli and his friend Giulio Figarolo di Gropello, a fellow lieutenant from Piedmont, amused themselves with mechanical experiments. Gropello was the kind of person who jumped off a roof to test a parachute, with unpleasant consequences.

"The surface, according to my calculations, was more than enough to carry my airborne weight," he told Agnelli. "Luckily the top of the farm was no higher than six meters from the ground. I climbed to the top and jumped. What a flight! I found myself on the ground much more quickly than I had thought, and with a broken leg."[35]

Agnelli, not the type to leap off a roof in a test flight, told him: "Your inventions are too dangerous. I would be happy if we could just nail down perpetual motion."[36]

The friends, both landowners, were keen to develop motorized locomotion that could be used in agriculture. After hearing about a certain German named Daimler who had invented an engine, Agnelli paid a visit to the workshop of an Italian professor at the nearby University of Padua, Enrico Bernardi, who was developing an internal combustion engine that would later be patented. Agnelli witnessed Bernardi's tests, which were made between 1887 and 1889, and "returned home enthusiastic about the man and his research."[37] Bernardi's three-wheeled car, which was made in 1894 and reached speeds of 35 kilometers per hour, now sits almost forgotten in the university's museum.

Bernardi's experiments seem to have emboldened Agnelli and his friend Gropello to try some tinkering of their own—they managed to blow up their workshop by trying to run a Daimler engine that had been scrapped, when they tried to rig up a carburetor for it.[38]

Scientific knowledge traveled quickly in those days, so Italy did not lag far behind other European countries in terms of technical know-how.[39] Turin was not short of garage tinkerers who dreamed of building a faster motorcar, which explained why Italy's auto industry was fast out of the gate when the time came. What it needed—and lacked—were capital, industrial vision, and managerial expertise. Bernardi, like many inventors, had none of these. Italy's auto industry would therefore pass Padua by. But Bernardi's meeting with Agnelli obviously had an effect on the young man's decision to leave the military.

"We could justifiably ask ourselves whether the young Torinese military officer would have made that decision if he had not met Enrico Bernardi, if he hadn't had access to his storerooms, if he hadn't experienced the inspiration of scientific trial and error,"[40] writes Silvio Pozzani.

Agnelli's military experience gave him access to an elite social class that would otherwise have been barred to him by the customs of the day. It would also stick with him until his dying day, making a lasting impact on his future, on that of Fiat, and on the dynasty he founded. Life in the cavalry gave him early managerial experience in commanding large groups of people, as he later would in Fiat's factories, walking the floors as if he were inspecting troops. This sense of military discipline and duty stuck with him and was the characteristic that later members of the Agnelli dynasty would recall the most.

■ ■ ■

Giovanni Agnelli made his first trip to the United States in 1906 for the opening of a Fiat dealership on Broadway in New York,[41] where Fiat had started to export automobiles, and visited Detroit as well. The latter city was in full-blown auto gold rush mode, with literally dozens of companies springing up and closing each year as fortunes were made and lost.[42]

Unfortunately, Agnelli did not keep a diary of his travels or write his memoirs. He was likely to have visited the red brick Ford plant on Piquette Avenue, where the Model N, a precursor to the Model T, had just been launched.[43] Ford had just gained full control of the company that bore his name, and was hell-bent on realizing his dream.

"We're going to expand this company, and see it grow in leaps and bounds," he told an employee in July 1906. "The proper system, as I have in mind, is going to get the car to the people."[44]

Ford, during the period of Agnelli's visit, was already working on the Model T, and the factory managers—along with their competitors— were already experimenting with moving the auto chassis around the factory in a sort of rudimentary assembly line. Ford spent most of his time in the drafting room, the experimental department, or the power room. Showing signs of a habit that foreshadowed later trouble, he would let correspondence pile up on his desk, including important letters. His son Edsel, age 12, would sometimes come in after school to help out with his mail.[45]

Agnelli visited Ford again in 1909, and in 1911 and 1912. It was the start of a long friendship that continued with both men's grandsons, Gianni and Henry Ford II.

After that, he stopped looking at what was happening in Paris; he realized that personalized production for elite buyers, the business model for the French industry, sooner or later would be outdated, wrote Italo Pietra in *I Tre Agnelli*.[46]

During his 1912 trip to Detroit, Agnelli saw a new factory that was already one of the wonders of the industrialized world: Henry Ford's Model T plant in Highland Park. Dubbed the "Crystal Palace" by locals during its construction for the huge amount of glass in its roof and walls, the Albert Kahn–designed plant was a sort of cathedral for the motorcar.[47] The building was visionary not only in its size, but in its organization. Each floor of the factory did a different task, with production starting on the top floor and ending at the bottom. A year after Agnelli's visit, in the fall of 1913, after years of experimentation, the first assembly line finally took shape.

Giovanni Agnelli would soon copy not only Ford's assembly line but the entire Highland Park factory as well. Agnelli immediately recognized that Ford's early production experiments were just what Italy needed, since the poor, agricultural country could not afford the luxury of hand-produced automobiles. Ford was the man he admired most, and on his desk Agnelli kept a photograph of himself and Henry Ford standing side by side—both men in three-piece suits and sharing an intense, rather dour air.[48]

Fiat set up its first, rudimentary assembly line in 1912.[49] Its shift to what could then be considered large-scale production, as well as an increase in factory space, positioned the company to reap advantages when Italy went into World War I in 1915. Its first car off the new assembly line, the Tipo Zero, presented in 1912, was a success. It was an economical car for its time, and it was small. It had four comfortable cowhide seats, a folding windshield, and a roof fitted with side curtains.

"The Zero marked the introduction of two factors that were to be the foundation stone of Fiat's success: standardized production and the popular car," wrote Riccardo Felicioli in *Fiat: 1899–1999*."[50]

The Zero summed up the young company's game plan, which was to make standardized, midpriced cars. That strategy forced Fiat into highly targeted business, technical, and financial decisions, which, in turn, made it stand out from its 40-odd competitors of the era. The decision made Fiat's cars rather staid. But it also meant that by the outbreak of World War II there would be only three Italian car companies left: Fiat, Lancia, and Alfa Romeo (which had support from the state).[51] By its 100th anniversary, Fiat would own all three. But that success was cut short when Fiat shifted to wartime production.

Agnelli took a cautious attitude toward Italy's entry into the war, not least because it limited the company from exporting to countries where it did business.[52] However, he was not above exploiting wartime advantages for Fiat's benefit. By the end of the war, Fiat had become Italy's third-largest industry; its workforce had ballooned to 40,000 from 4,000. Fat with war profits and trophy winnings from a defeated Austria, Agnelli at age 50 had become one of Italy's most powerful men. By 1918, Fiat was the largest producer of vehicles in Europe, manufacturing 70,862 cars between 1915 and 1918, compared to 3,300 per year before the start of the war.[53]

"Giovanni Agnelli was a genius. He understood that, at his time, America was the leader in creating the social and economic conditions by which workers could buy a car. It's a social and political climate that needed to be created," said Carlo de Benedetti, a Turin native who briefly ran Fiat and later turned Olivetti into a leading computer maker.

■ ■ ■

On the morning of September 1, 1920, after 20 years of company growth, Giovanni Agnelli, for the first time—but not the last—lost control of Fiat.

After months of strikes, factories all over northern Italy announced a factory lockout overnight. All of Europe had been crippled by labor unrest, sparked by the Bolshevik Revolution in Russia and the privations of war. Up until late into the night of August 31, Agnelli believed that the government would send troops to defend the factories.[54] But when he awoke the following morning, he found that the government had changed its mind. Or perhaps Agnelli had misread the situation.

"It would have been civil war," Prime Minister Giolitti later told Parliament.[55]

The next morning, Fiat workers streamed through the gates as usual, took up their places, and then sat down, crossed their arms, and refused to work until they received orders from the Workers' Council.[56] All over Italy, an estimated half a million workers did the same thing. The "occupation" would last the entire month.

Italy seemed to be on the verge of its own October Revolution. "Proletariat of Italy: Get Organized, Get Disciplined, Get Armed," screamed Socialist daily *Avanti!* in a banner headline on September 7.

At Fiat Centro, its largest workshop, Giovanni Parodi, secretary of the Internal Commission, was named its new manager by the Workers' Council. He walked the floor telling workers to be disciplined, to stay armed, and to continue their obstruction. He now ran the factory. Parodi, a World War I veteran, had been a member of the Socialist Party since 1905 and was also a union leader.

"Workers! It is time to show that you are able to accurately run the workshop without the supervision of the boss. Your Internal Commission will look out for your interests and will know when to contact you at the right moment," read the first statement on the first day of the worker-run Fiat.

The workers' councils were the idea of Antonio Gramsci, one of the founding theorists of Italy's Communist Party, who saw them as a way of bringing the Russian soviet councils to Italy.

In Turin, 185 factories were occupied that day, without bloodshed. Management had largely abandoned the plants; the technical staff who remained (at the request of their supervisors, who did not want to abandon the factory altogether) were generally allowed to come and go as they pleased. As night fell, armed "Red Guard" sentinels kept watch from the roof. At Lingotto, police attempted to break into the factory to confiscate weapons, but came away empty-handed because the guns were stashed away in various factories.[57]

During the first week, the pace of production slowed but Fiat's factories continued to produce automobiles. At Fiat Centro, about 37 cars were made a day compared to the usual 67 or 68. Trucks rolled in and out of the factory gates. Workers hung red flags out here and there, but mostly just focused on running the factory; they were searched going in and out by the Red Guards to make sure they weren't stealing. No alcoholic beverages were allowed.[58]

In Turin, workers were already starting to suggest at factory councils and union meetings that they set up a sales organization to sell the automobiles the worker-run factories were producing. But the Federazione Impiegati Operai Metallurgici (FIOM), the largest metal-working union, was against it.

"Production is owned by the collectivity and as such must be administered by the organs that represent the collective interest," it said in a statement, *Avanti!* reported September 5, adding that FIOM aimed that the factory inventory would be used for trading with Soviet Russia.

On the first Red Sunday, the Fiat Workers' Council admonished its comrades that "there must be no revelry" on their day off.

"The workers must demonstrate their seriousness," *Avanti!* said.

Fiat Brevetti, or patent office, went one better, calling workers into the factory on Sunday.

"Show that you are not afraid of fatigue, discomfort and danger for the emancipation from the capitalist scum!" said Brevetti's Workers' Council. Earlier that week, workers had discovered "black lists" in the Fiat management offices, with names of workers who were subversive and should be fired.[59] They found little else of value, since management had taken all the cash and important documents with them.

The occupation showed that Gramsci's Workers' Councils were successful enough at running a big industrial concern like Fiat. But as the days wore on, the lack of political organization and resources took its toll. The workers occupying Fiat Centro had just 5,000 rounds of ammunition—enough to defend the factory, but hardly enough to start a revolution.

Agnelli and his workers reached a compromise showing he was open to giving them control of running the factory.

"The preparation for a revolution was nonexistent," wrote Paolo Spriano,[60] Italy's foremost historian of the labor movement. "In military terms, there was not even the embryo of a central organization."

Political support for the movement was divided. The union and the Socialist Party could not agree on how to proceed. The Confederation of Italian Labor and the Socialist Party put the question to a vote in a conference in Milan on September 9 and 10, at which the union had the majority of the assembly. The revolution lost.[61] Giolitti's government stepped in at that point to broker wage talks.

On September 30, at 11:30 A.M., Agnelli came back to his office at Fiat. He was greeted by jeers and whistles from workers, along with cries of "Long live the Soviet!"[62] When he arrived in his office, the portrait of the king had been replaced with an image of Lenin.[63]

The day before, Agnelli had made a surprising move. At a board meeting on September 29, he had proposed to turn Fiat into a worker's cooperative.

"Awaiting a response, neither myself nor the director general can remain in their post," he said.

A tactical move? A sincere offer? Only Agnelli knew for sure. He was voted back in at a shareholders' meeting on October 26 to 28.[64]

From 1921, Fiat set up a mutual society to help workers pay for medical and legal assistance. The first Fiat summer camp for workers' children was set up in 1924, at Challand Saint Victor in the Alps outside Turin. One on the seaside followed in 1933. Through the years, Fiat developed a sort of internal cradle-to-grave corporate welfare state.

The factory occupation played a part in social changes that led to a revolution of another kind. Benito Mussolini, with the backing of landowners and other members of the ruling class, made his March on Rome two years later, on October 28, 1922. Italy spent the next 20 years under a Fascist dictatorship, a political force that took its strength from "the resentment of little men in a society that crushed them between the rock of big business on one side and the hard place of rising mass labor movements on the other."[65]

In the fall of 1923, Mussolini was relaxing at a gala dinner at the Hotel d'Europe in downtown Turin after a visit to the new Fiat factory earlier that day. The crème de la crème of Turin's business and social circles turned out for the glittering occasion, the men dressed in tailcoats and the women in evening gowns.

After dinner, Mussolini and his entourage went to stand on the balcony to watch a nighttime parade of people bearing flaming torches in his honor in Piazza Castello below. The square was illuminated by the torches and by fountains of fireworks, which lit up the royal palace opposite the square from the hotel. The small group was joined by Agnelli, his white tailcoat highlighted by the red and white ribbon of his Corona d'Italia medal, a royal honor, on his chest. Agnelli had just been named a senator by Mussolini's newly minted regime a few months before, and would henceforth be called *il Senatore* by his family and biographers.

"Satisfied, are you?" Agnelli said to Cesare Maria de Vecchi, Mussolini's mustachioed strongman in Turin and one of his four *quadrumiviri* who had led the March on Rome.[66]

"For tonight and today, but not with your comments this morning at Fiat," de Vecchi replied.

Agnelli countered, "But at Fiat it went just fine. . . ."

"It depends on your point of view," de Vecchi retorted.

Mussolini stood back and watched the argument develop, his arms folded across his chest.

Agnelli knew very well what de Vecchi was getting at. Mussolini had come to Turin to visit Agnelli's latest wonder: a huge, pale, five-story factory called the Lingotto where the clattering assembly line was churning out cars using the latest methods from the United States of America. The day before the visit, Agnelli had met with his Internal Committee at the factory and told them, "There are three ways to handle this visit: applaud, stay quiet, or sabotage it. I will let you choose between the first two." As Il Duce strutted through the factory, workers on the assembly line had watched in silence.[67] It was a slap in the face.

"At Fiat, Il Duce was given a fine—splendid—welcome," Agnelli insisted. "Just ask him."

"Compare this show of support, so warm and enthusiastic, with the gray and gelid one this morning," de Vecchi continued, not backing down. Neither did Agnelli.

"I have contributed just as much if not more to the splendid success of this demonstration of national solidarity than you have," he said. The two men started arguing in earnest, and de Vecchi finally got the better of him. Agnelli took the cigar from his mouth, tore it to pieces, and stalked out.

Agnelli's haughty attitude demonstrated that he was an industrial force to be reckoned with, even by someone as all-powerful as Mussolini. Agnelli did not become a member of the Fascist party until 1932. All the same, as the years rolled by Agnelli, *il Senatore*, did not disdain receiving help or favors from the regime, like when Mussolini banned Ford from building cars at its factory in Trieste in northern Italy in 1931. When Mussolini increased import tariffs on cars in 1930 by more than 100 percent, particularly hitting Ford and Chevrolet and greatly benefiting Fiat, Agnelli was quoted in *Time* magazine as saying, "I have promised the government not to take advantage of the cessation of American competition by increasing the prices of Fiat cars."[68]

Nor did he disdain in 1932 from lobbying Mussolini for tax breaks for a new small "people's car" called the Balilla, a name plucked from Italian history for the Fascist youth organization's young scouts.[69] "We businessmen are for the government by definition," said Agnelli when asked.[70] Such cynicism, while shared by other businessmen of the era, earned Italy's industrial class a withering reprimand from anti-Fascist economist Luigi Einaudi. He wrote an open letter in *Corriere della Sera* in the summer of 1924 after the murder of Giacomo Matteotti, a Socialist opponent of the regime, blasting the entrepreneurial class for complacency.[71]

For Agnelli, no price was too small to pay if it meant that Fiat could continue to grow into the international colossus he envisioned. Thus began a sort of 20-year-long tug-of-war between two men who each realized that the other was too strong to bend completely to his will.

"The boss of Rome and the boss of Turin ended up almost seeming like Siamese twins who were separated at birth," writes Agnelli biographer Marie-France Pochna.[72]

The Balilla was Fiat's first real attempt to make a people's car. It was roomy (considering its size), faster, cheaper, and much lighter than its predecessors. In the mid-1930s, car design underwent something of revolution, benefiting from a better understanding of the interplay between aerodynamics and styling. Fiat pushed forward with its goal of an efficient small car—along with a number of other European manufacturers—and that effort bore fruit in 1936 with the Fiat 500, which was immediately and affectionately nicknamed "Topolino," or "Mickey Mouse." The 500 was the smallest and most economical mass-market car ever made up to that time. It had four cylinders, instead of two, like some of its European rivals. And it had a curvy design that departed from the boxier look of the Balilla.

■ ■ ■

Once Agnelli had created an international automotive heavyweight, his next ambition was to lock up its control for him and his growing family by creating the Istituto Finanziario Industriale (IFI), a holding company, in 1927. Agnelli was now dizzyingly wealthy; IFI had investments in some 30 companies spanning mining, mechanics, chemicals, insurance, aeronautics, and shipping.[73] The first shareholders were Agnelli, his son Edoardo, and a group of corporate allies including Milan's Pirelli family. In 1932, IFI's statutes were changed so that any shareholder selling a stake had to first offer it to other shareholders. The twin engines of Fiat, already diversified into marine, air, and auto engines as well as other related businesses, and IFI, with its growing portfolio of investments, were the launchpad for the Agnelli family's later dominance of Italy's economy, which would reach its peak in the late 1980s.

In 1935, Agnelli lost his son Edoardo in a freak accident flying back in a plane to Turin after a carefree day on the beach with family members at their summer home in Forte dei Marmi. Giovanni traveled to Genoa, the site of the accident, where he identified his son in the morgue. In a grim ritual that would be repeated by his grandsons Gianni and Umberto many years later, Agnelli was forced to stand before his son's dead body. His military training did not desert him. He stood in silence for 10 minutes.[74]

The accident changed the family's fate. Agnelli, as old age approached, had already decided that his son Edoardo needed help running such a big company and had named Vittorio Valletta as one of Fiat's top managers. It would prove to be an excellent move, sparing Fiat the sort of warfare that went on at the Ford Motor Company between Henry and his son Edsel, which had left the company prey to a ruthless and dangerous manager. Valletta, a short, stocky man with a horsey smile, ran Fiat with an iron fist until the mid-1960s, taking it through the difficult war years, through reconstruction, and into Italy's economic boom.

"The Agnellis retained their economic and political power by creating and perpetuating, through acumen, intelligence, and force, an aura of familial legitimacy. This contrasts strongly with the more typical story of the Fords, where outsiders and family members repeatedly clashed over control," writes David Landes in the book *Dynasties*.[75]

The future of the Agnelli dynasty, however, was now on the shoulders of a very young man. Deprived of an heir, Giovanni began to groom his grandson Gianni, just 14, to one day take over the company. Gianni, in turn, would revere him throughout his adult life, keeping his photograph in his office just as old Agnelli had kept Henry Ford's.

■ ■ ■

On April 30, 1945, Edmondo Schmidt di Friedberg, the young son of a Fiat executive, saw a strange car appear in Turin's Piazza Castello that looked like a box mounted on four high wheels.[76] He later learned it was called a "general purpose" vehicle, or a "jeep" for short.

"They won the war with *these*?" Edmondo thought to himself.

The four men on board stopped and fiddled briefly with the vehicle's radiotelephone. Then they drove once around the square, and left. The U.S. Fifth Army had arrived in Turin!

Edmondo was not just a passive bystander. His father, and Fiat, had played an active role in Italy's war effort before, during, *and* after its surrender.

In the days after the Allies liberated Turin, Carlo Schmidt, Edoardo's father, acted as a mediator in the surrender of the retreating German commander, Hans Schlemmer, to the U.S. colonel leading the 15th Allied Army Group.

"Doesn't it seem a little bit beneath him, for a German general, the signature of an American *colonel*?" Schlemmer's aide-de-camp couldn't resist saying to Schmidt and his party when they served him the papers at the Castello Mazzè outside Turin.[77]

Between 1941 and 1943, Edoardo's father, Carlo, had fed Agnelli intelligence from Berlin after Carlo's nomination as an economic attaché at the Italian embassy. He warned the aging industrialist's right-hand man, Vittorio Valletta, about "a huge amount of illusions surrounding the overpowering invincibility of our ally."[78]

"Those responsible for the economic life of our nation . . . must be placed in a position whereby they can contribute to forming public opinion about the real facts," Schmidt had written in one of many memos, and Fiat had not wasted time in making contact with the British and American forces.

After Italy surrendered on September 8, 1943, the country was divided in two. The northern half, down to Rome, was occupied by the Germans. One of Agnelli's first actions after the surrender was to send Carlo Schmidt to Rome to "put himself at the disposition of the Italian government in all areas where Fiat could help the national cause and to work in close collaboration with the Allies," Schmidt's son Edoardo later wrote in his memoirs.[79] For this purpose, Schmidt was given the sum of 20 million lire to spend on his secret mission.[80]

During the months before the end of the war, the Agnelli family almost lost control of Fiat for the second time in 25 years. Valletta and Agnelli had carried out a delicate balancing act during the German occupation that began in September 1943. The German commanders from the start of 1944 pressed Fiat to supply their army with tanks, airplane engines, and trucks, under threat of moving the factory and its workers to Germany. So Valletta complied. But secretly, he began supplying money, trucks, and gasoline to the partisans and other liberation movements, risking being shut down, jailed, or worse by the Germans if they discovered what he was doing. Mussolini's Salò Republic aimed to confiscate and socialize Italian industry, and Mussolini, as yet, could not yet be ignored. The Allies, for their part, wanted Fiat's factories to run as little as possible.

In the spring of 1944, Fiat executive Paolo Ragazzi was ordered to act as a liaison with the U.S. and British forces. With Valletta's permission, he set up a radio station inside Fiat's factory. By August, he was operating out of a Fiat office in downtown Turin, also equipped with a radio.[81]

In April 1944, Giancarlo Camerana, Fiat vice-chairman and Giovanni Agnelli's grandson by marriage, contacted Allen Dulles's Office of Strategic Services (OSS) office in Berne to fill him in on Fiat's plans for closer commercial ties with the United States, rather than with Great Britain, after the war.[82] Meanwhile, Schmidt in Rome had been discovered, and was sitting in jail.

At the same time, Agnelli and Valletta increasingly supported the resistance movement, funneling funds to the partisans who fought with the Allied armies clawing their way up the Italian boot from the south. "Valletta and Agnelli's actions demonstrate they had an overall plan that went above and beyond saving the company and the people who worked there, and was intended to lay the groundwork for a restoration of the social order with the support of the Anglo-Americans," writes military historian Gianni Oliva.[83]

Their support of the partisans wasn't enough. At the end of November 1944, Valletta was declared a traitor for having collaborated with the German occupiers by the Piedmont section of the Comitato di Liberazione Nazionale (CLN), the committee that acted as Italy's government during the German occupation, and would therefore be arrested and have to stand trial at the end of the war.[84]

On March 18, 1945, a regional commission overseeing the purges of Fascist and Nazi collaborators ruled that Agnelli's, Camerana's, and Valletta's properties be confiscated "for having actively taken part in the political life of Fascism through their many visible demonstrations of support and propaganda" as well as for having benefited economically.

On April 23—about a week before Turin was liberated by the Americans—Valletta was arrested. He was freed and went back to Fiat's Mirafiori factory, but it was too dangerous for him to stay. He could be shot by partisans for having collaborated with Mussolini and the Germans. The ever-useful Schmidt smuggled him back out again as the Germans retreated, killing two workers posted outside.[85] After handing managing powers of Fiat over to the *comitato operaio*, or workers' council,[86] Valletta bided his time in semihiding in an office he set up in downturn Turin. It was a difficult period. During a visit to the home of one of his friends in Turin, his dreadful appearance ("seeing his darkened face, wearing a raincoat of indefinable color and a hat too large pulled down over his head") he was kept waiting on the doorstep because the child who answered the door thought he might be a beggar.[87]

Valletta appealed his case, and the hearings took place starting in May 1945. As evidence, he submitted letters of thanks from Colonel Harold Stevens of the British intelligence service and from the U.S. OSS headquarters detachment for his help in organizing clandestine resistance. He also submitted telegrams from the Gestapo asking for his arrest (on October 10, 1943).[88]

A 23-page defense memo dated May 13, 1945, scrupulously notes the sums given by the Agnelli family to the partisans ("over 100 million") in the form of logistical and medical assistance ("worth about 500 million") starting September 8, 1943, the date of Italy's surrender, as well as Fiat's donations of food and clothing to deprived workers.[89] Witnesses appearing in the trial overwhelmingly supported Valletta's case.

Allied command in Turin took an immediate interest in Valletta's case and pushed for a speedy trial, even going so far as to nominate him to a committee of industrialists set up in Milan that summer. The Italian government also became interested in his case, and Foreign Minister Alcide De Gasperi pressured the CLN on his behalf. The archbishop of Turin chipped in his two cents, telling both the CLN and Allied forces that Valletta was the right man to run Fiat.[90] By July 1946, Valletta was flying up and down Italy in an Allied military jet. He was soon cleared.

If Valletta and Agnelli had not succeeded on playing a "double or triple game,"[91] Fiat could have been expropriated after the war, and both could have been jailed. The family would have lost control of the company.

Giovanni Agnelli died on the evening of December 16, 1945, at age 79, in his home, just as he was about to be cleared of wartime Fascist collaboration.

■ ■ ■

For a man who had dedicated his entire life to building Fiat and who had enjoyed almost unlimited power, Giovanni Agnelli's last days must have been a huge disappointment. His tiny funeral of just a few dozen people was an unusually gloomy affair as the procession paused in front of his ruined Mirafiori factory on its way to Villar Perosa.

"Really, to think of everything he had done in his life made us feel incredibly sad," recalled Gianni Agnelli years later.[92]

One of Giovanni's last acts had been to convene an IFI board meeting so that the Agnelli family holding company could approve plans to rebuild Mirafiori. More importantly, he made a decision that would guarantee the dynasty's stability for the next generation. He divided his estate into equal parts among son Edoardo's seven children (the Agnelli side) and daughter Aniceta's five children (the Nasi side). Almost equal parts, that is. Gianni got a double share, assuring his position as future leader.[93] Gianni's goal would be to make Fiat prosper while keeping it in family hands. He would almost lose control of the company two more times.

And he would then reign uncontested until his death.

# Chapter 3

# From Salad to Skinny-Dipping

On May 24, 1899, the Principessa Massimo, from one of Rome's oldest aristocratic families, left her palace in a horse-drawn carriage encrusted with gold and crystal, crossed the Piazza Venezia, and climbed Rome's highest hill to attend the baptism of her granddaughter, Virginia Bourbon del Monte di San Faustino. Virginia was also a princess, but of a lesser sort.[1] Her proud parents were Carlo Bourbon del Monte, a melancholy aristocrat whose main achievement in life was bringing the sport of polo to Rome, and a lively, eccentric American from New York City, Jane Campbell, who was known to all by the unlikely moniker of "Princess Jane."

Little Virginia grew up in the Palazzo Barberini, a building so spectacular it makes the House of Savoy's royal palace in Turin look dreary. Now a museum, the Palazzo Barberini's airy, three-story façade is covered in glittering windows the same size as the arches in the Coliseum.

The palace was commissioned by Maffeo Barberini after becoming Pope Urban VIII in 1623, so that he and his relatives could live in style befitting a prince of the Church. Not exactly modest, the Barberini Pope ordered the two top architects of his day, Borromini and Bernini, to each create a staircase for the palace's two wings. One staircase is elliptical, and the other is rectangular. Only the Bernini staircase at St. Peter's itself is grander.

A vast cultural gulf separates Giovanni Agnelli, the humorless auto baron who argued with Mussolini and ate the same vegetable salad at home every day at lunch, from his grandson Gianni Agnelli, who is possibly the only industrialist in the world ever photographed jumping naked into the water from his yacht. The link between them is Virginia Bourbon del Monte and Edoardo Agnelli. The elder Agnelli left the couple a fortune and a company, and they parlayed the Senator's money into social status and a racy style that Gianni later successfully exploited in ways his grumpy grandfather could never have dreamed of.

■ ■ ■

Edoardo was tall, lanky, and slightly stooping, and loved to make fun of people.[2] Virginia took after her mother. Jane Campbell's life in Rome was the twin of Isabelle Archer's in *The Portrait of a Lady*, the Henry James novel in which a young American is unleashed on Europe to seek her destiny. Only Jane's had a much happier ending.

"Born plain Jane Campbell in Bernardsville, N.J., she married a prince, [and] became the sharp-tongued social queen of Rome for nearly half a century," *Time* magazine noted in her obituary in 1938.[3] Jane's parents were neither rich enough nor influential enough to win a place in New York high society alongside the Astors and the Vanderbilts. Denied a debutante ball by her father, the free-spirited and enterprising young lady decided to seek her fortune in Rome, where she stayed with her aunt and uncle on Rome's main square and parlayed her considerable wit and charm into major social standing. She inherited her aunt's fortune.

Living among faded papal splendor, Virginia and her brother Ranieri seemed to have had happy childhoods—or at least that's how Princess Jane recalls it. "The years at Palazzo Barberini, with Carlo and my children, were my golden age: what I regret today is that I didn't enjoy my family enough because I was too busy having fun," she wrote in her memoirs.[4]

Virginia, by all accounts, inherited her mother's love of entertaining, her high spirits, and her sense of humor. She was incredibly charming. But there was something unsettling about Virginia as well. She was even more headstrong than Princess Jane, who claimed she fought with Prince Carlo once a week.[5] A photograph of her at age 17 captures Virginia's unusual and almost disturbing charm: her hair loose around her shoulders, dressed in a masculine suit, she is petting a leopard and studying it with an intense, mournful look on her young face.

"Her face was not one of those that betrays an ordinary or common destiny," her mother Jane wrote. "Virginia certainly would not have been satisfied with the things that made other women happy."[6]

Edoardo Agnelli began spending time at the San Faustino household in order to play bridge, one of Jane's favorite pastimes. Jane soon realized, however, that it was not the cards that interested him most. One day, after having watched yet again the young Fiat heir pass an entire afternoon and evening chatting with Virginia, Jane informed Virginia that the amount of time she was spending with Edoardo was likely to cause gossip.

"He asked me to marry him, and I said yes, because I love him," Virginia informed her mother.[7]

Virginia's blithe acceptance of his proposal without consulting her mother was an early example of her lifelong fascination with flouting the rigid traditions that governed upper-class existence. It would later cause her great pain.

Jane seemed to like her new son-in-law, Edoardo. But her first meeting with the elder Agnelli left her perplexed.

"I read in his metallic blue eyes a seriousness that disturbed me, and I cannot say how desolated I was by this, because I wanted to have good relations with my daughter's family," she wrote. At family events, he avoided spending time with her by pretending not to understand her Italian.[8]

Princess Jane was no pushover herself. A friend of her daughter-in-law Katherine Sage recalls her in the mid-1920s as "an absolute terror," and "very formidable, very imposing." Her direct, rather imperious gaze was set off by a Queen Mary of Scots style widow's peak headdress that she wore after her husband's death. In the summer, she dressed in all white, and in the winter, in black.[9]

Edoardo and Virginia were married on June 8, 1919, a warm, sunny day. Showing the sure touch for scene setting that she would display again and again throughout her life, Virginia picked one of Rome's most dramatic churches, Santa Maria degli Angeli e degli Martiri. Built on top of the majestic ruins of the Baths of Diocletian from the designs of Michelangelo, the church is one of the few places where the ghost of ancient Rome lives on in modern days through the genius of the Renaissance. The Baths of Diocletian, built in 298 AD when the Roman Empire was near its peak, were massive, extending far beyond the Piazza della Repubblica that now sits in front of the church. Michelangelo, as did many other architects of his day, took pride in reaching the same grand scale as did the masters of old. As a consequence, Santa Maria degli Angeli is one of Rome's largest churches. Princess Jane chided Virginia that it would be empty.

"It will be full, because I want to invite all of the poor people from the soup kitchens" where she had worked with Jane during the war, Virginia told her.[10]

And she did.

The church was so packed that the bride and groom had a hard time making their way from the altar to the exit.[11] Afterward, the couple entertained 150 guests in the Palazzo Barberini and 300 more in the soup kitchen on Via Mantova at Virginia's request.[12] They left for their honeymoon in Venice in a custom-made Fiat car. The couple settled in Turin, in a mansion in the center of town that Virginia redecorated.

Together, Edoardo and Virginia were a sort of Roaring Twenties version of Elizabeth Taylor and Richard Burton, the sort of couple that in a later age would become standard tabloid fodder: they had a magnetic combination of good looks, aristocratic connections, and new money.

Virginia and Edoardo threw glittering parties at their mansion on Corso Oporto attended by Crown Prince Umberto of Savoy and his wife Maria José wearing a diamond diadem, another of the era's golden couples. These highly formal evenings were right out of a painting by John Singer Sargent or F. Scott Fitzgerald's The Great Gatsby.

Men wore tails and women dressed in bare-shouldered evening gowns with swept-up hair.

Crown Prince Umberto of Savoy and Maria José were similar to Edoardo and Virginia in many ways. Both couples loved to practice a fashionable new sport called skiing in the winter at Sestriere, near Turin, where Virginia and Edoardo spearheaded the building and decorating of a glamorous new hotel to create a resort that competed with St. Moritz.

The Crown Prince Umberto was tall, slim, and dashing in military dress on horseback reviewing the royal troops. He also cut a fine figure with Maria José at the beach in swimming suits, or dressed as Bedouins on a vacation in Libya, an Italian colony.[13]

Both men took advantage of the new set of pleasures offered by modern life in the 1920s. At the same time, both Edoardo and Umberto were educated according to the strict Piedmontese military tradition, mixing duty and sacrifice with the wild hedonism of the era. Last but not least, both were heirs to the throne—one literally, one figuratively—who had overbearing fathers who overshadowed their sons. And both young men came to tragic ends.

Edoardo and Virginia also crossed paths regularly with Benito Mussolini's daughter, Edda Ciano, and her husband, Galeazzo Ciano, another ill-fated, glamorous couple of the day. The two couples also saw each other at Forte dei Marmi, a seaside resort. While his father Giovanni kept his haughty distance from the regime except when he wanted to ask it for favors, Edoardo financed Mussolini's Blackshirts.[14]

Edoardo didn't play much of a role in Fiat. Instead, he pushed the family into new businesses: tourism and sports. His purchase of the Juventus soccer team was probably the most important step in making the Agnelli clan into Italy's First Family. He didn't just buy the team; he built it up into a winning machine at a time when soccer was just becoming a mass sport.

Edoardo embraced the high life with the same gusto that his father showed in embracing the auto business. On vacation in St. Moritz in March 1929, he arrived with Virginia and one of their children, installed them in the five-star Grand Hotel Suvretta in a suite, and took a room for himself at the Palace Hotel. Every day, he hired two ski instructors. And every night he went to the bar at the Palace Hotel and partied, drank, danced, and played poker for huge sums until the early hours of the morning.[15]

"Avv. Agnelli (Edoardo) spent liberally and stood out for his extravagance and gallantry, creating envy among some of the members of the high-born and wealthy hotel patrons, in the sense that His Royal Highness (Prince Umberto) was expected to be among them," a police informer wrote in a report dated March 12, 1929.[16]

When the crown prince arrived, Edoardo organized a gala dinner in his honor in a private room, inviting the Duke of Sangro of Naples, bobsledding champion Italo Casini, Prince and Princess Borbone di Parma, Court and Countess Del Torso di Udine, and other nobles and industrialists who were vacationing at the hotel. The dinner was paid for by Agnelli and the Duke of Sangro.

Edoardo Agnelli lost 17,000 French francs in a single night of baccarat to an American guest named Lyle Samuel, who died the next day on the bobsled run.

Edoardo's lifestyle caused gossip in Turin, attracted attention, and created family problems. The couple was spied on by Mussolini's police. And so was *il Senatore*.

"Everyone in Turin knows about the family council meeting held at the Agnelli home, which was attended by [family friend] Marchese Cinzano and the Princess San Faustino, to talk about very serious events that have involved Agnelli's son," said a police report on January 27, 1931.

Virginia was also the subject of malicious gossip in Turin. She didn't like it there, and the feeling was mutual. Her mother-in-law, Clara, never accepted her.[17]

"She was criticized because she walked down the street without a hat; because she was capable of saying the worst swearwords with an angelic smile, and because she refused to listen to the gossip of the ugly old Torinese ladies," wrote one of her daughters, Susanna Agnelli, in her memoirs.[18]

■ ■ ■

Sestriere was not the only resort that the fashionable couple put on the map. Their villa in Forte dei Marmi, on the Tuscan seaside north of

Rome, turned the village from an artists' colony into the glitzy shopping mecca for Russian millionaires it is today.

The Agnelli family's sentimental life revolved around summer in Forte. Virginia and Edoardo's seven children, and their grandchildren, spent many summers playing there with their friends. The Agnelli's private beach—another rarity in Italy, where most available sand is covered with armchairs and umbrellas—was furnished with two huge tents, one for adults and one for children. Their governess, Miss Parker, allowed them in the water for only half an hour before lunch.

Miss Parker was strict, and instilled a British stiff-upper-lip education that would later serve Gianni Agnelli well. It fit in neatly with his father Edoardo's rigid education and strict parenting. Young Gianni was mischievous and needed a firm hand. Virginia, however, was permissive and would let her brood do whatever they wanted, just like she did. She found it completely normal to sunbathe nude in their garden at Forte, have tea naked in St. Moritz in the sun, or walk around her Rome apartment, in later days, without a stitch of clothing on.

"When I was a girl in the 1960s even after the Agnellis had stopped coming here, they were still one of the main topics of conversation," one longtime villa owner recalled.

It's hard to imagine Forte dei Marmi as it looked when the Agnellis built their home in the 1930s. The low-lying coast was covered with a pine forest bordering a wide sandy beach, and framed by the Apuan Alps where the white Carrara marble quarried by Michelangelo is still visible to bathers as they float in the shallow, clear blue water. Forte dei Marmi was originally nothing more than a red brick fort built by a Tuscan duke to protect the coast; the wooden dock jutting into the sea was the final destination for blocks of marble dragged by teams of oxen down from the quarries. This stretch of green coast was a nature lover's paradise, completely different in feel from nearby Viareggio and its strip of grand hotels built to mimic the great bathing resorts of the French Riviera. Picking it as their summer retreat set the family apart in terms of taste and style from other industrialists of the day.

Virginia and Edoardo's summer house was surrounded by a huge garden, and was decorated in a casual, eclectic mix of light-colored ceramic tiles made on the Amalfi coast near Sorrento and delicate floral fabrics imported from Arthur Sanderson in London. The kids would play on the beach, and Virginia would supervise, wrapped in an African cloth as a beach cover-up.[19] "It was simple, and some of the sheets were mended; that was their style," recalled a guest who spent time there in the 1950s. But the house's most noted feature was not the mended sheets. It is the only one along the entire coast from Massa Carrara to Viareggio that has a tunnel passing under the road, connecting the garden directly to the beach—an early example of the Agnelli family's formidable clout.

"When the family built the villa, there was no paved road along the seaside," explained Learco Melegari, director of the Hotel Augustus, formerly Villa Agnelli. "When the road was paved, they wanted a tunnel. And they were the only ones to get one."

Susanna Agnelli recalls the days at Forte as a sort of idyllic endless summer. "We stopped to watch the fishermen on the beach drag their nets out of the sea," she wrote affectionately about summers at Forte in her memoirs. "Finally the net appeared. You could hear it roiling and breathing before you could see it, full of its load of fish: jellyfish, sole, scorfani, cuttlefish, and sometimes a starfish. I was enchanted by the light, the odor, and the beauty of it. My father asked a fisherman to bring the smallest fish to our house to eat fried, at breakfast."[20]

It was returning home on such a day that Edoardo Agnelli died in a freak seaplane accident, en route to Genoa on his way back home after a weekend at Forte dei Marmi with Susanna, Gianni, and Princess Jane.

"In a Fiat plane and with Ferrarin as pilot, I am ready to go anywhere," Edoardo told Susanna and others at lunch before he left on July 14, 1935.[21]

The most likely cause of the accident was most likely a log or floating object in the water at the port of Genoa, where the seaplane landed, according to a newspaper report of the police investigation.[22]

"The pilot recalls that Agnelli, as soon as they touched water, complimented him on the landing and stood up to take a look," the paper wrote. "At that instant, the plane flipped over violently."

Ferrarin landed in the water unharmed, but Agnelli was struck by the propeller on the back of the head, dying instantly. Princess Jane took the phone call at Villa Agnelli with the horrible news.

■ ■ ■

Back in Turin, the Agnelli mansion on Corso Oporto was thrown open to the public, its doors draped in black in a sign of mourning. People poured in despite the sweltering heat to pay their respects to Edoardo, who lay in an open casket in a drawing room. Gianni, age 14, and Virginia were overwhelmed by the number of people coming and going, and shortly withdrew to be alone in their rooms.[23]

Crown Prince Umberto came to pay his respects the next day for a private Mass at the family home before the group left for the funeral procession. The crown prince was the godfather of the smallest Agnelli child, Umberto, who was also his namesake and not even one year old.

When Virginia and her seven children arrived at Villar Perosa for the burial, they were greeted by *il Senatore*, who stopped in silence, rooted to the spot, as the young widow approached surrounded by his grandchildren. Tears began to flow down his cheeks.

"You musn't, *Senatore*, you musn't!" Virginia cried.[24] He shook his head and walked away. The family asked the parish priest not to toll the bells for Edoardo because it would upset Clara, his mother.[25]

After the accident, at age 35, Virginia did not suddenly settle down to live the life of a respectable widow.

■ ■ ■

Edoardo Agnelli died in the summer of 1935; by the end of the year, or sometime early in 1936,[26] the family had a new companion. He was a writer who also lived in Forte, under house arrest for anti-Fascist activity after having criticized Mussolini's regime. His name was Curzio Malaparte; he was an adventurer who had fought in the brutal trenches of World War I, embraced fascism, and then rejected it. His dispatches from the savagery of Russian front, *Kaputt*, as well as his sardonic chronicle of American-occupied Naples, *La Pelle*, would later become best sellers across Europe and pave the way for writers like Ryszard Kapuscinski and Joseph Heller.[27]

It was Princess Jane, a woman who "collects human beings as others collect postage stamps or moths," according to the Countess Sermoneta,[28] who spotted him walking up and down the beach with his white dog.

"Aren't you Malaparte?" she said after having had a servant call him over to her tent. "Come over here. I want you to talk to me. You are very good-looking."

Indeed he was. He had slicked-back black hair, a body that glistened with suntan oil, and shaved armpits.[29] Imagine Rudolph Valentino as a war hero and best-selling author, and then mix in a whiff of danger from being an enemy of the Fascist regime. He had just been freed from a prison on the island of Lipari. Gianni Agnelli pretty much hated him on sight.

"He was slick, perfumed, and wore a powder-blue jacket with gold buttons. Always making puns that I found far from amusing," he told an interviewer in 1976.[30]

He was also entertaining, and soon had the Agnelli women enthralled.

"He took us by bicycle to Massa to eat salami," recalled Clara Agnelli, an exotic sort of treat for the pampered children.

Virginia and Curzio were soon discussing marriage.[31]

Virginia Agnelli could not have found a more controversial lover if she had put an ad in the paper. Curzio Malaparte was not only an enemy of Mussolini's and a former prisoner. He was an adversary of none other than Giovanni Agnelli, Virginia's father-in-law, who had fired him as editor of the Agnelli-owned newspaper *La Stampa* in the early 1930s. His dismissal of Malaparte was even ruder than his firing of Aristide Faccioli, the engineer from Fiat's early days.

"Here's your envelope with your money," Agnelli told Malaparte. "I kindly request that you return the envelope."[32]

Virginia was about to discover that dynasties confer great wealth and privilege, but members are not allowed to make their own choices about how to live their own lives and with whom. The men are expected to work for the family firm, unless of course they do not. And women generally are expected to follow convention and raise well-prepared young heirs. Or at least pretend to.

On December 19, 1936, a courthouse official knocked on Virginia Agnelli's door and handed her butler a court order to leave the house immediately.[33] Turin's Tribunale per I Minorenni (juvenile court) had awarded custody of Virginia and Edoardo's seven children to none other than *il Senatore*, Giovanni Agnelli. The order granted Virginia permission to see the children two days out of every 15 in a place picked by Agnelli, and forbade her from taking them away from Turin without his permission.[34]

The reason? "The mother, shortly after the death of her husband, entered a relationship that is still ongoing, the effects of which cannot avoid having a serious impact on the material, moral, and educational well-being of the minors," the court order said.

Instead of leaving, she got on the phone. She called her lawyers, and then called Mussolini's office to make an appointment with the one man in Italy who was surely more powerful than her father-in-law.

"Put on your coats," she then told her children.[35]

Virginia and her brood, nervous and "feeling like refugees," in the words of her daughter Susanna, boarded a train bound for Rome, where Virginia had rented a villa overlooking the city. Shortly after leaving the station in Genoa, the train ground to a halt and was searched by police. They soon found what they were looking for.

"It would be better if you all got off the train," the officer said, pointing to the children. "You must understand, madam, given the circumstances, these children have been kidnapped."[36] The Agnelli children were loaded into cars and taken to a luxury hotel in Genoa awaiting collection by their grandfather.[37] Virginia, meanwhile, traveled to Rome for a meeting with Il Duce.[38]

She had to wait for hours. But finally Mussolini received her in his office in the Palazzo Venezia, the dark-brown Renaissance palace that had served as the embassy of the Venetian Republic and a residence of the Pope up until 1797.

When Virginia was at last shown in, it seemed to take her forever to cross the cavernous room, with tall columns adorning the walls and frescoes painted by Andrea Mantegna, to Il Duce's desk in the corner. Mussolini heard her out. Virginia told him it was unfair to take her children away from her simply because she had a lover. Though sympathetic, he seemed to do little to help her.[39] The legal battle over custody of the Agnelli children was only starting.

"I am completely broken in two, I didn't think such a thing was possible. But I love you," Virginia wrote Malaparte in a letter on Christmas Eve.[40]

Back in Turin, the children were looked after by their governess, Miss Parker, and two other nannies. Every so often they were invited to Agnelli's house for a meal, where they sat in stony silence.

Virginia filed an appeal on May 8, 1937. Her legal strategy was clever: her lawyers argued that since she had moved to Rome, it was the Rome court and not Turin that should decide her case. But what seemed to tip the scales was the behavior of the Senator's grandchildren themselves. Their opposition to his plan showed him how clearly they loved their mother. Susanna was particularly stubborn. One day she went out into the mansion's courtyard and screamed to her neighbors that she wanted to return to live with her mother, and didn't stop until her grandfather threatened to send her to boarding school.[41]

Finally the Fiat founder changed his mind. Virginia's legal battle, and a visit from her son Gianni to plead her case, finally tipped the scales. Old Agnelli listened, and then told Gianni that if the children loved their mother so much, well then, in some way, maybe she wasn't that bad. Virginia had won. By all accounts, including Gianni's, the auto baron and his heir had a very close relationship during Gianni's teenage years, right up to the time Gianni left for the war.

They made peace at a dinner, where Virginia was all smiles.

"You're so young and so beautiful," the Senator told her. "And your children love you. I think you should leave Italy for a while. Go ahead, Virginia—find yourself a nice place in the South of France where you can go for summer vacation. Have fun and relax. It will be a change for the children, and they will enjoy it."[42]

Virginia rented a huge, rambling house in Cap Martin and set up camp with her maids, cooks, nannies, drivers, and Fiat cars. Chaos reigned supreme. The house was full of visitors coming and going. Susanna and Gianni, neither of them with a driving license, took the family cars cruising up and down the Côte d'Azur. Virginia went out every night. Susanna and her sisters went around wearing short shorts that barely covered their behinds, and long hair that came to the end of their shorts. Princess Jane was horrified one morning when she came for a visit and caught the children half dressed lounging around in their beds drinking pineapple juice and champagne.

"Champagne? At breakfast?" she asked.

"Why not? It's good," came the reply, at which Princess Jane stalked over to Virginia's room, threw open the door, and said, "Virginia! You must be completely mad!"[43]

This schizophrenic sort of upbringing—a strict father, a British nanny, a domineering grandfather, and then a several years running riot with a totally permissive mother—created a family of individuals who later each went their own way but were at the same time extremely close. And it seems to have made Gianni Agnelli prize a certain reserve about his emotional experiences that would last his entire life.[44]

More importantly, Gianni was skillful enough to adopt the discipline of his grandfather while retaining the esthetic sense of his mother, which was what made his personality so interesting as he grew to maturity after returning home from the war. Seeing how his mother had flouted the rules of bourgeois morality, Gianni created his own sort of morality for himself, based on esthetics, manners, and a detached, aristocratic point of view. For all his life, he never pretended to be faithful to his wife. But he always wanted to be faithful to his idea of elegance.

"Agnelli would lead a perfectly uninhibited life, but his elegance would always remain intact," wrote French author Marie-France Pochna in her excellent biography, *Agnelli, L'Irresistibile* (*Agnelli, the Irresistible*).[45]

■ ■ ■

One day in the spring of 1944, as the war was drawing to an end, Virginia Agnelli sat talking in the garden of her villa overlooking Rome to the dark-haired, effeminate Colonel Eugen Dollmann, a Nazi officer of the occupying German forces who acted as a go-between among the SS, the Fascist hierarchy, the Roman aristocracy, and the Vatican.

"The war is going to end soon, my dear Colonel, if we can believe the Allied propaganda, and I think we can," Virginia would have said, as they both looked out over the domes of the city below. "The Germans are going to retreat from Rome soon. You know that as well as I do." Virginia told Dollmann she thought that they should try to find a way to convince the German army, as it retreated, to surrender Rome quickly and without street-to-street combat that would damage the city's historic and religious treasures.[46]

The setting made their conversation something more than theoretical. The villa, called Bosco Parrasio, built into the Gianicolo Hill, was one of Rome's most striking residences. A purple hyacinth crept up the side of a large patio that formed an open-air theater modeled after ancient Greece. The terraced garden paths, dotted with fountains and benches, ran down the hill to a huge white gate. And the view out over the rooftops, domes, and ancient monuments of Rome, framed by the Alban Hills in the background, was one of the finest in all of Europe.

Italy was divided in two. The north was invaded by the German army in August 1943 after Italy's surrender, and governed by a Mussolini puppet government from Salò. Rome was an "open city," occupied by the Germans, who immediately began rounding up the Jewish population from Rome's historic Ghetto, bound for the Reich's concentration camps.

Virginia and Dollmann, a frequent visitor to Bosco Parrasio and rumored to be Virginia's lover, had many things in common. They both loved art and Rome's ancient splendor, and they shared a similar sense of humor. They both operated at the highest social level. They met after Dollmann helped free Virginia from her arrest at the end of 1943.[47] She was ransomed through bribes with money from Fiat delivered by Schmidt.

Virginia was convinced that the pair needed to engineer a meeting between a high-level Nazi officer and Pope Pius XII at the Vatican. General Karl Wolff, who was in charge of the SS and therefore the security of occupied Italy, would probably be the right person. The pair decided that Virginia Agnelli would use her connections among Roman aristocracy, traditionally close to the Church, to procure a secret meeting with the Pope. If they succeeded, Wolff would be told at the last minute.[48]

Virginia was thinking of more than simply saving the Sistine Chapel from Hitler's wrath when the Germans retreated sometime in what looked to be the near future. She was also interested in "seeking mediators in northern Italy," she told Dollmann. She was probably thinking about protecting Fiat and her family. Virginia's father-in-law had already established contact with Allen Dulles's OSS in Berne in the fall of 1943. In the Allies' view, Agnelli was useful but politically compromised in Italy after the war because of his association with Mussolini. But Virginia was not. Perhaps she and the elder Agnelli were working together. Even if they weren't, they were both working toward the same goal.

From Dollmann's point of view, keeping the Coliseum, the Vatican, and the ruins of ancient Rome intact was a worthy aim. So was easing the Germans out of northern Italy without a fight. It meant shortening the war and preventing Hitler from carrying out his plans to hole up in the Alps with a group of war-hardened loyalists and fight to the bitter end. Wolff and Dollmann realized that the war, in a certain sense, was already lost to them, and wanted to avoid more destruction.[49] Their first attempt, through Giovanni Ruspoli, failed. But Virginia persisted, and succeeded in convincing Cardinal Caccia Dominioni to act as mediator.

"Tomorrow at noon, the Pope wants to talk to the General," Virginia told Dollmann by phone.[50]

On May 10, 1944, General Wolff crossed St. Peter's square with Colonel Dollmann, wearing ill-fitting civilian clothes he had hastily borrowed from Dollmann in order not to be recognized. The meeting had been arranged without the knowledge of the Vatican's ambassador to Germany. Instead, Wolff was accompanied to the Pope's antechamber by Father Pankratius Pfeiffer, a German priest who acted as a liaison between the Vatican and the Nazi occupiers.[51]

The Pope began the secret meeting by asking what Wolff thought of the situation in Germany. Wolff filled him in on the domestic and foreign political situation, as well as the military outlook, and told the Pontiff he was worried that the country would be worn out by a useless war between Germany and the Western powers. Worse still, Europe would be exhausted while the war could continue to rage in the Far East. The Pope, said Wolff, was the only person who could intervene to get the warring powers to hasten an end to the war, which Wolff added must be ended in the most honorable way possible, since he didn't want to be considered a traitor. All the same, he wanted to carry out his military duties in the most humane way possible, Wolff told the Pope.

."To achieve this, I am prepared to risk my life and that of my family, because that is what's at stake if my intentions are misunderstood," Wolff told the Pope, according to Wolff's testimony in 1972.[52]

The Pope replied that it was not easy to gauge the Allies' willingness to enter peace talks, because of anti-Nazi and anti-German sentiment. All the same, he promised to keep the channel with Wolff open, through Cardinal Schuster in Milan.

"How much injustice, how many crimes, how many offenses to the Christian spirit of love for our fellow human beings, how many misunderstandings could have been avoided, had you only come to me sooner!" said the Pope.[53]

The audience ended. As Wolff turned to go, he instinctively raised his arm in the Nazi salute. Father Pfeiffer took him by the arm, murmuring, "I am sure the Holy Father understood your gesture in the right way."[54]

Wolff did begin to discuss a German surrender secretly with Allen Dulles, dubbed "Operation Sunrise," in March 1945, and he pointed to his meeting in 1944 with the Pope to show he was in good faith and had the Pope's imprimatur.[55] Rome fell on June 4, 1944, and the German forces in Italy surrendered on May 2, 1945. The Church protected the elder Agnelli. Cardinal Schuster of Milan was a key player in the German retreat in the North, and the cardinal asked that Agnelli not be arrested.[56]

Agnelli and the Pope had a very important aim in common: to keep Italy from being run by the Communist Party after the war. Agnelli feared that the Communist Party would nationalize Fiat; it was already being managed by a committee that answered to the CLN, Italy's de facto government.[57] The Church and the Communist Party were natural enemies. Pope Pius XII feared a leftist takeover of Rome.[58]

The U.S. government, already anxious about a Communist threat in Eastern Europe, also shared Agnelli's and the Pope's aim. Stalin and the United States were already vying to reach Trieste, on Italy's border with Yugoslavia.[59]

Postwar Italy's first elections were won by the Christian Democrats, and the new republic's foreign policy was firmly in the Atlantic camp. The dollars from the Marshall Plan soon rebuilt Fiat's factories. But Italy paid a heavy price for excluding the Partito Comunista Italiano, or Italian Communist Party, from public life in the coming decades, and the deep divisions left by the war were never healed.

■ ■ ■

Virginia and *il Senatore*, who were bitter adversaries after Edoardo's death, ended their lives working for the exact same cause: Italy's—and Fiat's—survival and reconstruction after World War II. Both played roles in laying the groundwork for Italy's future postwar prosperity as an ally of the United States (its wartime enemy). By doing so, they guaranteed that an Agnelli-owned Fiat would continue to sit at the center of Italy's economy after the war.

Virginia died in November 1945, in a car accident near Forte dei Marmi, about a month before *il Senatore*'s death. Jane Campbell had been right when she predicted that her daughter Virginia would not have "an ordinary or common destiny." Virginia and her husband stamped the Agnelli children with their own idiosyncratic style, which came from an unconventional search for freedom from tradition that would have made her more at home in the 1960s. Her aristocratic upbringing and habits, at the same time, gave the provincial Agnelli clan the polish that Gianni would later build on in his long career as jet-setter-cum-industrialist.

# Chapter 4

# Gianni Agnelli, King of a Republic

E arly in the summer of 1993, Bocconi business school professor Giuliano Urbani made a surprising discovery: the next time Italy went to the polls, the parliament would end up being controlled by the Democratic Party of the Left (Partito Democratico della Sinistra or PDS), the new name for Italy's Communist Party.

The good news was that Italy's revolving-door governments would be a thing of the past. The bad news—in some people's eyes, like Silvio Berlusconi's, for example—was that the study showed that Italy's PDS would win 65 percent of the seats with less than 30 percent of the votes. At a time when the Communist Party was on the wane even in Russia, one of the world's largest economies was likely to be governed by a political party that still displayed the hammer and sickle on its party logo. Urbani published his study in Italy's main business daily, *Il Sole-24 Ore*.

The bespectacled professor was promptly deluged with speaking invitations from worried business groups, including one from Gianni Agnelli, who asked Urbani to come to Turin to address Fiat's executive committee. Urbani and Agnelli knew each other well, since Agnelli had been inviting Urbani to dinners at his residence, Villa Frescot, to discuss politics since the mid-1960s. The business community was concerned that a PDS-dominated parliament could strengthen union influence, could delay Italy's entry into the euro, and could even press for nationalizations of key industries. Italy's political class had been shaken to its core over the past year by an uncompromising anticorruption probe that had also snared Italy's top businessmen—including a few at Fiat—in its net. State-owned industry had been a key source of kickbacks. Italy's establishment was leery of any party that advocated a role for the state in business. The centrist Christian Democrat (DC) party and its leftist ally, the Socialist party, would soon be decimated by the scandal. But the PDS, with fewer politicians involved, would survive.

As Urbani was leaving the room after his presentation at Fiat, Gianni Agnelli turned to him and asked, "Did you speak to Silvio Berlusconi about this?" Agnelli knew that no one had more to lose from a PDS-led parliament than Berlusconi, the left-wing party's public enemy number one; the PDS had battled his swift growth into a media baron at every step. Plus, the TV tycoon had been toying with the idea of stepping somehow into the political void, and Agnelli's excellent radar had picked up on it.[1]

"I don't even know him," Urbani replied.

Two days later Urbani's phone rang, and Berlusconi was on the line. "I heard you did an interesting study," he told the stunned professor. "Can we talk about it?"

"Who do you think gave him my number? Agnelli!" Urbani recalled with a smile.

The rest, as they say, is history. At a meeting in his villa outside Milan that summer, Berlusconi told Urbani he was toying with the idea of founding a party, but did not intend to lead it or run it. By fall, Urbani was working on the political platform for the party that became Forza Italia, which Berlusconi created using managers from his Fininvest SpA holding company. Urbani later became a minister in Berlusconi's first government in 1994.

The anecdote speaks volumes about Agnelli's ability to pull strings behind the scenes in Italy to influence events in the way that best suited Fiat's interests. While he spent most of his career advocating cooperation with the Partito Comunista Italiano, he clearly was not keen to see the country take the risk of a PDS-dominated parliament. Agnelli managed to guide the flow of political events without ever directly entering the fray. For most of his life, he acted as Italy's unofficial foreign ambassador, particularly for business and political relations between the United States and Italy. John F. Kennedy and Henry Kissinger consulted him on Italian politics.[2]

■ ■ ■

At the end of World War II, Gianni Agnelli returned home to Turin after fighting in Tunisia and Russia alongside the Fascist army, and then fighting in Italy with U.S. General Mark Clark's Fifth Army. He was very much alone. His grandfather, tired, friendless, and worn out, died just a month after Gianni's mother Virginia in 1945, leaving Gianni, at age 24, to lead his family and Fiat. The young Agnelli was overwhelmed by the destruction of the war. Fiat's state-of-the-art new Mirafiori factory, his grandfather's pride and joy, was a bombed-out hulk. The Agnelli estate in nearby Villar Perosa was also damaged. He was weighed down by responsibility for his six brothers and sisters, and deeply worried by Fiat's uncertain fate.

"When I arrived in Turin, I was greeted by a sea of red flags," he later recalled. "I felt a certain amount of joy, but also a certain amount of fear . . . there were so many kids . . . and everything needed to be rebuilt."[3]

The "sea of red flags" Gianni saw were worrying to him for good reason. The war had left Italy not only physically destroyed, but politically divided. The Italian Communist Party, or PCI, had earned widespread support for its brave leadership of the partisan uprising that helped the Allies push back the Germans during the final phase of the war, which restored a modicum of pride to a humiliated nation. But industrialists like Agnelli, as well as Allied leaders themselves, were worried that the PCI could emerge as the main political force in postwar Italy. The young Agnelli faced a serious risk that a new left-wing government could nationalize Fiat. And in a broader sense, Italy was on the dividing line of the Iron Curtain. It bordered on Yugoslavia.

Italy did not "go red" or suffer a right-wing coup like Greece. In December 1944 Italian politics had already assumed the shape it would maintain for the following 50 years. The Christian Democrat party ruled Italy, supported by the Church and the Allies, and the PCI collaborated with it "based on the conviction that without working with the Catholics it was impossible to bring about the transformation of Italian society, which for the PCI must come about through democratic means," wrote Giorgio Galli in *La Storia Della DC*.[4] This formula lead to deadlock and stasis alternating with bursts of political violence, and finally, after the DC had long outlived its usefulness as an anticommunist bulwark, the party was swept away in the corruption scandals of the 1990s, making room for Silvio Berlusconi's own peculiar brand of electronic autocracy.

The young heir now faced a life-changing decision. He could stay in Turin, become Fiat chairman, and guide his grandfather's right-hand man Vittorio Valletta in rebuilding bombed-out Fiat factories and reestablishing the family company's footing in an economy destroyed by war. About one-third of Italy's industrial and material wealth had been lost, and its national income had fallen by half.[5] Or he could follow the advice of his grandfather, who had told him before he died to take a few years off before diving into the business. He picked the second alternative.

Agnelli then embarked on what *Time* magazine later called "a full career in the gossip pages"[6] before finally settling down to run Fiat 20 years later. He was young, handsome, and armed with an income of more than a million dollars a year,[7] and the sunny shores of southern France beckoned after years at war. He had a smile that lit up the room. Who could resist?

"I came out of the war and wanted to enjoy myself," he recalled. "I looked after my business, I knew what was going on. . . . I had an eye on things but they didn't totally absorb me. Those were lovely years, you know, between 1948 and 1953, just after the war."[8]

He later said he was too young to be chairman and didn't want to be under Valletta's tutorship.[9] It's also likely that Gianni made a calculated choice. Without a father or grandfather to guide him, it made sense to let Valletta run the company for a while rather than spend his energy in a power struggle trying to wrest control from the supremely capable, authoritarian executive. Later events showed he had been right in realizing that Valletta had no intention of relinquishing his grip on the company's day-to-day management.

Gianni's choice was a classic one for any second- or third-generation member of an industrial dynasty. By the time the company is handed over to the sons and grandsons of a founder, the exciting, history-in-the-making phase is usually over. That leaves the grandson or later generations with the more ho-hum task of financing and running an established business. The psychological pressure to live up to their parents, while not having any freedom to make a choice of their own, can be overwhelming. Many dynastical descendants shun the boredom of the family business and choose to spend most of their time enjoying their wealth far away from the factory floor, letting the company be run by hired hands. Gianni was no exception. But his grandfather, and his own military training, had instilled in him a sense of duty so strong that he eventually was pulled back to Turin, as the company and his responsibility began to exert a gravitational pull strong enough to overpower his glittering lifestyle on the Riviera. When Gianni finally settled down as Fiat chief, he was able to combine his corporate duties with a sense of glamour and fun. This is what made him unique.

Gianni was not the wealthiest or most influential of the world's business leaders, and the Agnellis are not the most powerful of the world's automotive dynasties. That honor would probably belong to the Piech-Porsche clan of Germany, who reign over Volkswagen. But Agnelli was one of the few industrialists who looked as good in a tuxedo as he did in jeans, and who combined the panache of James Bond with the power of Rome's first emperor, Augustus. He cultivated the Italian art of *sprezzatura*, or making things look easy. He seemed to wear his power naturally.

"The thing I like least about power is the image that a person could want it or love it," Agnelli told an interviewer in 1984,[10] when he ruled over an empire spanning insurance, publishing, finance, retail, wine, soccer, chemicals, construction, cars, and much more besides.

Count Baldassare Castiglione, who coined the term *sprezzatura* in his Renaissance-era best-selling handbook of manners, advised his readers to strive for naturalness and effortless mastery. An Italian will never admit it, but making things look easy is hard work. In Agnelli's case, beneath the charm and the movie-star smile lurked a steely and calculating resolve. Gianni had cultivated his image and used it to increase his power within his family, in Italy, and abroad. He used that celebrity, his connections, and the prestige they brought to steer Fiat through the second half of the twentieth century so that he could entrust the company to his own heirs like his grandfather had before him.

Gianni Agnelli paid a price for his seemingly effortless charm. Behind his jet-set comings and goings, and the fawning magazine profiles celebrating his quirky and eccentric sartorial tastes and his intimate tête-à-têtes with world leaders, lay a devastation of family tragedy and dysfunction. He was a man who inherited wealth, fame, and power, but left a shattered family behind him. And the company didn't fare so well, either.

■ ■ ■

On a summer's day in 1948, a pretty, red-haired British aristocrat named Pamela Digby Churchill was sitting on the terrace of L'Horizon, Prince Aly Kahn's villa on the French Riviera, wondering what to do with herself. Her fling with Aly had just ended, and he was traveling in Spain with Rita Hayworth while guests at his villa enjoyed themselves swimming, boating, and swooshing down the 25-foot slide from the pool into the Mediterranean.

Her ex-husband Randolph, the son of British Prime Minister Winston Churchill, had just informed her he was on his way to the villa to collect her. She didn't want that. She sat down for lunch at the buffet, grumpy and despairing. Her eye was caught by a motor launch pulling up to the dock with two young men in it.

"*Buon giorno, cara,*" the handsome one said, smiling. "My name is Gianni Agnelli."[11]

Pamela had fled a predictable existence as a provincial English country aristocrat in much the same way that Gianni's grandfather had fled Villar Perosa. It didn't take her long to find adventure. When she was 19 and working at the Foreign Office in London, Winston Churchill's son Randolph called her and asked her out on a blind date. She accepted, and they were almost immediately married. Pamela was soon living with her father-in-law Winston Churchill at 10 Downing Street and acting as an informal liaison with American officers. By the time she met Gianni, who was 27, Pamela was on the rebound from a deeply disappointing rejection by CBS radio correspondent Edward R. Murrow.

The pair hit it off. Gianni was friendly, easygoing, and fun. Pamela had a voluptuous figure, was worldly-wise, and flirted with him in a direct manner he was unaccustomed to. Their affair started on a spur-of-the-moment boat trip from the South of France to the island of Capri and continued for years.

France's Côte d'Azur, though still beautiful and still blue, is now lined with skyscrapers, and St. Tropez each summer is invaded by fleets of mega-yachts and all-night revelers who guzzle overpriced champagne and scarf recreational drugs in an orgy of conspicuous consumption. But in the late 1940s, when Gianni and Pamela met, this stretch of coastline was still an exclusive, sexy, sun-kissed getaway dotted with tiny, colorful ports, bobbing little fishing boats, and beaches with crystal-clear blue water. By midcentury, it had become an exclusive playground where European old money mingled with Hollywood stars. French actress Brigitte Bardot introduced the world to the bikini as she cavorted on the beach at St. Tropez, fresh from *And God Created Woman* in 1956. That same year, Prince Rainier and Grace Kelly met and married in nearby Monte Carlo, enchanting millions with their storybook romance.

Gianni and Pamela set up house in the summer months in 1949 and 1950 in a rented villa on Cap d'Antibes called Chateau de la Garoupe.[12] The 20-bedroom villa, almost as large as Buckingham Palace, was bought by Russian president Vladimir Putin in 2001.[13] Pamela gave Gianni the social entrée he lacked, since the whiff of Mussolini's regime still clung to Italy, and spent his money lavishly to fill Chateau de la Garoupe with interesting guests who never lacked for creature comforts.

Winston Churchill was not amused. Pamela was the mother of his grandson Winston, his namesake.

"What's this I hear about Pamela taking up with an Italian motor mechanic?" he asked.[14] But later he was charmed. Gianni lavished attention on young Winston. He would take him snorkeling and give him $100 each time he saw him, a friend of Winston's recalled.[15] Gianni commuted back and forth between his office in Turin, where he had mostly ceremonial duties, and the South of France.

The social scene was a heady mix of retired Hollywood moguls like Jack Warner and Darryl Zanuck, who supplied a steady stream of pretty young starlets; current heartthrobs like swashbuckling film star Errol Flynn, whose drunken parties aboard his schooner *Zaca* were legendary; minor European royalty like Prince Rainier; fabulously wealthy Greek shipping magnates Starvros Niarchos and Aristotle Onassis; and rich, darkly handsome playboys Porfirio Rubirosa and Aly Khan. Khan was in the middle of getting his divorce from Rita Hayworth, and Rubirosa was a legendary lover who was cited in two divorce cases and has a pepper grinder named after a part of his anatomy (for its length). A young John Kennedy and his sister Kick also used the Riviera during those years as their stomping ground.

Pamela introduced Agnelli to Franklin D. Roosevelt Jr., whom Pamela knew from her days in London during the war. Agnelli later awarded Roosevelt with a Fiat distributorship in North America. According to Agnelli's aunt, Lydia Redmond, the Roosevelt connection "got Gianni in with the U.S. government, which gave an enormous loan to Fiat after the war."[16]

When Gianni bought a villa in 1951, he chose one that demonstrated what would become his signature good taste, and made a statement about the provincial young auto heir's social ambitions. He bought the French Riviera's most lavish estate, Villa Leopolda, a 28-room residence built by King Leopold II of Belgium in 1902, a trophy property that made the Agnellis' Villar Perosa look like a country cottage.

On a hill commanding a sweeping view of the sparkling blue Mediterranean and Cap Ferrat below, the 20-acre estate was dotted with cypress and olive groves nestled around on oval pool. Not only was the villa sumptuous, but it was also star-crossed. King Leopold II of Belgium, founder of the Belgian Congo, built it with profits extracted from forced labor in his colony, for a mistress and lover in his aging years. The villa would later be owned by the Safras and be the site of a mysterious murder. Safra's widow reigned at Villa Leopolda for years until she sold it to a mysterious Russian buyer who paid a reported 500 million euros, a world record.

Pamela was deeply in love, but Gianni was never faithful.[17] She told him right from the start that she wanted to marry, and he told her it was impossible.

"An Italian wife would stay with him no matter how he behaved. But if he married her, he told Pamela, she would eventually find his behavior intolerable and leave," wrote David Ogden in his biography of Pamela Churchill.

Early on, Pamela had an abortion. Gianni took her to a Swiss clinic, and then met her the next day at the Villa d'Este hotel on Lake Como, "where he told her about a gorgeous model he had picked up the previous evening," Ogden writes.[18]

Still, Pam struggled to accept Gianni's ways. By the fourth year of their romance, the affair was becoming strained.

■ ■ ■

Gianni Agnelli's life in the fast lane came to a screeching halt, literally, in 1952, when he drove his car into a butcher's truck after a night of partying. Roaring down the hillside at the crack of dawn after a fight with Pamela, who had discovered him in the embrace of a beautiful young brunette,[19] his reflexes impaired by cocaine and alcohol,[20] he broke his leg in seven places, and injured the three passengers in the butcher's truck.

Recovery was slow, and his injuries gruesome. Gangrene set in, and he almost lost his leg. He had plenty of time to think. His sisters, who did not approve of his relationship with Pamela, persuaded their friend Marella Caracciolo to visit Gianni often while he was recovering.[21]

Marella, like Gianni's mother Virginia, was the daughter of an American woman and a prince, with a doe-eyed gaze that made her look like an Italian version of Audrey Hepburn. She had been in love with Gianni for years. Agnelli later claimed it wasn't the accident that changed his life; it was turning 30.[22] Either way, his "Riviera Rat Pack" phase had helped him leave the narrow world of the Turin of his childhood, where his parents entertained the future king and queen but were still quite provincial. Now it was time to move on.

Gianni and Marella married in 1953. Gianni wore a morning coat and looked nervous, still walking on crutches from his accident. She wore a long satin gown that emphasized her stunning figure and long neck, and was two months pregnant.

"Marriage may have been the wisest move Gianni ever made," said William Paley, the founder of the CBS network and an old friend from Gianni's Riviera days.[23]

Pamela and Gianni's affair had been winding down for some time, and Marella's pregnancy gave him a chance to end it. He sold his apartment next door to Pamela's in Paris and made a substantial financial settlement with her, writes Sally Bedell Smith in her biography of Pamela.[24] They remained friends for the rest of their lives.

The couple began to come to New York in the late 1950s, where they would hang out at the home of Henry Fonda and Afdera Franchetti, the bewitching Venetian baroness who claimed she inspired the Renata character in Ernest Hemingway's *Across the River and into the Trees*.[25] David Rockefeller, whom Gianni met in Italy in 1957 when they watched the Sputnik launch together at a conference, was a social mentor and became a close friend. Their social circle in New York included the Kennedys, the Rockefellers, Jacob Javits, Gunther Sachs, the Fords, Onassis, Niarchos, the Rothschilds, the Flicks, the Paleys, Andrey Meyer, and the Thyssens, as well as Oscar de la Renta and Italian friends like Mario d'Urso.

It was the Agnellis who introduced Jack and Jackie to an aging Winston Churchill on the Riviera in 1958, Jackie later recalled.[26]

The Agnellis had both money *and* taste. Marella was named to the International Best Dressed list in 1963, and was inducted into its Hall of Fame alongside Babe Paley, Gloria Guinness, Jackie Kennedy, Brooke Astor, and many of her other glamorous and beautiful socialite friends. Gianni Agnelli is on the same list, for men. They were one of the few couples to make both the men's and women's lists (along with the Duke and Duchess of Windsor).

Gianni certainly knew how to have fun. A lover of the period recalled the start of a typical weekend: "One time he called me on the phone and said, 'Put on your bathing suit. I'll be by soon to pick you up.'

We got on a helicopter, whizzed over from Milan to the South of France, and flew out over the water. 'Jump!' he said. And we did, right into the sea."

Marella created a group of perfect homes for the couple and their two children, Edoardo and Margherita, in Turin, St. Moritz, Rome, Marrakesh, and New York, and proceeded to fill them with a world-class art collection that later came partly to roost at the Lingotto factory's rooftop museum.

She picked Renzo Mongiardino as her decorator, a master of making Europe's grand old homes in stately palazzos look comfortable, cozy, and intimate yet theatrical and tasteful at the same time. He could mix the extravagant and the historical with little touches that made the room seem welcoming rather than imposing.

"She will forever be remembered by people interested in style and taste for her Avedon photograph," said Amy Fine Collins, a *Vanity Fair* special correspondent. "She had taste and simplicity, and held up the better half of Agnelli. It must have secured him in work and in social life. She was elegant in a way that you don't ever see people aspire to understand today."

But the world's top decorator cannot design a perfect marriage. Marella put up with his affairs, even having his lovers over to their dinner parties. Sometimes, however, she would lose her temper. One family friend recalls seeing her curse "It's that asshole again" and slam the phone down on one of Gianni's good-time bachelor friends when he called to see if Gianni wanted to go out for the night. She spent as much energy trying to keep up with Agnelli's restless lifestyle as she did tolerating his roving eye.[27]

■ ■ ■

The Agnellis are often compared to the Kennedys, since both families are powerful dynasties that combine a mix of glamour and tragedy. The two families started socializing in the 1960s and continue to be in contact up to the present day.

On August 7, 1962, Jacqueline and Caroline Kennedy flew to Italy for a summer vacation, in a specially prepared "bedroom" converted from a first-class four-seat section of a commercial airliner.[28] When a tired Jackie and Caroline arrived by car from Naples, the town of Ravello on the Amalfi coast pulled out all the stops to greet them, decking itself out with red, green, blue, and white lights and signs of "Welcome Jackie." Police shouted, "No photographs!" to the jostling scrum of photographers.[29] The mayor of Ravello, Lorenzo Mansi, gave a little speech outside the entrance of the villa.

"*Grazie mille*," said Jackie.[30]

Jackie's sister, Lee Radziwill, was staying on the Amalfi coast and had invited a group of friends, including Gianni and Marella, to join them in a few days' time on their yacht for a bit of sailing. Jackie was looking forward to a relaxing month of swimming, chatting with Lee, and socializing with their friends. Marilyn Monroe had been found dead August 5, just days before Jackie left.

The comparison between the Kennedys and the Agnellis is apt in more ways than one. Jacqueline and Marella were both married to men who were repeatedly and openly unfaithful, and both women accepted it as the status quo of their era and social class. Both Gianni's and John's infidelities took place in a world before the round-the-clock television and Internet news cycle, when powerful men were accorded privacy by a deferential press. They both took advantage of it to the full. Last but not least, both men chose women—Marella and Jackie—who helped polish their husbands' image in a way that was key to their careers.

Jackie's trip to Italy was the subject of mild sniping in some sections of the U.S. press, which deemed it unsuitable for the First Lady to be so far away from her husband. Jackie, though closely guarded, was able to slip away from her escort a few days after she arrived to have a nightcap with Lee and Gianni at on outdoor café in Ravello before their guards caught on.[31]

The comings and goings of the photogenic group were soon splashed all over the international press. Jackie's routine was simple: Every day she would travel by car or boat from Villa Episcopio to Conca de' Marini, a pristine little bay protected by Secret Service agents. There she would meet Lee and a group of other friends, including Sandro d'Urso and Lee's husband, Prince Stanislas Radziwill, and go waterskiing or swimming.

Jackie's trip to Capri August 13 with Gianni and Marella on their yacht, the *Agneta*, got tongues wagging. Jackie stole away from Ravello on a speedboat and rendezvoused with the *Agneta* at sea, according to one account. On the cruise over, she and the other guests were serenaded by an Italian singer accompanied by mandolins. After a day spent shopping and snacking at Villa Vivara, where she was welcomed by Count Silvio Medici de' Menezes and his wife, Irene Galitzine, the group went to a nightclub where they danced the cha-cha until the wee hours. She was having such a good time that weekend that she extended her trip for another week.

Jack got jealous—which may have been the intent. "Less Agnelli and more Caroline," her husband, the U.S. president, cabled to her.[32]

Members of their circle disagree on whether Jackie and Gianni had an affair. They were under the eyes of not only Gianni's wife Marella, but a host of Secret Service agents as well. It will remain a mystery. She burned her love letters, including a missive from Gianni, before she died,[33] one biographer writes.

"It was not like Gianni to have an affair with Jackie," said Countess Marina Cicogna, a friend of Gianni's. "He didn't want to be involved in things that were complicated, and that would have been complicated."[34]

A British tabloid, *The Daily Mail*, claimed that Jackie confessed in a series of taped interviews with Arthur Schlesinger, Jr., shortly after her husband's death, to having an affair with Gianni—as well as movie star William Holden—in retaliation for JFK's own numerous flings.[35]

But if she did confess, that part of the conversation was not made public in the tapes.

On the other hand, Jackie's sister, Lee Radziwell, had a crush on Gianni and pursued him avidly, much to Gianni's chagrin, recalled a friend.

■ ■ ■

One fall afternoon in 1989, Thomas Davis, a men's wardrobe consultant at Brooks Brothers in midtown Manhattan, got a call from the housekeeper of Gianni Agnelli's Park Avenue residence, Mrs. Pardo, telling him Gianni would be over soon to visit the store. Usually she simply ordered shirts in solid colors—never stripes—that Agnelli liked, blue, white, and beige; had six or a dozen of each delivered to his apartment; and then shipped them off to his homes in Rome, Paris, Turin, and Argentina. Gianni traveled without luggage and didn't carry cash.

Davis was pleased. The tall, gentlemanly African-American had worked at the store since 1967, missing Ralph Lauren—who had also walked those Madison Avenue floors—by just a few years. He had supplied Gianni's shirts since the start of the 1980s. But he had not yet had the pleasure of meeting Mr. Agnelli in person.

Gianni pulled up to the austere-looking stone-clad store in his chauffeur-driven gray Alfa Romeo. He left the driver at the curb and entered with a bodyguard and his butler, Bruno, who traveled from Turin with him on Gianni's visits to New York. Bruno and Gianni's chef always accompanied him to New York, where Gianni entertained a mix of old friends like Henry Kissinger and models Heidi Klum and Elle MacPherson. He also liked to see shows on Broadway and walk in nearby Central Park.

As Davis walked Agnelli around the store's five floors during a two-hour visit, he was impressed by how open and friendly he was. He stopped often to admire this shirt or that jacket. He didn't want any special treatment. All he wanted to do was enjoy himself, stopping to chat for quite a while with the Italian tailors. His own suits were made back in Italy, at Caraceni, but he liked to mix and match ready-made shirts from Brooks Brothers with them. Purchases that didn't need altering were boxed up and stashed back in the gray Alfa.

Agnelli had started shopping at Brooks Brothers in the 1960s, possibly stealing a page from JFK's book. Agnelli adopted some of his New England preppy clothing habits, although adding a dash of his own Latin flair. The signature quirk was his trademark.

"He never liked to look too neat; always a little jaunty, a little rakish," recalled Davis.

Gianni Agnelli was very clever about style. He was one of the first business leaders to realize that in the age of photography having a visual signifier increased his own personal power. Although he was following a long line of political and religious leaders before him, Agnelli took this age-old practice to new heights. He started style trends like wearing his watch over his shirtsleeve, or leaving the buttons on his Brooks Brothers button-down shirts undone. At a Fourth of July party aboard Malcolm Forbes's boat in 1991, instead of wearing a blazer and suit like the other men, "Agnelli came in a worn denim shirt, blue jeans, and a red cowboy bandana. His watch was atop his cuff. He was shod in dark brown suede desert boots. There wasn't a woman on board who could take her eyes off him," gossip columnist Liz Smith recalled.[36]

For men interested in matters of clothing, Agnelli remains iconic today.

"It's because he makes it look comfortable, and is still able to be well dressed," said Nick Sullivan, fashion director at *Esquire* magazine. "And that's why the way Italians dress is still very important, because they feel relaxed in the clothes. If you dress up, you dress up . . . but nobody really wants to dress like that anymore. It's the *sprezzatura*, the making it look easy."

■ ■ ■

Anyone who knew Gianni Agnelli agrees—he was charming, intelligent, curious, and always on the move.

"Gianni gave me a taste for life, for fun," Marella said in a rare interview.[37] "When he was young, it was like everything was always possible."

Agnelli's cultivated *sprezzatura* had its drawbacks. He affected a detached air that was often superficial at best, and at worst cynical. His off-the-cuff comments could be cruel. When his friend and role model JFK was assassinated, Gianni and a small group of friends were eating at Grappe d'Or in Lausanne, Switzerland. "He was already screwed anyway," said Gianni, referring to JFK's back troubles, which often kept him in pain. That was all he said. And he didn't go to the funeral.

Agnelli's one-liners were widely admired, but the cult of his image had negative effects, said Paolo Panerai, an Italian business news publisher and journalist.

"This continual search for the perfect one-liner . . . it's a problem. It's superficial. It's very damaging. It created the impression that everything can be waved away with a joke," he said. "He was not a profound man."

For example, when asked by a biographer at the end of the 1990s why the dynasty was struggling to keep pace with other automakers, Agnelli brushed off the doubts with a gesture, and then rolled up his sleeve to display a faded blue circle.

"You see this? It's a tattoo I got from a Tunisian fortune teller during the war," he said. "It has brought me luck. And luck . . ."[38]

Agnelli seemed to spend his life avoiding any sort of emotional contact whatsoever, including with his own children. He shrank from Marella when she threw a fit over his infidelity.

"You could never fight with him, because he would always turn it into a joke. He didn't want any trouble," recalled a longtime lover. But despite his public posturing as a cynic, Agnelli privately was a very sensitive man who was unable to impart any discipline to his children whatsoever, said a person who knew him well.

Whatever the case may be, his incessant work and then escape into play took its toll on Agnelli's relationship with his two children, Margherita and Edoardo. He spent little time with his children when they were small, and they suffered from his lack of attention.[39] This in turn created a serious problem for Fiat and for the Agnelli dynasty: Gianni had no suitable heir.

"One thing is true: I was always present," he told Arrigo Levi in 1983.[40] "When we were at war, I went. When it came time to get closer to the Americans, I was there. When Turin had problems, I was always there. We went through the difficult years of terrorism, and I didn't step away. There were also times in our lives, in our generation, easy times, when things were fun, and I had fun. I believe I was present as a witness to every single thing that happened during the forty years of my country's life."

■ ■ ■

Gianni's grandfather had almost lost control of Fiat twice, once to striking workers and once at the end of the war. The third time the family almost lost the company played out amid Italy's postwar descent into chaos in the late 1970s, more than a decade after Gianni took over as chairman.

Gianni Agnelli took over Fiat in 1966 from his grandfather's right-hand man, Vittorio Valletta, who had done an excellent job. The group's gross profit was two billion lire, and its total turnover was equivalent to 5 percent of Italy's gross domestic product (GDP). Fiat churned out 1,335,000 cars per year, in addition to trucks, motors, airplanes, tractors, and diesel engines. It sold more cars than Volkswagen did.[41] It was an old-fashioned, centralized company where secretaries didn't dare to wear pants and were forbidden to wear lipstick.[42]

Yet Agnelli's choice of timing to take up the mantle of Italy's leading industrialist could not have been worse. Italy's economic boom was peaking, and the country's never-ending series of coalition governments of the same parties over and over again were incapable of dealing with the hangover. Italian workers started striking in 1968, and they didn't stop until 1980.

Fiat launched the 500 in 1957, and the little car soon became the symbol of Italy's economic boom, earning itself a halolike glow in Italy's collective memory. Italy was rebuilt from a humiliating and disastrous war by Marshall Plan money from the United States, as well as the hard work and ingenuity of the Italians themselves, led by industrialists like Agnelli, Adriano Olivetti, Leopoldo Pirelli, and Enrico Mattei. A land more known for art and music became a player in industry in the space of two decades.

The boom gave poor southerners the chance to flee unemployment by coming north to the humming factories in Turin and Milan. Their ancestors would have left for the United States, Australia, or Switzerland. Now, instead, they ended up at the foothills of the Alps as Fiat workers. Like the Great Migration in the United States, when a million and a half African Americans left their sharecropping holdings in the South to seek jobs in the factories of Chicago, Detroit, New York, and Cleveland in the years between 1910 and 1930,[43] Italy's northbound wave brought social change. Like blacks in the United States, Italy's southerners suffered from discrimination, exploitation, and poor working conditions. Like blacks in the United States, the migration was spontaneous and relied on informal kinship networks rather than help from state or local authorities. And like blacks in the United States, the migrants from Italy's south eventually fought back.

Alfano Bonaventura was one of those migrants. In March 1964, Bonaventura traveled to Turin from Basilicata, a region in the instep of Italy's boot. Basilicata's poverty stood out even by the standards of Italy's south. Perched mostly high in the Apennines, it was simply empty. There were few cities, roads, schools, or factories. The choice was stark: either emigrate or spend a life trying to coax crops out of a rocky hillside.

Once in Turin, Bonaventura stayed at the home of family friends from Melfi for two weeks until he finally found a one-room unheated apartment—and he considered himself lucky. He got a job at Fiat's Mirafiori factory, becoming one of the 65,000 workers who entered the 42 gates of the gargantuan plant on the outskirts of Turin each day.

"The people who didn't find a place to live slept on benches in front of the Porta Nuova train station," he said, recalling those years.[44] "I knew a guy who slept in a Fiat 500 parked in front of the factory. . . . Here it was just Fiat, Fiat, Fiat. They were interested in production, production, production. They didn't care where we lived, about our problems with housing."

Another southerner from Basilicata, Giovanni D'Onofrio, also came to Turin in those years.[45] Signs hanging in windows saying "We don't rent to southerners" were common. As soon as he found a room, people from his town of Laurenzana in Basilicata turned up on his doorstep asking to stay while they looked for work. Conditions at Fiat were strict. And at the factory, the Piedmontese workers would make him the butt of jokes.

"At Mirafiori I was making bumpers for the 500. I made 180 bumpers each hour. Workers didn't have so many rights back then," said D'Onofrio. "There were no breaks to go to the bathroom. If you needed to pee, you had to ask for a break and wait until someone could substitute you, and the guards followed you to the bathroom."

Bonaventura and D'Onofrio were part of Italy's boom, when the economy grew more than 6 percent each year from 1959 to 1962. In the space of a single generation, the country went from Vittorio De Sica's 1948 classic *The Bicycle Thief*, where an entire family's livelihood is fragile enough to be ruined by the disappearance of a bicycle, to the glittering Via Veneto of Federico Fellini's *La Dolce Vita* in 1960, where an affluent consumer society represented by Marcello Mastroianni has lost its moral bearings.

The explosive mix of slowing economy, a reaction against Fiat's heavy-handed anti-union tactics, and poor living conditions meant that by the end of the 1960s Turin's big factories were a tinderbox.

Agnelli realized too late that Fiat should have paid more attention to the social needs of its workforce.[46] Italy's politicians, led by the Christian Democrat party, squandered the possibility for social reform during the boom that might have resulted in fewer strikes in the 1970s. Italy was no longer a country where farmers in Basilicata had marched during the war demanding a new pair of shoes, or where half of the people in Calabria were illiterate.[47]

■ ■ ■

The strikes started in 1968, two years after Gianni took over, building upon an earlier period of unrest in the early 1960s. But these strikes were different. The workers' movement, this time, was joined by the students who were pouring into Italy's universities. Outside the gates of the Pirelli factory in Milan, students electrified by third-world revolutionary Marxism and the events of Paris in 1968 joined forces with workers tired of the inertia of the PCI and the labor unions, and created the first United Base Committee (CUB), which answered neither to the union nor to the factory commissions.[48]

Gianni and Umberto, who had joined him as chief executive in 1970, could not control the labor unrest that stalled the production lines in Fiat's factories. Gianni's strategy of compromise with unions did not bring labor peace.

"The combination of strikes and an absentee rate of as much as 14 percent cost Fiat an estimated 130,000 cars in lost production in 1969," writes Alan Friedman in *Agnelli and the Network of Italian Power*.[49] "By 1972, the group was losing 150,000 cars and was using its plants at only three-quarters capacity. In 1973, Fiat suffered its first operating loss, and was forced to withhold dividend payments for the first time since the end of the Second World War."

In 1975, Gianni and the Communist head of Italy's largest labor union, Luciano Lama, signed a historic agreement to index workers' wages to inflation. With it, Agnelli hoped he would finally buy the labor peace he needed to get Fiat back under control again. He was wrong.

The unrest soon morphed into something more sinister. In 1970s, the Red Brigades terrorist group was founded. From 1975 to 1980, 27 Fiat managers were wounded by the Red Brigades and other terrorist groups. Four were killed. Gianni and Umberto traveled under heavy police protection. Fiat's factories were targeted for arson, and a number of managers' cars were destroyed.[50]

"For the entire 1970s, middle management watched helplessly as their friends and colleagues were wounded and killed by terrorists," said a former manager who lived through that period. "Those of us who were potential targets had to go to work with a police escort, never knowing when we said goodbye to our wives and children if it would be the last time. I don't want to be pathetic—Fiat survived because we kept a stiff upper lip."

*Esquire* in 1978 called Gianni Agnelli "the most prominent capitalist in a nation that has the most powerful communist party in the world."[51]

"When Italy was rebuilt in the 1950s, we would have thought it was for good," Agnelli told *Esquire*. "It's surprising to find it in shambles, to have to start all over again."

The escalating spiral of violence culminated with the kidnapping and killing of Italy's Prime Minister, Aldo Moro, in the spring of 1978. At Fiat's factory in Stura, 5,000 workers gathered on the day of Moro's kidnapping to listen to a speech from the chief of the Communist trade union, the Italian General Confederation of Labour (CGIL), Bruno Trentin. The unions had put up a huge banner saying "Against all terrorism, to improve the state." Trentin denounced the kidnapping. But worker after worker, as each one got up to speak, did not.

"For thirty years we've suffered from terrorism in the factories, with fascist foremen, with pension payments that take months to arrive, with uncontrolled and forced migration . . .," said one, as reported in *La Repubblica*. "I don't condemn the Red Brigades and I don't condemn anyone. I am against terrorism, but I know that what we need here, immediately, are reforms."[52]

Between strikes and terrorism, Fiat was slowly bleeding to death.

■ ■ ■

On September 21, 1979, Fiat CEO Cesare Romiti's car phone rang as he was on his way to Turin's Caselle airport. It was Umberto Agnelli.

"Romiti, fifteen minutes ago they killed Ghiglieno," he said.

Romiti's veins turned to ice. He ordered his driver to turn around and head to the Ghiglieno home on Via Petrarca in Turin.[53]

Sometime between 8:15 A.M. and 8:30 A.M., as Fiat manager Carlo Ghiglieno and his wife were leaving their home after his morning espresso, he was gunned down by Prima Linea terrorists.[54] His wife witnessed the killing. His two sons, aged 21 and 24, arrived on the scene within minutes.

It was not the first time Romiti had been at the scene of a terrorist shooting. The vice-editor of Turin's *La Stampa*, the Turin daily owned by Fiat, had been killed two years earlier. Carlo Casalegno had been shot four times in the face and died 13 days later. Romiti had learned two things then: stay detached, and don't be afraid.

That evening Romiti visited Ghiglieno's widow Matilde and her two sons at their home. The funeral was attended by Italy's Prime Minister Francesco Cossiga and Labor Minister Enzo Scotti. Scotti dropped by Romiti's office before he returned to Rome.

"What can I do to help?" Scotti asked. "What can we do about this?"[55]

Romiti shook his head. It was up to Fiat to act. And he already knew what to do.

The square-jawed, gravel-voiced Romiti had joined Fiat in 1974, recruited by the Agnellis from a job at state holding company IRI in Rome at the suggestion of Mediobanca's Enrico Cuccia to put Fiat's finances in order. The overcentralized company was reeling from the oil shock of 1973. It was heavily in debt and crippled by strikes. Romiti had a very Roman blend of a jovial backslapping manner combined with a worldly cynicism and an ability to be brutally tough. The crisis provided him with the opportunity to take control of the situation. He would keep control for decades to come, right up until he retired in 1998.

On October 9, Fiat notified 61 workers who had been identified as suspected terrorists that they were fired.[56] Fiat long knew it had terrorist cells operating in its factories. Now it finally drew the line. The decision had been made September 1, before Ghiglieno's murder, by Romiti and other top management, with the assent of Gianni Agnelli.

Romiti knew the action would ignite a storm of protest, and he was right. Prime Minister Cossiga, when informed of the decision, was lukewarm.

"Do what you need to do," Cossiga said unenthusiastically.

Union chief Lama told Romiti that Fiat had to find "valid justi-fication" to fire the workers it suspected of being terrorists. He was right. Workers could appeal to a special labor court and be reinstated if they could prove Fiat was wrong.

"Or we succeed, or Fiat goes under," he told Agnelli.

Romiti was galvanized by the battle. He literally saw it as a war to "take back" Fiat.

"I felt like we were on the right side," he said years later. "Fiat had 350,000 workers around the world, and in Turin alone about 100,000. I felt we had to win."

In 1980, Fiat decided it had to cut its labor force to adapt to changing market conditions and to take back control of its factories. Umberto Agnelli gave a newspaper interview in which he said Fiat had the right to act unilaterally to make as many staff cuts as it needed to. In the resulting furor, he stepped down as Fiat CEO, giving Romiti a free hand. No large employer had ever tried to make so many layoffs at once.[57]

The announcement of some 15,000 job cuts was made September 11, 1980. Workers went on strike, and stayed on strike for 35 days. Romiti dug in his heels. Cleverly, he had already stocked Fiat's dealerships with cars, even bringing back unsold stock from overseas.[58] In the end, salvation came from an unlikely source: a middle manager named Luigi Arisio. His "right to work" meeting at Turin's Teatro Nuovo turned into a huge demonstration, the "March of the 40,000," on October 14, 1980, that made Italian labor history.

The tide had turned. The Agnellis had come close to losing Fiat another time, and had succeeded in saving the company from collapse by stepping back and letting a professional manager take over.

■ ■ ■

The sentimentalism so absent in his relationships with his children colored Agnelli's management decisions in later years at Fiat. He couldn't seem to bring himself to make the tough managerial decisions that the company needed in the late 1990s to become competitive like it had been in its glory days of the 1980s. Faced with the undeniable evidence that Fiat was too small to compete with the new auto giants like DaimlerChrysler emerging from a round of mergers, Agnelli opted for a halfway solution that later proved to be a ball and chain.

On March 13, 2000, Fiat Chairman Paolo Fresco, General Motors Chairman and CEO John Smith, and GM's Chief Operating Officer, Rick Wagoner, held a press conference at Lingotto's conference room in Turin, which was beamed live to journalists in Detroit.

Under the accord, GM acquired a 20 percent stake in Fiat Auto, and Fiat, in turn, the world's seventh-largest carmaker, became GM's single largest stakeholder.

"Automaking today is a truly global affair," Smith told the press conference.[59]

For GM, the alliance was a first feather in Rick Wagoner's cap after he had been named CEO-designate, just before his 47th birthday. One of his first goals as GM chief was to expand international operations, and the Fiat deal, announced in March 2000, seemed to come at just the right time for him.[60] It would help GM cut costs. Fiat's small diesel engines were just what GM needed in Europe, Wagoner thought.

Fiat was hardly considered a prize at that point. Its auto operations were losing money. Fiat's globalization strategy, based on a so-called world car, had flopped when emerging markets went into a tailspin, at a time when the world car industry was bulking up in a mergers and acquisitions musical chairs that saw BMW snap up Rover and Daimler-Benz pair up with Chrysler. Fiat would be unable to survive on its own in such a scenario. It needed to move fast. And it did.

Gianni had given Fresco the task of finding a buyer for the auto unit. Fresco came back with not one offer but three. GM was prepared to buy all of Fiat Auto in exchange for either $12 billion in cash or 22 to 23 percent of GM.[61] GM also was willing to buy just a small part of Fiat's car unit, with an option to acquire the rest of it at a later date. At the same time, Fresco had an offer from DaimlerChrysler to buy all of Fiat Auto in exchange for $10 billion to $12 billion.

Gianni turned Daimler down in favor of the smaller deal with GM and the right to eventually sell the Detroit colossus the rest of Fiat Auto from 2004. Fresco, speaking at the press conference, said the put option was "a parachute."

"We have no intention of using it," he said.[62]

Gianni justified his decision in an interview the next day with the family-owned paper, *La Stampa*.

"I can't go and retire to the island of Tonga with a backpack loaded down with billions of German marks," Gianni said, explaining why he didn't sell Fiat Auto to DaimlerChrysler when he had the chance. "Our job is to make cars, to make the cars of the future."[63]

The deal called for Fiat and GM to set up joint ventures in power trains—engines, transmissions, and drive shafts—and in diesel engines. Platform sharing, which is where any real savings would occur, was postponed to a later date.

Gianni was pleased. "If I had been told when I was a boy I would one day be a partner of General Motors, I would never have believed it," he said in an interview.[64]

The day before the deal had been announced was Gianni's 79th birthday, a Sunday. He spent it doing his favorite things—a bit of skiing in St. Moritz, watching the Fiat-owned Ferrari racing team win a race on television, and then flying back to Turin for a bit of work.[65]

■ ■ ■

Like his grandfather, Gianni Agnelli twice narrowly avoided losing control of the family company. Once was during the economic chaos of the 1970s. The second time was much later, in the early years of Fiat's second century, when Fiat's financial and industrial distress threatened the company's survival.

"The only way I will go out of the auto industry is feet first," he said to a relative.

By the time his grandson John Elkann inherited control in 2003, Fiat was in such bad shape that old Giovanni Agnelli would have hardly recognized it. Gianni had accomplished his goal of conserving his inheritance, but just barely.

# Chapter 5

# A Lament like a River

A few hours before lunchtime on November 15, 2000, Gianni Agnelli was in his office working when he got the sort of phone call that no parent ever wants to receive. Minutes later, he and Turin's chief of police, Nicola Cavaliere, entered the Turin-Savona tollway and drove south until they got off at Fossano, and then wound down the hill to reach a field on the pebbly bank of the Stura River below. As they bounced along the dirt road leading to the riverbank, Gianni asked the chief of police if it could have been an accident. He couldn't believe it was true.[1]

There, on the ground, underneath a plastic cloth, lay the lifeless, bruised body of Gianni's son Edoardo, 46. Edoardo's car, a Fiat Chroma, was parked on the highway viaduct that soared some 26 stories above their heads. Cavaliere pulled back the cloth, and Agnelli nodded. Yes, it was his son. Gianni did not say a word.

Cavaliere filled Agnelli in on what had happened. At 10:20 A.M., a highway worker named Carlo Franchini had seen a Fiat Chroma parked on the viaduct, with its motor off and hazard lights flashing. Franchini saw the body lying below and notified the police at 10:30 A.M. Police found Edoardo's driver's license at the scene. Hence the phone call.

"I would ask you only one favor: if you could see to it that—with full respect for proper procedure—everything is done in the least time and with the most attention possible," Agnelli asked Cavaliere.[2]

Like his grandfather before him, Gianni was forced to identify his son's body after a gruesome accident. And, like his grandfather, he remained perfectly composed.

Gianni stayed for half an hour to take care of the necessary formalities. Younger brother Umberto soon joined him. Umberto had lost his own son, Giovanni Alberto—"Giovannino" to his family—just three years earlier, and now was witnessing his brother go through the same anguish he had. The two brothers reacted with their usual Piedmontese composure. The family was not one given to great public or private displays of emotion. Gianni and Umberto had always been close, and now were drawn together by the loss of their sons. At this point, both had lost their natural heirs. That loss would force Gianni—three years later, on his deathbed—to ask Umberto to take over the chairmanship of Fiat in an attempt to keep it in family hands.

"This is more responsibility for you," had been Umberto's curt greeting to Andrea, his only remaining son, the day after Giovannino died.

Edoardo had left no suicide note, and people close to him later told the police he had given no indication he was planning to do anything self-destructive or indeed out of the ordinary. The police investigation into Edoardo's final days turned up nothing more than the routine of a wealthy, unemployed adult: daily meetings with a computer technician, discussions on Islamic theology with an Iranian carpet merchant called Hussein, and meetings with old friends.

But two things he did were out of the ordinary. For each of the past three days, Edoardo had gotten up early, gotten dressed, and driven over the same bridge where he finally met his death on November 15.[3] And three days before he died, he gave a photograph of himself to his father and to another person close to the family. He was standing on a bridge, in a suit, looking formal and slightly pleased with himself.

"I want you to remember me like this," he told the person, who at the time hadn't understood why.

Edoardo Agnelli had woken up early that morning, read the Italian papers, and then left his residence, Villa Sole, which is located just a few steps away from his parents' home, alone at about 7:20 A.M.[4] He had dressed carelessly, wearing his pajama top as a shirt underneath a corduroy blazer. He asked his security guard, Gilberto Ghedini, to get his car ready, telling him he was going to visit Superga, a nearby hilltop with a fantastic view over Turin. But that's not where he went.

Nothing in any of Edoardo's actions that morning seemed the least bit unusual. He drove down the narrow winding street Strada San Vito, in the exclusive hillside enclave where Turin's wealthy reside, and entered the Turin-Savona toll road. At 9:00 A.M. he called Ghedini, and asked for a password for the car phone. Edoardo phoned Ghedini two more times, once to ask if everything was okay, and the second time to ask him to call the dentist to postpone his appointment to the following day. Ghedini called him back to say he'd spoken to the dentist, and Edoardo told him he would be out for a bit longer.

Edoardo also called Alberto Bini, a social worker whom he saw daily, for a chat and asked him whether he had been able to set up a meeting with the mayor of Turin for November 17. Edoardo wanted to talk to him about renovating an old building on his property. Bini had met with Edoardo for a few hours each day for the past 10 years at the request of Edoardo's mother, Marella, after Edoardo was arrested for possession of drugs in Kenya in 1990.[5] Edoardo told Bini he would phone him later to set up an appointment with him for that afternoon.

In the coming days, Edoardo had been planning to spend some time in a prayer retreat at a sixteenth-century monastery in Umbria. He had spent recent evenings talking in English on the phone or sending e-mails. His passwords were all names like "Amon Ra," "Sun Ra," and "Jedi." The last thing he had read on his computer was a text by Nostradamus, as police discovered when they searched his villa on the day of his suicide.

The last time his cousin Lupo Rattazzi had seen him, five days before his death, he had talked a lot about money, and was very worried about his finances.[6] Another friend recalled that he had started to spend a lot of time alone in the Agnelli family vault at Villar Perosa, next to his cousin's tomb.[7]

Edoardo Agnelli died because of "grave wounds caused by the impact of his body with the ground, after having fallen 80 meters (262 feet)," while still alive, according to a report by Marco Ellena, the doctor from the public health office of nearby Cuneo who examined his body.[8] An autopsy would have revealed internal injuries that "could only be formulated in a hypothetical manner" from an external examination, but "would have not resulted in any further elements regarding the identification of cause of death which, as has already been mentioned above, was due to a grave trauma of the head, face and chest."[9] Police found nothing unusual in his car beyond his phones, cigarettes, walking stick, address book, bottles of mineral water, and so on.

Gianni Agnelli got his wish, as always. The body was buried quickly, without an autopsy. Edoardo was laid to rest in the family vault next to his cousin Giovannino, at Villar Perosa, in the cemetery perched above the immaculate grounds of the Agnelli family villa, with its reflecting pond, helipad, fruit trees, and little chapel; the cemetery view looks down over the town itself and the soccer field where Juventus holds its first practice of the season. It looks past the ball bearing factory founded by his father's grandfather, and, finally, looks out at the timeless tree-covered hills of the Chisone river valley.

A few weeks later, the public prosecutor working on the case, Riccardo Bausone, finished a brief investigation into "unknown persons" regarding Edoardo Agnelli's death. The purpose of the investigation was to see if Edoardo had acted alone in his suicide. Bausone concluded that he did, and asked that the case be closed. And it was.

Edoardo's conversion to Islam, although he did not practice, and the speed surrounding his burial have fueled a conspiracy theory that he might not have committed suicide. Marco Bava, a Turin-based financial consultant and friend of Edoardo, filed a complaint in the days immediately following Edoardo's death asking for an investigation.[10] His request was turned down, but Bava has continued to be vocal about his beliefs.

"Our Darwinian side would say he was not strong enough; our compassionate side would say his father was the one who was not strong enough," wrote Marco Ferrante in *Casa Agnelli*.[11]

Edoardo's suicide forced Gianni to confront his very public failure as a father. He couldn't just brush it away or distract himself from it with one of his spur-of-the-minute trips. This sadness weighed him down and made him feel old.

"This is a failure," Gianni told Lupo Rattazzi the day Edoardo died—meaning, this is my failure.

One can only imagine Gianni's grief that day, and in the days to come. Spanish poet Federico Garcia Lorca captures the horror of experiencing the violent death of a loved one in his moving 1937 classic elegy "Lament for Ignacio Sanchez." First there is the surreal feeling of disbelief, where time seems to stop as the human mind struggles to grasp the mystery and finality of death. In the poem's first part, "Codiga (Code) and Death," Lorca obsessively repeats the time of day—five o'clock in the afternoon—when Ignacio, a celebrated bullfighter, was fatally gored by a bull on an August afternoon in 1934. This depicts the trance-like unbelieving state that suddenly bereaved people naturally fall back on as a coping mechanism. Gianni would have done the same.

Disbelief gives way to denial as Lorca's poem continues, with the writer refusing to look at his fallen friend's spilled blood staining the sands of the bullfighting arena after his body is carried away. In the poem's third part, Lorca is forced to confront the hollowed features of Ignacio's corpse as he is laid out during the wake, and invokes "a lament like a river" as he finally gives vent to the deluge of grief and anguish engulfing him. The poem ends with the acceptance of the conclusiveness of death, and a bittersweet recollection of the memory of Ignacio's now-vanished vitality.

■ ■ ■

Edoardo Agnelli lived in a unique sort of hell. Single and unemployed, he had chosen to stay just a stone's throw from his parents and was kept on a very short leash. He was financially dependent on them, and they controlled his funds, which made him complain bitterly.[12] He had no children and had never been married. His family had interests in publishing, sports, automobiles, and much else besides, but he had been unable to carve out even a minor sort of role within the vast Agnelli empire. His interest in religion and the arts never led him anywhere else but trips to India, Iran, and Africa; to his uncle's estate in Tuscany; and to spaces within his own mind and his own soul. Nor could he cut the umbilical cord connecting him with his parents and go live, say, in New York, where he was born.

Unsuited for business and not disciplined enough to buckle down and conquer the skills and mastery of detail needed to govern any of his family's enterprises, he failed to reconcile the difference between what he was and what he thought other people expected him to be.

"He had accepted the fact he wasn't the heir to Gianni Agnelli," said Lupo Rattazzi, his cousin. "He struggled with it more and more. And the more time passed, the more difficult it became."

Intelligent, cultivated, and a bit of a snob, Edoardo Agnelli would have perhaps been happier as a dandy back in the days of Lord Byron and Oscar Wilde. He walked with a walking stick even when he didn't need one. He spoke Italian with an *erre moscia*, or soft *r*, French-style, like his father. As a young man he had the ethereal beauty of a Renaissance painting. But his physical decline over the years was disconcerting. At times he would wear a long, unkempt beard, with a tailored suit. During his last few months, he was overweight and had an absent stare.[13]

Gianni and Edoardo had a difficult relationship right from the start. Gianni was the sort of risk taker who liked to measure his limits by, say, not turning back in the face of one of those sudden storms that can come up when sailing across the Mediterranean from Liguria to France.[14] Edoardo as a boy was physically uncoordinated, would trip over his own feet, and was too afraid to even leap from the family yacht into the water, earning only his father's scorn. Gianni spent little time with Edoardo and Margherita when they were growing up, people close to the family say, raising them in the aristocratic tradition whereby children were cared for by nannies and were brought to see their parents only for a kiss goodnight. The family did not often have meals together. In his later years, Edoardo took to calling the family's butler each day for an update on news of Gianni.

"It was like something straight out of the film *The King's Speech*," said a family member, referring to the Oscar-winning film about King George VI. Edoardo's biographer, Marco Bernardini, a sports journalist, tells a heartbreaking tale of Edoardo at age nine that he says was recounted to him by Margherita. The young boy was told by his father to have dinner early and then get ready to go to a Juventus soccer game. Gianni would come by the mansion at Villar Perosa and pick him up. Edoardo wolfed down his dinner, and then waited around with a black-and-white Juventus scarf around his neck. But evening turned to nightfall and his father never turned up. Edoardo woke up the next day with his clothes on and with the scarf still around his neck.[15]

Margherita and Edoardo were close, but Margherita used to physically torment him, according to one witness, doing things like pulling the curtain sash from the window and hitting him with it, or chasing after him with a toy gun during a game of soldiers.

Edoardo, who was born in the United States, earned a degree in history from Princeton University, where he also studied theology and philosophy. His father did not fully agree with his choice.[16]

After finishing his studies, Edoardo took a long trip to India to reflect on his life. He also visited Rome frequently, where he hung out with a group of hip young aristocrats. The handsome, long-haired Count Gelasio Gaetani Lovatelli d'Aragona, an expert in fine wines, and his three brothers were like Edoardo's second family. The group would relax together at the Tenuta di Argiano, a cypress-lined estate in the Tuscan hills near Siena that first started producing wine during the Renaissance for the Pecci family.[17]

When Edoardo returned to Italy from India, he started training to work in the family business, taking a job at IFI, the Agnelli holding company that controlled IFIL. He also worked at Lehman Brothers in New York, for Mario d'Urso, a close family friend.

"For a few months, he was very good and attended meetings on time and was very interested," d'Urso recalled. "Then, when I came back from vacation, he was no longer interested."

Edoardo's first big step into the family arena was his appointment to the board of the Juventus soccer team along with his cousin Giovanni Alberto, who was 10 years his junior. Juventus is something far more than a business to the Agnelli clan. Gianni and Umberto both genuinely loved the team, as a fan would. During an important game in April 1986, Edoardo appeared in the dugout with the coach and players, giving advice, perhaps trying to imitate his father. He was hoping to have a managerial role running the team, like his father and grandfather Edoardo before him.

But Edoardo put a foot badly wrong soon afterward when he gave an interview to *Tuttosport* in which he laid out his strategy for the team and made the mistake of saying the Juventus president Giampiero

Boniperti was "tired out," hinting perhaps he should resign. All hell broke loose the next day. Boniperti was furious. The journalist, Marco Bernardini, was "invited" to the Agnelli family law firm and "asked" to retract the story. He refused.[18]

Later that year, Edoardo attracted the wrong sort of attention in another public appearance. On October 27, 1986, Pope John Paul II hosted the first World Day of Prayer for Peace, leading world religious leaders in a day of prayer and fasting. Edoardo attended, and gave two long interviews to two Italian media outlets, the left-wing newspaper *Manifesto* and the weekly news magazine *Panorama*, about his own religious views.

Religion is "a private relationship between God and myself," he said.[19]

More worryingly for the heir to one of the world's automotive dynasties, he said that it was "utopian to think that capitalism would last forever" and added that he wanted to spend his time thinking about matters related to "religion, philosophy and fundamental values" because "it's no longer enough just to produce automobiles well." All the same, he did not intend to step back from a role in Fiat, he said.

"It is my intention to accept all the responsibility that awaits the owner of a big industrial group like ours," he said.

Three years later he was arrested for possession of a minuscule quantity of heroin in Kenya. Charges were later dropped.

Edoardo's friend Gelasio Gaetani recounts an episode that speaks volumes about the hazards of being Gianni Agnelli's son, and also about the pitfalls of Edoardo's approach. During a vacation on the Greek island of Mykonos, the pair was driving a Jeep past the NATO base when Gelasio stopped and told the guard at the gate that Edoardo Agnelli wanted to ride on one of the base's fighter planes. The guard replied that only the general could make that sort of decision, and went to fetch him. The general came down to the gate and, after a short back-and-forth with Gelasio, sent them away.[20] But if it had been Gianni himself who wanted to take a spin on a fighter plane, the request would probably have been granted. Gianni had position, fame, and vast personal charm.

A family friend who used to speak frequently to Edoardo about his problems recalls how upset he was when Gianni picked Giovannino to groom for a management role at the company. After Edoardo was imprisoned in Kenya, the friend received a call from Gianni asking him not to talk to Edoardo anymore to give him advice.

"Gianni was ashamed," the person said. Gianni, despite his jet-set image, was a tough-minded man who by age 25 had already fought on both sides of World War II. Another person close to the family disputes the claim that Gianni neglected Edoardo. Gianni continually challenged Edoardo to make decisions about his future, but Edoardo always evaded him.

Gianni was deeply disappointed with Edoardo, who he realized would never accept his military sort of discipline, and would frequently discuss him with certain friends.

Marella seems to also have been an absentee parent. They were both concerned about his drug use, but in a cold and distant sort of way. After the Kenya drug arrest, Edoardo was continually watched by minders. But to speak to his father at home, he had to go through the Villa Frescot switchboard, because he was not given his father's direct number. It was a family accustomed to power and uncomfortable with affection.

"Edoardo suffered a lot from having a father who didn't care about him and a mother who was more interested in running after the father trying not to lose him," said a family friend.

■ ■ ■

Edoardo's suicide created an eerie pattern of unnatural death in the Agnelli family tree. Edoardo had been named for his grandfather, who had died in a freak seaplane accident in 1935. Senatore Agnelli had been forced to identify his son's dead body in a morgue in Genoa. And Gianni, in a grotesque coincidence, also had to identify his son's body after Edoardo's suicide. In both cases, the death of the legal heir to the controlling stake of Fiat passed to the grandson rather than the son. In Senatore Agnelli's case, it was to Gianni. And in Gianni's case, it would be to his daughter's son, John Elkann. Gianni, however, did not wait until Edoardo's death to anoint his successor to run the company.

It's unclear when Gianni first realized that Edoardo was not fit to control Fiat. Certainly his arrest in 1990 on drug charges in Kenya was the point of no return.

But it had been clear for many years that Edoardo had always been interested in the arts and religious studies rather than in business. Edoardo's unsuitability to run Italy's largest company was a serious setback for Gianni, because Italian inheritance laws force parents to leave their property to their surviving children (and their wives or husbands if they are married). In other words, Gianni, by law, was not free to pick an heir. So when Edoardo would inherit the company, sometime in the future, Fiat would be controlled by an outspoken critic of capitalism, a man with eccentric religious views, and one who passed his days writing long, detailed letters to business leaders and heads of state offering unrequested advice.[21]

Gianni appeared to have never considered Margherita for the top job at Fiat. Family tradition ruled out women from taking any management role, and she never showed any interest, picking painting and child-rearing over studying. Gianni began to groom Umberto's son Giovanni Alberto for a top role at Fiat from 1993 when he was named to Fiat's board, causing Edoardo deep pain, according to family members. Giovannino was also named chairman of scooter-maker Piaggio.

Giovannino and Edoardo were very close. But when Giovannino came to Turin for his first board meeting, he made the faux pas of not going to visit or phone Edoardo. As a payback, Edoardo wrote him a scathing letter, attaching a copy of a "welcome letter" he wrote to another new Fiat board member the day after the meeting.

"Unfortunately I cannot extend you the same welcome," Edoardo wrote to his cousin, using the formal *Lei* reserved for superiors and the elderly. "The reason, if you permit, can be found in the fact that you neither informed me nor warned me when you came to Turin where, as you know, I currently reside. This act, considering that we belong to the Family and are both members of the controlling block of shares [of] a limited partnership as well as direct shareholders of Fiat, can be defined or interpreted as an act of negligence towards, if not downright inobservance of, the fundamental rules governing these matters."[22]

Edoardo had been informed by the family of Gianni's decision to name Giovannino to the board, and he was furious. He boycotted Giovannino's wedding in 1996.

It is easy to see how Edoardo could be jealous of his cousin. Giovanni Alberto was young, handsome, and athletic. He looked sort of like John F. Kennedy Jr. He had been in the military, like his father and his uncle, and their revered grandfather. He was probably one of the world's most eligible bachelors until he married a blonde American heiress, Avery Howe, in 1996. He had star power, and seemed to be positioning himself as a leader of a new, more market-friendly generation of Italian family capitalists.

"The establishment should follow the rules of the market more because more competition is good for consumers, industry and investors," he told the *International Herald Tribune* in an interview that made waves in Italy. "The establishment includes, of course, my own family. I cannot exempt Fiat from what I am saying."[23]

By the time Giovanni Alberto was diagnosed with cancer in 1997, the pair had made up. Giovannino seemed protective of Edoardo. Had the younger cousin lived, he might have taken Edoardo under his wing and funded his pet project, a charity foundation.

"If Giovannino were alive today, I think Edoardo would be too," said Edoardo's biographer, Marco Bernardini. "Giovannino understood Edoardo's needs. He wouldn't have abandoned him. He would have helped him set up his foundation."

But if it was relatively easy for Edoardo and Giovannino to mend their bridges, Edoardo probably never forgave his father for publicly pushing him aside for a second time after Giovannino's death.

■ ■ ■

A year after Giovannino was named to Fiat's board in 1993—the start of a long process seemingly leading to the chairman's spot one day—John Elkann came to Turin from Paris to study engineering at Turin's Politecnico, the city's engineering and architecture university. The bland, modern tan stone building in downtown Turin had churned out engineers for Fiat's top ranks for as long as the company had been in business. In fact, it had been around for longer than Fiat. It started as a civil engineering school in 1859 to train the House of Savoy military how to build bridges.[24] Gianni Agnelli believed that the school was one of the three pillars of Turin's industrial success.[25] The main lecture hall is named after Fiat founder Giovanni Agnelli.

John didn't come to Turin explicitly in order to work at Fiat, in the sense that he didn't feel entitled to a job, but he didn't rule it out. A Fiat manager who worked with him at the time recalled he was very keen to learn the skills for a job at the company.

"He came to work at Fiat," the executive said.

John had overruled his grandfather in his choice of curriculum and of school. Gianni thought the young man should study business at Milan's Bocconi University. But John liked science and wanted to do engineering. He picked a degree in industrial engineering, which combined a traditional engineering curriculum with economics, political economy, and law. The goal of the course is to create an engineer with a bit of management background.

He favored the Politecnico over a more prestigious place like a U.S. Ivy League university, Oxford, or Cambridge because it was important for him to be in Turin, near Fiat. Apart from visits during the summer he had never lived in Italy, even though both of his parents were from Turin. He had grown up all over the world, never in one place for long. His English had an odd, unplaceable accent. If he didn't try to connect with his Italian heritage now, he figured, he might never get the chance.

At that point, he faced a tricky political decision. Which set of grandparents should he live with? Moreover, how could he find the time and concentration to study if he lived at Villa Frescot? The Agnelli family villa certainly had plenty of space, but Gianni and Marella's globe-trotting lifestyle—as well as all the entertaining they did—was not conducive to studying. Avoiding the issue entirely, he decided to live in a dormitory called Villa San Giuseppe, run by a priest named Fratello Igino. Instead of living in a mansion with a private guard at the gate, John's home in Turin was on the second floor in a red brick building overlooking a garden with 180 other students. His room, at the end of a long corridor, had a single bed and a desk. He had his own shower, but not his own bathroom. And first-year students couldn't have a car.

Instead, John drove around on a motorcycle. When one of his fellow students at San Giuseppe was hurt playing a game of soccer, John loaded him onto the motorbike and brought him to Turin's Molinette hospital, earning him a traffic ticket from the police.

Dorm life was quite an adjustment at first. In Paris he could come and go as he pleased, despite the fact he was only a teenager. In Turin, it was dinner in the dorm and then lights out at 10 P.M. He took his laundry home to Villa Frescot on weekends for it to be washed.

But it was fun. When students passed their exams, they were invited into Fratello Igino's office to drink a toast with something he called "Ambrosia."

John was a good student but did not stand out academically, one of his professors recalled. What struck him instead were John's good manners and the way he fit in with other students. John was strong-willed and methodical. He and Fiat chairman Cesare Romiti laid out a year-by-year study plan that John followed scrupulously.

Even though John's education was outwardly pretty normal, he hardly lived the life of the average university student. He started seeing his grandfather Gianni a few times each week, sometimes being whisked off by plane to see a Juventus game in some European capital.

Glamorous episodes like that were rare, however. During the summer of 1997, he worked on an assembly line in a Fiat plant in Tychy, Poland. But John didn't just punch a time card all summer until he went back to Turin. He redesigned the headlight assembly station, and came up with a more efficient way to deliver small parts to the assembly line. On a larger scale, he set up a competition for workers at the plant to come up with the best ways to eliminate quality defects. The competition initially involved two assembly lines, and by 2005 had been extended to the entire plant.

He also worked in a dealership in France and at a component factory in England, where he lived with a British family.[26] He was gradually sucked into Fiat's orbit as he met Fiat's management team one by one. Holidays were few, because if he wasn't studying he was off working at one of Fiat's plants somewhere. If he wasn't working, he divided his time between his family (he was a son of divorced parents) and skiing with friends in Sestriere. As a crown prince in training, John's college life had little room for the spontaneous, goofy fun that he enjoyed at Villa San Giuseppe. Instead, like many industrial and royal heirs before him, John was learning that belonging to a dynasty involves discipline and self-sacrifice. Personal preferences and inclinations must be set aside for the good of the family, the company, and the country.

If John was going to follow in the footsteps of his grandfather and great-great grandfather, he needed to learn the fine art of balancing self-indulgence and self-repression in the service of duty. Gianni had been a master at this trade-off. His eccentric habit of continually flitting from Turin to Paris, say, for a party, or to the seaside and back, was a way of letting off steam and marking off some sort of private space. His excesses never made their way into the press, which before the advent of the 24/7 news cycle was still deferential to the privacy of the powerful industrialist. More to the point, Agnelli controlled large swathes of it.

Gianni thought the best way to prepare for manhood was through acts of physical courage. Edoardo did not seem to agree, but John was always ready to take up his grandfather's challenges. Gianni's idea of a fun outing with his grandson was to take him skiing in March or April, and then down to the seaside—by helicopter, one assumes—for a dip in the freezing cold water, and then back to Turin.[27] One of John's earliest memories of his grandfather was skiing at St. Moritz. Gianni would push him to pick the trickiest way down the mountain. Years later, Gianni urged John to test himself on the St. Moritz Cresta skeleton run, where adrenaline lovers have been plunging headfirst on a tiny sled down a chute of ice for over 100 years.

"People under the age of 18 weren't supposed to do it, but my grandfather got special permission for me to take my first trip at age 16," John recalled.[28]

His life as a student became even more unusual on April 10, 1996, when his grandfather awarded him ownership of a 24.87 percent stake in Dicembre, the unlisted financial holding that owned Gianni's controlling" stake in Fiat. It was the year Gianni stepped down as chairman. Edoardo had been offered shares in Dicembre and had not accepted them, furious. Edoardo never went on the record saying why he refused the shares, but a person close to the family thinks it was in protest over not being picked as a successor to his father.

"He suspected a trap," his cousin Lupo Rattazzi said.[29]

■ ■ ■

On December 13, 1997, when Giovannino died of cancer, John's life changed forever. Before Giovannino died, Gianni invited John to Villa

Frescot for lunch. After they were finished, he asked John to stay for a chat. Gianni remarked on what a sad moment it was for the family. Then he got right to the point.

"I think you are the best person to represent the family on Fiat's board," he told John, who was 21.

John was surprised, and honored. Gianni had never discussed this with him before, although John sometimes got the feeling his grandfather had been gauging him.

Gianni had decided to act quickly to nip any speculation about family succession in the bud.[30] He had wanted John to be the family heir for some time.

Less than a week after his cousin's death, John went back to Villa Frescot, this time for his first Fiat board meeting. His grandmother Marella's gardens below the house were mostly bare, except for the soft orange fruit hanging from the cachi trees, which stood out against the dark, somber December tones. John had dressed with care in order to make a good impression on the big day, and had no idea what to expect. Unusually, the board was meeting around the Agnellis' dining room table, because Gianni had broken his leg—for the fifth time!—after tripping on a step, and was on crutches. John was tongue-tied from shyness, and fortunately didn't have to make a speech. The butler showed him through the little room Marella sometimes used to make phone calls from a wicker couch and into the dining room; John crossed the creaky parquet floor and took his seat, underneath a Monet painting of a snowy pond. He received a warm welcome.

John was curious to understand what his responsibilities as a board member would be. He knew one thing already. It meant that he was being named publicly to take over as the head of the next generation of the family.

"He is young, but he has already shown he has outstanding ability and moral qualities," Gianni told his board. "I think John's nomination to the board is the most meaningful way to demonstrate, also symbolically, the continuity of the family's close involvement with Fiat."[31]

His decision, which Gianni believed was best for the company, proved to be painful for many of the people involved, both immediately and later. For Edoardo, who had not been informed by Gianni of his decision, it was like reopening an old wound.[32] Edoardo's reaction was scathing. He criticized the move as being "along the lines of Caligula making his horse a Senator."[33]

"I think John Elkann was like getting a second rib taken out," said Lapo 10 years later. "But he realized that the position was not the right one for him. It wasn't power or the management role that created problems for him. It seemed like in emotional terms, the son was being pushed aside."[34]

■ ■ ■

By the time John graduated in 2000, a month after Edoardo's suicide, he was a public figure. Italian students have to defend their thesis in public oral examinations in front of a board of professors. Often, this event is attended by family and friends. In John's case, it was also covered by a national newspaper.

"We're not celebrating, because the family is still in mourning," John's father, Alain Elkann, told *La Repubblica*.

John's thesis was on the topic "Reverse Auctions Online, a New Negotiating Tool," and he was voted 95 points out of 110. His mother, Margherita Agnelli, was in the audience, along with a "mysterious and beautiful young woman who could be either a cousin or a friend," wrote *La Repubblica*.[35] Fiat CEO Paolo Cantarella was there, too.

John, for his part, had the luxury of being schooled in a long tradition dating back through his family and—by extension—to the House of Savoy's militaristic practice of centuries past. But as he would find out later, the press would no longer treat all the heirs of the House of Agnelli with kid gloves like they had the *Avvocato*. Times had changed.

Certainly Casa Agnelli was not as rigid and old-fashioned as Casa Savoia, where the crown price was not allowed to mix in politics until he inherited the throne and, like other members of court, could speak to his father, the king, only if addressed by him.[36] Crown Prince Umberto was known for his extramarital affairs and looked glamorous when photographed on vacation in Bedouin gear with his wife, Maria Josè—unlike his father the king, who was short and squat and wore an old-fashioned mustache.

But the life of any member of a royal family is mainly made up of a never-ending stream of tiresome ceremonies filled with small talk, handshakes, and photo ops. Discipline trumped self-indulgence at every turn. Crown Prince Umberto was able to eat an entire plate of roasted grasshoppers served to him by an Arab sheik on an official trip to the Mideast sometime in the 1930s "without making so much as a single grimace," a historian recalled.[37]

Therein lies the difference between John and Edoardo: John, at a young age, was willing to make a life choice that would force him to eat metaphorical plates of roasted grasshoppers not once but many, many times over. Edoardo, for reasons only he could know, was not.

# Chapter 6

# Only One Person Rules at a Time

Exactly one month after Gianni Agnelli's death, Margherita and Marella, his two surviving heirs, walked through the glass-walled, marble-paved lobby of a notary's office in downtown Turin to complete the paperwork related to Gianni's will. Margherita and her frail and elderly mother had just attended a Mass in Gianni's memory at the Santuario della Consolata, a shrine dedicated to the Virgin Mary, where the memorial services for Edoardo and Giovanni Alberto had also been held. A crowd of people crammed inside the church, and waited outside on the steps to grasp Donna Marella's hand. The outpouring of grief was just like it had been at the funeral.[1]

When Margherita arrived, she found Gianluigi Gabetti, Gianni Agnelli's longtime business adviser, who had come back out of retirement at Umberto's request, and lawyer Franzo Grande Stevens, waiting for her.[2] She had been assured by Gabetti there was nothing special to sign.[3] Her son, John Elkann, was there, too. Margherita was somewhat perplexed by John's presence.[4] The reason John was there would soon become clear.

A few days earlier Margherita had called Gabetti and said she wanted "everything to be in place" for the meeting, so he called the notary's office and made sure there were two witnesses present to conform with the correct procedure. The paperwork was being done that day because Margherita, who lived in Switzerland, was in Turin for the Mass.

Margherita should not have been all that surprised to see John at the notary office that day. Her father Gianni had made it clear in writing in 1996 that he wanted John to inherit his stake in the unlisted company through which he controlled Fiat, where John was already a shareholder.[5] Family tradition held that only one person could rule at a time. After all, that's how Giovanni had done things; he had left Gianni a share in the company that was twice as big as everyone else's. And the system had worked well. So far.

The will itself was fairly standard, as was to be expected, since inheritance in Italy is very tightly defined. The deceased's fortune is divided into equal portions among the living heirs, plus one other portion that the deceased may dispose of in the way he or she best sees fit according to his or her instructions. This so-called *disponibile* portion is taken from the assets of the other heirs after the estate has been divided.

Gianni's estate was assigned 50/50 to his two heirs, Margherita and Marella. He left his hilltop home and Villa Frescot with all its furnishings to Marella, Margherita, and Edoardo (who died in 2000, after the will was written in 1999). Marella had "use" of the house, and the two children were given ownership. He also left Villar Perosa, the country mansion that had been in his family since before his grandfather's day, to his three heirs. He left the Rome townhouse on the Quirinal hill opposite the presidential palace, with a stunning view over the domes and rooftops of the city, to Marella. Last but not least, he left a small villa near their Turin residence to Edoardo, where he would stay until his suicide.

Margherita was immediately suspicious, as she later stated when the events of that day ended up in court. Her father had eight homes, but the will mentioned only four. What about the Park Avenue apartment in New York, the pink chalet with green shutters in St. Moritz where Marella lived every summer, or the apartment in Paris? And there was no mention of the former convent in Corsica, which was one of Gianni's favorite places. In whose name were they registered? she wondered.[6] For that matter, was there a list or catalog of her father's art collection, with its Klimts, its Bacons, its Picassos, Klees, Warhols, and Lichtensteins?

Nevertheless, Margherita didn't raise any questions at that point and signed the papers.

However, Margherita, for her part, claimed she never signed the paperwork for the wills. "I am not signing," she said, according to author Gigi Moncalvo's record of the event, "because no records or documentation of my father's total assets had been made available. I don't understand the reason for this unexplainable behavior."[7] Marella signed the papers.

Margherita had touched a raw nerve. Gianni's daughter had received 100 million euros from her father in 1999 as a gift, sent to an account in Switzerland from money that her father held offshore.[8] Edoardo, for his part, had refused his gift. It was her right to know how much he held. Margherita had moved to Switzerland and bought herself the villa on the shores of Lake Geneva with the money. Actually, she had been obliged to move to Switzerland in order to receive her father's gift. And she suspected that he had given away a lot more money while he was still alive to friends and lovers.[9]

If Margherita started asking questions—such as a full accounting of the estate—she would have been playing with fire. The last thing the family needed after Gianni's death, with Fiat losing money, lacking management, and with seemingly few prospects for recovery other than a sale to General Motors, were revelations that the man who had been dubbed "Italy's uncrowned king" had presumably accumulated a secret fortune and had hidden it from the Italian tax authorities.

There had been whispers and hints in the past that Gianni may have had a pot of money hidden offshore. In 1994, a Turin magistrate had tried without success to prove that Gianni kept a secret Swiss bank account that he used to make an off-the-books payment for Juventus to a soccer player, Dino Baggio.[10] But a Swiss notary, Hans-Rudolf Staiger, came forward and said the account belonged to him, and Gianni had simply used that account to make a "personal donation."

Gabetti and Grande Stevens could not help Margherita even if they had wanted to, as they had never received any sort of formal authorization from Gianni to deal with his personal finances.[11] Gabetti was surprised by Margherita's suspicions.[12] Nor was it in Marella's interest—as later would become clear—to take Margherita's side in such a delicate matter.

But the meeting was only just getting started.

After recording the contents of the will as a matter of public record, the notary, Ettore Morone, turned to a different matter of business. It was a shareholders' meeting of Dicembre, the company created by Gianni back in April 1996 to hold his majority stake in the GA&C limited partnership through which the family, in turn, controlled IFI, then IFIL, and then finally Fiat. Dicembre was a *società semplice*, a type of unlisted company that gives shareholders wide leeway in writing up the statutes.

The complicated ownership structure through a cascade of companies is a common practice in Italy, locking up control of market-listed family empires away from the unwanted advances of hostile takeovers. The family is able to tap the capital markets to raise cash for investment and expansion, but at the same time the structure cuts down on the risk that one day it could lose control in a takeover battle.

In this case, the chain of interlocking companies served another, more important, purpose. The aptly named Dicembre, which means December in Italian, had statutes with a clause that gave Gianni Agnelli sole administrative control over the unlisted company, "without exception," according to Article 9.

The statutes also gave him the power to name John Elkann as the one to inherit control of Dicembre after his death.

"In the event that Gianni Agnelli dies or is somehow unable to discharge his duties, the same administrative powers in the same position and prerogatives will be assumed by John Philip Elkann," the statute reads.

The statute had been approved by all of Dicembre's eight shareholders in 1996, including Margherita.

Dicembre had already caused a rift in the family in 1996, when Edoardo refused to accept his stake in the company because John had been included as a shareholder. So the stake tagged for Edoardo still belonged to Gianni and was therefore part of the estate. Now Dicembre was about to cause trouble again.

Morone started by reading a letter Gianni had written in July 1996, before entering the operating room for heart surgery. It was after Dicembre had been set up. Gianni was 75 at the time and had already had heart surgery once, so he wasn't taking any chances.

"Having acknowledged the refusal of my son Edoardo to accept my donation of a stake equal to that offered to other family members, and accepted by them, I hereby leave to my aforementioned son assets other than the stake in Dicembre of the same value as my remaining stake," the handwritten letter said. "I leave my aforementioned remaining stake to my grandson John Philip Elkann, while the value of the right to the stake of my legal heirs must be paid for with assets other than stakes of Dicembre."

The transfer of property is one of the most difficult challenges facing any family company, and in Italy it was further complicated by the fact that inheritance law calls for the estate to be split among the heirs. But such a split would not be good for Fiat, especially in its weakened state in 2003.

Margherita had known of Gianni's wishes at the time, and went along with them. She signed the Dicembre statutes. After all, it was what he wanted, and John was her son. The letter had no legal value since it was written before the will, but Gianni's intentions in it were clear.

At that point in the meeting, a second set of papers was placed on the table for signatures. Margherita read through them and was incredulous.[13] The atmosphere in the room grew tense. The papers said Marella was donating her shares in Dicembre to her grandson John. Grande Stevens took the floor to explain.

"In making this donation, Donna Marella is interpreting the wishes of her recently departed husband," Grande Stevens said.

Margherita was visibly upset. By donating her shares to John to guarantee he was given control of Fiat, Marella had just ambushed Margherita.

According to the Dicembre statutes, Marella, Margherita, and John were to divide up Gianni's stake. That meant after Gianni's death, they were each to have 33.3 percent. Had they proceeded according to Italian inheritance law, Margherita and Marella would have divided up Gianni's stake between them, giving them more than John. But in

Gianni's letter in 1996 and the company statutes,[14] and by naming John to the boards of Fiat and the family limited partnership, Gianni clearly indicated he wanted John to control Fiat.

The Dicembre statutes did not violate Italian law, since they said that Gianni's heirs could be compensated for not receiving his stake by being paid with the equivalent value in other assets.

But in order to carry out Gianni's wishes to transfer his stake to John, Marella was now donating her own stake to John, before inheriting her share of Gianni's stake. Marella's sudden gift would deprive Margherita from inheriting Marella's stake after the elderly woman died. Gianni had never transferred his stake to John when Gianni was alive, despite all of his signals. Now, it was being done after his death. It was Margherita's right to inherit her half of Gianni's stake, and for some reason, her mother had not seen fit to let her have that right. Nor did his advisers seem to trust Margherita with the responsibility to hold the stake.

"Why are you doing this?" Margherita asked her mother.[15]

Margherita refused to sign these papers. But her signature was not needed; Marella's and John's would do, along with the signatures of Grande Stevens and Gabetti, who (with foresight) each had been given one share in Dicembre.

Margherita turned to Marella and said, "Mother, do you understand what you are doing? Explain to me that you understand the consequences. Why did you not tell me anything?"[16] She also had a reprimand for John, her son, who had just there and then become Fiat's controlling shareholder.

Gabetti stood up.

"I would be glad to sign as a witness, because in so doing I am witnessing the fact that Marella meets the expectations of her husband," Gabetti said, walking over to the table and signing.

It is unclear whether her father or her mother filled Margherita in. Gianni was likely to have made an oral request to Marella before he died for her to donate the Dicembre shares to John, a close family member said. But he was also likely to have dodged the responsibility of informing Margherita, who was often volatile.

"At the end of his life, Gianni was tired and didn't want to talk about the inheritance," the person said. "He sensed it could be controversial and didn't want to face it."

Nor did Gianni's advisers, Grande Stevens and Gabetti, ever fill Margherita in on the financial consequences of Gianni's death.

"These people operated in a culture of secrecy for so many years," said a financial adviser to Margherita. "In Italy it was impossible to do business if you didn't keep it secret. Business here is mixed with politics. Plus secrecy is also necessary because you don't want to be a target of organized crime."

But another family member said that Margherita had been informed, and was angry about Gianni's decision. By asking Marella to give her stake in Dicembre to John, Gianni had in essence cut out Margherita's other seven children from ever having a stake, since Margherita could never inherit it herself and leave it to her children. In this version of the story, her confrontation with her mother over Gianni's will grew out of her dissatisfaction with her parents' decision. Leaving Margherita, John, and Marella with equal stakes was a risk that Gianni didn't feel he could take. How could he? At Fiat, only one person could rule at a time. That was the tradition, and it had always worked.

Whatever the case, one thing is clear. Gianni and his advisers badly misread Margherita's reaction. Instead of signing the papers and going along with the plan, she dug in her heels. She did not believe her mother had decided to donate her shares to John on her own, and later said her father's advisers were making a power grab.

And then there was the matter of the inheritance. She was aware that her father kept money hidden in offshore bank accounts outside of Italy, and did not understand why it was being kept secret from her now. She was being treated in a high-handed manner, like a child. They had pushed it too far. The blunder would cost them dearly.

■ ■ ■

If her brother Edoardo's emotional life could be summed up by the hours he sat on his bed as a young boy with a Juventus scarf around his neck, waiting to go to a soccer game with a father who never arrived, Margherita's life also had its own emblematic episode.

It was in 1974, when Margherita was 19. Her father was in his office at Villa Frescot working on the speech he would be giving as the president of Italy's main business lobby, Confindustria. The door flew open and in walked Margherita, with a completely shaved head.

"What on earth have you done?!" Agnelli exclaimed.

"I am glad you noticed me," she replied, and turned on her heel and left.

Edoardo seemed to have crumbled under the pressure of not feeling able to live up to Gianni's myth. Margherita, who was never considered for any sort of responsible role at the company, was under less pressure and therefore freer to create her own life for herself. She was sent to boarding school in England, and when she came back to Italy, studied art briefly in Rome, where she insisted on not living in her parents' apartment on the Quirinal hill, hidden behind a huge wall with a grand double staircase leading up to a white stone gate a stone's throw away from the presidential palace.[17] She stayed instead with her Aunt Suni, who had a place in the same building.

"She shunned her mother's elegance, refusing to care about the least detail of how she looked," wrote Pochna in her biography of Gianni, *Agnelli, L'Irresistibile*. "She dressed not only like a hippie, but also just threw on any old thing she had in her closet."[18]

She embarked on her adult life by marrying young, a year after the head-shaving incident. On September 11, 1975, Margherita and Alain Elkann, a handsome young writer from a prominent Italo-French Jewish family, were wed at Villar Perosa. Elkann's father, Jean-Paul Elkann, was chief rabbi of Paris. His mother, Carla Ovazza, came from a Torinese banking family.[19] Margherita's wedding photograph shows her with short hair in a pink Yves Saint Laurent dress, grinning, discreetly covering her pregnancy. John would be born in April the following year. Gianni, by her side, is expressionless.

"It was not the wedding Gianni would have wanted; she wore neither a white dress nor was married in church," wrote Agnelli biographer Pochna.

Gianni presided over the wedding in his capacity as mayor of Villar Perosa, with photographs of *il Senatore* and his son Edoardo gazing down from the wall in city hall.[20]

She skipped university and had three children in quick succession: John in 1976, and then Lapo and Ginevra in 1977 and 1979. The couple moved to London, and separated in 1980. Margherita stayed in London to raise her three children, working part-time at a private kindergarten, La Petit École Française, where she became friendly with the founder, Anne Henderson Stewart. It was through Anne that Margherita met the man who would become her second husband, Serge de Pahlen, a Russian count, who became the father of a new family of five more children. They were married in 1985.[21]

Serge was from an old aristocratic family who left Russia after the Revolution. His mother was born in Paris in 1918, where Serge grew up. When he met Margherita, he was working at the French engineering firm Technip. The couple moved to Brazil with John, Lapo, and Ginevra. Their first of five children was born in 1983, in Rio de Janeiro. Margherita seemed happy to have created the sort of family life she had lacked. Serge began to work for Fiat in 1985, after the couple's wedding, and they moved the family to London, and then later to Paris. In 1998,[22] they moved to Allaman, Switzerland, a town on Lake Geneva famous for its huge castle.

"I know my last name is Agnelli, but I have tried to create a life for myself on my own, and not on the basis of how the media wanted to see me," she told an interviewer in 1997 at the opening of an exhibition of her paintings in Venice.[23]

In the mid-1970s, the decision to groom a woman for a place at Italy's largest company would have been a bold break from tradition. Instead, Margherita painted and wrote poetry, and her public appearances were limited to readings of her work or the occasional painting exhibition. Like her brother Edoardo, she took a great interest in spiritual and religious matters. She painted Russian-style religious icons, taught by Father George Drobot at the St. Sergius Orthodox Theological Institute in Paris, a religious school operated by the Russian Orthodox Church.

In 1997 she wrote and illustrated a children's book based on the Bible story of Jonas and the whale, published by Mondadori, Italy's largest publisher. At the book's presentation in Milan in December that year, Monsignor Gianfranco Ravasi, an expert in Bible studies, praised Margherita as "a true storyteller." After the presentation, family and friends gathered at the home of Mondadori's first wife, Paola Zanussi, one of Italy's *grandes dames* and granddaughter of the founder of the Zanussi home appliance company. Her Milan apartment had been decorated by Renzo Mongiardino, like the Agnelli family home in Turin.

Margherita never sought the limelight in matters regarding Fiat, and often used her married name. A few days after her book presentation, she was asked to comment on John's nomination to Fiat's board, and politely declined.[24]

■ ■ ■

In April 2003, two months after the opening of the will, Emanuele Gamna, a lawyer, received a phone call from a very agitated Margherita. The pair had known each other socially for years, and were on friendly terms.

"You have always given me very good advice, and now I need it more than ever—I am in a terrible situation!" she began abruptly.[25] Gamna asked her to explain what she meant.

"The situation about my father's estate is complicated, but his people in Turin are treating me like an idiot—and worse still, like an outsider, as if I don't have any right to know anything, even if as an heiress, never mind being the daughter," she started.

"I have hired a lawyer in Switzerland, but I need one in Turin," she continued. "I need someone who can talk to Gabetti, and to my mother, about this prickly subject. . . . That's why I thought of you, because you know everyone, and my father thought highly of you. Plus you have an excellent relationship with my mother and with Gabetti."

A few days later, Margherita and her old acquaintance Emanuele met in secret in Milan, in the deserted bar of the Grand Hotel de Milan.

Margherita had an ace up her sleeve—or more like a hand grenade! The head of the Agnelli family's financial consultant, Sigfried Maron, had visited her home in Switzerland in March and shown her a list of Liechtenstein-based foundations worth a total of 600 million euros.[26] The foundations had strange names like Alkyone, Calamus, FIMA, Sikestone, CS-Account, and Sigma. They belonged to Marella, given to her by Gianni. So Margherita had been right in assuming that her father had offshore assets that were hidden from her when the will was opened. Amazingly, no one in the family had informed her about the existence of her father's 600 million euros. Margherita was both hurt and furious, according to a person who worked closely with her in the following years.

The list was used by Margherita and Gamna as a sort of treasure map to build a picture of her father's full wealth. As they sat amid the potted palm trees in the stately elegance of the back rooms of the Grand Hotel de Milan, a strategy took shape. Margherita and Gamna believed her father was likely to have donated up to another 600 million euros to third parties, as was his right.[27] She did not plan to challenge Gianni's crystal-clear intention to have John inherit his controlling stake in Fiat.

However, Margherita, for her part, had no intention of simply rolling over and letting her legal rights as Gianni's heir be trampled on. She wanted to inherit her full portion of the estate. And she also planned to contest the Dicembre statute that called for Gianni's stake in the company to be divided three ways—between Marella, John, and Margherita—instead of between the two legal heirs, in accordance with Italian law, so that she would inherit her fair stake, even though the company statutes gave her no say in its management whatsoever.[28]

But first things first.

"In that first meeting we agreed that the most urgent priority was to gain an exhaustive inventory of the estate," Gamna, who would later have a spectacular falling-out with Margherita, wrote in his 2011 memoir.[29]

Margherita and Gamna began a series of negotiations with Marella's lawyer, Grande Stevens. Stevens had resigned as executor of the estate to represent Marella. A full list of paintings emerged, and Marella was willing to come to terms. Talks between the two sides moved forward in an atmosphere of distrust, suspicion, and genuine lack of understanding. Had Margherita been more trusting of her father's advisers, perhaps she could have simply waited to discover the true extent of Gianni's estate when she inherited it from her mother. And had Gianni's advisers trusted her more, they would have perhaps been more forthcoming.

"I realized, perhaps a bit late, that the older generation in Turin for the past 30 or 40 years is accustomed to exercising unquestioned power, and to impose solutions by force: they are structurally set up, or even programmed, to never be contradicted, and convinced that every time you don't bow to one of their orders you are offending the majesty of their king; a person who, in their not completely disinterested eyes, is equivalent with the universal good," wrote Gamna.[30]

By October, Gamna and Margherita had come up with an estimate for what they believed was the true value of Gianni's estate, including real estate, offshore funds, and the art collection: about 2.5 billion euros. After subtracting the one-third of the estate that Gianni would have been free to leave to others, the amount to be divided between Marella and Margherita would provide them about 800 million euros each.[31]

By the end of the year mother, daughter, and attorneys had come to an agreement: Margherita would inherit all of the offshore funds in the list given to her back in March, or about 550 million euros, plus 37.5 percent of Dicembre (worth 105 million euros), and about 240 million euros in real estate and paintings, plus other assets. The total was about 1.2 billion euros. In exchange, she agreed to make an annual payment to Marella of 7 million euros and a few paintings she was particularly fond of.[32] Margherita renounced any right to further question her mother about her father's offshore wealth.[33] She received the lion's share of the offshore funds, in exchange for the annual payment to Marella, because she gave up any claim to Marella's inheritance after her mother's death. They both renounced any right to any donations Gianni might have made to third parties.[34] And Margherita sold her stake in Dicembre to Marella, cutting Margherita's ties to Fiat.

Mother and daughter signed their agreement in March 2004. Margherita wanted to make peace.[35] Happy with her inheritance—for the time being—she worked on patching up relations with her aunt Suni, her cousins, and her daughter Ginevra.[36] John's wedding was slated for September, and she wanted to bury the hatchet and celebrate with the rest of her huge clan at what would be the first wedding of the new generation of Agnellis.[37]

# Chapter 7

# The Wedding of the Year

I t was September 2, 2004, and John Elkann and Lavinia Borromeo's wedding was just two days away. Alfredo Ratti, a stout man with a snow white beard and pale blue eyes, decided it was time for his team of 15 florists to start arranging the hundreds of fresh plants and flowers that had been brought by boat to the tiny islands of Isola Bella and Isola Madre on Lake Maggiore.

Lake Como may be more glamorous, because its stunning shoreline of steep green hills plunging into dark, placid water has attracted the likes of Gianni Versace and George Clooney. But Lake Maggiore has something Como does not: not one but two palaces on twin islands, one a riot of Baroque fantasy with a wedding-cake garden and the other immersed in the silent calm of an otherworldly botanical garden where white peacocks and shiny-plumed pheasants stroll.

Ratti had already been at work for a week setting up the various arches, trellises, vases, wreathes, and table centerpieces for what newspapers had already dubbed "the wedding of the year," working in tandem with tastemaker Beppe Modenese, one of the most powerful men in Italy's fashion industry. The jasmine plants had to be affixed one by one, by hand, to the arch set up over the altar of the tiny family chapel on Isola Madre—which had been in the Borromeo family since the 1600s—that would transform the inside and outside of the church into what Ratti knew would be an oasis of perfumed bliss.

Ratti and Modenese thought the flowers should be simple, since the two islands were already pleasure gardens in and of themselves. Modenese's idea was "to add beauty to beauty." Both the bride and groom wanted the wedding to be elegant, but not showy. They were in good hands with the tall, dapper Modenese, who had been organizing fashion events for decades. Lavinia's aunt, Principessa Bona Borromeo, who worked with them on the cancer charity she ran, had asked him to help out. They all recognized that there was no way this wedding could be a small and intimate family affair. The young scion of Europe's most famous automotive dynasty was marrying a princess who had a family name attached to more residences than even the Agnellis owned: an incomplete list would count six castles, three palaces, one museum, a college, and four villas.

The wedding announcement was simple enough: "Lavinia Borromeo Arese Taverna and John Elkann announce their marriage. The wedding will take place in the chapel on the Isola Madre." The invitations were made by Raimondi di Pettinaroli, the engraver that had been serving Milanese nobility since 1776.

Tongues started wagging almost immediately. Why were the couple's parents not mentioned in the announcement? Would Margherita Agnelli be coming? Had she and John made peace? Was Margherita still on bad terms with Marella? How much did she get from her inheritance? Margherita put out a statement before the wedding, saying she had found "a fair solution in the interest of all my children" to questions surrounding her inheritance.

More than just the whispered gossip, the young couple also had to endure some misguided snobby sniping about their choice to create a gift registry at La Rinascente, the Italian department store, along with a more select group of antique dealers.[1] The couple chose it simply because it was part of the Fiat group.

Indeed, despite their high-powered family backgrounds, both John and Lavinia, 26, avoided the limelight when they could. By marrying a princess, John was continuing a family tradition. The Borromeo family had made its fortune in banking in the 1400s before being given a title by the Duke of Milan. Like all Italian nobility of the time, the Borromeos had their share of cardinals, bishops, and saints. One of her ancestors, San Carlo Borromeo, named Archbishop of Milan in 1566, lies entombed in Milan's Duomo. But unlike many of the princes of the Church, San Carlo and his cousin, cardinal Federico Borromeo, founder of a precious Milan library in 1609 that later evolved into a painting museum, are still remembered today for their good works.

Lavinia, or Lavi, as her family called her,[2] was more often photographed in jeans and sneakers than in designer clothes, despite having tried a few turns on the runway and then having worked briefly for Giorgio Armani.

John and Lavinia's wedding did not try to upstage the setting. The Isola Bella was spectacular enough, with its 10-tier statue- and obelisk-topped terraced garden, hovering just off the coast of the lake like a carnival float set adrift from its parade. The family chapel on the Isola Madre, with just four rows of pews, would not hold more than just family and friends. But for the dinner and party on the Isola Bella, 700 bankers, politicians, models, and European aristocracy would descend on the small lakeside resort of Stresa for the occasion. The two islands were closed to tourists, and the town would be cordoned off by police.

■ ■ ■

At around 6:30 P.M. on September 4, Lavinia walked down the steps of Palazzo Borromeo—the smaller one, on the Isola Madre—wearing an ivory silk mikado wedding gown designed by Valentino that had taken 15 seamstresses two months to make, a veil that had been in the family forever, and a diamond tiara lent to her by her paternal grandmother, Ida. Her long blonde hair was gathered discreetly behind her bare neck.[3]

She made her way down the back steps, past the lemon trees and roses that Ratti had woven along the stone balustrade, toward the terracotta-trimmed little neo-Gothic chapel, escorted by her tanned, white-haired father, Carlo. A bouquet of white roses and gardenias tumbled from her hands in a cascade to below her knees, accentuating her tall frame. Below her, gathered around the circular lily pond outside the church, was a sea of upturned faces. She had always dreamed of getting married in that church. She had known John since she was 20 years old, and it was the first serious relationship for both of them. John, dressed in a morning suit from Anderson and Sheppard on London's Savile Row, a white gardenia in his buttonhole, stood outside the church, beaming.

John and his family had gathered the evening before at the five-star Grand Hotel Des Illes Borromees in Stresa, where a mix of royalty, American financiers (like Vanderbilt, Morgan, Carnegie, and Rockefeller), and, later, writers like Ernest Hemingway had been coming to vacation since 1863. John met up with them for a dinner organized by Ginevra and her cousins. The next day, John and his family met in the hotel's painstakingly restored lobby to take the boat over while the bride got ready. Nicola and Carlo Caracciolo, Marella Agnelli's two brothers, were already waiting in the lobby for Marella when she arrived, looking super-chic in an understated beige silk Armani pantsuit woven with silver thread.[4]

Ginevra, Lapo, and their cousin Alessandro Nasi were particularly excited, since it was the first wedding of someone from their generation of the family. The three Elkann children were close, perhaps partly as a result of being raised in Brazil, London, Paris, and New York. When they spoke to one another, they switched from French to Italian back and forth indiscriminately. They were also close to their father, Alain, often spending time with him on weekends at his home near Turin, where he still kept their old bedrooms. Before the wedding, Alain had organized an engagement party at his home in Moncalieri so the two families could get to know one another.

A pink-hatted Margherita and her husband Serge were next to arrive, with their five children in tow. Margherita and Marella embraced warmly.[5] Together they walked to the hotel embarcadero, where they boarded a boat to the applause of the photographers.

The church was only large enough for John, Lavinia, their witnesses, their closest family members, and two priests. The religious rites were Catholic. It was the first wedding that Principessa Bona Borromeo could ever recall being held in the chapel.[6]

After the couple exchanged vows, the guests witnessed another emotional moment when John gave Margherita a long hug.[7] John and Lavinia had hoped the wedding would make the family happy again. The family had endured four funerals in the last seven years, and the last one—Umberto's—was still fresh in everyone's mind. The family tragedies had taken their toll on Fiat, too, plunging the automaker into crippling management churn at a time when it could least afford it. Margherita's long-drawn-out negotiations with Marella over her inheritance had put a strain on all of them. Right then, it looked like the wedding had succeeded in bringing everyone together. Ginevra was happy to see the family all together again, even if it was to be short-lived.

There was time for a toast in the gardens, which had been assembled by Count Vitaliano IX Borromeo by importing plants from greenhouses all over the world. Guests commented on how radiant the bride looked and how nice it was for the family to be together again. Lavinia was not often photographed smiling, but today she was giddy with joy. Guests walked or minced along the gravel walkways past the oleanders and palms down to the boat launch for the short trip to Isola Bella, as swallows darted around, screeching. John and Lavinia climbed into the vintage wooden motorboat from the 1920s, with flowers on the prow, and set off for the Isola Bella as the light began to turn pink and fade gently into dusk.[8]

In a country its inhabitants call *il Bel Paese* with more than its fair share of enchanting places, the Isola Bella (Beautiful Island) lives up to its name. The architects who built it back in the mid-1600s wanted to make it look like an imaginary ship, with the landing pier in front of the palace as a prow, and the terraced pyramid forming the ship's bridge at the back. Not even the two little cafés, the touristy restaurant, or the closed-up stalls that usually sold soccer shirts, straw hats, Lake Maggiore tea towels, and beach dresses could diminish the scene's charm as John and Lavinia pulled up in their boat.

They crossed the little square in front of the island's church, entered the palace, and walked up the grand staircase studded with giant crests of Italian noble families along the walls, past their initials made from white roses. They walked through the Sala della Medaglie, decorated with gilded medallions depicting the life of San Carlo Borromeo, and a portrait of Count Vitaliano, the builder of the palace, wearing a ruffled collar and long, curly brown hair tucked in the corner. The robin's egg blue Salone Grande, with its four-story ceiling and windows looking out onto the lake, had been transformed into a deluxe restaurant.

But instead of stopping, they were headed through to the garden. So they strolled though the Music Room, Napoleon's room, the Work Room—where the scent of grass from the lawn drifted in through the open windows—the Ballroom, the Conversation Room, and finally past the collection of sixteenth-century tapestries depicting lions, leopards, and unicorns devouring each other, where Ratti had opted for a soothing row of green potted palms, with flowers at the base. The long gallery led out into courtyard, where steps took the couple and their guests up to the formal garden for drinks before dinner.

The guest list was a who's who of Italian politics, industry, and finance, with a smattering of European royalty thrown in and a sprinkling of supermodels to top it all off. Italian Prime Minister Silvio Berlusconi arrived from a conference in Cernobbio on nearby Lake Como with his undersecretary, Gianni Letta, and his spokesman, Paolo Bonaiuti.

Never one to hide from the cameras, Berlusconi stopped to tell journalists the wedding was wonderful and "is an event of peace that we all really need."[9]

Fiat CEO Sergio Marchionne was there, along with Chairman Luca di Montezemolo, his wife Ludovica, and their two children Matteo and Clementina, as well as past Fiat executives Cesare Romiti, Paolo Fresco, and Gabriele Galateri. All of Italy's top bankers were there, including Mario Draghi, the head of the Bank of Italy, and Mario Monti, who had just stepped down as the European Union's competition commissioner. Designer Valentino arrived with his companion and business manager, Giancarlo Giammetti, along with Matteo Marzotto, Valentino director general and a relative of Lavinia's by marriage (who gave her wedding dress to her as a gift; she, in turn, donated a sum to Matteo's favorite charity). Other younger members of Italian industrial dynasties came, too: Alessandro Benetton, Guido

Barilla, and the younger Merlonis. Model Elle MacPherson (whose first child had been baptized by Gianni Agnelli) wore a long yellow gown, and was photographed with Carla Bruni in midnight blue.

Lavinia, though she had removed her diamond tiara, was not the only crowned head at the reception. Maria Gabriella of Savoy, the daughter of the last king of Italy, was there, along with her nephew, Prince Serge of Yugoslavia.[10]

Guests snacked on hot and cold hors d'oeuvres, like stuffed olives and crispy fried sage or skewers of shrimp, and sipped Veuve Cliquot champagne or Italian prosecco from Aneri. The perfectly manicured gardens were filled with the sound of laughter and clinking glasses. Many climbed to the top of the pyramid of terraces for the view out over the lake, as well as to take in the multilevel amphitheater on the other side on the way back down, decorated with seashells, a statue of Neptune, and a cupid riding a unicorn. As the daylight faded, the sky turned from deep blue to pink, and then finally darkened, and the lights along the shoreline started to blink on, reflecting against the black waters of the lake.

In the kitchens set up in the palace's cool basement grottoes, which usually housed a collection of prehistoric pottery, caterer Ernesto Mauro and his staff worked furiously. They had been preparing for five days, and had transported all the refrigerators, ovens, and utensils necessary to feed 700 people from Milan.[11]

At 9 P.M., guests sat down at tables set with pale yellow tablecloths and decorated with lemons and other citrus fruits, recalling the Borromeo family crest.[12] The flowers had been designed to echo the different stucco decorations in each room. Lavinia took off her veil and was seated with John at the table of honor, with family members and the couple's witnesses. Twenty sommeliers in tuxedos served the wine, and 120 waiters roamed the rooms making sure the guests had everything they needed. For a first course, guests could choose *sformato di riso*, pesto, or *agnolotti* (or have all three!), followed by a choice of veal, tiny Milanese cutlets, or lamb chops.

The trickiest part of such a big wedding was the cake. It had to feed 700 people. Pastry chef Enrico Parassina took the door measurements again and again, and fretted about moving a huge cake up a flight of 20 stairs from the grottoes to the upstairs rooms. After several tests—especially around curves—the chef decided that only by making a narrower cake could he feel confident that his creation would make the journey safe and sound.[13]

And what a cake! Carried by four men, the monumental concoction was amazing to behold: a white chocolate Lingotto factory surmounted by a cupid riding a unicorn, in a nod to the Borromeo and Agnelli families' origins. When the time came to name their children, though, John and Lavinia steered clear of family names and picked Leone and Oceano.

The pastry chef may have fretted about carrying the cake up the stairs, but he could do nothing about the brief rain shower that threatened to turn his creation into mush. Luckily it didn't. John and Lavinia took the rain in good spirits. After all, *sposa bagnata, sposa fortunata*, according to the Italian saying. A rained-on bride is a lucky bride.

■ ■ ■

John and Lavinia got their wish; their wedding was indeed a happy time for the family and seemed to presage better things. By the spring of 2005, Fiat had turned the corner, although it was not obvious yet at the time of the wedding. But Gianni's death had changed the family dynamics forever.

Margherita's son Lapo nearly died of a drug overdose in the fall of 2005, three days after his birthday. His life was saved by a call from a transsexual prostitute, who called the police, telling them to come quickly because a VIP was in trouble.

The Italian press had a field day, granting Lapo and his family none of the discretion that had been shown the *Avvocato* in his day. Times had changed. The inheritance battle carried out by Margherita, mixed with Fiat's problems and Lapo's now-public weaknesses, created an impression that the Agnelli dynasty's power and allure were fading.

"Lapo's drug moment was like Prince Charles' tampon moment," said British journalist William Ward, referring to a wiretap of an intimate conversation between the prince and then-lover Camilla Parker Bowles that seriously dented his regal prestige.

But it was not Lapo, who inherited Gianni's verve and style, who knocked the family from its pedestal for good. That honor went to Margherita. On May 30, 2007, she launched a devastating lawsuit against Gianluigi Gabetti, Franzo Grande Stevens, and Marella Agnelli. On the day of the suit, John found out Margherita had decided to tell her story to the *Wall Street Journal*, which ran it the next day under the headline "House of Agnelli Divided."[14]

Margherita's suit sought a full and complete reckoning of what she alleged were offshore assets hidden by her father's advisers, contesting the agreement she had reached with her mother back in 2004. Gabetti and Grande Stevens told the court that Gianni Agnelli managed his personal assets on his own and without help from them.[15] The suit was dismissed in 2010.

"The court's verdict brings to an end an episode that has been sad and painful for all of us," said Marella in a statement in March 2010. "Now I hope with all my heart that peace and affection will return and that we can look calmly to the future for the good of the family."[16]

Undaunted, Margherita pressed on, filing an appeal in January 2011 after naming her third set of lawyers. The case is still ongoing. In addition to all the bad publicity, the lawsuit had another negative effect as well. The attention attracted by the inheritance battle caught the interest of the Italian internal revenue service after Margherita and Marella's 2004 settlement was finalized, resulting in a whopping 100 million euro fine for unpaid taxes.

■ ■ ■

Gianni and Marella's children had both committed deeply destructive acts against their parents. Edoardo's was self-destructive, a gesture of despair and possibly recrimination. Margherita, instead, made a violent assault on her family's authority and prestige. In the process, she turned them against her and thereby perpetuated an unhappy cycle of family dysfunction for her.

John said he was saddened by Margherita's lawsuit, which has damaged his relationship with her. He has had time to reflect on the nature of family businesses and draw some conclusions.

"Families and businesses are very different by nature," he said in a speech in Chicago at the Family Business Network's annual summit in 2010. "The value of a family is about being equal and helping one another. Instead, a business is about performance and hierarchy. These two worlds operate and function differently. The lesson is ultimately that when a family and a business function, they function together. You have to have a family that works, and a business that works."

# Part II

# THE POWER OF
# AN INDIVIDUAL

# Chapter 8

# Unfixable Fiat

Gianluigi Gabetti, Gabriele Galateri, John Elkann, and Luigi Gubitosi, Fiat Group's treasurer, were having a working lunch around the lone table in IFIL's small corporate dining room, talking about Fiat's finances. It had been clear to all of them since the start of that year that Fiat was not in good shape, and it looked like the company would lose money again in 2002.

The automaker's latest model, the Stilo, had missed its targets. The attempt at making a Fiat to compete with Volkswagen's Golf had not been a success. The dot-com bubble had burst in 2000. And the world economy was in a tailspin following the September 11, 2001, terrorist attack on New York's World Trade Center. It looked like the company was going to need some sort of a loan or fresh capital. But Fiat's latest capital increase had just taken place in 2001. Neither the family nor shareholders would want to put in more cash. Their conversation was interrupted by a phone call from Fiat Chairman Paolo Fresco, in Rome.

"Our talks with the banks for new financing are speeding up. You need to drop what you're doing and come to Rome," he told them. "We have to nail down a solution this weekend."

It was a Friday on the last weekend in May. Nail it down they did.

■ ■ ■

Fiat's management, creditor banks, and the nervously watching Italian government were about to experience what U.S. President Obama's Presidential Task Force on the Auto Industry had learned in 2009: an indebted automaker saddled with overcapacity and shrinking market share cannot be saved by throwing cash into its maw. Plant closures and layoffs are not enough; top management has to go. Unless the underlying structural issues are fixed with management changes, asset sales, debt reduction, and a rethink of the way the company does business, the car company will just chew through the cash. The size of the industrial machine and the slow return on capital will guarantee that. And when the cash runs out, the machine simply stops, leaving tens of thousands of workers jobless. So the bank (or government) that steps up to the plate must also assume the responsibility of attaching strings to the money.

But what sort of strings? Fiat's management was about to find out.

Fiat's problem was more than just a lack of attractive new car models. It was overleveraged, having borrowed to finance acquisitions intended to diversify out of the auto business to offset Fiat Auto's weak position. For example, Fiat had bought Case New Holland for about $4.6 billion, in a bid to become a big player in agricultural machinery. The move would later pay off. In Fresco's mind, it was part of a strategy to sell Fiat Auto. But right now, it was debt sitting on the company's balance sheet.

The meeting in Rome was spurred by talk that the Bank of Italy intended to ask Fiat's creditor banks to consolidate all of their risk exposure to Fiat on their balance sheets. The Bank of Italy wanted the Italian banks' exposure to Fiat "to return back down to physiologically normal levels,"[1] to use business paper Il Sole-24 Ore's euphemism.

Fiat's total financial debt at that point was 35.5 billion euros, of which 19 billion was in the hands of Italian banks,[2] on total sales of 58 billion euros in 2001, 24.4 billion euros of which came from automobiles. The rest of the debt was in bonds held by national and international banks.[3] Fresco had been meeting with the banks since the spring of 2002 to find a solution. Fiat knew it risked a downgrade on its debt, which would be devastating for its creditor banks because of all the loans they held.

Fiat's debt was not saddled with covenants that could trigger a default, but management knew that liquidity issues would eventually start spooking its banks. Fiat had been placed on credit watch for a possible debt downgrade by ratings agency Moody's at the end of February, and by Standard & Poor's at the end of April. It risked seeing its bonds tumble into "junk" status. It needed to find a way to move debt from its balance sheet.

Fresco had been in Milan on Thursday with Fiat's adviser Gerardo Braggiotti, head of European operations at Lazard Europa Ltd, going over the outlines of the loan. And on Friday, he traveled to Rome to present it to Prime Minister Berlusconi. Berlusconi and Treasury Minister Giulio Tremonti, along with the Bank of Italy, were worried about the overexposure of Italian banks to a single client, Fiat, and the impact it could have on the Italian banking system and on the country's economy if Fiat started to circle the drain.

The outlines of the loan at that point had already been hammered out: Fiat's bankers were asking for it to speed up and increase its planned asset sales. The company was already trying to find a buyer for Magneti Marelli, its components maker. Fresco had promised to raise 2 billion euros from asset sales that year.[4] Now, other Fiat assets would need to be put on the block, too, like its insurance unit Toro Assicurazioni, and its Fiat Avio aerospace company. It would also have to sell 51 percent of Fidis, its car financing unit, thus removing its debt from Fiat's balance sheet. Fiat would also have to part with Edison, its energy company. Last but not least, the banks were insisting that the Agnelli family invest money in recapitalizing Fiat.

Despite Berlusconi's posturing about saving jobs and Fiat remaining Italian, Fiat's survival was now in the hands of a new generation of Italian bankers: Corrado Passera at IntesaBCI and Matteo Arpe at Banca di Roma. Alessandro Profumo of UniCredit joined the talks in the following days.

■ ■ ■

Fiat's crisis in 2002, brewing for years, came to head at a time when Italy's banking establishment, like its political class, had been transformed. In the past, when Fiat—or any other Italian company, for that matter—needed cash, it went to one place: Milanese investment bank Mediobanca. Mediobanca's founder, Enrico Cuccia, was often referred to as "the high priest of Italian finance." The secretive blue-eyed Sicilian had created a successful system that had helped Italian companies grow after the war despite the country's tiny capital markets and state-owned crony-capitalist banking system.

Cuccia's many critics say the bank's practice of locking up family control by using devices like cascading holding companies (also referred to as Chinese boxes), cross shareholdings, and voting pacts violated the spirit, if not the rules, of a free market and held Italy back from developing a more egalitarian system. His supporters say that if it hadn't been for Cuccia, the Italian state holding company Istituto per la Ricostruzione Industriale (IRI) would have gobbled up even more of the economy than it already had. Either way, when it came time to defuse a potential systemic banking crisis as Fiat slid near the brink in 2002, Mediobanca never even made it to the table at the meeting at Banca IMI that day. Mediobanca's way of dealing with overly indebted companies in the past had been like a surgeon amputating a limb to save a patient. When family-owned conglomerate Ferruzzi Finanziaria could no longer pay interest on its debt in 1993, Mediobanca led a restructuring of Italy's second-largest private company that called for creditor banks to swap their debt for equity. The family was forced out, and Mediobanca-picked management was brought in. The banks got stuck as shareholders for years.

In Fiat's case, Mediobanca had held talks with the government and the Bank of Italy on something similar, and Italy's commercial banks were determined to block it.

"Mediobanca was going around talking to the government and other institutions in Rome saying Fiat was in such a difficult situation that it needed absolute restructuring," one of the bankers involved recalled. "We were not convinced this was the case. And we decided we didn't want Mediobanca in the deal."

The last thing Italy's commercial banks wanted was to get stuck swapping their debt for equity in the automaker without ending up with any influence. So the banks decided to move quickly, preempting any attempt by Mediobanca to gain control of the situation. They succeeded, sending out a strong signal that a changing of the guard was taking place in Italian banking.

Matteo Arpe, who looked like Luke Skywalker dressed in a business suit, was the youngest of the trio and the whiz kid of Italian finance. He shot to international prominence by being one of the brains behind Roberto Colaninno in his bold bid for phone company Telecom Italia in 1999. Arpe had left Mediobanca after clashing with Cuccia's successor, Vincenzo Maranghi, in 2000, headed for a top job at Lehman Brothers in Europe. Two years later, he left to take on Capitalia, another formerly state-owned bank that was struggling under the weight of a huge bad loan book. Arpe had staked his reputation on the bank's turnaround with an ambitious plan to make it profitable by 2004.

Corrado Passera was the only one of the three with experience in industry and services as well as banking. During the 1990s, Passera had worked at Olivetti, the computer maker, when it was still controlled by Carlo de Benedetti. Before coming to IntesaBCI, his most recent task had been to drag Italy's antiquated postal system into the computer age, which he did, giving its drab post offices a much-needed face-lift in the process. His reassuring manner, ability to get along with everyone, and vast network of contacts often made him rumored to be in the running for a ministerial job whenever there was a new government.

Profumo, at 46, tall and prematurely gray, was the most outspoken of the three bankers about Italy's need to modernize the way it did business. Raised in Palermo, he moved to Milan when he was 19 and worked his way through college as a bank clerk. After a stint at McKinsey & Company as a consultant, he became Credito Italiano CEO in 1997 and built it up into Italy's second-largest bank. He had already clashed with Mediobanca more than once in his career by the fall of 2002.[5]

In Rome, Fresco and a group of bankers had convened in Banca IMI's offices in the Palazzo Bonaparte, so-called because Napoleon's mother had lived there from 1818 until her death. Her green-shuttered balcony, where she sat to watch the carriages roll by on the Via del Corso below, is still there today. Berlusconi's private residence, Palazzo Grazioli, stands nearby, guarded by vans of armed policemen.

Gubitosi, Elkann, and Galateri arrived in downtown Rome, their drivers whizzing round the circular Piazza Venezia past the oversized national monument the Romans call "the typewriter," past the tip of the ruins of the ancient Roman Forum, and past the balcony of Palazzo Venezia, where Mussolini was filmed haranguing the crowds in old black-and-white newsreels, to stop in front of Banca IMI's building. They walked past the stone plaque telling visitors that Napoleon's mother had died here, through the iron gate and the little marble-paved courtyard, and up a flight of stairs to the *piano nobile*. The bank's offices that boasted an impressive, monumental frescoed ceiling. The place was packed with people: CEOs of the three main banks; representatives from Merrill Lynch, an adviser to Fiat; and lawyers.

Neither Cantarella, Fiat's CEO, nor Damien Clermont, Fiat's CFO, were present, sending a clear signal they were out. Cantarella's star had been fading since October 2001, when Fiat had told analysts it would miss its financial targets that year for the first time since 1993, the company's previous crisis.[6]

"No one said it at the meeting, but it was clear that separate conversations about Cantarella and Clermont's resignation had already taken place at that point," said a person who was there.

More than a loan, Fiat needed capital. The ratings agencies would not be placated by a traditional loan, since they were beginning to question Fiat's long-term viability in terms of repayment. So the financing was a so-called mandatory convertible loan in which the banks would lend Fiat three billion euros. In return, Fiat promised to repay in 2005. If it couldn't, the banks were forced to convert their debt to equity by buying up shares to be issued at a certain price in a capital increase, in which the Agnelli family could take part as well.

Passera was the unofficial leader of the talks, since his bank would have the largest portion on the loan. Arpe, for his part, was good on technical details and was well schooled in the ways of Mediobanca, having begun his career there at age 22 at the side of Enrico Cuccia. The old-style way of doing deals would have been for the banks to swap their debt for equity and Mediobanca to appoint a new manager. Instead, this time, the approach would be a bit softer. The banks would provide capital and require discipline from management in terms of fixing the business, leaving it up to the family to decide whether to name a new CEO. The banks did not ask to name management, nor did they ask for board seats. They did, however, make it clear that they didn't think the current management was getting results and advocated what one banker called "a smooth management change." Such a change would be up to the family to decide.

The meeting that night lasted until 3 A.M. Sandwiches were brought in. Fiat did not resist the banks' conditions. It was the price of the share conversion that turned out to be a sticking point.

Braggiotti, Fiat's adviser, had worked with Arpe at Mediobanca. They spoke the same language and were steeped in the same traditions. Braggiotti's grandfather and father were both bankers, and he probably knew more about European banking and its secrets than anyone in the room. Both had broken with Mediobanca and struck out on their own. Braggiotti, a dark-haired man whose deal-room poker face was a mask of impish amusement, was older and smoother than Arpe.

Braggiotti argued that the shares should be priced at 15.50 euros, which was what they had sold for at a one billion euro capital increase in December 2001.

"Our original idea was to do it at 15.50, and the capital increase was at 15.50," he argued.

Arpe rejected that price, saying, "There is no connection between that price and the market value."

The shares were at 13 euros. The pair argued back and forth, in what sometimes looked to others present like a duel over who had greater mastery of the technical details of the complicated and unusual deal. Arpe was arguing for a price of the six-month average from March to September 2005. Clearly, the lower the price was, the more shares would have to be issued in the capital increase in 2005 needed to convert the loan to equity. And the more shares that were issued, the more the Agnellis' ownership would be diluted.

Fresco and Galateri, in turn, huddled with Gubitosi, who along with Braggiotti was the main negotiator for Fiat. Arpe was very sharp technically, but lacked the seniority necessary to sway the other bankers at the table. For this, Passera was crucial, often calling for breaks during which the finance men would go discuss the point of contention among themselves.

In the end, they came to a compromise that satisfied both sides. It was the average of the two: 15.50 euros and the average share price for six months below the conversion.

John Elkann, 26, looked on. He had decided to end his job with the corporate audit staff at General Electric early to come back and work at Fiat as the crisis in Turin worsened. His grandfather Gianni had flown to New York for cancer treatment earlier that month. John wanted to get up to speed as quickly as possible on the company's problems by working alongside Paolo Fresco, Gabriele Galateri, and Gianluigi Gabetti.

What he saw worried him. At the same time, he was convinced that he was doing the best thing by coming back to Italy. He needed to gain the knowledge that would enable him to protect the company's and his family's interests.

That weekend's discussion was not the sort any owner of any company enjoyed having, but for the time being, the transaction was beneficial to John and his family. After all, a debt conversion or capital increase would have diluted the family's ownership immediately. With the mandatory equity conversion in 2005, the company would gain time in the hope that its restructuring plan would work. For John, the three-year deadline for the conversion seemed a long way off. A lot could happen before then.

The logic of selling cash-cow businesses to prop up a core unit, Fiat Auto, that was bleeding cash was against the basic premises of business principles for running a publicly traded company. For a family-owned company like Fiat, though, the family was prepared—and even obliged, in a way—to stick it out.

The meeting resumed on Saturday, and again ran late into the night.

By Sunday, the bankers, Fiat executives, and their lawyers had a deal, a two-page framework agreement. It said that Fiat agreed to sell a 51 percent stake in Fidis to the banks, giving it 7 billion euros in liquidity, and that the banks could ask Fiat to sell other assets. They flew up to Turin for the signing.

"Fiat never went to the banks," said a person who took part in the meetings, with a sly smile. "It was the banks who came to Fiat."

All the same, the Agnellis had just backed a financing deal that potentially meant the banks would own more of Fiat, in 2005, than the family would.

■ ■ ■

On October 13, 2002, a Lancia Thesis sedan drove past the police guard outside Prime Minister Silvio Berlusconi's 147-room villa, which sits behind a green metal gate amid the suburban and industrial sprawl that has gobbled up the countryside outside Milan. Unlike Agnelli, who had inherited Villar Perosa from his grandfather, Berlusconi had purchased this villa in the 1970s along with its Tintoretto, its Tiepolo, and an entire collection of paintings, furniture, and books.[7] He had used it for business ever since, and continued to use it for government business after he entered politics.

Inside the car was Gabriele Galateri, who had been named Fiat CEO after Paolo Cantarella was asked to leave as part of Fiat's three billion euro bank loan in May. Berlusconi arrived late and in a German car, seriously irritating some members of the Fiat delegation. The two cars parked in the gravel parking area on the street side of the villa. Galateri, along with Chairman Paolo Fresco and Fiat Auto Chief Giancarlo Boschetti, were shown into a large dining room with a big table seating 20 people in the center. Berlusconi, with Treasury Minister Giulio Tremonti and Treasury Director General Domenico Siniscalco, sat down on one side, and the Fiat group on the other.

The tone was cordial, but this was not a social visit. Galateri and Fresco had come, at Berlusconi's invitation, to discuss Fiat's latest turn-around plan to lay off more than 8,000 workers and close a money-losing plant in Sicily. Fiat needed the government's support, since the labor ministry would have to declare a "state of crisis" in order for Fiat to tap a special state fund for layoffs. The fund is made up of contributions from Italian companies, and it pays 80 percent of a worker's full salary while laid off, typically for a 12-month period. Usually in these cases the government gets involved in a three-way collective bargaining round.

■ ■ ■

Less than 10 years had passed since Gianni Agnelli had played match-maker for Silvio Berlusconi and Giuliano Urbani, the professor who became the idea man for the media mogul's new political party. In that short time, though, Italy and Fiat had changed. Back then it had been Agnelli, king of Italy's business establishment, giving Berlusconi, a parvenu, a hand. Now the tables had turned.

Fiat was accustomed to getting its way with Italy's weak governments, which, for the company, was a double-edged sword. Fiat, back in the days when it accounted for 5 percent of the Italian economy, had always been able to count on the government to give it a hand. In 1986, the government had put Alfa Romeo up for sale in one of its first-ever privatizations. Fiat had elbowed aside Ford and grabbed the prize at the last minute. Import restrictions on Japanese cars had been extended until 1999. In 1997, when Fiat needed a boost, the government obliged by giving a one-off tax break to people who bought new cars. But the incentives had backfired for Fiat, which ended up losing market share to its competitors because it didn't have models people wanted to buy. Worse still, the incentives actually weakened demand in the coming years.

Fiat's previous chairman, Cesare Romiti, knew how to navigate the corridors of power in Rome: ride through like a bulldozer. It was Romiti who had thrown his weight around to get the Italian government to sell Alfa Romeo to Fiat. Fiat, historically, has had a much bigger share of its domestic auto market than its competitors in Europe and the United States have had in theirs. As recently as 1990, Fiat *on its own* had more than a 50 percent market share in Italy.[8] The company's focus in that sort of situation was to protect its home market at all costs, something Romiti excelled at doing. And it was worth the politicians' while as well, since Fiat was such a big employer.

Those days were over now. Fiat was still heavily dependent—too dependent—on its home market. About 39 percent of the 2.1 million cars sold in 2001 in Italy had been to Fiat—a much larger share than other automakers had of their home markets. But the globalization carried out by Fresco and Cantarella in the 1990s meant that more than half of Fiat's workers were now outside Italy. That meant a lot less weight to throw around at Berlusconi's villa at Arcore that day.

Plus, Berlusconi had been voted into office largely by professionals and small businesses. Indeed, some members of his coalition made no secret of their dislike of how Italian left-leaning governments of the past had given Fiat and other big companies a hand—like Prodi did in 1997 with incentives. While hardly an economic conservative like Margaret Thatcher, Berlusconi's government had clashed with unions in the past over labor flexibility.

The political balance had changed in another way, too. Gone were the weak and revolving-door governments of the past that had no choice but to curry favor with Fiat in order to win electoral support from left-wing trade unions. Berlusconi had been voted into office with a strong right-wing majority, and his government allies were reliable. That gave him a freer hand in dealing with Fiat than his predecessors had had.

As the meeting got under way, Fresco and Galateri walked Berlusconi through the company's latest financial results. They didn't look good. The third quarter results would probably come in significantly under the forecast.[9] Fiat's market share and sales would, clearly, be declining in 2002 compared to the year before. The three billion euro loan gave the company breathing room. But it still needed to cut costs, since its market share was shrinking.

Galateri had stepped in as chief executive at the request of Umberto Agnelli, with a mandate to take a close look at Fiat's finances and come up with an assessment of what it would take to fix the company. He and Umberto had done an excellent job at IFIL through the years, and he had the family's total trust. But he had made no attempt to hide the fact that he was not an industrial manager. And the problems he found at Fiat were overwhelming, though he didn't say that publicly.

The two executives repeated for Berlusconi what they had told Economy Minister Tremonti the week before. Discussion then moved to how to save a company that was a cornerstone of Italy's economy.

It was clear that the two sides of the table were far apart. Fresco's recommendation was to spin off Fiat Auto to protect the profitable parts of the company's other businesses. Fresco wanted to get rid of the money-losing car factories and make the rest of the company into a top-notch energy and capital goods business. He was open to government investment in the auto unit, once it had been spun off from the rest.

Tremonti, for his part, was already looking at ways that the government could directly put equity into Fiat. He was ready to consider a state investment in a spun-off Fiat Auto, and had a CEO in mind. The ministry would later sound out European Union Competition Commissioner Mario Monti about whether the state could invest in Fiat, and would receive a preliminary green light, as long as it was done in terms of market conditions and not as state aid.

Fresco's position was, more or less, "We don't need or want government help." After all, the Italian state's record as an investor was hardly stellar. And the Agnelli family did not want the government to be an investor in their company.

Tremonti suggested Fiat do the exact opposite of what Fresco was proposing. The government thought the family should sell off Fiat's good businesses and then pour taxpayer and Agnelli money into the struggling auto unit in order to protect jobs. In the government's view, Fiat was a strategic national asset and Fresco and the family were sort of in denial about what needed to be done.

Berlusconi's insistence that the Agnelli family pony up some cash to help save Fiat shed a harsh spotlight on one of the unpalatable truths of family capitalism, Italian style. Italian family owners had scarce access to capital in Italy's shallow financial markets, and were accustomed to controlling the boards of their companies while putting up very little cash through alliances brokered by Mediobanca. The Agnellis had been no exception.

Now, Berlusconi told Fresco and Galateri, the family had plenty of assets inside and outside Fiat it could spin off or shift around to create a new company in which the government could invest. Berlusconi also laid down a second condition for government help: Fiat's managers had to pare back the number of layoffs in their industrial plan, particularly in factories in Italy's poorer South.[10] And Fiat had to "stay Italian." This request was old-style political meddling, pure and simple.

Paolo Fresco was frustrated by the visit, and by the entire exercise. He had been meeting with Berlusconi off and on since spring, and he wasn't hearing anything new.

"He thinks that because he was successful in a couple of national businesses, he can run a business as different as a car company," he thought.

Fresco correctly sensed that there was very little that Berlusconi could actually do at this point. Most of the drastic measures that would eventually help bring Fiat's car business back to health were already spelled out in the agreement between Fiat and its creditor banks that Fresco, Galateri, Gubitosi, and others had negotiated in May.

Tremonti's idea of a government investment in Fiat never got off the ground. Fiat didn't want it, its creditor banks didn't want it, and the family didn't want it. The men sitting around Berlusconi's dining room table that day were all doing what came naturally to them. Fresco, Galateri, and Boschetti wanted to keep their company free of state intervention. Berlusconi, Tremonti, and Siniscalco wanted to avoid the economic turmoil that would come with a Fiat collapse. Like President Obama in 2009, their natural instinct was to offer government help to keep it afloat.

The three government officials were right about Fiat's management being in denial. Fresco and Galateri, each for his own reasons, had unrealistic views about their ability to influence the outcome at Fiat. Fiat's management was being ground up like hamburger meat by Fiat's industrial problems, and seemed to be under the illusion it was doing the right thing. And at its most basic level, the company was floundering because the founding family believed it was their responsibility to run the business but had been unable to do it properly.

■ ■ ■

Just as many of General Motors' top managers came from the Midwest, Fiat's top ranks were often recruited from the towns in the hills outside Turin, and often educated at the city's polytechnic university, the Politecnico di Torino. This provincialism was personified by Fiat CEO Paolo Cantarella, who was born in Vercelli, near Turin, and used to like to chat sometimes in Piedmontese dialect with some of Fiat's managers or staff. It was his way of showing where the company's roots were.

The affable, friendly Cantarella, who trained as an engineer, was a true car nut who reveled in details like gas caps and door handles. He loved nothing more than to whip out a pencil and sketch new models for Gianni Agnelli.[11] His career at the company marched in lockstep with that of Cesare Romiti, Fiat's tough-talking former CEO and, later, chairman, who ruled with an iron fist for 25 years.

When Romiti retired, Gianni Agnelli brought in Paolo Fresco as chairman, giving him a mandate to make Fiat into a global player just like Fresco had helped Jack Welch make General Electric into one of the world's most successful conglomerates. The company's auto unit needed an alliance partner, and Fresco was told by Gianni to find one. Fiat's other businesses needed to become either number one or number two in their areas. Last but not least, Fresco was given a free hand to make acquisitions that would diversify Fiat's revenue to offset the ups and downs of the auto unit.

Fresco drew up a list of his objectives at Fiat. The list was ambitious, amounting to a total cultural overhaul. At the top was "Change culture from local to global; from closed to open." "Hack away at internal bureaucracy" was also high on the list, as was "Move from vertical to horizontal."

But two things hindered Fresco's plans. One was the Fiat culture itself. In General Electric, if he called a meeting, five people would show up, they would make a decision, and they would then move on to the next thing. The Italian business culture was different. At Fiat, the meeting would drag on without people reaching a conclusion. Under Cantarella, the Savoy-bred virtues of duty and discipline atrophied into an overly rigid and bureaucratic culture in which managers shirked making decisions. One Fiat engineer who arrived in 2004 recalled that his technical staff used to send him meeting minutes for his approval.

"They were used to a culture of extremely centralized decision making," he recalled. "They came to me with screws to approve; they came to me with technical details."

What Fresco didn't bargain for was a lack of clear definition between his job and Cantarella's. Cantarella had been an excellent head of Fiat Auto, but as a CEO he was unable to delegate or take advice. He meddled in engineering and car design, dismissed test results showing that consumers didn't like the Multipla,[12] a funny-looking but innovative people mover, while Fiat ignored the SUV boom.

But even if he had clicked with Cantarella, the pair had inherited a company that hadn't had the right management for years. As a result, by the time Romiti left in 1998 and Paolo Fresco came in as chairman, Fiat Auto was strong in some markets like Brazil and Poland, but the collapse of emerging markets had derailed its "world car" strategy of making a small, specially designed car to tap growing global auto demand. Its product pipeline was thin and overly focused on compact cars. Fiat was not big enough to compete against the other automotive giants at a time when companies were merging.

Moreover, the competitive scenario in Europe had changed in the 1990s. The market had segmented into many different smaller clusters, with niche cars attracting buyers. Italy was forced to open its borders to Japanese imports, finally, in 1993 with the Common Market. Last but not least, South Korean producers started aiming at the segments where Fiat had previously ruled.[13]

Fiat was coddled by the government in the 1990s, with state investments for its plants in southern Italy, for research, and then for car sales incentives. Fiat's state-of-the-art factory in Melfi, Basilicata, was built with contributions from the state for research. This did the company no favors. The "Bribesville" corruption scandal that decimated Italy's political and business class in the 1990s touched Fiat as well when Cesare Romiti was placed under investigation, sapping morale and distracting management. Romiti was found guilty of false accounting in 1997, and the ruling was upheld by Italy's Supreme Court in 2000.[14]

"From a strategic point of view, Fiat's biggest weakness was a strong predominance of an engineering-based culture at the expense of the company's other functions and of a lack of awareness of what the market wanted," wrote Giuseppe Volpato, a professor at Venice's Ca' Foscari University specializing in industrial management.[15]

■ ■ ■

One afternoon in mid-December, Fiat CEO Gabriele Galateri received a call from Umberto asking if he could drop by his office at IFIL in downtown Turin. The pair had worked side by side in IFIL for over 15 years. Now for the past five months, Galateri, at the family's request, had moved over to the CEO office on the fourth floor of the Lingotto. Galateri rode down the long stretch of Via Nizza in his car, and parked in the courtyard at IFIL. As Galateri settled into the chair in Umberto's office, he noticed Umberto's manner was unusually cool.[16]

Galateri—a tall, urbane, and low-key *Torinese*—had told Umberto previously that he would not be able to make any progress at Fiat. He had just lived through hell week, ordering 8,100 layoffs and witnessing the collapse of talks between the unions and the government. He was suffering from the stress, and he had shared his concern with Umberto. He wanted to resign.

At their meeting that day, Umberto told Galateri he was free to resign as CEO. A replacement had been found. It would not be appropriate for

Galateri to take his old job back at IFIL. But something suitable would come up, certainly, elsewhere in the Agnelli family's vast holdings in the months to come.

Galateri left the office wondering what had happened to make Umberto make such a sudden decision.[17] He was relieved to be rid of the nightmare of Fiat's turnaround, with the political interference and media spotlight.[18] And the company needed an executive with a proven track record at turnarounds.

On Sunday, Galateri spoke with Umberto again and then decided to call Gianni to ask him for an explanation. Gianni said he knew nothing about Umberto's decision.

"I have to see my brother at five o'clock," he said. "Then you'll come over to dinner in the evening like you do every Sunday and we'll clear everything up."[19]

That evening, Galateri and his wife Evelina entered the gate of Villa Frescot, and the guard waved him by. He made the sharp turn of the drive and parked his car in the little courtyard between the peach-colored villa and its twin, called *il rustico* (the cottage).

The family butler told Galateri that Gianni was unwell, and would receive him in an upstairs study. Evelina waited downstairs, chatting with Marella in the living room. The two men sat in the leather-and-wood-paneled study, with its charmingly worn sofas giving it a comfortable feeling. Gianni cleared matters up, but not it the way Galateri had hoped. He told Galateri that it was better if their paths separated at that point. Fresco would be asked to leave, replaced by corporate fix-it man Enrico Bondi as CEO and Gianluigi Gabetti, one of the family's closest advisers, as chairman.

The matter had to be rushed because of the upcoming board meeting and the traditional year-end management meeting, Gianni said.

Galateri, at that point, decided not to stay for dinner. He and his wife Evelina left the house with the empty table set, ready and waiting, and Marella Agnelli close to tears.[20]

"Galateri had wanted to get out, but all the same, he took it badly," said a former executive. "Like a good lieutenant, he said 'I obey.'"

Galateri landed on his feet. Not more than four months later, he was named chairman of Mediobanca, the influential Milanese investment bank in which Fiat had a small stake.

Up until that moment, Fiat's problems in 2002 had been a matter of concern for investors, workers, and the government—anyone with a stake in the company's well-being. But when Umberto decided to accept Galateri's resignation, the chaos that ensued made Fiat a laughing-stock, a target for financial analysts, comedians, and left-wing newspaper editorialists to take potshots at. It ceased being a company that Italians were rooting for and became a dead man walking.

The family had not been able to find the right management to carry out the asset sales and restructuring plan that it had prom-ised the banks it would deliver as part of the three billion euro loan package.

Umberto Agnelli's plan to change Fiat's management had implications that neither Fresco nor Fiat's creditor banks liked the looks of. Umberto's choice, Enrico Bondi, had made a name for himself in business circles by carrying out open-heart surgery on ailing companies Ferruzzi, Telecom Italia, and, later, Parmalat after it went bust in 2003. It was precisely the fate of Ferruzzi that Fiat's banks had fought so hard to avoid! Now to have Bondi running Fiat was the last thing Profumo, Arpe, and Passera wanted.[21]

"The idea of Bondi's appointment as Fiat CEO was met with huge resistance by the banks," said one of Fiat's bankers.

To make matters worse, it appeared that Berlusconi was putting pressure on Umberto to make the changes, and Mediobanca was also advising him, promising the Agnelli family the bank would find a way to refinance Fiat that wouldn't involve the family putting up any cash. In other words, it was a return to the bad old days of Italian business—government meddling, with Mediobanca calling the shots.[22]

Fresco found out about Galateri's resignation—and Umberto's desire to replace Fresco with Gabetti—by reading it in the papers. He had planned to step down next year, anyway, when he turned 70. But there was no way he was going to be dismissed like a family butler.

The day of the announcement that Galateri had resigned, Fresco blew off steam in conversation with Rome daily *La Repubblica*'s editor Ezio Mauro, calling Umberto Agnelli "arrogant" and saying Berlusconi "must be crazy."

"From the very first day of the Fiat crisis, we were part of a circus that for me was totally incomprehensible . . . subject to a lynching at the hands of the media and politicians," he said. "Actually it was more of a political lynching, if I were to be sincere . . . each day another minister jumped all over us, talking one piece of crap after another."[23]

The interview was a sort of pop milestone in Italy's corporate culture as the first time the chairman of a blue-chip company used the words *piece of crap* in print.

When Umberto Agnelli called him that day, Fresco challenged Umberto's right to force him out.

"I have a responsibility to the board and to shareholders. I will convene the board and ask that this gets put to a vote. I will not resign," he told Umberto. "What authority do you have to ask me to resign?"

"I am chairman of IFI," Umberto reminded him, referring to the Agnelli family-owned holding company through which they controlled Fiat.

"The family controls Fiat with a very small equity stake." Fresco replied. "I need to take care of the remaining shareholders. If the board tells me to resign, I will."

Umberto's coup never took place, because it never even came to a vote at the board meeting midmonth. Fresco emerged with the backing of the board, and with the support of Umberto. But the changes were simply delayed. In just over a month's time, Fresco handed in his resignation the day after Gianni's funeral.

■ ■ ■

Fiat's option to sell Fiat Auto to General Motors was often invoked as the magic formula in 2002 to give Fiat a quick and painless exit from its problems. In reality the partnership was not working very well. This was obvious when Fiat and General Motors executives gathered in early 2003 at the super-luxurious Hotel George V Paris for one of their periodic steering committee meetings.

A Goteborg-based team of Italian, Swedish, American, and German engineers had been working on a premium vehicle platform, or large-car architecture, that could be shared among Fiat's Alfa Romeo, the GM-owned Saab, and GM's new Cadillac. The idea behind platform sharing is to use the same car floor plans across different models and brands, thus saving money and speeding up development times.

Automakers were all plagued by the same problem: it could cost more than a billion dollars to develop a car from scratch, and there was no way to tell if that money could ever be recouped. But if they could team up and share the costs of a car's underbelly, which often included parts that the customer didn't see, the manufacturers would save money. Fiat and GM had agreed to make a small car platform, called the SCCS, which was later used for the Opel Corsa and the Fiat Grande Punto. Work on the large car platform had been coming along well—up to that point.

At the meeting, GM chief Rick Wagoner, Fiat Auto's Giancarlo Boschetti, Fiat's head of business development Alfredo Altavilla, and GM's Bob Lutz gathered in one of the hotel's conference rooms to take stock of progress.

"You know what, you guys, I don't like this platform; it's gonna be useless for GM," said Bob Lutz, who was smoking one of his beloved cigars. "We're withdrawing from the project."

The Fiat people exchanged glances. Bob Lutz was a Detroit legend, a car guy's car guy, and when he spoke people tended to listen.

"Bob, we've been working on this project for two years to get economies of scale," Boschetti said. "What do you mean, you are walking away?"

"Yeah," said Lutz. "We want to do this on our own. I don't care how long it took. I just care about product. Talk to Rick."

And the case was closed.

As a result, Fiat ended up using the platform for its Alfa 156 model, but it was the only car that was developed off that platform. So GM funded its share of development and got no benefits. Fiat, for its part, shared just the engineering costs and was forced to give up any economies of scale that would have come from sharing the car built on this platform.

GM pulled the plug as part of a larger plan to cut costs at Saab, which was losing money. But Fiat was particularly vulnerable to its larger partner's decisions, and the difficulties in sharing platforms hurt Fiat in an area where it was already weak. Fiat planned to reduce the number of platforms it used to build its vehicles from 15 to nine, but was still far from achieving this goal.[24] A quick look at the numbers tells the story.

At the time of the meeting, Fiat was building two million units off of the 15 platforms, which works out to 136,000 cars for each platform. Of those 15 platforms, only three were shared with another automaker.

"And the reality is much worse in places," *Automotive News Europe* noted in 2003.[25] Many of the two million cars Fiat sold were four low-cost, low-margin models. Fiat's two highest-volume platforms at the time of its meeting with GM in Paris were the B platform for its small cars, accounting for a full one-quarter of its volume, plus the Palio world car platform, which accounted for another 15 percent of sales.[26]

Fiat's luxury cars, meanwhile, accounted for just a fraction of that volume. The Lancia Thesis and the Alfa Romeo 166 were made from different platforms, and accounted for just 4,227 and 8,175 vehicles, respectively.

Worse still, in terms of efficiency the C-frame platform Fiat developed for the Stilo was not planned to be used for its next medium-sized car at the end of the decade. Fiat planned to switch to a new GM-Fiat platform. Fiat's face-lift of the Stilo, slated for mid-2004, was probably the last time Fiat had planned to use that C-frame platform. The episode in Paris shed a harsh spotlight on the state of Fiat and GM's partnership and how it went wrong. Fiat's executives, at first, had been thrilled with the GM alliance.

"GM was perceived as a toy store of all technical and technological devices available in the marketplace," said a long-time Fiat executive. "So we thought we had been underinvesting for a number of years because of our crisis, if we partner with them we could go cherry-pick anything we need—which turned out to be one of the worst and most dangerous mistakes in the industry of all time."

The purchasing joint venture got off to a good start, because cost savings from the economies of scale were easy to deliver. Calling a supplier and saying that the company would double its orders if the supplier cut prices 5 percent was not difficult. But sharing technology or platforms turned out to be an obstacle course. By late 2002, it was clear to Fiat executives that GM was disorganized, didn't share information across geographical regions, and was divided into fiefdoms, each presided over by a jealous executive. There was no carryover of programs from one region to another.

That sort of attitude is "one of the reasons why GM went bankrupt," said a Fiat executive many years later with the benefit of hindsight.

But the basic problem was rooted in GM's attitude toward Fiat. The two partners' sizes, and their relative statuses on the industry totem pole, made for an unequal alliance.

"The GM people's attitude made it difficult," said another Fiat executive. "GM had 20 percent of Fiat Auto, and Fiat had a 6 percent stake in GM. Fiat was GM's largest single shareholder. Yet GM acted like Fiat was theirs from day one."

# Chapter 9

# Running on Empty

S ome time in the middle of 2002, Fiat Auto's head of advanced design, Roberto Giolito, gathered his team in what he called the "loft" at Mirafiori, an area located just behind the marble-floored executive offices at Fiat's grungy, gargantuan factory on the outskirts of Turin.

"Let's start with a blank sheet," he told the group, a handful of whom were young trainees he had recruited himself in trips to the top design schools across Europe and the United States. "We have to build the new Fiat 500. I want it to be extremely contemporary and modern. No retro styling allowed." The project was called the Trepiuno.

Giolito, a soft-spoken man with curly gray hair who is often seen in a black T-shirt, a black jacket, and black jeans, had gained acclaim or notoriety in the auto world—depending on your point of view—for having created the Fiat Multipla. With his trendy good looks, slightly vague air, and phrases like "we have to clothe the car," he looked like he would have been more at home having cocktails in the bar at Milan's design museum, the Triennale, and not in a makeshift office at Fiat's neglected flagship. Yet here he was, trying to explain his design philosophy to a group of people about to undertake the most ambitious project of his life: create a new Fiat 500.

Despite Giolito's often tortured constructions of speech, the idea he was trying to convey that day was as simple as the motto of his favorite designer, Achille Castiglioni: Design demands observation.[1] Castiglioni was brilliant at using examples from everyday life to make simple, stunning objects, like his Arco floor lamp, which was inspired by a street light. The 1962 stainless steel lamp has found its way into the Museum of Modern Art's permanent collection and is to this day still arching its way over couches and tables on its thin stalk in homes across Europe and America. Giolito's task that day was to get his group to understand that to make the new 500, they would have to look around them at what was going on in the streets and in people's minds *right now.*

His Multipla was a good example of what he meant. Launched in 1998, the Multipla was a daringly designed small minivan that people either loved or hated. From the outside, it looked simply weird. The car's front end had the crushed-up face of a pug dog. But once inside, the two rows of three seats each meant a lot of people could fit comfortably into its small space. The British *Top Gear* show named it the Ugliest Car of 1999; the same year the Museum of Modern Art included it in an exhibition entitled "Different Roads—Automobiles for the Next Century."

Both the Multipla and now the 500 were new versions of earlier hits from Fiat's past and its knack for making small, cleverly designed, economical vehicles. The 1998 Multipla reached back to an ungainly six-seater, the Fiat 600 Multipla, built starting in the mid-1950s. The cars were a sort of early precursor to the minivan. In Rome, they were a familiar sight ferrying around groups of nuns. The 1957 Fiat Nuova 500, in turn, was a postwar version of the company's Fascist-era 1936 Topolino, which had been Italy's first true people's car.

But when Roberto Giolito set about designing the 1998 Multipla, he started from scratch. Now he was determined that his team would do the same thing with the 500.

Fiat's troubles, in Giolito's view, looked worse from the outside than they did to him and his eager new recruits in the loft. *BusinessWeek* had featured Fiat on its cover in May, with the headline "Fiat: Running on Empty."[2] "Management is in turmoil. Cash is low. And there's no hot model in sight," the cover read. It was hard to argue with its assessment. Fiat went on to lose 4.3 billion euros in 2002, the largest loss in its history. Sales of its cars fell 9.4 percent. It was not exactly the ideal atmosphere to design a hot new car.

Giolito knew that Fiat's ability to make cars was as solid as ever, despite the flop of the Stilo. He just had to prove it. And now he had his chance. He had just been made head of Fiat Advanced Design, which was a newly formed design group and a big step forward for him. The idea was to create a unit that could work directly with the rest of the company. As head of Advanced Design, Giolito would now be working directly with the brand managers, with marketing, and with engineers. He wouldn't be just a pencil. He would be look-ing at strategic issues now, too, and at stuff like how car sharing will affect business trends in the future. To staff his new group, Giolito created a Milan-based program in which 25 young interns from design and communications would spend three months training at a studio in Italy's design capital. At the end of the three months, three would be picked to come to Turin and join the team.

Giolito was too busy to worry about the executives over at the Lingotto—their comings and goings with bankers, the revolving-door management, Gianni Agnelli's illness, and the rest.

His new group was fired up. How will we improve the aerody-namics? How will it be more than just a new covering for the same old small box? How will we make it comfortable?

Giolito had his team start with what he called "the communications side," rather than getting right to work on sketching. He instructed them to start by answering the question, "What should a modern 500 be?" and then proceed by taking away everything that was unnecessary.

To get the group looking outside the company for ideas, like he always did, he had master designer Alessandro Mendini compose a briefing and present it at Mirafiori. Mendini, whose work ranges from buildings to a corkscrew shaped like a woman for Alessi, arrived with a video presentation touching on 1960s design themes from the United States and Italy, ranging from art and architecture to design and graphics. The presentation was a touchstone for Giolito's team as they started sketching concepts for the Trepiuno.

His main challenge as they got started was to politely beat back all the requests he had from Fiat 500 aficionados inside and outside the company, who would make requests like "You absolutely have to keep the little vents on the back hood." Giolito just kept saying no, no, no. Plus, his designers were coming up with ideas that looked too much like the Nuova 500 car from 1957 designed by Giacosa, which had overtaken even the 600 in terms of popularity. Sometimes he had to kill their sketches.

The project's original name, the Trepiuno, referred to the idea of fitting three adults plus one more into the small car's interior without making them feel crammed. The exterior, though, was based on the 500's instantly recognizable half-of-a-pear shape.

■ ■ ■

A week before Christmas in 2003, some 600 people crammed into a courtyard at Corso Como 10 in Milan. From the outside, the pale yellow building doesn't look much different from the other traditional ones alongside it on a street running to the squat and ugly Garibaldi train station. Once you get past the plants that discretely block the view of the courtyard, however, an expensive boutique, an art gallery, and a chic café await. During Milan's fashion week—when buyers, press, and executives descend on the city to view runway shows of upcoming collections—Corso Como and the nearby Le Langhe restaurant become fashion central.

The crowd that evening was for a party, hosted by *Vogue*, to celebrate the launch of a zippered sweatshirt with a vintage Fiat logo emblazoned across the chest in huge letters.[3] The company had done little to distinguish itself in the time since Umberto and his new CEO, Giuseppe Morchio, had taken over. In midyear, it had unveiled its latest recovery plan that called for closing 12 of its 138 factories worldwide, raising almost two billion euros in cash, and investing in new car models.[4] Fiat's image was at low ebb. It was hardly the time to throw a party for a young, hip crowd of television celebrities, fashionistas, models, and heirs and heiresses to Italy's industrial fortunes,[5] and even less likely that they would turn up. But turn up they did.

Lapo Elkann, Gianni's red-haired, blue-eyed 26-year-old grandson, was the driving force in the events that led up to that evening. The idea of attempting to put the words *Fiat* and *hip* in the same sentence would not have occurred to many people that year, but Lapo had been working on this project for months. He left his high-profile job in New York City as Henry Kissinger's personal assistant to come back to Italy in 2002 to spend time with his grandfather during Gianni's illness, and to work at Fiat at a time when the company's future was shaky.

When Lapo got to Fiat in mid-2002, conditions were "difficult, complicated, harsh, and hard," he recalled later. Lapo was working in the marketing department, but the auto company had few cars to market. His goal was to maximize his results on a shoestring budget. His main challenge was to be creative while being fearless. And his first task at hand was to bring back a sense of pride to the people inside the company, starting with the workers on the factory floor.

Lapo decorated his office in Mirafiori with photographs of Winston Churchill, Mao, and New York City. What he found at Fiat was a company full of people who were deeply fearful about the future, and who passionately wanted to see the company pull through. He found a design team steeped in heritage, and a brand that could tap into deep wellsprings of pride, affection, and innovation. All auto companies are populated by employees who are car nuts and wild about the company they work for. Fiat had all that and was a national icon and a municipal institution to boot.

The best way to counteract the fear, Lapo wagered, was with energy of the sort that comes from having a project, a plan. He had given up a life in New York where he could have made a future far away from Fiat and the family name. Now, he threw himself into his task as if he were married to the company itself. When politicians attacked Fiat or analysts slammed the company's management, the anger he felt galvanized him to do more. And the experience of being in the trenches only made what he was trying to do more of a challenge.

The idea to bring some freshness back to the brand seemed as natural to him as picking up the logo out of Fiat's archives. In the months leading up to the launch party, Lapo tested the sweatshirt himself, wearing it around town to see people's reactions. Some people liked it, but some didn't.

He went to longtime friend Franca Sozzani, the editor of Italian *Vogue*, with his idea for a launch party. Together they came up with the idea to involve her sister Carla, who owned Corso Como 10.

Lapo had already inherited his grandfather Gianni's place on the celebrity pages because of his penchant for sharp-looking clothes and even sharper-looking women. He also had Gianni's gift for making everyone, from a head of state to a waiter, feel at ease. That night he was a ball of energy, welcoming guests with a nonstop stream of chatter. He spent the evening flitting to and from the side of his girlfriend, Martina Stella, a former Miss Italia who later had a role in the movie *Ocean's Twelve*. But the evening, for him, was all about work.

John Elkann was among those in the crowd, and could see that his brother's efforts were paying off. The two were close, and had both come back to work at Fiat in 2002—John because he had been groomed to do so eventually, and Lapo out of affection for their grandfather—but their personalities could not have been more different. John seemed to turn each word over in his mind before he said it, while words tumbled out of Lapo's mouth. John preferred to avoid the limelight, while Lapo seemed to be drawn to it. John inherited Gianni's serious, dutiful side, while Lapo inherited Gianni's style and wit.

The event was a success. Photos started circulating of Lapo, John, and John's girlfriend Lavinia Borromeo wearing the sweatshirts. All three were young and good-looking, and wore their sweatshirts with a certain attitude. The limited-edition sweatshirts sold like hotcakes at 215 euros apiece. This was no free giveaway from a car dealer. It was an instant fashion item. Lapo had scored a home run with a bold stroke. He had turned himself into a brand testimonial for Fiat, at a time when the company's image was at an all-time low. It was a gutsy move, and he pulled it off.

Maybe there was some of *il Senatore*'s street-fighting spirit left in the Agnelli clan yet.

■ ■ ■

On the second day of the Geneva Auto Show in March 2004 as designer Roberto Giolito walked through the big glass doors of the ugly, modern convention center on his way to the Fiat stand, he reflexively grabbed a copy of the show's daily tabloid paper. Splashed across the front page was a jaunty photo of the Trepiuno, zipping off the page at an angle.

"Bull's-eye!" he thought, amazed.

He had known the car was good, but nothing had prepared him for the buzz it created at the show. Granted, the Fiat stand stood out this year. One of his Advanced Design interns had come up with the idea to scatter iconic Italian furniture around the stand, emphasizing the link between the Trepiuno and the best of Italy's design tradition. And the decision to show a car in white was eye-catching, he had to admit. In an exhibition hall full of row upon row of SUVs and sleek silver sedans, the cute little white car stood out in the crowd.

"If this is the wave of the future, we can't wait," gushed the *Detroit News* about Fiat's new "Beanie Baby–like" car in its postshow wrap-up review.[6]

The Fiat stand was packed with a mix of press as Giolito got there, already camped out waiting for Umberto Agnelli, now Fiat chairman, and CEO Giuseppe Morchio, who had eventually replaced Cantarella after his ouster, to arrive later that morning. Umberto had brought Morchio on board in February 2003, replacing co-CEOs Fresco and Alessandro Barberis and making him Fiat's fourth CEO in nine months. Lapo Elkann, who was deeply committed to the Trepiuno because it dovetailed with his branding vision, was thrilled with the media reaction. He had spent hours discussing marketing ideas with Giolito and had pushed hard for the car inside the company. But he was upset that the concept still had no green light from Morchio.

When Morchio and Umberto arrived, they went from car to car, stopping to be photographed by the swarms of photographers as journalists jostled to ask questions.

"I am pleased with the work carried out by management, but I will be even more pleased when the company resumes paying a dividend," said Umberto. "My brother Gianni would be happy to see this progress and with the hope of seeing Fiat back on its feet and capable of producing profits in a reasonable time span."[7]

When it came time to show off the Trepiuno in Geneva, Morchio could feel reasonably confident: the company had lost less money in the first two months of 2004 than it had the year before, his early figures were showing. And Fiat's market share had grown in February, he told journalists. He was right about the profit figures, because when results were released in May, Fiat's first quarter loss had narrowed to just 212 million euros, from a loss of nearly 700 million euros for the first quarter in 2003.

And in terms of cars, Fiat had gotten its mojo back. The restyled Fiat Punto and Fiat's Nuova Panda had been Italy's top sellers for months. The Lancia Ypsilon, presented at Geneva in 2003, won the European Automotive Design Award. The Panda was named the Car of the Year in 2004 by trade journalists for combining small car size with the roominess of a much larger model, confirming "the reputation of the Italian manufacturer to make clever, practical small cars and offer them at very competitive prices."[8] Morchio was optimistic enough at Geneva to confirm his target of breaking even for the entire year.

Morchio was beaming as journalists clustered around him with questions. His eyes sparkled with energy behind his small round glasses. He was very pleased with the Trepiuno, he told them. But he stopped short from saying that the Fiat 500 concept would get the green light, despite all the hullaballoo surrounding it. "We have a minicar slated for 2008," he said. "We have the resources to invest, but we have to make sure we have an adequate return on capital."

The answer was typical of Morchio, an engineer by training. He was a strong believer in research and development, but he was also a keen numbers cruncher. At Fiat, he walked around with a 600-page black leather folder containing the company's financial projections.[9]

Morchio, at age 56, had a track record at tire and cable maker Pirelli that was nothing less than stellar. He had joined Pirelli in 1980, six years after earning a degree in mechanical engineering from Genoa Polytechnic. After a stint in the tires division, he joined the cables unit in 1993 and built it up to become one of the world's leaders. A sale of Pirelli's photonics unit at the top of the dot-com bubble in 2000 had left Morchio with some $150 million in stock options,[10] a payday so big that it was the talk of the Milan financial world for literally weeks. It also left Morchio wanting the top job at Pirelli, which was not available. It belonged to Marco Tronchetti Provera, Pirelli's chief shareholder, who asked Morchio to leave at the end of 2000.

One of his first moves after taking over Fiat's CEO office at the Lingotto was to sell off Fiat's airline engine division, Fiat Avio; its insurance unit, Toro; and 51 percent of Fidis, its financing arm, under the terms of the three billion euro loan in 2002. By June 2003, he

Gianni Agnelli, head of Fiat, stands beside a Fiat Tipo on the lawn of the family's estate in Villar Perosa near Turin in 1988. Agnelli's fashion quirks, like his unbuttoned shirt collar in this photo, were legendary.
*Photo credit:* © Vittoriano Rastelli/Corbis

Fiat Chairman John Elkann (*left*) and CEO Sergio Marchionne (*right*) during the presentation of the new Lancia Ypsilon at Turin's Automobile Museum on May 25, 2011—one day after Chrysler repaid its loans to the U.S. and Canadian governments. John is wearing a "PAID" button.
*Photo credit:* © Di Marco/epa/Corbis

Before becoming one of Fiat's founding partners, Giovanni Agnelli served as an officer in the Italian cavalry starting in 1889. The military experience stayed with him for the rest of his life, and was repeated by his son and grandson.
*Photo credit:* Centro Storico Fiat

Marella and Gianni Agnelli arriving at Truman Capote's Black and White Ball in the Grand Ballroom at the Plaza Hotel in New York (1966). They were one of the few couples, along with the Duke and Duchess of Windsor, to both appear on the International Best Dressed list.
*Photo credit:* © Condé Nast Archive/Corbis

Gianni Agnelli (*right*) and his cousin Giovanni Nasi (*left*) playing at the
Agnelli residence. Gianni had a privileged upbringing, but had lost both
parents by the age of 24.
*Photo credit:* Centro Storico Fiat

Umberto Agnelli (*right*) and his son Giovanni Alberto (*left*), who died of
cancer in 1997 while he was being groomed for a leadership role in Fiat.
His sudden death left a gap in the Agnelli family's dynastic succession.
*Photo credit:* Centro Storico Fiat

U.S. First Lady Jacqueline Kennedy (*center*) on a daylong cruise aboard a yacht owned by the Agnelli family in 1962. The Agnellis are often compared to the Kennedys, since both are powerful, glamorous dynasties steeped in tragedy. The two families socialized for years, and are still in contact.
*Photo credit:* © Bettmann/Corbis

Gianluigi Gabetti (*standing*) and Gianni Agnelli (*seated*) share a joke during a pause at IFI. Gabetti was Agnelli's closest financial adviser for over 30 years.
*Photo credit:* Centro Storico Fiat

Sergio Marchionne makes his first speech at Chrysler on June 10, 2009, as employees wonder what the company's latest owner has in store.
*Photo credit:* Chrysler Group LLC

Roberto Giolito, who in 2007 led the team that redesigned the Fiat 500, the iconic car that symbolized both Italy's postwar recovery and Fiat's resurgence.
*Photo credit:* Centro Storico Fiat

Sergio Marchionne (*right*) and General Holiefield (*left*), vice president of the United Auto Workers. As part of the Chrysler deal, the UAW accepted a two-tier wage system whereby new hourly workers would get paid less than older ones in a move seen as critical for the industry's recovery.
*Photo credit:* Chrysler Group LLC

Fiat CEO Sergio Marchionne (*left*) and Ferrari Chairman Luca Cordero di Montezemolo (*right*) arrive at an annual meeting of market regulator Consob at the Milan Stock Exchange (July 3, 2006). This is one of the last times Marchionne was photographed in a suit and tie.
*Photo credit:* © Daniele La Monaca/X01660/Reuters/Corbis

John Elkann and Princess Lavinia Borromeo leave the Borromeo family chapel on their wedding day on September 4, 2004, on the Isola Madre at Lake Maggiore. It was Italy's equivalent of a royal wedding, with 700 guests.
*Photo credit:* Photo courtesy of the Agnelli family archive

Ford Motor Company Chairman and CEO Alan Mulally (*left*), Chrysler Chairman and CEO Robert Nardelli (*center*), and General Motors Chairman and CEO G. Richard Wagoner (*right*) make their case for federal assistance at a Senate hearing on November 18, 2008.
*Photo credit:* © Matthew Cavanaugh/epa/Corbis

John Elkann makes his first address at the Fiat Group's general meeting as chairman, in March 2011. John became Fiat vice chairman in 2004, helping to manage Fiat's turnaround with Sergio Marchionne. In 2008, John played an active role in Fiat's search for a partner, which led it to the alliance with Chrysler in 2009. Named chairman in 2009, John oversaw the splitting of Fiat into two companies.
*Photo credit:* © Di Marco/epa/Corbis

The Agnelli family—Gianni, Marella, Edoardo, Margherita, and Margherita's children and a Caracciolo cousin—at Villar Perosa in 1986. Neither Margherita nor Edoardo showed interest in running the family business.
*Photo credit:* Centro Storico Fiat

had unveiled a four-year turnaround plan—Fiat's second in just six months—aimed at breaking even in 2004 and returning to net profit in 2005. The plan called for Fiat to close 12 plants out of its 138 world-wide and to invest 17 billion euros in new models and research spending between 2003 and 2006. It aimed to slash 12,300 jobs out of a worldwide total of 170,000. And it planned to raise nine billion euros in asset sales and by selling new shares to help finance it all.[11] By the end of 2003, Fiat's loss had narrowed to 1.9 billion euros for the year (which Fiat called "a year of transition"), compared to 4.3 billion euros for the year before.

But Morchio was not popular in Fiat. His abrasive and critical manner grated on Fiat's longtime management. Perhaps he may have been perceived by some inside the company as the banks' man placed by Fiat's creditors in the corner office to sell off Fiat's crown jewels. In any case, at the Geneva car show he still thought he was holding a good hand of cards.

■ ■ ■

A month after the Geneva Auto Show, Umberto Agnelli criticized the company's past management—and, indirectly, his brother Gianni's stewardship—in an unusually frank speech in April 2004 at the Lingotto.

"Our core business—the automobile—has suffered from inadequate attention and has burned through a vast amount of resources," he said, speaking to a business group at the Lingotto Fiere.[12] "In the meantime, to strengthen other sectors of its activity, the Group undertook a series of high-priced acquisitions that because of the dynamic economy offered expectations of high growth."

Umberto had always been painted as the brother who wanted to sell Fiat Auto. He had pointed out time and time again what he saw were its problems. He knew better than anyone how much money the family had lost year after year at Fiat Auto. But it was also true that he loved the car business deeply. Now, he wanted to brush aside any lingering doubt that Fiat wanted to keep its car business. At Geneva, Fiat's commitment to making new cars had come through loud and clear.

"The Group makes cars, industrial vehicles, tractors, and construction equipment," he continued. "This is our past, and this will be our future, and we are focusing every last bit of our energy on it."

Freed of the towering figure of Gianni Agnelli, the charismatic guardian of the company's past, Umberto concentrated all his energy on the company's future. Everything the Agnelli family had—the money, the social prestige, the political clout, Juventus, Ferrari—they owed to Fiat, and Umberto felt it was his duty to make sure that the company survived. He simply would not contemplate anything less. He focused on achieving his goal step by step, methodically, one day at a time, as he always had. He stuck to his routine, arriving in the office early and going home to eat dinner with his family every night.

Under Umberto's guidance, the family also changed the way it picked its next manager. When he took over as chairman in early 2003, leading his list was a search for a CEO, and—for the first time—the candidate's track record would be more important than his credentials as an Agnelli family loyalist, a Mediobanca pick, or a longtime Fiat man.

But Fiat was still steeped in the same House of Savoy era militaristic culture that its founder Giovanni Agnelli, the former cavalry officer, had first instilled more than 100 years ago. While Fiat's respect for its rigidly hierarchical traditions and its management's sense of duty to the company had undeniably gotten it rebuilt after World War II and helped it through the dark years of terrorism, its leadership had now grown too unaccustomed to taking individual responsibility.

A former manager who joined Fiat in 1977 recalls that it was still populated with *cavalieri*, or "knights," a Valletta-era institution honoring Fiat workers who started their careers on the shop floor.

"These were people with no doctorate or even maybe no university degree," the ex-manager recalled. "But they were people who built up and belonged to the company. They were absolutely loyal to the company and to the family. This allowed Fiat to face a lot of hardship and come out with success."

By the mid-1990s, the *cavalieri* and others like them who had originally been a strength of the company started to turn into a weakness as it expanded into global markets. The manager the company sent to head up its human resources (HR) office in India did not speak English.[13]

When he gave his speech in April 2004, Umberto already knew he would not be around to see Fiat's renaissance. In February, at the age of 69, he had discovered he had cancer.

Umberto's illness had been apparent to a coworker in mid-January, when the Fiat chairman visited Italy's foreign ministry in Rome to attend a roundtable conference on Japan.

"The ministry has a huge long staircase leading up to it, and Umberto had to stop two or three times to catch his breath," the person recalled. "He tried to cover it up by saying 'Just a minute, I'm having a problem with my knee.' But that's when I first realized he had a serious health problem."

Umberto had bravely accepted his brother's request to try to save the family car business. He did his duty. He faced death stoically, and was lucid up until the very end. He was aware that fate had granted him wealth and privilege with one hand, and with the other had taken away his beloved son Giovanni Alberto at an early age and was now, again, dealing his remaining family another very harsh blow.

He died on May 28, 2004, only 16 months after his brother Gianni. Having two family leaders die in such a short time was a huge trauma for the Agnellis and, surprisingly, the family had no succession plan in place to fill Umberto's shoes.

Umberto's passing was a trauma for Fiat's workers as well, but for a different reason. Umberto's death, in a sense, was more tragic than Gianni's, because it made the lack of family leadership glaringly evident at a time when the company was fighting for its life. It created yet another emergency just when the company needed it the least.

"Gianni Agnelli was a legend, but Umberto Agnelli could have been an additional safeguard for us," said a woman who worked on the Lancia Thesis line as she left Mirafiori after the news of Umberto's death was announced. "Now we just have to hope."[14]

Unlike the media glare that accompanied Gianni's funeral, which had been televised live on television, the family decided Umberto's ceremony was to be a private event.[15] The mayor of Turin declared a day of mourning, and flags flew at half-mast.[16] Workers at Fiat's factories observed a minute of silence. The family-owned Turin newspaper La Stampa published a special edition.

The day after Umberto died, thousands of Italians filed past his casket to pay their respects just as they had done for Gianni just over a year ago. Umberto's casket, covered with white peonies, lay in a makeshift chapel in the Fiat history museum, which is housed in its first factory. A military guard of honor stood outside the museum. Another guard of honor stood inside. The casket was flanked by 15 flower wreaths and colorful banners from the cities of Turin and Sestriere, the Turin province, the Region of Piedmont, Fiat's management, and the Juventus soccer team.[17]

Many of the workers who filed by the coffin expressed worry about the future of the company.

"This man wasn't as visible as his brother Gianni, but is one who worked and gave a lot to Fiat, to Turin, and to Italy," said Joaquino Contracchio, a retired Fiat worker. "When his brother Gianni died we knew there was still Umberto to take over. I don't know if the younger members of the family can replace them."[18]

Fiat CEO Giuseppe Morchio had been the first to arrive to pay his respects to Umberto. He stayed by the coffin all day, shaking hands with everyone from local people to visiting politicians from Rome.[19] People later remarked that Morchio's behavior was a bit strange—that he was acting like a family member. No one really knew what to make of it.

Umberto's widow Allegra arrived next, with their two children, Andrea and Anna. John and Lapo Elkann followed. Lapo was accompanied by Gianluigi Gabetti.[20] The rest of the family, along with ex–Fiat CEO Paolo Cantarella and former Foreign Minister Renato Ruggiero, were clustered around the casket for most of the morning. When the players from the Agnelli-owned soccer team Juventus arrived, Allegra Agnelli could not hold back the tears.[21] The team stood for 10 minutes in silence. Last to arrive was Prime Minister Silvio Berlusconi, who talked to Allegra and Morchio for nearly half an hour.

"Our wish is that his work can continue and that Fiat can return to being a leader," Berlusconi said to Umberto's widow.

■ ■ ■

The week before Umberto died, with an emergency looming, IFIL Chairman Gianluigi Gabetti and John Elkann agreed that John should go to Geneva, Switzerland, on a mission: to sound out Sergio Marchionne, the Italian-Canadian chief of SGS, a quality inspection company that was the Agnelli family's largest investment after Fiat. Marchionne was on Fiat's board, and Gabetti had his eye on him as a possible candidate to replace Morchio should the overreaching manager suddenly decide to walk.

John and Sergio were acquainted from serving on Fiat's board, but didn't really know each other. Umberto had spotted Marchionne's managerial talent while he was at SGS, and had him named to the carmaker's board in 2003. Although he was a well-known figure in Swiss business circles for his blunt style and impressive results at aluminum maker Alusuisse, Marchionne was unknown in Italy and an auto industry outsider. The Agnelli family had him on their radar, but he was not a family associate born and bred in Turin, like a Galateri or a Cantarella. As a candidate to run Fiat, he was the proverbial long shot.

The unlikely pair settled in at a table at Windows, a gourmet restaurant in Geneva's sumptuous Hotel d'Angleterre with stunning views out over Geneva's lake and beyond to Mont Blanc, the highest mountain in the Alps. The two men couldn't have been more different. John, tall, thin, always looks impeccably dressed and is a taciturn person whose careful choice of words gives the impression that he is shy. Sergio, perennially rumpled, has an offbeat charisma and a knack for coining odd expressions ("a zoo-ish clan"). John, who didn't normally smoke, was smoking that evening. At the end of the dinner, over grappa, John brought up the topic of what to do about filling Umberto's place when the time came. John asked Sergio what he thought.

"You've gotta get ready to be chairman," Sergio told John, outlining a scenario whereby John could be backed up by a vice chairman who could help him navigate the role as he found his footing. Gabetti would be perfect. "You need someone who can legitimize you in that role. You're still young."

John's head bobbed in agreement. The two batted around a possible Elkann chairmanship for a bit, and then John put his cards on the table. There was a problem, he said. Morchio wanted to become chairman and as well as CEO. John believed that Morchio was trying to take advantage of the family's weakness, and John was determined not to let him.

Then John dropped the bomb. "Can you help me by becoming CEO of Fiat?" John asked Sergio. The normally hypertalkative Marchionne was stunned speechless.

When he recovered his composure, Marchionne's first reaction was to try to talk the young Fiat heir out of the idea. Marchionne knew from being on Fiat's board, and from taking a long, hard look at its financials as a member of its audit committee, that Fiat was in deep trouble despite Umberto and Morchio's efforts. Morchio's targets weren't stacking up in terms of Fiat's actual operations, as far as Marchionne could tell. More importantly, Marchionne knew that a new CEO—and more management churn—was the last thing that Fiat needed.

"You need to make this thing with Morchio work," Sergio told John. "There's a limit to the number of earthquakes a house can take."

John's serious face grew even more grim. "This lack of a game plan is making the situation become unmanageable," he admitted.

Marchionne offered to act as an intermediary between Morchio and the family, but John brushed him off, saying, "That's being handled." The dinner was over, and one last grappa was downed. The pair agreed that in the worst-case scenario, Marchionne would be available to take over. Marchionne, at that point, was a second choice. Sergio asked for some time to think it through.

A few days later, Marchionne was watching the BBC newscast when a flash headline crossed the screen: Umberto Agnelli had died. His time for thinking it through was up.

He spent the next few days on the phone with John, who kept him updated on events back in Turin. Becoming the chief executive of Fiat would be taking on a huge risk; Marchionne knew that Fiat was bleeding cash, and there was nothing he saw in the company in terms of raw material that made him optimistic that it could be turned around.

Risk was something Marchionne knew well. He had first learned about it playing poker with his father back in Canada. It gave him an adrenaline rush. The most important thing about risk, though, was the calculation. The rush itself could be distracting or destructive. Much more interesting was weighing out all the aspects, and trying to stay calm. The cards. The moves. The consequences. Work it all out ahead of time, and then see if you were right or wrong. And in the business world, it was more or less the same thing, he had learned. Only this time it was impossible to stay detached from the risk and its consequences.

"It was the most emotional decision in my life," he said later. "Fiat is an institution. If you are born Italian, you don't say no to the institution."

■ ■ ■

As Gianluigi Gabetti stood outside the church at Villar Perosa waiting for the funeral to begin, chatting with Franzo Grande Stevens, the family lawyer, they were approached by one of Morchio's closest associates with a message for the white-haired lawyer.

"*Dottor* Morchio asks that *Avvocato* Grande Stevens, as secretary of the Fiat board, kindly call a board meeting for tomorrow at 3 P.M.," the person told the stunned pair.

"What the hell do you want to have a board meeting for?" Gabetti muttered to himself. He frowned and entered the church, the gears in his mind whirring.

Gabetti could guess why Morchio was in a hurry to call the board meeting. The annual meeting of the Bank of Italy, one of Italy's most time-hallowed public rituals, was the next day. The governor of Italy's central bank, one of the country's most revered institutions, had been giving this speech since the days after World War II. It was a solemn occasion, like the Vatican Mass on Christmas day. Gabetti suspected that Morchio wanted to call the board meeting so that he could propose naming himself chairman, taking advantage of the family's disarray. The chairmanship, until Paolo Fresco stepped down just over a year ago, had almost always been held by a family member. If Fiat didn't send a chairman to the Bank of Italy event, it would look terrible for the company. Gabetti knew in his gut that Morchio was right about that part. Where he disagreed was in Morchio's idea of combining the two positions. It would simply give Morchio too much power.

Morchio, for his part, was aware that the family had not been able to identify one of its own members to become chairman. He had told Umberto at one point that he was ready to buy shares in IFI, IFIL's parent company, in order to show his support for the company.[22] And with Gabetti, he had floated a trial balloon about a possible candidacy for chairman.

Gabetti had promised Umberto Agnelli he would be his eyes and ears. "Stay alert," Umberto had asked Gabetti when he told him he had cancer, "and watch over Fiat." The man who had spent his entire adult life helping the Agnelli family out of tight spots was not about to fall asleep on the job—and on the day of Umberto's funeral no less.

The Agnellis, unlike other automotive dynasties such as the Ford family, had a long history of highly civilized management transitions, with the family firmly in the driver's seat when it came to picking and dismissing its managers. But the family right now was leaderless. Umberto had called him out of retirement in Switzerland precisely for a moment like this, Gabetti realized. By virtue of his status as an honorary family member, he would simply have to pick up the fallen scepter before someone else did. And use it. Fast.

The white-haired octogenarian stood outside the door to the chapel as the family filed out and shared with John the news about Morchio wanting to call a board meeting and the executive's possible reasons for it.

The danger, Gabetti said to John, was that "if Morchio becomes the sole leader, and doesn't want to tell us something, we will never know." John and Gabetti had been planning what to do if something like this were to happen. John had traveled to Geneva to sound out Sergio Marchionne about becoming CEO, and Gabetti had been dealing with Morchio and the family.

"Please don't go away—we have to discuss something very important about the future of Fiat," the pair said to each family member on their way out, asking them to gather at IFIL's offices in downtown Turin the next day, Sunday, at 10 A.M.

On Sunday, the family settled into the IFIL boardroom. The company's offices had a gray, gloomy painting of a greyhound sprinting across several panels on a wall. As the dog traveled from top to bottom of the painting, it decomposed into bits and pieces. The artwork had been a favorite of Gianni's. The dog could stand for a company, which needed to stay alert or perish. Or it could represent the perils of stock market speculation. And on that day, it brought to mind the possible fate of the Agnelli family itself. As the family settled in, Gabetti, who was chairing the meeting, told them that Morchio had asked to call a board meeting later that day, and about the CEO's desire to add the duties of chairman—a role traditionally reserved for a family member or a handpicked executive.

"This is the situation we're facing," he told the 20 or so family members gathered in IFIL's boardroom. "Fiat governance has always had a chairman and a chief executive. The role of chairman is to represent the main shareholder, and the CEO is the one who handles operations of the company." It's not a good idea to have one person be both the chairman and the chief executive, he explained. It simply gives that person too much power.

"So given the situation, we would propose nominating Luca di Montezemolo as chairman," Gabetti concluded.

Next to Gabetti and Gabriele Galateri, Montezemolo was one of the group managers who were closest to the family. He had first joined Ferrari in 1973, and had been socializing with Susanna's son Cristiano since they were both young men. A respected business leader, charismatic speaker, and possessor of dress sense that rivaled Gianni Agnelli's own, Montezemolo, 57, had just been named chairman of Italy's Confindustria, the national business lobby. He was a perfect choice, the family had no doubt.

John then took the floor. As Fiat's main shareholder, the decision was his to make. He had no question in his mind: the answer to the question "Do you want Morchio as Fiat chairman?" was a resounding "No." Morchio was trying to take advantage of the family in a moment of weakness, and there was simply no reason the family should roll over and let him do that, John thought.

The former Pirelli chief had seriously misjudged the Agnelli family's toughness, as well as the loyalty of its longtime managers like Gabetti and Montezemolo. John's "no" was a watershed. His period of training, which started with his appointment to Fiat's board in 1997, was now about to come to an end. Being a shareholder meant deciding who would run the group. It was time for him to make an important decision, and he made it.

"The idea of naming Morchio as chairman is unacceptable to me," he told the group. The family listened. Susanna, in her role as family elder, then spoke for the group.

"Thank you," she said. "We want Gabetti to become head of the family's limited partnership, replacing Umberto. And we would like to nominate Luca Cordero di Montezemolo as chairman. Please give Morchio our full appreciation."

Luca di Montezemolo was already on the Fiat board, named by Umberto along with Sergio Marchionne. Someone suggested they call him on speakerphone then and there, to ask him to serve as chairman. The Ferrari executive was driving when the call came through, and pulled over to take the call.

"If the family wants me to do this, I will," he said.

At that point, talk moved to the topic of appointing a vice chairman. Andrea Agnelli, Umberto's son, suggested that John was the right person for that role. John, according to tradition, would one day be chairman. The idea of having him earn his chops working with Montezemolo seemed like a good idea to Andrea.

John became vice chairman of Fiat, of IFIL, and of the family limited partnership, Gianni Agnelli & C.

The family meeting wasn't over yet. "What if Morchio doesn't accept this?" Susanna asked.

"John and I have someone in mind who can step in as CEO should Morchio refuse to stay on," Gabetti said. "At present, though, we can't tell you who it is. We have promised that person confidentiality until the appointment, if it happens, is official."

Gabetti knew he and John were asking the family to simply trust them on this. It was asking a lot. But he had served the Agnelli family loyally since 1971, and they had no reason not to trust him.

All his life, Gabetti had done his best to do his duty to the family. What would Gianni or Umberto say if they were here now, and an outsider wanted to grab control of the company that they loved? That he loved? The idea was unthinkable.[23] He had to stay on the inside and in control.

The meeting broke up. Gabetti and John had just a few minutes to make the trip across town to the Lingotto, where the board was waiting as Morchio had requested. They would have the thankless task of informing Morchio that the family had picked a chairman, and that the person was not Morchio. The Lingotto was deserted on a Sunday. The pair parked their cars in the underground parking lot and took the elevator to the fourth floor. Gabetti and Morchio met in an empty office near the Sala Agnelli, the large room used for board meetings. Gabetti told Morchio that the family had given him the approval to appoint Montezemolo as chairman at the board meeting due to start right about now. In fact, the board members were all waiting down the hall.

"*Dottor* Gabetti, I intend to suggest to the board that I stand as chairman, in the absence of another candidate, should an external— and by that I mean a nonfamily member—be considered for the role," Morchio told Gabetti. "There is a strong argument for joining the two roles, since it would give maximum momentum to the group's recovery efforts."

After three years, he would step down in favor of John Elkann, Morchio told him.

Gabetti informed him that the family had already decided on Montezemolo as chairman. Gabetti asked Morchio to stay on as CEO.

"I am sure you will accept," Gabetti said.

Morchio realized that without the support of Umberto Agnelli, who had hired him, he had no one backing him and might as well resign. He stood up.

"I would rather go," he said abruptly to Gabetti, and walked out of the room. "I am not feeling well."

"I would be happy to ask to delay the board meeting until you are feeling better," Gabetti offered.

"That won't be necessary," Morchio said.

At the Sala Agnelli, Angelo Benessia was waiting to start the board meeting, stepping temporarily into the chairman's role. The group was seated around the huge table that was the only piece of furniture in the spartan room, killing time waiting for Morchio to arrive. Finally, Lodovico Passerin d'Entrèves, executive assistant to the chairman and head of public relations, came into the room bearing a message.

"Morchio doesn't feel well; he is leaving," he said.

As those around the table discussed what to do next, they heard the sound of a helicopter taking off from the helipad on the Lingotto roof. It was Morchio, leaving. He resigned later, by fax, forgoing his exit bonus.

■ ■ ■

The Agnelli family, led by Gianluigi Gabetti, had just successfully fended off what it saw as an attack. And now it had a new CEO. Again.

On June 1, 2004, Fiat sent out a brief statement: "The board of directors, which met today in a meeting chaired by Luca Cordero di Montezemolo, named Sergio Marchionne as chief executive officer, having served on the board since May 2003 as an independent director."

Fiat's new management was the equivalent of a second-string baseball team: Marchionne (who had no auto industry experience) had been tapped only after Morchio's power grab made the family suspicious; Montezemolo was not a family member and was a stopgap for John, who was still considered too young to be Fiat chairman; and John himself had been officially picked as heir by his grandfather after John's cousin Giovanni Alberto died unexpectedly of cancer. Even Gabetti was something of a second choice; Umberto had called him out of retirement to run IFIL in a pinch because he "had no one else."

Hardly a dream team.

# Chapter 10

# You Deal with It, and You Move On

S ergio Marchionne may have been the Agnelli family's plan B pick to run Fiat at that point, but it would soon become apparent that his background, upbringing, and personality made him one of a kind to lead the long, hard slog ahead. His international upbringing and experience were the perfect antidote to Turin's provincialism, and clicked with John's globe-trotting childhood. He was steeped in a rigid work ethic by his disciplinarian parents. Last but not least, he was the rare executive who not only was numerate but also had a fine-tuned sense of what made people tick.

Marchionne was born on June 17, 1952, in Chieti, a small, charming, and ancient hill town near the Adriatic coast halfway down the Italian boot. His father was an officer in Italy's military police, the *carabiniere*, and his mother, Maria Zuccon, hailed from a village in what is now Croatia. The family was comfortable, and Sergio had a happy childhood, with trips to the nearby seaside in the summer and plenty of cousins from his father's huge family always around to pass the time with. But his childhood was not exactly carefree. His parents were strict, and dark memories of hardship and suffering in World War II were still fresh. Neither of his parents discussed what had happened openly. But Sergio had been able to piece it together from bits of overheard conversation and from his own observations. The rest he learned from his mother, but only much, much later. He never would have heard the word *foibe*, and about the massacres that took place there, because it was a taboo topic in Italy until recently.

Sergio's mother Maria grew up in Carnizza, or what is now called Krnica, where her parents owned a big shop on the main square where people from nearby towns and workers from the coal mines at Arsia and Arbone came to buy fabric, clothing, and supplies. Maria's family was Italian, and her family lived side by side with Slovenians and Croats as people in Istria had for centuries in the Austro-Hungarian Empire, which granted each community a fair amount of administrative, cultural, and religious freedom.[1] But when Maria was a girl, that peaceful coexistence started to degenerate.

Istria, a peninsula sticking out into the Adriatic opposite Venice, had been Venetian before passing to Austria-Hungary, and it became Italian after World War I. The Fascist government began a series of policies to "Italianize" the area that forced the local Slavic population to speak and worship in Italian. As the years went by, the policy became increasingly brutal, sparking strong anti-Italian sentiment and fanning the fires of a nascent Slovene and Croat nationalism. When Mussolini's Blackshirts burned down a Slovenian cultural center in Trieste in 1922, houses were also set on fire in Maria's village and the nearby Mackoije.[2]

Despite the growing tensions, Maria's life carried on as before. During the summers, she and her sister Anna would walk under the piercing heat of the Mediterranean sun to the sound of cicadas to swim in the crystal-clear blue water at the nearby seaside, and explore the little caves along the coast.[3] Anna and Maria's two brothers helped out in the family shop, but Anna was the one who showed real talent with clients. She and Maria went to Trieste, a cosmopolitan city that was the Austrian seaport, to order new merchandise for the shop, and each time Maria bought a new hat.[4]

Maria met Concezio, who was from Abruzzo, when he was stationed at Carnizza. On one of their early outings, Concezio took Maria shopping in Trieste at a fancy department store, where she spent more on silk scarves in a single outing than Concezio earned as an entire month as a *carabiniere*. Concezio was worried that Maria would never be happy on his small salary. He had been saving up to buy a home for his family since he was 18. Maria's sister Anna fell in love with Concezio's friend.

But when the war broke out, Maria's village and others like it were caught up in one of the cruelest conflicts of a war that already stands out for its brutality. The local Croatian and Slovenian population had been hardened by two decades of Fascist "Italianization," with arrests, shootings, and deportations. Then, on April 6, 1941, the Germans invaded Yugoslavia, which was partitioned into territories occupied by Germany, Italy, Bulgaria, and Hungary. The carving up of Yugoslavia into war booty had a lethal effect on the local ethnic groups, which were scattered across the divided-up regions like salt and pepper. An estimated 300,000 to 500,000 Serbs were massacred by Croats from 1941 to 1945.[5] But the Albanians also took advantage to eliminate Serbs as well, and there were other massacres in Bosnia-Herzegovina. The spiral of ethnic violence soon became a sort of war within a war.

In the Italian-controlled areas, like where Maria's family lived, a resistance movement formed in the summer of 1941 that combined Slovene nationalism with communist ideology that Mussolini's army tried with all its might to stamp out with increasingly repressive methods. The Italian army was authorized to round up and imprison entire villages or areas "for prevention, precaution, or repression, categories of individuals from the city or the countryside," according to an Italian armed forces memo.[6] Tens of thousands of partisans were deported by the Italian occupiers to labor camps, some of which were set up on islands in the Adriatic that are now a peaceful, unspoiled vacation paradise, where they often died of malnutrition. Italians also adopted cruel German methods. In Podhum, where Slovene partisans killed an elementary schoolteacher and his wife, the prefect of Fiume ordered 91 hostages to be shot in reprisal on June 13, 1942.[7]

But the escalating spiral of violence only served to strengthen the resistance movement, "creating the equation of Italian = fascism = repression"[8] and setting the scene for worse things to come.

On September 8, 1943, Italy announced it had signed an armistice with the Allies. Italy's prime minister and king fled to set up a new government in Brindisi, leaving northern Italy leaderless and its army without clear orders. German troops quickly took over Italian territories as Italy's army, with some notable courageous exceptions, dissolved like sugar in a coffee cup.

While the war ground into its final stages for the rest of Italy, for Maria and her family it would drag on and on. After the Italians surrendered, the Wehrmacht occupied Trieste and the Istrian cities of Pola and Fiume. But it could not penetrate into the countryside beyond, leaving a sudden power vacuum that was quickly filled by Tito's partisans, who scooped up arms left behind by departing Italian troops and quickly started rounding up those they deemed to be "enemies of the people." The vacuum was also filled by local farmers and townspeople acting on their own, in a lawless environment where looting, score settling, and random violence were the order of the day.

During those chaotic days, a group of men came to the Zuccon family home and arrested Maria's father, who was 49. Maria's brother, who had been away fighting, had arrived home from the front. He went out looking for their father, and never came back. Maria and her sister Anna took refuge in the countryside with their grandfather. The Zuccons' store was looted and confiscated.

That fall, all across Istria, thousands of Italian citizens were killed and thrown into *foibe*, or deep, vertical caves that had been carved into the soft white limestone by the region's underground rivers over the centuries. Most had been executed first, but many were still alive. Some were former Fascist officers, bureaucrats, officials, or judges. Others were bankers or insurance agents. Some, like Maria's father, were simply guilty of being well-off.

"After we walked for about a kilometer, we stopped at the foot of a hill where someone roped a rock weighing about 20 kilograms to our tied-up hands with wire," Giovanni Radetticchio, a survivor of one of the massacres, said in a newspaper account published in 1946. "Then we were pushed over towards the opening of the *foiba*, with its terrifying black opening looming beneath our feet. One of our group, out of his mind for the torture he had already endured, threw himself into the abyss on his own, yelling. One of the partisans, standing up with his rifle pointed at a nearby rock, ordered us to do the same. Since I didn't move, he fired at me. And that's when the marvel happened: the bullet, instead of hitting me, broke the wire holding the rock to my wrists. So when I jumped into the *foiba*, the rock simply rolled away. . . . I fell down into the river, and popped up floating. So I hid behind a rock. They threw four more people down after they shot them. And I heard the murderers say, 'next time let's throw them down from over here, it's easier.' "9

■ ■ ■

Maria and Concezio got married in April 1947, and left for Rome. Maria's life in Italy was much different from the one she had known in Istria. Her husband had nine brothers and sisters, and she had a steady stream of relatives coming and going. She got used to preparing huge impromptu meals for Concezio's various relatives on holidays and birthdays. She adapted to living on Concezio's small salary. But the prosperity she had known before the war was gone. The young couple's savings were wiped out by the lira devaluation in November 1947. Instead of the new house they had dreamed of, Concezio and Maria went out and bought each other a pair of new shoes. That's all the money would buy.

"I still remember the look of resilience on my mother's face when my parents told me that story," Marchionne recalled. "You deal with it, and you move on." Sergio inherited his parents' ability to take hardship in stride, their toughness, and their resilience.

Sergio and his older sister Luciana's parents drilled the values of discipline and hard work into their two children. Education was a top priority. Happily, Sergio's elementary school teacher noticed he had an unusual talent: he could add up numbers in his head with amazing speed.

"Mr. Marchionne, you should do everything possible to give your son a good education; he has many talents and it would be a great pity not to cultivate them," she said to Marchionne's father.10

It was Sergio's mother Maria, however, who pushed for the family to go to Canada. Anna and her husband had moved to Canada after the war, and Maria had gone to visit them once. Concezio was not keen to move, but Maria convinced him.

Thus the Marchionne family moved to Toronto, Canada, when Sergio was 14. It was 1966 and the Beatles, Barbra Streisand, Harry

Belafonte, the Rolling Stones, and Herb Albert were sharing space on the radio airwaves. Maria's sister Anna, in keeping with the family tradition, had opened a bridal shop called Pola Ladies' Wear. The Marchionne family went to live next door to Sergio's aunt in an apartment above the shop. Sergio's first impressions of Canada were the big American cars and the brightly colored Fruit Loops cereal.[11]

"Who would eat these in the morning?" he wondered.

He spoke no English.

"I missed out on six years of girls," he recalled later. "I made up for it."[12]

Marchionne quit school when he was 16, and finished high school as a private student. He was younger than the rest of his class, and had a hard time fitting in. His father was a disciplinarian, and the young Sergio wanted to do things his own way. He was a rebel. But Sergio and his father had one thing, at least, in common: a love of poker. The pair used to spend hours together playing cards at the *carabinieri* social club founded by Concezio in Toronto.

Marchionne's first experience as a boss came early, when he managed a bank branch at a savings and loan at the age of 18. He had been itching to finish school and get to work. He quickly grasped the ins and outs of the bank branch. But management skills eluded him.

"I was a horrible shit," he recalled.

The early experience of being a manager taught him that being overly authoritarian got results, but the price was too high. It also made him realize he wanted to study. He wanted to catch up to his sister Luciana. At age 28, Luciana was already a fully tenured professor of Italian studies at Erindale College at the University of Toronto. She had degrees in Italian studies and Latin, had already published a book on Italian writer and political activist Natalia Ginzburg in 1978, and was working on two more.[13] Luciana spoke and wrote ancient Greek fluently. She was popular with her students, and had her own radio and television programs.

She was on her way to a brilliant academic career, but Sergio never got a chance to catch up. Luciana died of cancer at age 32.

Sergio's love of studying could have sent him into a career in academia instead of management. Instead, he stuck to business, even though his first experience as a manager, at a bank branch, had left him uncomfortable—a feeling that really didn't disappear until he went back to university. After degrees in philosophy, law, and business, the man who would later save Italy's car industry began his business career with a job as an accountant at Deloitte Haskins & Sells, at the age of 31. He was a quick study, mastering the ins and outs of deferred tax accounting. He was already starting to wonder what to do next.

Sure enough, his attention was soon grabbed by something very interesting going on at Deloitte that had nothing to do with taxes. The biggest leveraged buyout ever in Canada was taking place beneath his nose, at one of Deloitte's clients. Mardon Packaging International was being sold by its owner, BAT Group, for some $250 million. The buyer was a group of British and Canadian managers from Mardon. To make the purchase they loaded up on debt, set up a new group (Lawson Mardon), and aimed to pay back to loan with the company's cash flow. It was the 1980s, and the leveraged buyout boom was riding high. Marchionne joined the new company in 1985 as group controller and then director of corporate development.

It was a hands-on education in finance that gave Marchionne the first hint of what his calling in life would be. He wanted to become a better chief financial officer (CFO), and buckled down and finished his law degree. He stayed at Lawson Mardon until 1988, and returned in 1992.

In his four-year absence from Lawson, he worked as executive vice president of Glenex Industries, and then president of finance and CFO of Acklands Ltd, where the company's owner recalls him as having a "magic touch" for deal making.

"His biggest negotiating talent is that he is able to put himself completely in the shoes of the person on the other side of the table," recalled K. Rai Sahi, former chief shareholder of Acklands and now chairman of Morguard.[14]

Lawson called him back, and he went, this time as the group's number two—as vice president of legal development, CFO, and group secretary. His hard work was paying off. In 1992, the company had about 7,400 employees and did about 1.2 billion Canadian dollars in annual sales.

Marchionne and his wife Orlandina's first son, Alessio Giacomo, was born in 1989, and his second, Jonathan Tyler, was born in 1994.

In 1994 Lawson was acquired by Alusuisse Lonza of Switzerland, a midsize aluminum, packaging, and chemicals group whose main shareholder was a billionaire German aristocrat, Baron August von Finck, after Lawson's main shareholder, Cragnotti & Partners Capital Investment SA, started talks to sell its stake to the Swiss company in November 1993.[15] After the deal went through, Marchionne realized he was now on death row. The deal was closed in January and he was meant to leave by July. He was named "chief of special programs," which was a polite way of giving him a title until he could be moved out. But as the months wore on, the Alusuisse management realized that Marchionne was not only a crack negotiator, but someone who could outlawyer the lawyers and tear through balance sheets like they were Twinkies. He also knew packaging inside and out, which accounted for about a third of Alusuisse's revenue. Marchionne and his family moved to Switzerland, where he became a resident in low-tax Zug.

The business culture in Switzerland was different from and more formal than what he was used to. To underline his place in the pecking order, when he arrived in Zurich he was given a tiny office opposite the bathroom. The formality, at first, was jarring. But he grew to like how well everything worked in Switzerland, and how accountable people were at the company and in general. Marchionne dug into his job with his usual intensity, and his new bosses were impressed by his hard work. He was named CFO by the end of the year, and also appointed to the Alusuisse executive committee. He was appointed CEO of Alusuisse in 1996, at age 44.

By that time, he already had a good reputation with investors for delivering on his financial targets and was seen as a good communicator.

"His dynamism, openness and concentration on increasing value for shareholders" had attracted investors, an analyst at Bank Julius Baer told the *Wall Street Journal* in November 1996 when Marchionne's appointment was announced.[16]

■ ■ ■

Once settling into the corner office, Marchionne reorganized Alusuisse by selling off several businesses, mostly in packaging. He then reorganized the company's three units into six tightly focused groups. To investors, he pledged to increase profits by 10 percent each year and to double the company's revenue in the next five years from about $5.5 billion in 1997 through acquisitions in packaging, food wraps, and chemicals.[17]

His commitment to increasing the market value of the company attracted the eye of Martin Ebner, a bow-tied investor who in the 1990s was known as the Warren Buffett of Switzerland. By the end of Marchionne's first full year, Ebner had built up a stake of 6.3 percent.[18] Ebner had become a force for change in Swiss business circles in 1994 when he took on the financial establishment with a high-profile battle in favor of greater shareholder rights at UBS. His critics dismissed him as a raider only interested in walking away with a capital gain.

Marchionne led Alusuisse—renamed Algroup—into the merger merry-go-round that dominated business strategy of the late 1990s as companies bulked up for globalization and to better compete in the single-currency European market. But months-long talks with Germany's Viag AG fell apart in early 1999 after Viag demanded a higher valuation for its shares in an all-paper share-swap deal, despite the fact that Alusuisse was more profitable.

"We're not going to reskin this dead cat," he said when asked if the decision to walk away from the talks was final.

Martin Ebner, who by now owned 22 percent in Alusuisse and had become chairman, didn't seem to mind that the deal had fallen through.

"The bet we're making on Alusuisse is a bet on Mr. Marchionne," he told the *Wall Street Journal* in the summer of 1999.[19]

Ebner and Marchionne made an interesting couple. Both aimed to maximize shareholder value and stood out in the staid Swiss business world as outsiders. Ebner spurred Marchionne on to find a new merger partner. And Marchionne was nothing if not fast. He believed that a failure to find a merger partner in the rapidly consolidating commodity business of aluminum would lead to the stragglers' marginalization.[20] The industry was plagued by falling prices and overcapacity, especially after low-cost Russian producers started piling in. It was a view he would later take in 2008, when the auto industry demand collapsed.

Marchionne's financial and strategic skills made his investors into fans. But his subordinates, at times, were not as keen. His impatience and temper could make those who reported to him fearful, one said.

"He's a control freak and he can't take criticism," said Vincent Assini, the former head of Alusuisse's aluminum division who left in 1996. It should be noted that Marchionne had succeeded Assini's mentor.[21]

Just five months after the collapse of the Viag talks, Marchionne was back at the drawing board. Algroup and two other companies, France's Pechiney and Canada's Alcan, unveiled a three-way merger August 11, 1999, in Zurich that would create the world's largest aluminum maker. At Marchionne's insistence, Algroup signed a separate agreement with Alcan to make sure that the pair would merge even if Pechiney did not received clearance to go ahead.

As part of the deal, Algroup's chemicals unit, Lonza, was to be spun off into a separate group. Algroup was the smallest of the three in terms of sales, even though it was valued by the market at more than the other two. A committee was formed to decide who would run the new aluminum giant. The CEOs from each company were interviewed by the board, which included Martin Ebner.[22] Marchionne was not picked as CEO. He stepped aside and went to run Lonza, with Martin Ebner as his chairman. The three-way merger became a two-party deal between Alcan and Algroup after Pechiney dropped out in April 2000 when the deal encountered antitrust problems in Europe.[23]

■ ■ ■

The first time Marchionne met Umberto Agnelli was in 2000, at the IFIL offices on Corso Matteotti. Baron von Finck organized the meeting. Umberto was casting around for a manager who could revive the fortunes of SGS, a Swiss-based provider of goods certification and inspection services. The company that year had lost a chunk of business when its government contracts dried up. Marchionne, for his part, was looking for something new after his stint at Lonza. He had been passed over for the top job at the aluminum merger he had engineered.

"You've got to meet this guy," von Finck told Umberto. "He can fix SGS."

The meeting lasted an hour and a half. Marchionne told Umberto that he thought SGS had great potential, but that the company needed to go through a painful restructuring to reset the base of its businesses. Marchionne's job at Alusuisse was done. They started negotiating a contract in the fall of 2000. He was appointed to the SGS board in 2001, and joined as CEO in January 2002.

For 20 years, Sergio had worked for the same company, hopping from Toronto to Zurich when Lawson was bought by Algroup and then to Lonza when it became a separate company after the Algroup and Alcan merger. Now it was time for a change.

■ ■ ■

One day in July 2004, Luca de Meo, a sharp young marketing executive at Fiat's Lancia brand, heard a knock on the door of his office at the Mirafiori factory. It was Sergio Marchionne, who had been CEO for about a month, on one of his walkabouts. De Meo had to hide his surprise. To see the new head of Fiat come from the executive offices at Lingotto to Mirafiori, inside the belly of the whale, going door to door, was unheard of.

"This is like something out of a science fiction film," he thought.[24]

De Meo had joined Fiat in 2001, and had spent his first few months at the company wondering if he had made the biggest mistake of his career. Fiat looked like a defeated company. But the launch of Lancia's new city car, the Ypsilon, had gone well.

"Mind if I come in? So tell me, what do you do here?" Marchionne asked, without much of a preamble, his eyes boring into de Meo's face like a laser beam.

That scene was repeated again and again in those summer months in 2004 as Marchionne scoured the company's ranks to pick the people to build his new flat team and put an end to the "great man" era of Fiat management where the CEO made all the decisions on his own. He did the interviews himself, bypassing the human resources department, which in Italian companies are all-powerful because of employees' high level of guaranteed job security. He was looking for people who wanted to lead. At the end of his series of walkabouts, he would give 2,000 executives early retirement packages.[25]

In late July, Marchionne gathered together the core of what would later become his team of executives; they met at the Grand Hotel du Golf in Crans-Montana, an Alpine resort where the executives hunkered down in a conference room as golfers played outside in the crisp

Alpine air under the glorious summer sun. The idea was to get the group to come up with a plan for Fiat. First, Marchionne had asked them what they thought Fiat needed to do next. Then he asked them what they expected of him. And on the last day, he held a collective session on where Fiat should be in three years.

By the end of the weekend, the group had hammered out the targets to present to Fiat's long-suffering shareholders, and they had kicked around some ideas to reorganize Fiat Auto.

When Marchionne was done with his tour at the end of August, he had a pretty good idea of who was "a sclerotic," in his words, and who were the risk takers he could rely on to rewrite Fiat's playbook. He put the risk takers in charge. By the time he was done assembling his new team, Marchionne's Fiat had shed parts of its century-old Piedmontese skin like a mummy getting a body scrub.

"What happened in August 2004 was Marchionne got rid of at least a couple of layers in the organization overnight," said a longtime Fiat manager. "He got rid of the people who had already lost the game in their own minds, and gave freedom to a bunch of young managers that had nothing to lose. Having nothing to lose gives you tremendous energy."

As Marchionne trudged through Fiat plants around Italy and across the globe, the stakes of his wager started to become clearer to him. Before he could win at this particular round of poker, he needed to get senior management to join the game. Many of them probably wanted to sit it out until they could see results, he wagered. That's not what he needed. If he could get a handful of top people on board with his targets, he figured he could drag them along until the results started to show.

But he certainly wouldn't get them on board the way the company was organized now. The core of his plan was to make a new committee called the Group Executive Council (GEC). The idea was to get all the decision makers for the different areas of the Fiat Group's businesses into one room, around the same table, and on the same page. Simple. None of this "my secretary will speak to your secretary and set up an appointment" stuff. Once that was done, the group could focus on making Fiat more efficient and quicker, and exploit synergies across its businesses. Fiat had no structure for group purchasing, for example.

In terms of operations, the GEC brought together the heads of Fiat Auto, tractors unit CNH, truck unit IVECO, parts unit Magneti Marelli,

Comau (robotics), Teksid (steel), research, and business solutions. The rest of the GEC was made up of the heads of HR, finance, purchasing, public relations, and business development. And of course Marchionne.

"It was really the creation of the GEC that made the difference," said a longtime Fiat group executive. "He killed the committees. It ended the bureaucracy. The GEC met one weekend each month, and decided all the investments then and there."

Fiat was losing millions of euros per day when Marchionne joined.

"When you're losing that kind of money each day, and you wake up in the morning, you know you're not going to have a good day," he recalled later.

■ ■ ■

On September 1, 2004, just a few months after he took over, Marchionne unveiled his 24-person management team for Fiat Auto, the cash-bleeding car unit that was burning millions of euros per day.

Why was Fiat losing so much money? When an automaker gets a model wrong and it flops on the market, not only does it lose the billions of dollars, euros, or yen it invested over the years to design, engineer, produce, and market the vehicle; it also continues to bleed money for the entire time the bomb is sitting, unloved, in showrooms and on dealer lots, while its competitors are out there making money by selling cars in that same segment. It will be years before the bomb can be replaced with something new and, hopefully, sexier. So not only do unsuccessful models force automakers to lose money on development costs; they are also a bleed on operations going forward. Cost cutting, at that point, would not solve Fiat's problems. Marchionne had to attack the way that Fiat made the decisions that went into the product.

He had spent most of August in Turin getting up to speed, because he intended to keep his promise in July to move quickly with a cultural change at Fiat. Ten of the 24 people were under 45.

At one of the first meetings of newly appointed group, Marchionne gave a presentation that started with a cover of *Fortune* magazine. The headline of the January 13, 2003, issue read, "*Arrivederci* Fiat? Losses are mounting. Workers are up in arms. The board is in revolt. Will Fiat exit the car business?" Underneath, the cover illustration was an upside-down Fiat 500.

"This cover illustrates our situation today," he told his new team. "I totally believe we have a chance to relaunch the company. If you follow me, you will see that within three years we will see the same magazine with the 500 right side up."

It might have seemed like an idle boast coming from a manager with no experience in the car business to make to a room full of Fiat executives. But Marchionne was able to deliver on this promise for a very simple reason: groups of highly talented people can solve problems that totally transcend their leader's knowledge of the topic if the leader has picked the right mix of people. After Marchionne had assembled his team of Fiat brand managers, production experts, engineers, marketers, and product managers on September 1, his message was simple: "Now we need to dare. Think out of the box. Take a total risk."

Marchionne's new team reported to Fiat Auto CEO Herbert Demel, who was also made head of the Fiat brand temporarily, concentrating a tremendous amount of power in his hands. The heads of Fiat's five platforms, along with all the brand leaders, would now report directly to Demel instead of to the head of engineering. The team included Luca de Meo, whom he promoted to run the Lancia brand, and Gianni Agnelli's grandson Lapo Elkann, John Elkann's younger brother, who became head of brand promotion for all three brands—Fiat, Lancia, and Alfa Romeo. Alfredo Altavilla was also a clear winner. He emerged with two jobs instead of one—moving up to the position of head of business development as well as the head of Fiat Powertrain. Only one person came from outside the company.

Daniele Bandiera, a longtime Fiat man who was involved in building Fiat's heavily automated Melfi showpiece factory, was confirmed at Alfa Romeo.

Last but not least, Angioletta Boero, a woman, was named to top management for the first time in Fiat's history.

Under the previous system introduced in 2002, Fiat's three brands were three separate business units, each run as separate fiefdoms. Each business unit did its own purchasing, hiring, finances, and development. The result was high costs, bureaucracy, and inefficiency. "They didn't even share one screw," noted an amazed engineer who arrived at the company in the fall of 2004. Contrary to common industry practice, the brands did not share platforms between them, either.

Marchionne's reorganization hardly set the financial markets on fire.

"Just because you change your management doesn't mean that customers will start buying your cars," said analyst Adam Jonas at Morgan Stanley in London. "But it does address some of what Marchionne said at his first meeting with analysts."[26]

But by eliminating the business units, he addressed one of the key reasons why Fiat Auto was losing money. Instead of bringing Fiat closer to its customers, the business units were run by car guys who were in love with the technical content of the automobile. Frequently they were executives from the engineering department, and they did not involve marketing or other parts of the company in their decisions. Car development pre-Marchionne had revolved around the *iniziativa di vettura*, a new vehicle program for each model that contained the design, finance and investment, and business case. After it went through the development process at the business unit, it was handed over to marketing with instructions on how many units marketing had to sell, at what price, and to whom. Post-Marchionne, the new vehicle program was handed over to the brand managers, who had to convince the marketing, product, design, and sales people that their business case made sense to them *before* it was greenlighted, not after. Most of the new team came from inside Fiat. Marchionne had found them on his walkabouts, and promoted them to roles they would never have been able to dream of in the old House of Savoy style Fiat.

The timetable was tight. The company needed to get new product out into the marketplace as soon as possible before it collapsed, and it needed to come up with head-turning ads on a tiny budget.

Marchionne's managers on both sides of the Atlantic get a nostalgic, happy look in their eyes when they start talking about their experience of working in these small groups. Long hours and the occasional bout of verbal abuse do not seem to cancel the sheer thrill of the corporate reinvention that these groups unleashed under Marchionne's leadership. His ability to make snap strategic decisions on the back of presentations by his management team quickly won them over.

"We were ready to go to our death following him," recalled a former brand manager. "There was adrenaline. And each time he punched you out, you learned something."

■ ■ ■

If Marchionne has a management bible, it is Warren Bennis's 1997 book *Organizing Genius: The Secrets of Creative Collaboration.* One of his favorite passages in it is a quote from an article about Walt Disney that ran in *National Geographic* in August 1963:

> "You know, I was stumped one day when a little boy asked, 'Do you draw Mickey Mouse?'" Walt Disney said. "I had to admit I do not draw anymore. 'Then you think up all the jokes and the ideas?' 'No,' I said, 'I don't do that.' Finally, he looked at me and said 'Mr. Disney, what do you do?'
>
> "'Well,' I said, 'sometimes I think of myself as a little bee. I go from one area of the studio to another and gather pollen and sort of stimulate everybody.' I guess that's the job I do. I certainly don't consider myself a businessman, and I never did believe I was worth anything as an artist."[27]

Most groups have a potential for greatness that never quite takes off. But every so often, the right person comes along who can put together a handful of superb people, set an impossible goal, engage them in a holy war, and let them rip. It happened at Disney when the company created the first-ever feature film. It happened at Apple, with the Manhattan Project, and at Xerox PARC. And it happened at Fiat starting in the fall of 2004.

"Our attitude was, we have a 50 percent chance of making it and a 50 percent chance of dying," recalls a former advertising executive. "If we die, let's at least make sure we do it with enough honor to get remembered for it."

Time after time, Marchionne pushed what he called "the kids" to rip up piece after piece of Fiat and reinvent it. Decision-making processes had to be shortened.

"We said to ourselves, why go in with a 250-page PowerPoint presentation? Let's go to him with just a chart," recalls the former adman. "We had to work two weeks all night for a one-hour meeting. He is great at asking questions. You had to be simple, detached, and with a story to tell."

Life as one of "the kids" was not easy. The Fiat Auto management committee met once a week, often on weekends. The meetings were held in English, the language Marchionne spoke when he arrived. Remarks from Marchionne like "Even my fucking Labrador would understand that" were the order of the day. One false step during the early days could lead to an on-the-spot firing, like the unfortunate head of a Fiat-owned dealerships during a Sunday meeting when he presented his midyear budget numbers in the Lingotto's big meeting room on the fourth floor.

"Despite extremely challenging market conditions, I managed to improve our loss from 180 million euros to 120 million euros," the executive said with a hint of pride.

Marchionne interrupted him.

"Well, well, well, look here," he began. "We have a person who wakes up in the morning, and as he is getting ready for work, looks into the mirror when he is shaving and says, 'Great! Instead of losing 180 million, I am losing just 120.'"

The executive started to look pale. Marchionne turned to the rest of the group. "I don't need people in here who are happy to lose money. I want people who culturally are all about making money, not losing it." Then he turned to the unfortunate executive and said, "You are free to go." He was fired to make a point.

Top executives were not spared the same treatment. The first high-profile casualty in Marchionne's management came in mid-October, when Daniele Bandiera was abruptly fired by phone just hours after he told journalists at a press conference in Naples that Fiat had invested 60 million euros in the new Alfa Romeo 147 model, which he was preparing to launch in November. Bandiera had acquired the habit of going over Demel's head under Morchio, and both Marchionne and Demel clearly wanted to stop it. Bandiera was replaced by a former Rolls-Royce executive, Karl-Heinz Kalbfell. However, he didn't last long, either.

Marchionne's team quickly realized that their boss prized debate and conflicting views as good for business, and wanted meetings to continue until a decision had been reached. They also came to dread being put on the spot, which could lead to a brutal dressing-down and even an on-the-spot firing.

There were moments when "you have to throw yourself down on the ground and pretend you are dead. That's the moment when you get saved. Because if he is looking at you, and you say something, forget it," said a former brand manager.

No one was spared from Marchionne's drumbeat of "faster, faster, faster"—not even Demel himself. Tension between Marchionne and Demel began to leak out into the press as soon as early November.[28] The two had a fundamental difference on their approach to the auto industry. Demel, an engineer by training, had a deeply ingrained respect for tried-and-true production processes. He was not comfortable with Marchionne's "let's rip it up" approach.

At a Fiat Auto meeting in mid-November, Marchionne was forced to deny those rumors of Demel leaving as "pure crap." Marchionne said, with Demel looking on, that he had taken control of the sales and network development outside Italy.

"He cannot do everything alone," he said.

Marchionne started sniping at Demel, whom he admired as an engineer, in management meetings. "We need to cut our time-to-market by half," Marchionne would say. "Impossible," Demel would reply. And he was right. The manufacturing process of an automobile is complicated and very difficult to compress without taking risks, which Marchionne was willing to take. "Let's take the risk. We're about to die," he would say. "At least we'll go down kicking." But that wasn't Demel's way. He was a great engineer, but Marchionne needed someone who could also run people.

Fiat announced Demel's resignation in February 2005. Marchionne stepped in as head of Fiat Auto. Along with unleashing the power of his management group both at Fiat Auto and at the GEC, which was officially unveiled in November 2004, Marchionne knew during the early months at the company that his success at Fiat depended on many things that were out of his control.

First and foremost, he had to simply hope that the car market didn't collapse. Second, he had to successfully pry a juicy cash settlement out of GM in exchange for Fiat giving up its right to sell the car unit to GM in 2005. Separating Fiat from GM would give the company its freedom back. Third, he was operating on an assumption that Fiat would not pay back the three billion euro convertible loan to Italian banks due in 2005. The nonrepayment would force the banks to convert their debt to equity, thereby diluting the Agnelli family's ownership. But Fiat simply didn't have the cash to repay the loan. It was useless to fret over it.

Last, he was crafting his financial targets by making an against-the-odds bet that the brand equity of Fiat could somehow recover with the upcoming launches of the Punto, the Brava, and the 500. That would be the hardest part for him. But if he could find a guy to do a bunch of ads that really tapped into the deep wellspring of feeling for Fiat, the way he had seen it on television at Gianni Agnelli's funeral, to tap into that thing he felt himself when he said yes to John Elkann . . . well . . . maybe he'd have a half-assed chance, he wagered.

■ ■ ■

Harald Wester joined Fiat as head of engineering and design for the car unit in November 2004, and two months later he was sure he had made the completely wrong decision. His offices were in the brown brick Engineering and Design building along one of Mirafiori's gloomy little streets, which were named Viale 1, Viale 2, Viale 3, and so on. It looked like an elementary school. Everything was gray, dark, old, and dirty. Even if he left his house smiling in the morning, he lost 10 percent of his energy once he went through the factory gates. And once he went through the door to his building—well, forget it.

The green-eyed 46-year-old German had worked his entire life at Volkswagen, Audi, Ferrari, and most recently, Magna. Ah, Ferrari. Just a few months earlier, Ferrari had unveiled a new 22 million euro[29] research center designed by architect Massimiliano Fuksas, made from steel and glass, with reflecting pools on the mezzanine so that more light could filter into the meeting rooms. Coming to Fiat—even though they were part of the same group—was like leaving a golf course to live in a desert. Wester had thought long and hard about giving up life in paradise to come help fix Fiat. And he said yes only because the HR chief had promised him that some big organizational changes were coming through. And if it didn't work out, he could always go somewhere else.

And now here he was stuck in what looked like an elementary school on Viale 8. One of his first moves was to give the place a face-lift, a paint job in sun yellow. But Fiat didn't even have the money to foot the bill for a professional paint job. So Wester, a trim, energetic man with a spring in his step, bought the paint himself and convinced his staff to do the work. He stopped working for a week to oversee the project. When it was done, the whole place looked different. It might not be a 22 million euro steel and glass paradise like where he would be if he still worked at Ferrari. But it was a lot better than it had been.

When Wester arrived, his former colleague at VW, Herbert Demel, was already struggling at Fiat Auto. Marchionne was growing impatient with Demel's by-the-book approach. But the new Fiat CEO had no engineering background and no automotive experience, so he relied on Demel, and then increasingly on Wester, to execute his vision.

The first thing Wester had done was to report to work in October, two weeks early, to interview his staff of 120 engineers and designers. After he finished all of his interviews, Wester redesigned his organization, creating a new team that pulled in people from five or six business units of the company, plus international sources. By mid-December his new team of 52 was in place.

What he found shocked him and mirrored Mirafiori's neglect. It was far worse than he had imagined. Fiat had been divided into business units, which were run separately. They were all supported by a sort of centralized product and process engineering department, a sort of captive engineering service provider that had no power, voice, or input. In terms of auto development, Fiat did not have the precise processes or methodologies in place for gauging a potential new model's buyer and market. The engineering and commercial side of auto companies usually worked together. And, last but not least, competitors were benchmarked in terms of quality and model offerings. None of this was going on at Fiat.

It was as if the company had missed out on the 1990s. A lost decade. Wester's mission was clear: revitalize and empower this key core of Fiat Auto, which had been simply destroyed over the past 10 years.

But it needed more than just than simply revitalizing a weakened department. The rest of the European auto industry was converging onto standardized platform and parts sharing. At VW, a Golf and an Audi 3 could share everything from nuts and bolts to heating units, door handles, and rearview mirrors. But at Fiat, none of that was happening. The new Stilo in 2001 had shared exactly zero parts with other Fiat models. It was the exact opposite of what he had seen at his previous employers and what was the standard procedure at pretty much any carmaker. He would really have to start from scratch. It was mind-boggling.

"How could this company have been so stupid?" he wondered.

Painting over the dirt and grime on the walls was easier for Wester than overcoming the inertia and the old mind-set of Fiat.

His new team did not coalesce overnight. Some members had been working on Fiats, and some on Alfas. And each thought the others were "complete idiots," Wester recalled. It was difficult for them to come to grips with the idea that they could share parts and standardize procedures and not sacrifice brand identity.

Plus, his new team was used to "the boss" making all the decisions. He explained in staff meeting after staff meeting in the bright yellow conference room opposite his office that from now on, decision making would not be centralized, and that the best way to run things was to delegate technical decisions down to the level of maximum competence.

Wester's first project was the launch of the new Grande Punto in September 2005. Most of the car was already defined, so all he could do was make some safety changes to make sure it got a five-star European rating.

His first big project was the replacement for the ill-fated Stilo, a mid-size car in a segment where Fiat is traditionally weak. The replacement's name would be the Bravo. The product steering committee, which included Marchionne and Demel, was in the final stages of approving the new Bravo before Wester's arrival. One of the options the group was hashing out at the Fiat styling center, which also needed a face-lift, was to do a low-cost and cheerful restyling, not an entirely new car. The advantage was that it would be quick and cheap at a time when Fiat was bleeding cash. The disadvantage was that it would be like combing the hair on a corpse.

Wester didn't like the restyling idea.

"It would have been nice to have this car on the road now," Wester said to his colleagues. "But in two years' time, forget it."

The Bravo discussion in the product steering committee became "what can we do if we don't do the face-lift?" Fiat Chairman Luca di Montezemolo was also involved in the talks. The decision was made, at a meeting in February 2006, to kill the face-lift and make a new car.

But there was a small problem. The car was due to enter production in July 2007. That didn't leave enough time to make a new one.

"How quickly can we have a new car?" Marchionne asked Wester.

"It will take 36 months," said Wester, giving the standard answer.

There was a significant level of desperation in the air, he noted.

"We won't be here in 36 months," said Marchionne. "I need it in 18."

Instead of balking, Wester committed to proposing a different styling of the car in just two and a half months. And said he would look at coming up with a way to drastically slash the car's development time. But how?

Wester set up a team to look at what other industries did, which met in the conference room off of his office. On weekends, it used space heaters to ward off the chill.

Wester's specialization as an engineer was in computer simulation of test crashes. He was also versed in aeronautics, as well as vehicles. He had worked with those systems for years at the start of his career when he was at VW. Automakers used computer simulation as a backup, a sort of virtual parallel to real-world design. But in the aeronautics business, makers of big commercial jetliners were forced to use computer simulation. If it was good enough for them, Wester thought, why not for Fiat? What if Fiat were to just junk the real-world design and shift the whole thing over to computer simulation? No one except Fiat had been desperate enough to try it. Wester was willing. He trusted the tools, and he didn't really have a choice.

■ ■ ■

One day toward the end of 2005, Sergio Marchionne threw a surprise party for "the kids" in the Sala Nasi, a meeting room down the corridor from his office. After 17 quarters of losses, Fiat Auto, the industry laughingstock, had returned a profit.

To celebrate, he ordered a cake decorated with the profit figure on it: 21 million euros. And champagne. There were no speeches, just a celebration. People didn't cry like they had when Fiat finished up with GM. But they came close.

To lighten up the atmosphere, Marchionne had a video made called "Operazione: Carmageddeon" with a countdown to the profit number.

"September, 2004," the video began, opening with a scene from the Bruce Willis movie *Armageddon*, as the words "Fiat Crisis Unit" flashed across the screen. A narrator intoned: "The situation was getting worse. It was a red alert. Dr. Mark called his team. Twenty-four men, ready for anything, from PR to design. That day, Operation: Carmageddeon began."

Marchionne and his management team's pictures flashed across the screen, alternating with scenes of Bruce Willis dressed in a space suit. Marchionne was wearing a suit in the picture, but sometimes in the office when he had no appointments he wore just a sweater with no jacket. It was much more comfortable.

"Results were not long in coming," the video continued, cutting to scenes of a zippy orange Punto on a highway. "But there was no time to celebrate. The kids pushed ahead. Third quarter was one success after another."

A classic happy ending, the video noted.

"The first challenge has been won, but their competition is still alive and kicking. Dr. Mark and his men will have to face even tougher tests ahead. Good work, kids. You've earned . . . a 10-minute break."

# Chapter 11

# Sergio Marchionne's Two-Billion-Dollar Bet

O n July 26, 2004, financial analysts and business journalists convened near the town of Balocco, a village tucked away between the rice paddies that stretch along the Po River valley between Turin and Milan. Both Balocco, just off the highway exit, and nearby Bastia had seen better days. The brick façade of the church at Balocco looked like the decoration had fallen off long ago. The little castle tower presided over an empty square. At Bastia, the scene was even more desolate. An old Fascist slogan was still visible on the side of a farm building underneath the coat of white paint: "We Don't Want War, Nor Do We Fear It. Mussolini." The castle of the Piazza Castello was crumbling, and the area in front had been turned into an impromptu parking lot for two huge tractors.

The out-of-town visitors were headed for Fiat's test track nearby. Analysts and press who had been hoping for a sumptuous spread of the Piedmont's finest food and wines were disappointed. Instead, they were welcomed into a sweltering industrial hangar without the usual trimmings and finery. The muggy heat was oppressive, made worse by the mosquitoes buzzing from the nearby rice paddies. Most of the analysts making the trek that day thought the company's future was hopeless, although a handful of investors had Sergio Marchionne on their radar screens because of his success at turning around Swiss company SGS.[1]

Marchionne was Fiat's fifth CEO in two years. Financial investors had been writing off Fiat as a basket case since 2001 because of bad management and shrinking market share. The few who had buy ratings on the stock, like Philippe Houchois at UBS, were optimistic only because they wagered that the company couldn't get any worse. Marchionne had impressed investors with his sharp work at SGS, but it was far from clear whether his fix-up job there would be sustainable. Alusuisse had fallen apart after he left. In most people's eyes, he had been a talented manager at mid-capitalization companies who was now making a leap into the big time.

One thing was immediately clear: the waste and extravagance of previous Fiat events, when Cantarella and Fresco would hop over from nearby Turin in a helicopter, were a thing of the past. Gone too were the bright red Ferrari baseball caps and bottles of high-priced Brunello wine that Fiat used to lavish on its guests. This event was much more sober, Houchois thought, and the huge space looked like a barn.

Marchionne had already lived through a failed presentation, at a debt refinancing in the early 1990s in London that didn't net him a single dime in new loans. Since then, he had developed a relaxed, off-the-cuff, no-notes speaking style that was extremely effective. He did not stick to his slides. With his shaggy hair and glasses, he had a deep resonating voice that was hypnotizing, sort of like a DJ on a late-night jazz music program.

"Unfortunately there are more negatives on these slides than positives," said Marchionne as he launched into a five-hour marathon, speaking tieless in the summer heat.[2] "I think that the 2003 plan was sound, but the time lines were unrealistic. I think the ability to turn around Auto as quickly as the plan envisioned is certainly not doable. More fundamental than this is . . . the organizational structure that was put in place to deal with the challenge is fundamentally and totally inadequate."

Marchionne's bid to win over his audience by criticizing Fiat's former management was not subtle, but it got their attention. Here was something different. This guy was slamming all the cronies that the Agnelli family had put in place over the previous years, thought the Reuters correspondent, Jane Barrett. He really gets it.

"It was pitch-perfect, every slide," recalled Christopher Emsden, a journalist who covered the event for Dow Jones Newswires. "He has a real skill with the question-and-answer banter."

Marchionne's insistence that the put option to force GM to buy Fiat Auto was valid was what made the headline in *The Wall Street Journal* the next day.[3] Most of the focus in the coming days was on the put option that gave Fiat the power to sell Fiat Auto to GM. Marchionne took a strong stand, indicating he would do everything in his power to extract a cash settlement from GM by the end of 2004 or early in 2005. GM's position was that the put had no value. A battle loomed.

But the most important change he unveiled was one that seemed far less dramatic at the time.

"We need to open up the whole house and the process of decision making so that people who do make a difference can matter," he said.[4]

Marchionne planned to remake Fiat from the top down in two ways. The first was the bland-sounding Group Executive Council—the GEC, which with Italian pronunciation ended up sounding like "the Jack"—which would run Fiat. He also unveiled a new structure at Fiat Auto. Both turned out to be Marchionne's secret weapons. These two small groups functioned as a mix of war council, battering ram pounding Fiat into shape, workhorse pushed to exhaustion, and turbocharged engine that Marchionne ran in the sixth gear. Fiat's new structure was often called "flat," but that word didn't really capture its dynamism or its interconnected nature. He would later import the "small group" idea to Chrysler, where it evolved into a matrixed management organization that gave the company the speed it needed to come out of bankruptcy like a rocket.

The presentation was a success. Marchionne came across as serious, principled, and substantial, UBS's Houchois recalled. Even Marchionne's frank admission that the auto unit's recovery would be a year behind schedule, posting a small operating loss in 2005, was well received. Fiat Auto and the group itself would not go into the black until 2006, he said.

The stock ended the day with a gain of 2.2 percent. After the presentation was over, anyone who wanted to could test-drive anything from a Ferrari to a CNH combine harvester, or simply grab a drink. Marchionne stood around and mingled with journalists, shaking people's hands and accepting kind words from well-wishers.

■ ■ ■

Along with convincing investors he was on the right track, stopping the losses at Fiat Auto and dragging the group's corporate culture into the twenty-first century, Marchionne faced another immediate challenge in the fall of 2004: how to extricate Fiat from its partnership with General Motors.

A week before Marchionne's humid meeting with investors amid the rice fields outside Turin, on July 17, 2004, General Motors CEO Rick Wagoner Jr., Fiat Auto chief Herbert Demel, Alfredo Altavilla, and a handful of other executives gathered at the Townsend Hotel in Birmingham, Michigan, for one of the steering committee meetings that the two automotive partners held every quarter to make business decisions. Birmingham's curving streets, rolling hills, and huge trees, as well as its chic shopping district and the luxurious hotel, have made it the favorite place to live for the Motor City's top executives, including Rick Wagoner.[5]

The Townsend's dark, faux-English country manor interior—with its marble floors, heavy chandeliers, and oil paintings of white-wigged aristocrats—was a welcome contrast to the humid July heat outside. The meeting was the first one attended by Marchionne, who had been at the job for just over a month. Marchionne arrived when the others were already waiting.

"I am sorry I am completely underdressed," he said, apologizing for his lack of tie and the sweater. "The airline lost my luggage."

As the meeting got under way, Marchionne sat quietly and listened. He had been briefed the day before by Demel and Altavilla, when he had quickly grasped the issues plaguing the dysfunctional partnership. Some were already clear in his mind, like the fact that the alliance tied Fiat's hands. At the top of his agenda was what to do about the so-called put. As part of the two companies' alliance back in 2000, Fiat had negotiated a put option—the right to be able to sell 90 percent of Fiat Auto to GM. Fiat would be able to trigger the sale in December, in less than six months' time. There was no way that GM wanted that to happen. It had lost money in Europe for four years in a row.[6] GM's position was that the contract giving Fiat the right to unload the money-losing Fiat Auto onto GM's groaning balance sheet was no longer valid.

Marchionne could not help but notice the subtext of the meeting with GM: Fiat was treated as the junior partner.

"It was sort of like a wrestling match: there was the strong guy, kicking and punching, and then the weak guy trying to defend himself," said a Fiat executive who attended the meetings. "That was the pattern."

The July steering committee meeting at the Townsend was the first and last time Marchionne was quiet at a meeting with GM.

The next time the group gathered was at the George V Hotel Paris, during the auto show in September. Marchionne, Demel, and Altavilla were joined by Eugenio Razelli, who had been named vice president of business activity for Fiat SpA. The GM delegation was made up of Wagoner, GM Europe chief Fritz Henderson, and Maureen Kempston Darkes, president of GM South America.

The mood among automakers in Europe at the Paris show was gloomy. Car companies in Europe all faced the same problem: too many factories making cars for too few buyers. GM, in particular, was struggling. It hadn't posted an annual profit in Europe since 1999. The company was looking at plans to cut about 3,000 jobs in Europe, or the capacity of about two of its plants.[7]

When the discussion turned to the topic of making cuts to the capacity of the engine joint venture, Wagoner started to raise his voice. People at Fiat were used to getting pushed around by GM. But it was only Marchionne's second meeting with Wagoner, and he didn't see why Fiat's so-called partner should be abusive.

"I am going to ignore the belligerent nature of this comment," Marchionne told Wagoner, who changed his tone.

The put is "effective and exercisable," Marchionne continued. "If they want to take us to court they can take us to court."[8]

The meeting was a wake-up call to GM executives, who realized they were finally dealing with a CEO who could challenge their position. Wagoner's dealings with Giuseppe Morchio, Marchionne's predecessor, had been different. Morchio didn't really believe that Fiat could pry any money loose from GM in exchange for extracting them from their obligation to buy Fiat Auto. But Marchionne did.

After the meeting, Marchionne gave one of his impromptu press conferences to journalists camped outside the hotel.

"As far as I know today, there will be no further delay," he told reporters in regard to using the put option early the next year.

■ ■ ■

Executives picked to work with Marchionne that fall quickly learned that the company plane would become their second home. Fiat's rented jet had a bedroom, a bathroom, a four-seat area with a table, and two armchairs. Anyone on the plane realized that the books, papers, or magazines they had brought along were going to sit in their bags, unread.

Marchionne loved to play poker, and had been playing since he was a teenager. Passengers on the plane rarely escaped a game with the boss. One executive recalled playing cards for an entire Turin-to-Tokyo flight.

As soon as the plane started taxiing down the runway the cards were dealt out. If players weren't careful, cards on the table would slide into their laps during takeoff.

"Do you always want to sit there and act like a goddam intellectual the entire flight?" Marchionne asked an executive who had tried in vain to make it a habit to read.

New managers were not exempt.

"Hey kid, get *over* here," Marchionne said to one who had settled back in the chair with a set of Bose headphones and a stack of magazines.

Marchionne's poker-playing days go back to his early years in Toronto, when he would spend afternoons twice a week playing cards with his father and other retired former *carabinieri*.[9] Concezio Marchionne founded Canada's Associazione Nazionale Carabinieri in 1973, and for his son Sergio it became a sort of second home. Sergio soon became a better card player than his father. Concezio would get angry if he lost. But Sergio never blew his cool.

Not knowing how to play poker was no excuse. Marchionne patiently explained the rules, and other players were prohibited from harassing or taking advantage of the newcomer. No one played for money. Marchionne got irritated only if someone at the table played badly.

Just like Marchionne could listen to meetings of the Fiat Auto product or commercial committee for hours and not miss a trick, his eyes semiclosed behind a haze of cigarette smoke, so too could he remember every single card played in game after game.

In another illustration of how his mind operated on several levels at once, he could remember the cards that were played and still talk business the entire time. He used the game as a chance to assess a manager's appetite for risk, and to pick his or her brains for tidbits of information.

And so it would go until three or four hours before landing, when Marchionne would end the game, turn the heating in the plane down to freezing, and collapse into the bedroom to sleep.

■ ■ ■

After the steering committee meeting in Paris, Marchionne convened a small group to plot strategy in October in Turin. His goals were to get paid for releasing GM from the obligation to buy Fiat Auto and to free up Fiat Auto to do joint ventures around the world that would make its operations more efficient.

One of the first questions that emerged from the Fiat strategy meeting was how to get GM to the table. The U.S. automotive giant had either dodged or procrastinated on the issue. Sergio backed the idea of ramping up the pressure on GM and constantly was adamantly insisting in the press and in public statements that the put option had value.

"Part of the strategy was to have Sergio make a big nuisance of himself," said a person who took part in the meeting.

Privately, there was some concern that the put might not be enforced in a U.S. court. Prior to Marchionne's arrival, Fiat's management had lacked confidence that the company could withstand the strain of a long-drawn-out lawsuit in the United States. There was also some concern within Fiat's top ranks about whether a U.S. court would uphold a position that would hurt one of the country's biggest corporations.

Marchionne and his advisers were a bit more confident of their prospects. But they had some lingering concerns about whether the contract signed in 2000 was completely bulletproof. It would be better to avoid the courtroom if possible.

Marchionne, an external legal counsel, and Altavilla went through GM's corporate calendar for the next few months so that Fiat could send GM's executives a letter beforehand describing why it was so important for GM to remove this sword of Damocles hanging over its head sooner rather than later. That way, if GM executives were asked, they could no longer be dismissive of the put and say, "No one has asked us about that"; they would have to say, "No, we just got a letter, and we are still in talks about it."

At the strategy sessions, Marchionne and his advisers also considered the option of telling GM that it would exercise the right to unload Fiat Auto and all its woes on GM. Both Sergio and John Elkann, who participated in some of the sessions, were fairly unemotional about the prospect of triggering the sale, even though it was a political taboo in Italy.

GM was clearly wagering that Fiat wouldn't have the courage to hand over Fiat Auto, an Italian icon, to Detroit. Marchionne, the expert poker player, was clearly willing to call GM's bluff. Fiat's board, including John Elkann, gave him their backing. To support the scenario of the potential damage to GM to get stuck with Fiat Auto, Fiat started to tell GM and its financial advisers that Fiat's long-term liabilities could exceed assets by $20 billion.

"I think that was somewhat persuasive to them," said a person at the strategy session.

Fiat already had all the papers ready it needed to sue GM. The standstill agreement calling a time-out between the two companies expired on December 15 and was not extended, forcing the executives at the two companies into a round of one-on-one talks to reach an amicable agreement that would enable them to stay out of court. Time was running out to reach a deal, since Fiat could force GM to buy Fiat Auto anytime after January 24. GM had enough problems in Europe; Wagoner had already announced 12,000 staff cuts there. That loud ticking sound as the days passed toward the January deadline with Fiat was not a clock. It was a time bomb.

The stakes were high for Fiat as well. If it didn't reach a deal with GM and ended up in court, Fiat's operations would pretty much grind to a halt, seriously paralyzing the greatly weakened company.

At a board meeting on December 23, the board was fully supportive of Sergio's determination to keep pushing GM and to litigate if necessary.

The January deadline came and went, and the two sides were locked into a stalemate. The talks had boiled down to a brutally simple game of poker: Wagoner was betting that Marchionne and the Agnelli family wouldn't have the courage to face down the wrath of Italian public opinion if they forced GM to take Fiat Auto. Marchionne maintained that they did have the courage, and he was betting that Wagoner wouldn't have the guts to see if his position was nothing more than just an expert card player's bluff.

For Marchionne, it was a matter of survival. He had been at Fiat for six months at that point, and had a clearer idea of whether he could stop the losses that were slowly bleeding Fiat dry. He simply couldn't hang on to Fiat without being compensated for it. His asking price was $2 billion.

■ ■ ■

Finally, Marchionne, Altavilla, Wagoner, John Devine, GM's chief financial officer, and others gathered at New York law firm Sullivan & Cromwell's conference center in midtown Manhattan over Valentine's Day weekend in 2005 to put an end to their misery. On Saturday night, as the talks turned to details surrounding the price GM would pay Fiat for half of Fiat's diesel engine plant in Poland, Rick Wagoner made a special request. Duke University's Blue Devils were playing Maryland's Terrapins, and their white-hot games were gripping to their fans. Wagoner had graduated from Duke in 1975, and had been elected to its board of trustees in 2001. He urgently needed a television hooked up so he could watch his college team play ball.

"That's part of why it was all so surreal," recalled a person at the meeting. "There were some fairly tense talks going on, he was tearing up a part of his legacy, paying two billion dollars, and his main concern seemed to be about watching a college basketball game."

Marchionne had been right. The GM people would rather pay than risk to find out whether Marchionne was bluffing. Even people inside the company closest to Marchionne didn't see his hand.

Word started to leak out in Italy early Sunday morning that Marchionne had managed to pry a settlement out of GM for what might have been an Italian icon but was still a money-loser. Fiat's board approved the settlement on Sunday. Marchionne, Altavilla, and the rest of his small group celebrated by sharing a bottle of champagne on the ride on the CNH plane back from New York to Turin. They were exhausted, and the plane was cramped. After the pleasant fizzy sensation faded, Marchionne had a sobering thought. In the back of his mind, he always had an irrational belief that he could have dumped Fiat Auto into GM's unwilling hands had push come to shove, had things really gone badly. Now that camel that he had bargained so hard to buy in the souk was his.

"Now I own the camel," he thought. "It's not a great camel. And it's not getting any better while I sit here on this plane."

# Chapter 12

# A Completely Different Beast

On April 8, 2005, Fiat released a statement saying it was delaying its annual shareholders' meeting, which had been scheduled for May 10. The announcement was a misstep that had unintended consequences. Oddly, it gave no reason for the delay, nor did it set a new date. Fiat had made a lot of progress so far that year. Marchionne had pried $2 billion from General Motors. Analysts expected Fiat to turn a profit in 2005. To investors, the situation had looked reasonably under control.

Until now.

The delay announcement touched off a slide in the company's stock, which slipped 20 percent to 4.20 euros by April 20. Marchionne and a handful of Fiat managers bought Fiat stock as it fell, demonstrating they thought the shares were undervalued and they believed in the turnaround.[1]

The reason for Fiat's postponement of the shareholders' meeting was that Marchionne needed more time to negotiate an extension of the three billion euro bank loan that was coming due April 25. Fiat could not repay the loan, which it had taken out with eight banks, led by IntesaBCI, Banca di Roma, SanPaolo IMI, and UniCredito Italiano in 2002. Italy's four biggest banks held 69.9 percent of the loan. Four more banks—Banca Nazionale del Lavoro, Banca Monte dei Paschi, BNP Paribas, and ABN Amro—held the rest. On September 20, the eight creditor banks would convert their portions of the loan to equity, giving them a total of 26 percent in Fiat and diluting the Agnelli family's IFIL ownership from 30 percent to about 23 percent. IFIL had an option to buy shares in the capital increase that would cover the loan. But it would be expensive for IFIL to do so. The topic was a subject of debate in the family and of concern at IFIL. Fiat was showing signs of recovery, but it was not out of the woods yet.

Marchionne's plan to extend the life of the loan was called Project Moses. The idea was to convert the loan to equity as planned, and then re-create another debt instrument that would tide Fiat over a few more years until it could pay the banks off. But the banks were not interested. It made more sense for them to convert the loan, hold the shares, and gain voting rights on the stock. Each bank was free to decide to either keep the shares or sell them. At the current market price, they would be selling them at a loss. Around that same time, the banks told Marchionne they did not intend to renew a one billion euro backup credit line that was expiring in July. Why should they? Fiat's creditor banks wanted to have a clearer view of the fate of their loan before they went ahead with renewing the credit line.

"It was a way of putting pressure on the family to put more money into the company," said a person involved in the talks.

Fiat didn't need the one billion euro credit line, but if it didn't have one, the ratings agencies would be worried. Fiat was under pressure, and didn't have a lot of wiggle room. By mid-July, Fiat's finance staff with the help of Marchionne had found a group of 11 international banks and five Italian ones that had agreed to a three-year revolving credit facility.[2]

■ ■ ■

Gianluigi Gabetti got a phone call one Saturday in late April from Angelo Benessia, a Turin lawyer who sat on Fiat's board, that sent waves of panic rolling through Fiat for the next several days. For the second time in two years, Fiat had attracted the unwanted attention of vulture investors. But this time around, Gianni and Umberto were both gone. It fell to Gabetti, again to pick up the ball.

Gabetti and Benessia, who had close links with Turin bank SanPaolo IMI, one of Fiat's main creditors, exchanged pleasantries.

"I would like to tell you about an alternative to a direct investment by Fiat's creditor banks that could be of great interest," he said.

Benessia began to read Gabetti a letter sent to the CEOs of four banks that would soon be holding the largest stake in Fiat. It was an offer to buy the banks' stakes in Fiat at a price that was as much as 25 percent more than its current market value. It was signed by Ruggero Magnoni, a banker who was chairman of Lehman Brothers International Italy at the time. The offer wasn't exactly generous, but it certainly was clever. The shares were at an all-time low. The banks were already losing money on the loan, since the three billion euro loan that would be converted in September into a stake in Fiat was valued at a share price much higher than the four to five euros that the shares had been hovering at for most of the month. So the offer, for the banks, could be tempting.

Nor was the timing a coincidence. In just a few days, Fiat and the banks would announce their plans to convert the three billion euro loan into Fiat equity in September 2005.

The letter, Benessia continued, was a friendly offer from a group of "Italian and foreign private equity funds, Italian families with industrial interests, and institutional investors," represented by Lehman Brothers.[3]

"Lehman would also consider taking part in the investment," the letter said.

The new investors and IFIL would have 50 percent of Fiat, according to this plan, and "would have a strong managerial interest in Fiat as part of the agreement with IFIL."

That last phrase made Gabetti's ice-blue eyes narrow. The turn-around was on track, the management team believed. And so did Gabetti. The last thing he wanted was for a bunch of new people to come in and start tinkering around with Sergio's turnaround plan or, worse still, come in and break Fiat up and sell it off in pieces. Maserati. Ferrari. Iveco. It was unthinkable not only for himself, but for the city of Turin. For Italy. Fiat had survived terrorism, bombings, strikes, and the ups and downs of the car industry. The family was not going to roll over and let Fiat be taken over by a bunch of opportunists. Gabetti was certain of that. This was one of those moments where one had to go above and beyond the mere call of duty.[4]

Gianni, on his deathbed, asked his brother Umberto to become chairman because he figured Umberto would have a better chance of keeping Fiat in the family's hands. Now they were both gone. Last August Gabetti, who had never wanted to be in the limelight, had turned 80. But it was time to pull on the boxing gloves and enter the ring. He hung up the phone upset,[5] and started making calls. Who could be behind this, he wondered, suspecting it was Carlo De Benedetti, the former owner of Olivetti. (Much later, De Benedetti called him and said he was not involved.) Whoever it was, they "were ready to put the cake in the oven and bake it," Gabetti recalled later.[6] The timing was, to say the least, impeccable.

It might be difficult to track people down because of the holiday, but no matter. Marchionne and chief financial officer Luigi Gubitosi, who was out of town, were soon alerted and called to Turin for an urgent meeting. They briefly considered asking for a Fiat board meeting to examine the letter.

The Lehman letter created a sense of panic among Fiat's top management that day. Fiat was clearly facing intense pressure for a breakup. Now, as it started to show signs of life, the family's control of the company—and therefore its backing of Marchionne and his plan—was even more at risk than when Fiat was hovering near death's door. That greyhound in the painting in IFIL's boardroom couldn't afford to stumble now.

Back in February, John Elkann had asked Gabetti to look at ways to bring the family's ownership back up to 30 percent. No decision had been made, but the idea remained a topic of debate within the family. After all, it was far from clear that Fiat was out of the woods. Did it make sense to pour even more money into it? Some members of the family were skeptical. In December, Gabetti's right-hand man, Virgilio Marrone, had written Gabetti a note to say that the limited partnership would have to spend between 351 million euros and 497 million euros to bring IFIL's stake in Fiat back up to 30 percent.[7] The partnership had about 510 million euros.

Both Gabetti and Daniel Winteler, the IFIL CEO, were not so keen about it.[8] Perhaps IFIL should invest its money in other areas, the thought was at the time. But that was before Fiat's ridiculously cheap share price had attracted unwanted overtures from mysterious buyers angling for management control. And before Fiat's financial department was forced to go scrambling around to renew a credit line because its main creditors dragged their feet on deciding to renew it pending their other financing arrangements with the company. The banks said they didn't want any management say at Fiat. But could they be trusted? What if they started to throw their weight around? The family was under siege on several fronts. Sometime during the month of April, Gabetti had a change of heart about spending the money.[9]

■ ■ ■

On April 25, in Milan, Marchionne and Montezemolo met with the top management of Fiat's largest creditor banks: Corrado Passera of Banca Intesa (formerly IntesaBCI), Matteo Arpe of Capitalia (formerly Banca di Roma), Alfonso Iozzo of SanPaolo IMI, and Alessandro Profumo of UniCredito Italiano.

The meeting had been hastily shifted from Lazard's quarters in Milan's financial district, where hordes of journalists were camped out in front of the building, to an advertising sales office owned by La Stampa newspaper in a distinguished rust-colored palazzo opposite one of Christianity's oldest churches, the triangle-topped, red brick Basilica of Saint Ambrose.[10]

Marchionne kicked off the meeting by outlining Fiat's targets for 2007 and confirming that the company was on track to meet them.

After the meeting, Fiat made a statement telling the world what Marchionne had said all along: that the banks would convert the loan. Fiat could not repay the three billion euros it had borrowed in 2002, and on September 20, its creditor banks would convert their portions of the loan to equity.

"The Agnellis Step Down; The Scepter Passes to the Banks," wrote ANSA newswire that evening, after Fiat's statement. Italian newspapers next day put the story on the front page, some spinning the Agnelli angle harder than others. "Fiat Belongs to the Banks," blared *Finanza e Mercati*. "Banks Stand Alongside Fiat," wrote the *Corriere*, which is partly owned by the automotive company. "The majority of Fiat passes to the banks," said *Il Giornale*.

It had been almost a year since Umberto Agnelli died, leaving Fiat without an Agnelli at the helm for the first time since the end of World War II. To outsiders, it looked like the family had just been shoved aside by its creditors. Amazingly, its 2005 numbers were improving, and its financial debt would fall to six billion euros at the end of the year with the conversion of the bank loans. Gabetti voiced his confidence in Fiat in a newspaper interview a few days later, brushing aside suggestions that the family was in any way taking a backseat.

"We are determined to maintain the role of controlling shareholder of Fiat in the future," he told *Corriere della Sera*. "We will continue to act as controlling shareholders, and will try to deserve it."[11] He declined, however, to provide any details about how he would achieve that aim. His only reply was a cryptic one, spoken in English in the Italian-language interview.

Probably he didn't even fully know himself how he would pull it off.

"Only the future will tell what is needed," he said. And he denied that the group was looking at ways to raise IFIL's stake in Fiat—which, technically, was true.

Few people at that moment were willing to follow in Marchionne's footsteps and risk money on buying Fiat's stock. Gianluigi Gabetti was one exception. On April 25, he decided to bet half a billion euros that Fiat's stock would rally.

■ ■ ■

Since the end of January, two bankers at Merrill Lynch International (MLI) in Milan—Maurizio Tamagnini, managing director of investment banking at Merrill Lynch International, and Enrico Chiapparoli, director of investment banking—had been kicking around ideas about IFIL's upcoming dilution in Fiat. Fiat was a Merrill client. One of the ideas was an equity swap. Merrill Lynch could buy, say, 90 million shares on the open market—which would cost between 550 million and 600 million euros—hold them for a set period, and then sell them to IFIL. Virgilio Marrone, who had worked with Gabetti since 1971 and was CEO of IFI, which controls IFIL, had been keeping his eye on the stock price for months, in order to calculate how much it would cost IFIL in September to increase its stake back up to 30 percent so the family wouldn't lose control.[12]

As Fiat shares fell throughout April, Chiapparoli and Tamagnini saw an opportunity and asked for a meeting with Marrone at the bank's offices on Via dei Giardini in Milan. At the meeting, the bankers observed that Fiat's stock price did not reflect the group's prospects, in their view. Marrone agreed. Chiapparoli laid out the equity swap, pointing out how much it made sense in terms of price. Fiat and Merrill Lynch had already completed an equity swap together on General Motors shares in 2002, and Marrone was therefore familiar with how it worked.

Marrone consulted Gabetti about the swap. They both realized the deal was not right for IFIL, which took only long-term investments. But it could work for Exor, a nonlisted offshore financial holding company that was part of the Agnelli family holdings. Gabetti agreed it looked good, and told Marrone to pitch it to Exor CEO Ruy Brandolini. Brandolini was the son of the youngest of *il Senatore*'s four grand-daughters, Cristiana, and Count Brando Brandolini d'Adda, who handled the family's and the group's foreign investments.

Gabetti wagered that if speculators were starting to become attracted to Fiat because of its low share price, he could become a speculator, too. Gabetti believed Marchionne would make it. In a few weeks, Fiat was going to launch the Grande Punto, which would likely be a top seller. And if Marchionne didn't make it . . . well, the stock couldn't fall much lower than where it was right now.

On the morning of April 25, Marrone and Brandolini met at IFIL's offices on Corso Matteotti with three bankers from Merrill Lynch: Chiapparoli, Mike Hammond (head of Equity-Linked Capital Markets in London), and Glenn Fairbairn (a London-based derivatives team member who worked for Hammond). John Elkann stopped in to say hello and then left.

Hammond brought along a standard term sheet, and the men sat around the table and started filling in the possible conditions for an equity swap deal. Brandolini said that Exor was willing to spend its entire cash pile of about 500 million euros, buying 90 million shares, and to risk up to 50 million euros if the shares fell below their current price. The Exor executives asked that the purchase price not be above six euros per share.

Brandolini figured it was a good investment for Exor. After all, the stock couldn't go much lower. And hadn't Marchionne and all of his management team just demonstrated that they thought the same thing?[13]

"We would like this agreement to remain between us," Marrone said, pointing out that there was no obligation to disclose it by law in any case. "And please make sure you don't exceed daily average trading volumes when you buy up the stock."

Italian stock market rules called for a buyer to inform the market when it bought more than a 2 percent stake. But Merrill, like any other buyer, would be able to get around that rule by breaking up the Fiat stakes it would be purchasing and swapping them out with other counterparties.[14]

Marrone didn't want the market to catch on that Merrill Lynch was buying, lest it set off a speculative frenzy about a takeover bid.[15] That would do nothing but increase the stock price.

The Merrill bankers suggested wrapping up the trade on June 30, 2006, but the Exor executives asked Merrill to make the contract close at the end of December 2006.[16]

The term sheet called for the contract to be unwound with a cash settlement; in other words, Exor would not end up owning the actual Fiat stock. That meant it did not need to disclose the contract to the market, according to Italian stock market rules. It also gave Exor the right to ask for a physical delivery of shares instead of cash, if it wanted. In that case, if both parties agreed, Exor would end up holding a chunk of Fiat stock that it bought for no more than six euros per share.[17] That possibility was not discussed at the meeting.[18]

At the end of the meeting, Gabetti—who had since arrived just in time to sign—and Brandolini signed a preliminary term sheet on behalf of Exor, and Hammond signed for Merrill Lynch.

Merrill Lynch started buying the stock on April 26. In memos to Exor outlining its share purchases, the agreement was given the code name of "Distacom."

■ ■ ■

In mid-July, Fiat's shares started rallying, just as Gabetti and his advisers had hoped they would. Instead of being glad, though, Gabetti was worried.[19]

Marchionne had given a very, very bullish presentation to a group of fund managers at Milan investment bank Mediobanca on July 8, and Fiat's signs of recovery might be attracting a stake builder, Gabetti fretted. In September, the family's stake would fall to 22 percent from 30 percent. The 30 percent threshold was important. It meant that if another investor wanted to get control of the company, it had to buy more than 30 percent, therefore triggering an expensive bid for all of Fiat's stock. But if the family had just 22 percent, a bidder could outflank the family with a larger stake just under the 30 percent threshold, without having to buy up the whole company. It would be much cheaper for the predator.

Gabetti turned to Grande Stevens for help. The lawyer started to look at ways for IFIL to buy up the shares from Merrill Lynch instead of Exor buying them, as planned, and discussed ways to do this at a meeting in his office July 15 with Fairbairn and Chiapparoli from Merrill Lynch.

Grande Stevens, the dean of Italy's corporate lawyers, had started as Gianni Agnelli's counsel in the early 1960s. His legal expertise had served the family well ever since. In 1987 he created Giovanni Agnelli & C., the limited partnership that through the years had provided a forum for family decision making while leaving control in Gianni's hands. Unlike Gabetti and most of the Agnelli's inner circle, the dark-eyed Grande Stevens was from the south. One of his ancestors had been a British vice-consul in Gallipoli at the end of the 1800s, and a relative, Colonel

Harold Stevens, had read messages in code for Radio London during the war.

His legal expertise would serve the family well again now. At the July 15 meeting, Grande Stevens realized that the best way to proceed was to modify the equity swap contract from a "cash delivery" to a "physical delivery of shares." The key issue, at that point, was to come to an agreement with Merrill on terms, as well as with Consob, Italy's stock market regulator, on whether the changes would result in IFIL having to bid for all of Fiat's stock. The deal must also have the blessing of the family, Grande Stevens decided at that meeting, although the family could not be informed until the last minute to avoid leaks.

Fiat's market value at the end of June had been 4.7 billion euros. But with the shares now rallying, its market value was rising fast.

On August 12, Grande Stevens sent a draft of a letter to Consob asking for an opinion on whether the Agnelli group would need to bid for all of Fiat should it bring its stake back up to 30 percent after the banks converted their loan to equity on September 20. Grande Stevens had been meeting with officials at the market watchdog off and on since July 21 about his request for an opinion. Oddly, Consob officials never questioned Grande Stevens in depth about how IFIL planned to acquire the Fiat shares necessary to take its stake back up to 30 percent after the conversion of the bank loan to equity. And Grande Stevens, for his part, had so far never mentioned the existence of the equity swap between Exor and Merrill.

At this point, Merrill Lynch and Grande Stevens were already working on the draft version of what would eventually become the final equity swap contract giving IFIL the right to buy the shares held secretly by Exor. On August 24, in response to a disclosure request from Consob, IFIL issued a statement denying that it was looking at any plans in relation to the convertible loan, stating that it had no information regarding a reason for Fiat's share price rally, and reiterating its intention to remain Fiat's chief shareholder.

"IFIL will make any decisions regarding that matter at the most opportune moment," the company said in its August 24 press release.

When Claudio Salini, Consob's Markets Division chief, read the statement, he picked up the phone and called Grande Stevens.

"This looks a bit minimalist compared to what we expected, in light of some of our discussions during our meetings," he said.[20]

Grande Stevens replied that his involvement in drawing up the plan was "purely professional," referring to his role as the Agnelli family lawyer and ignoring the fact he was also on the IFIL board. IFIL CEO Daniel Winteler had not yet been informed of the plan. Clearly, Grande Stevens expected Salini to take his word that he had not discussed the plan with any of his other fellow IFIL board members—including Gabetti, who was IFIL chairman—and was simply acting as a family lawyer.

On September 15, at 10:30 P.M. local time, IFIL sent out a statement saying it maintained a 30.6 percent stake in Fiat. IFIL bought 82,250,000 Fiat shares from Exor at 6.50 euros each, for a total of 534.6 million euros. Exor, in turn, had bought them from MLI at 5.60 euros each. Exor, therefore, made a profit of 74 million euros on the transaction.

Earlier that day, Fiat said its board approved the capital increase at 10.28 euros per share, or the average of the agreed-on price of 14.4409 euros and the weighted average of official prices over the prior six months. As a result of the conversion, Fiat reduced its net debt by three billion euros.

The deal was a coup for IFIL, since it was able to scoop up Fiat shares at 6.50 euros each that cost the banks 10.28 euros. But it outraged just about everyone else, from investors to Consob itself, which began an investigation almost immediately.

Despite Consob's request—twice—to inform the market about why Fiat's shares were rising, IFIL had issued two statements saying it had no information about the matter.

Gabetti had to field angry questions from investors the next day on a conference call.

Traders "rolled their eyes at what many perceived as a clever but cynically orchestrated power play," reported Dow Jones Newswires.

Press commentators were outraged at what they saw as a blatant disregard for market communication.

"It is conceivable that the swap was no more than an informed bet," wrote *The Economist* afterward. "However, it is more plausible to see it as essential planning for the conversion of the loan in September, and the swap's original cash-settlement terms as an ingenious plan to avoid informing the market."[21]

Asked why he did not inform the market at the end of August about the draft contract dated July 29 that gave IFIL the right to take ownership of the 10 percent Fiat stake, Grande Stevens said the final decision hadn't been made at that point.

"It was only one of the things that I had been looking at, and we could have decided not to finalize it had Consob not exempted us from making a full takeover bid," Grande Stevens told *La Repubblica* newspaper.

Gabetti had asked Grande Stevens to look into ways to change the contract from a cash settlement to a physical delivery in mid-July. But the final decision had not been made until September.

So technically speaking, Grande Stevens's statement is correct, since IFIL had not yet decided to sign the equity swap contract giving it the right to take physical delivery of the shares at the time when the official statements had been made.

Consob started an investigation that fall, and on February 13, 2007, announced it was fining Gabetti, Grande Stevens, and Virgilio Marrone, plus IFIL and Giovanni Agnelli & C., a total of 16 million euros, its largest fine ever.[22] Consob also suspended the three from their posts for a period of six, four, and two months, respectively.

But their problems were by no means over. Gabetti and Grande Stevens were ordered to stand trial in Turin for market rigging on September 18, 2007. The trial would start in the autumn of 2008. Both men reacted in public with nothing less than good sportsmanship.

"If I had to go back in time, I would do it all over again, because otherwise we would have lost Fiat and with it thousands of jobs, which would have had serious consequences for Turin and for the nation," Grande Stevens said a month after the trial started.[23]

Gabetti was less effusive.

"It was an on-the-job accident, and that's how I am dealing with it," he said in November.[24]

■ ■ ■

In the summer of 2007, as Gabetti and Grande Stevens resigned themselves to enduring days and days in court in a few months' time, Turin was gearing up for a massive celebration.

On July 4, 2007, Fiat launched its new Fiat 500. When the original version of the minicar was launched 50 years before on July 4, 1957, a river of 500s streamed in a sort of military parade out of the Fiat factory gates, bearing a bevy of big-hatted beauty pageant contestants waving at passersby from their perches in the cars' canvas convertible tops down the Via Roma. When they reached their destination in Piazza San Carlo in downtown Turin, the tiny cars were inspected by a curious and delighted public. Marchionne and his team wanted to do something similar, something that everyone in Turin could be a part of.[25]

The 500 has a special place in the heart of almost every Italian. For many people in their 50s, it was probably the family's first-ever car. Even if it wasn't, it is connected in the national collective consciousness to Italy's economic boom in the 1950s, when the country went from an agricultural nation devastated by a war very few people wanted, to becoming one of the world's leading industrialized economies. More to the point, people who a generation ago were scratching out a living on the land could now enjoy the small luxuries of a consumer society.

"The year 1957 was the birth of the 500, and also the year when the quiz show 'Lascia o Raddoppia' took off," wrote *Corriere della Sera*'s television critic Aldo Grasso the day after the 2007 launch. "In 1957 therefore the miracle of Italian unification took place: families who owned a television set held court, bars are crammed with people, movie theaters are cannibalized by television, and streets are deserted, and televisions across the land are tuned in to new adventures in knowledge and of the road."[26]

Italy is a not a country given over to self-celebration. Most Italians are quicker to point out the shameful moments in their nation's history—such as Mussolini's 20-year dictatorship or Berlusconi's trial for allegedly having sex with an underage woman—rather than listing the many contributions Italians have made to art, culture, and the sciences through the centuries.

But July 4, 2007, was different. The celebrations started that morning, with games for children in the public squares. Some 7,000 people, half of them Fiat distributors, descended on Turin from 63 countries. Guests could browse an open-air market with knickknacks from the 1950s, have a toast with the 500 in Piazza San Carlo, or eat a car-themed meal at one of the five "slow food" *trattorie* scattered around the city.

At 5:00 P.M., Italian Prime Minister Romano Prodi touched down at the helipad on the roof of the Lingotto for a private viewing of the new car. Sergio Marchionne, John Elkann, and Luca di Montezemolo were on hand in the Renzo Piano–designed glass bubble near the helipad to welcome him. Gabetti, as usual, was not far away. Prodi sat behind the wheel, and also wanted to sit in the backseat with John, who is a head taller than Prodi.[27]

"Let's remember what people said about Fiat a few years back, and think of how different it is today," the Prime Minister told the scrum of press huddling around him, mashed against his bodyguards. "This is of enormous importance for Italy. And I am not saying this for free advertising, but out of a sense of gladness. This car had a huge symbolic value, which is to update a very original tradition."[28]

Labor Minister Cesare Damiani recounted how his first car had been a used Fiat 500, and he had driven it from Turin to Budapest and Vienna, and then back.

"It was a wonderful vacation," he said.[29]

Later that day, Fiat invited 90 people for dinner in the square in front of Palazzo Carignano, one of the birthplaces of modern Italy, and in front of Il Cambio, the restaurant where Count Cavour, the architect of Italian political union, used to eat. When John and Lavinia arrived in their blue Maserati at 8:00 P.M., the atmosphere had turned carnival-like. The handsome young couple—Lavinia was pregnant—were applauded by the crowd, and someone yelled out, "John, the 500 is spectacular!"[30] Marchionne, in his black sweater, and Luca di Montezemolo were also welcomed with applause from the crowd. Italy's business leaders and a handful of government ministers soon joined them, dining on risotto with saffron (with 500 saffron flowers) and the Turin classic, *vitello tonnato*. Each guest went away with a computer mouse in the shape of a 500.

The group made its way over to the banks of the Po River, which had been transformed into an open-air theater by Marco Bialich, the mastermind behind the closing ceremony of the Turin Winter Olympics in 2006. Some 12,000 people crammed into the stands to watch Lauryn Hill sing and a 500 swoop down from the sky. Gianni Agnelli's face appeared on a screen, talking about the 500. More applause. A Fellini-esque stage show featured a traffic cop, a Marilyn Monroe, a banquet, and a gangster in a sort of cheerful, surreal pastiche of Italian characters. For the grand finale, as fireworks lit up the sky, 40 new Fiat 500s drove around the city of Turin.[31] The event was broadcast live on Canale 5, Silvio Berlsconi's flagship television network.

After the fireworks were over, Marchionne and Fiat brand chief Luca de Meo decided to stroll back from the riverbank through the center of town for a last espresso. The people they passed in the street were applauding Marchionne like a rock star, de Meo recalled.[32]

Marchionne, with his trademark sweater, had now become recognizable in the same way as Gianni Agnelli, but with a completely different style. The last time he had worn a suit to an important event was in October 2006, when he was named a *Cavaliere del Lavoro* by Italy's president. A month later, he wore a sweater to a press conference, and had felt so comfortable that he decided to just wear one all the time.

Gabetti, with characteristic insight, said the show "combined the intelligence of the past with that of the present."[33] He was right. The Fiat 500 itself was designed to be a present-day interpretation of a certain moment in history, when a war-weary country ashamed of its political past finally embraced the future with optimism.

What was not obvious amid the fireworks and applause that night was that at some moment after Gianni Agnelli's death, Fiat had shed its skin and had become a completely different beast so that it could live on in a different form. Fiat's old motto was "Land, sky, and sea." In other words, be everywhere. Its new motto could be summed up as "Be fast, be focused, and be best." It was no longer a conglomerate, and was now just a moneymaking car company. Gone was the huge tentacled creature that had inhabited every corner of Italy's economy. Gone were companies like jet-engine maker Fiat Avio, insurer Toro Assicurazioni, department store chain la Rinascente, and many other things besides. Gone were the trips to Rome to demand or cajole or wring this or that concession or favor from the government. Gone, last but not least, was Fiat as a sort of royal court at the service of the king, Gianni. Most Italians would not have recognized Gabetti if he passed them by on the street. Yet the 83-year-old man had just successfully steered one of Italy's biggest companies through the shoals, even if he had to use methods that had made him run afoul of Italy's market regulator.

After Gianni Agnelli died, the Agnelli family had risked losing control of Fiat for the fourth time, at many different moments. Perhaps Giuseppe Morchio could have grabbed the reins away from the family. Perhaps the company's creditor banks could have taken control of Fiat, broken it up, and sold it. Or the government could have nationalized Fiat Auto. And certainly predators had been circling Fiat. Thanks largely to Gabetti's temporary leadership of the family, those potential threats never materialized.

Marchionne thanked him publicly in a speech to Fiat management three years later.

"If Fiat had the freedom to reinvent itself, we owe it to Gianluigi Gabetti's efforts to keep the role of the main shareholder in place," he said. "With his ability and courage, he gave the company the stability it needed to carry out our project and keep our promises."

Gianluigi had done his job very well. It was up to John and Sergio now to do the rest.

# Part III

# THE POWER OF
# A GOVERNMENT

# Chapter 13

# Skin in the Game

L ate in the morning on Thanksgiving Day 2008, Andrew Horrocks, a banker at UBS, was standing in his kitchen with oven mitts on his hands when he got a call from Europe, from his colleague at the Swiss investment bank. The deal between Fiat and Chrysler, which he and a few others had been working on since March, was "going live." They needed to switch into high gear. A conference call with Marchionne and his team was scheduled in an hour's time. For Andrew and his colleagues, the rest of the holiday weekend was punctuated by long-distance phone calls with Sergio Marchionne and Alfredo Altavilla, Fiat's chief deal maker, in Turin.

The U.S. auto industry was imploding. The credit crunch had dried up demand for new cars, leaving the automakers burning cash. Detroit's Big Three had traveled to Washington, D.C., earlier that month seeking emergency government aid, but they failed to make a convincing case. Instead, their testimony exposed them to criticism about Detroit's management failures and inability to compete in the marketplace.

Chrysler and General Motors were facing bankruptcy. In Washington, D.C., a top adviser to President-elect Barack Obama was already working by Thanksgiving on a policy memo saying that automakers would not make it without restructuring. But in order to survive until spring of next year, when the new administration would be up and running, Chrysler needed to demonstrate it had long-term viability in order to tap a loan that would be approved by President Bush during his final days before he left office. It was no secret that Chrysler needed an ally to help it share the investment needed to make it internationally competitive and give it the right vehicle mix. In other words, to survive, it needed a partner. And it needed one right now.

Fiat was its only prospect. And Fiat's plan was a naked reflection of harsh economic reality: in exchange for its engines, technology, and management expertise, it was angling for a stake in Chrysler—for free. Fiat had already batted around a few ideas with Chrysler's owner at that point, and with a top executive, Tom LaSorda.

"This is going to be intense," Alfredo Altavilla, Fiat's senior vice president in charge of business development, told Horrocks and the other bankers on the team on a conference call later that weekend.

Some of the bankers were doubtful it would ever work. Altavilla brushed them off.

"We're gonna *do* this deal. It *will work*," he said. "I've done cashless deals before."

Altavilla should know. His boy-next-door face hid a tenacious personality. Since 2005, when Fiat's alliance with General Motors had been dissolved, the jovial southern Italian had criss-crossed the globe as a sort of one-man mergers and acquisitions (M&A) band. Instead of looking for another big partnership, Marchionne told Altavilla to go out and strike selected deals to enter new markets or gain access to products that Fiat was lacking. Since Fiat had no money, it offered its own technology. Altavilla, a Fiat lifer whose father had run a Fiat dealership, had many doors slammed in his face during those years. However, he had done 24 deals in 24 months. He knew that Fiat had some damned good engines. Among his coups were a deal to supply diesel engines to Mercedes, and then a deal with Ford to share a platform for small cars.

The deal Marchionne had told Altavilla and his banking team to deliver was tricky, to say the least. It was one thing to offer to swap engine technology or share the insides of a car for free. It was another thing to ask for an entire car company.

Fiat was already in talks with Cerberus Capital Management, the private equity fund named after Greek mythology's three-headed canine guardian of Hell. Cerberus had bought the floundering Chrysler in May 2007 from Daimler AG for $7.4 billion, as the German carmaker scrambled to unload Chrysler in a hasty exit from its grand experiment in a global auto tie-up.

The three-headed dog's six eyes had seen that the credit bubble was popping, and the firm's management thought they could ride it out.[1] The timing of the Chrysler deal was horrendous. In June 2007, Bear Stearns was forced to bail out two of its hedge funds that had invested in collateralized debt obligations (CDOs), the first step in what later became the first big casualty of the financial crisis. The Cerberus deal left banks JPMorgan Chase, Goldman Sachs, and Citigroup sitting on $10 billion in debt.[2] Chrysler, too, became a casualty, as Cerberus slashed investment and started firing people. The company began to wither. The pipeline of new cars trickled to a halt.

By the time Fiat entered the scene in late 2008, Cerberus's equity value in Chrysler had already been wiped out. By the end of the year, Cerberus balked at putting any more money into Chrysler.[3] The company was staring into the abyss.

■ ■ ■

The phone call that derailed Andrew Horrocks's Thanksgiving Day came just over a week after the Big Three had gone to Congress in private jets to ask for bailout money, and just a few days after a decision made by out-going Treasury Secretary Hank Paulson to get more TARP money.

For the past several months, Paulson had been fighting to stabilize the financial system with a $700 billion fund called the Troubled Asset Relief Program (TARP). Congress had appropriated half of the money, and the Treasury was shoveling cash into Wall Street's crippled banks as fast as it could manage. Paulson was worried that if a few more financial giants failed, the Treasury would be unable to stave off a total, Great Depression style economic collapse, complete with bread lines, runs on the banks, political upheaval, and who knew what else.[4]

TARP was already unpopular; President George W. Bush was on his way out of office after the November 4 election had been won by Barack Obama, a little-known black Democratic senator who seemed to come out of nowhere. Winning approval from Congress to appropriate the next $350 billion in TARP funds would be the new president's first headache after he was inaugurated on January 20, only Paulson didn't think it could wait until then.[5]

Two days before Thanksgiving, Paulson called Rahm Emanuel, Obama's chief of staff, with a message that Emanuel was not happy to hear.

"We need to take down the last part of the TARP, and we can only do that with you and we need your help," Paulson said.

Emanuel told Paulson to speak to Larry Summers, who had just been named Obama's top economic adviser. Paulson got Summers on the line. After they had finished discussing TARP, Summers brought up the auto industry, to Paulson's surprise.

"You're not going to let the autos fail, are you?" Summers asked Paulson.[6]

No, Paulson was not. The Treasury secretary's staff had already held conversations with Chrysler executives in mid-October about how much cash the company would need to tide itself over until the presidential inauguration next year.

It was not surprising that the incoming Democrats were much more committed to helping the auto industry than Bush had been. But Bush's administration, too, had come to the conclusion that help should be given only on evidence of a major change in the way Detroit did business. And the Republicans knew that to get the remaining amount of the TARP funding approved by Congress they needed Democrats' votes.

"But they didn't want to help Detroit unless they could attach strings—they wanted the automakers to secure concessions from major stakeholders to ensure their long-term viability," wrote Steven Rattner, who led Obama's Task Force on the Auto Industry.[7]

Bush's advisers were worried that the incoming Democrats would "cave in to special interests," especially the United Auto Workers (UAW) union, according to Rattner. The funds must be made available, in Paulson's view, only if the automakers made the restructuring moves they needed to become competitive again. Anything less and they would remain wards of the state.[8]

The day before Thanksgiving, and a day after Paulson and Summers spoke about TARP, Summers called Steve Rattner, a private equity executive with more than 20 years' experience on Wall Street, just as Rattner was about to leave his office to take one of his sons to a Broadway matinee.

"I'm calling with a hypothetical question," Summers said to Rattner. "If you were asked to take on a six- to twelve-month assignment for the administration, would that be something that could work for you?"[9]

Rattner said yes, and started to put the word out with his contacts in Washington that he would be interested in putting his deal-making and financial expertise at the service of the new president, who would be juggling a housing crisis, a banking bailout, unprecedented fiscal challenges, and a devastated auto industry that was hovering near collapse.

Summers was clearly getting his ducks in a row to fight for and manage another looming cash injection for Detroit. At the end of November, Summers and his deputy, Jason Furman, started working on a 57-page memo on the economy for President-elect Obama ranging from TARP and the economic stimulus package to housing policy, the state of the auto industry, the deficit, regulatory reform, and budget savings.[10] It ended with an 11-page appendix with recommendations for items to be included in the stimulus bill that Obama later proposed in his first weeks in office. On autos, the memo said that the industry was clearly not going to make it and that it possibly needed bankruptcy to pull through.

Obama and his top advisers gathered to discuss the situation on December 16, 2008, in his team's transition headquarters in a snowy Chicago. Obama sat on one side of a square table, along with Vice President–elect Joe Biden, Summers, Emanuel, David Axelrod, Timothy Geithner, Christina Romer, Peter Orszag, Jared Bernstein, and several others.[11]

Summers (and Republican Senator Bob Corker before him) had come to the same conclusion that Fiat's creditor banks had in 2002: some auto companies needed more than just cash to survive, and it was useless to simply throw money down a rat hole. The weaker ones needed to rip up the way they did business and start all over again from a smaller footprint, or else they would be back at square one in a few years' time. The bank or, now, government had the responsibility of finding a way to make an investment that made market sense. By Christmas, an auto task force was already being put together by Obama's advisers.

Chrysler, for its part, kick-started the off-again, on-again talks with Fiat in late November because influential lawmakers and analysts believed Chrysler was not viable without a partner.[12]

When Chrysler's Robert Nardelli returned to Washington, D.C., on December 4 with GM's Rick Wagoner and Ford's Alan Mulally—this time by car rather than corporate jet—the Chrysler plan included a line saying Chrysler was focused on "developing partnerships, strategic alliances, or consolidation" as a way to expand its product portfolio.[13]

"Look, there's not a human being alive in the automobile world that thinks Chrysler is going to do anything other than finding somebody to marry and that this cash is here long enough for you to do that," U.S. Republican Senator Bob Corker told Nardelli at the hearing.[14]

It was still too soon on December 4 to talk publicly about Fiat, but the wheels were already in motion.

Congress dragged its feet, and ultimately rejected giving Chrysler and GM any loans. Instead, it was George Bush who approved a last-minute loan of $17.4 billion to GM and Chrysler on December 19, one of his final acts in office. The idea was to keep the car companies in business until the new government would come up with a long-term plan. In exchange for the cash, Chrysler and GM had until February 17 to come up with a so-called viability plan to return to profitability.

The deal memorandum between Fiat and Chrysler was signed December 29, and it was a key condition for Chrysler to receive its first slice of $4 billion in Treasury cash, which was released over the New Year's holiday.

Bob Nardelli and his staff had to labor mightily to meet that tight deadline and prepare all the necessary documents to receive the $4 billion.

The Loan and Security Agreement between Chrysler and the U.S. government freeing up $4 billion in loans dated December 31 specified that Chrysler had to achieve three conditions: long-term viability, international competitiveness, and energy-efficient vehicles. Fiat had the lowest carbon monoxide (CO) emissions in Europe. More specifically, the financing was granted in exchange for a viability plan that called for compliance to fuel emissions standards, production of advanced technology vehicles, a competitive product mix, and "an achievement of certain milestones."[15] Chrysler's management had admitted publicly that it needed a partner to achieve those things, and had been looking for one for all of 2008.

It wasn't Obama who pushed Chrysler into the arms of Fiat; it was Bush.

The idea that Fiat—a second-tier automaker that specialized in small cars—could not only fix Chrysler's problems but also somehow turn two weak automakers into a global competitor was audacious. And the plan to put a dollars-and-cents value of Fiat's diesel engines and powertrains as the basis for a barter deal and then somehow get a financial animal like Cerberus to sign on the dotted line seemed, well, impossible.

Instead, the three-headed hellhound would spawn a three-headed deal: Chrysler, Cerberus, and the U.S. government.

■ ■ ■

Sergio and Chrysler President and Vice Chairman Tom LaSorda, whose mandate was to find a partner or buyer for Chrysler, first met in Turin on March 12, 2008, when they announced Fiat's purchase of Chrysler's TriTech Motors, a maker of powertrains in Brazil. Signs of a slowdown in U.S. car sales were already starting to show as a destructive mix of high gasoline prices and unemployment caused by the financial crisis took its toll. The economic crisis was already obvious to Fiat's board that spring and would become the dominant topic of board meetings going forward.

Although Marchionne and LaSorda shared an alma mater in Windsor, Canada, where LaSorda was born and raised, their paths had never crossed. LaSorda's roots in the car industry went a lot deeper than Marchionne's. LaSorda was the third of nine children, and his father had been elected president of a UAW local in Windsor the same year that Tom graduated from the University of Windsor and joined General Motors.[16] He joined DaimlerChrysler in 2000, and spent most of his time working for Dieter Zetsche until the latter was promoted to become head of Daimler in 2006. LaSorda briefly replaced him, until Nardelli was tapped by Cerberus as CEO in August 2007.

After pleasantries were exchanged and the contract signed, Tom LaSorda made a suggestion during lunch.

"Why doesn't Fiat give a thought about taking a stake in Chrysler?" he said to Marchionne. They spent the rest of the lunch talking about how Fiat and Chrysler could partner for a small car in the United States.[17] Chrysler had been looking for a partner since the end of 2007, and was already in talks with Nissan-Renault.[18] Altavilla, who attended the lunch, was assigned by Marchionne to do follow-up for Fiat. Marchionne was definitely interested. He had been concerned for some time about Fiat's lack of scale, and wanted a presence in the U.S. market.

By April, talks between Fiat and Chrysler had broadened to include potential teamwork in other products beyond small cars, along with manufacturing and market areas.[19] Cerberus asked Fiat if it wanted to buy Daimler's 20 percent in Chrysler. UBS advised Fiat to wait, noting that the company's debt was already trading at a very low price, reflecting a possible default, and that equity holders would be at the back of the line of creditors in the event of a bankruptcy. By the summer of 2008, the companies had ordered their teams to look at the synergies of a full-blown partnership.

Bob Nardelli flew over to Italy to see Sergio in June to push talks further, meeting in his office at the Lingotto and then staying for lunch in the Fiat dining room.

"I will twist myself into a pretzel to help, but I can't do more than a small car platform," Marchionne told him. The two men had a handshake deal to work on making the 500 in Mexico.

LaSorda and Fiat were convinced that their companies were a good fit. Fiat was skilled at small, fuel-efficient cars, and Chrysler excelled at trucks and minivans. Chrysler would give Fiat access to the U.S. market for its sporty Alfa Romeos and the cuddly little Fiat 500, while Fiat's sales network in Latin America and Europe could be used to move Chrysler's minivans and Jeeps.

■ ■ ■

For Chrysler CEO Bob Nardelli, 2008 was a year in the trenches. Every Monday since he had come to Chrysler, he had been holding "war room" meetings in a conference room on the second floor in the Tech Center. Chrysler CFO Ron Kolka was responsible for selling $1.8 billion worth of assets, and he would usually walk the team through the latest update on where they stood. The wall was full of pieces of paper ripped off pads and stuck up from previous meetings. It was a standup meeting, to keep people focused. The meetings would last an hour or an hour and a half. Nardelli went around the room, calling on people one by one. How are we doing on our dealer development? On quality? On output? How much overtime was Chrysler doing?

The "war room" concept was introduced at business units throughout the company. At Mopar, the parts unit, for example, the standup meetings were run by a Mopar manager, but there was often a Cerberus person on hand looking on. They were useful at going through all the opportunities to grow the business—but only if those opportunities didn't call for investment.

"It was sort of like cutting your way into growth," recalled a former manager.

The idea was to cut costs in order to generate enough cash flow within the company for investment, and reduce the need for Cerberus to put in more cash. On a practical level, however, what employees saw dismayed them.

In March 2008, Cerberus abruptly said it would shut down the company's Carlsbad, California, car design studio, which had been opened by Chrysler in 1983 to tap into the West Coast's more freethinking car culture. The closure of the Pacifica Advance Product Design Studio sent a shudder through Chrysler. The decision looked hasty, and was not preceded by any sort of review of the studio's usefulness. It looked like Cerberus wanted to cash in on some California real estate.

Inside the company, the standup meetings and actions like the hasty disposal of Pacifica fueled speculation that the whole thing was up for sale. Nardelli had been dealt a very bad hand. When Nardelli had been asked by Cerberus in 2007 to run Chrysler, he was an automotive outsider with a reputation for improving the numbers at Home Depot during his seven-year stint as CEO. His alleged $210 million severance package from Home Depot had made him a lightning rod for criticism. A stint at Chrysler would offer him a chance both to redeem himself from having been ejected from the executive suite by Home Depot's board that was dissatisfied with a flat share price and a high-handed management style[20] and to go back to the basics he had learned from a long career at General Electric. Instead, he got hit by the tidal wave of economic misery caused by the credit crunch. As 2008 wore on, Bob Nardelli pored over the data that helped him understand what was shaping up to be the worst crisis in the auto industry since the oil shock of the 1970s.

The financial crisis had caused a speculative spike in fuel prices. U.S. consumers had enjoyed low pump prices for most of the decade, giving Detroit the luxury of being able to stuff showrooms with big, profitable, gas-guzzling trucks and SUVs. The drawback, of course, was that when gasoline prices rose and consumers started to balk at spending $80 to $100 to fill up the tanks of their Ford Explorers or Jeep Grand Cherokees, Detroit's Big Three were not ready with a smart lineup of small cars. And Chrysler—starved for investment under Cerberus— certainly didn't have them. Worse still, consumer credit was drying up, meaning that people could not get financing to buy new cars.

June's dreadful auto sales turned out to be a game changer for Detroit. On July 2, Merrill Lynch analyst John Murphy sent GM's stock plummeting to below $10 per share, its lowest price since 1954, when he released a research report that mentioned the dreaded "b" word—bankruptcy.

"We believe . . . that a bankruptcy is not impossible if the market continues to deteriorate and significant incremental capital is not raised," Murphy wrote.

The *Detroit Free Press* noted wryly that the last time GM's stock had traded below $10, "Dwight Eisenhower was president, power brakes were new and the Bel Air was the automaker's hot new car."[21]

LaSorda and his team contacted almost every major automaker in the world in 2008 about a partnership as that grim spring turned to a horrible summer. At the top of the list was Renault-Nissan, with a partnership that held out a tantalizing $11.8 billion in cash flow synergies, compared to the $3.7 billion later promised by Fiat over eight years.[22] Executives from the two companies held more than a half dozen face-to-face meetings in Auburn Hills, Paris, New York, and Tokyo, as well as weekly conference calls. They went through the entire mating ritual. The Chrysler executives had visited Renault-Nissan's design

center and test-driven their vehicles; Chrysler was going to produce
Nissan trucks and join its purchasing alliance; and a small car to be built
in Japan was in the works. By July, they had gotten as far as a term sheet.

At the same time, Cerberus and JPMorgan, its chief lender,
had come up with their own merger idea: a Chrysler-GM alliance.
Cerberus owned the financing arms of both GM and Chrysler. LaSorda
put in a call to GM's director of corporate planning, John Smith, whom
LaSorda knew from his years at GM. The two executives began leading
teams working toward what would have been a massive auto merger of
former competitors.[23]

But by October 31, 2008, GM's Rick Wagoner told Commerce
Secretary Carlos Gutierrez the deal was dead. Chrysler would have
been a millstone around a floundering GM's neck.[24]

Nardelli, U.S. Senator Corker, and JPMorgan liked the GM-Chrysler
deal, which would have offered $13 billion to $15 billion in synergies.
But the deal got killed by a mix of political naysaying and GM's own
problems.

A merger would have given GM some cash and created long-term
benefits in terms of cost sharing, but also would have resulted in the
closure of about seven of Chrysler's 14 assembly plants, and the elimi-
nation of 19 out of its 26 car and truck lines, according to a study
done by Grant Thornton at the time.[25]

"What is it that you don't understand?" U.S. Speaker of the House
Nancy Pelosi said to one person pitching her the deal. "We are not
going to ask for government money to eliminate U.S. jobs."

So Nardelli had to go back to the drawing board to resume his search
for a partner.[26] Fiat was pretty much his last hope. The Wednesday
before Thanksgiving, he had been forced to announce 5,000 more
layoffs.

■ ■ ■

When Fiat's group executive council (GEC) gathered in Ferrari's headquarters at Maranello near Modena in late September 2008, it was clear
that the agenda would not be routine. A meltdown of the U.S. financial system was under way. Lehman Brothers, which could no longer
fund itself, had been allowed to go bankrupt, and the ensuing market

turmoil was so severe that the U.S. government had done the previously unthinkable a week later and stepped in to take control of insurance giant American International Group (AIG).

Marchionne's driver drove through the Ferrari gates crowned with its yellow logo, past the Renzo Piano–designed wind tunnel, and parked the car outside the smoked-glass Centro Sviluppo Prodotto, where Ferrari engineers were busy inventing the next generation of high-performance cars and engines. Marchionne took the elevator up to the next floor and walked past the reflecting pool lined with white stones to the Sala Rossa. The place looked like a luxury hotel. Architect Massimiliano Fuksas had designed it to be restful, and it was. But business conditions were anything but.

The gathering storm had been visible since July, when U.S. auto demand crumbled. Fiat had been riding high, enjoying record earnings. But Marchionne realized that events taking place in the United States right now were changing the game. All of the issues that had plagued the industry—its overcapacity, its poor use of capital, its inefficiency, the crushingly high cost of investment for new models—were now going to become unsustainable. When the other executives from the GEC arrived, Marchionne launched into his short presentation.

"The financial crisis we're seeing in the U.S. right now is going to create problems for Fiat, which despite its network of product alliances is simply too small to survive this market turmoil," he said. "Fiat needs to radically change its alliance strategy. We've done everything we can on our own. If we're going to survive this one, we need a partner."

The problem of a partnership had dogged Fiat for years, or maybe even decades. Its linkup with General Motors in 2000 had looked like a good solution at the time, but had proved to be messy. After the partnership dissolved, Fiat's business development chief, Altavilla, had cobbled together a patchwork of alliances giving the automaker access to technologies or markets where it wasn't present.

Those alliances would no longer be enough, Marchionne said.

Looking out at the faces of the group's top executives gathered around the table, Marchionne could see that Altavilla was following his reasoning closely. After all, he had been involved in talks with Chrysler earlier this year on teaming up for a small car model. Eugenio Razelli, the head of Magneti Marelli, Fiat's parts division, was also nodding in agreement. Razelli had a window into his competitors' businesses because Fiat sold parts to them, and what he was seeing wasn't pretty.

Marchionne could also see from John Elkann's face that the young Agnelli heir agreed, which was no surprise, because they had already discussed it. This is the wake-up call, thought John Elkann. He knew from experience that Sergio was absolutely right.

John had sat on Fiat's board since he was 21 years old, and for the past 11 years he had invested an inordinate amount of blood, sweat, and tears trying—and succeeding, until now—to fix the family car business. Before Marchionne's arrival, he had spent more hours than he could count listening to executives discuss ways to compensate for car losses for one more quarter. Many times he had said to himself as he listened, "This problem is simply not being addressed."

He had also seen how past partnership talks in Fiat's postwar history—with Citroën, Ford, Chrysler, and Renault—had all fallen through over issues of control. Fiat Auto and Ford Europe, for example, had started talks to pool their operations in February 1985. Fiat's chief executive at the time, Cesare Romiti, had placed a condition: Fiat needed to have 51 percent. Talks quietly ended seven months later.[27] When Fiat finally did find a partner in 2000, GM, the alliance looked great on paper because it gave Fiat plenty of freedom. But John had witnessed firsthand the paralysis created by Fiat's alliance with GM, which his grandfather had picked over an outright sale because of his reluctance for the family to lose control. At some point, the issue of the family's control had to be taken out of the equation if it blocked a deal, in John's view. That time had arrived.

John was keen to consider a game-changing, transformational deal. He knew Fiat's turnaround—while impressive—was frail. Auto industry conditions guaranteed that. The big picture was that there were too many carmakers in Europe, and too much overcapacity in the United States. Fiat was not a player in the Far East. So sooner or later, even in good times, Fiat would probably have had to find a new partner.

Whereas his grandfather and grand-uncle had been unwilling or unable to make a decision that would change the shape of the company, he knew from the failed experience with GM that it was now probably the only hope for Fiat's survival. "I am in full agreement with Sergio,"

John said. "We need to move forward on looking for a partner. I will work with Sergio on looking at our best options."

In the weeks after the meeting that fall, Sergio and John started reviewing the best possible partnership options. They went through the entire list of candidates, from Honda to Peugeot to Ford to BMW. John sent out feelers to family-owned automakers and spoke with family members of the ones interested in speaking to him, like Peugeot.

Marchionne, for his part, met with chief executives and huddled with his investment bankers at UBS, looking at valuations and the best combinations. The two met internally many times that fall to review possible combinations and see if they made sense.

As John and Sergio continued their talks with potential partners that autumn, it became clear that governments were stepping in to support the auto industry, changing the equation. In some cases, like in France, it meant that potential partners could say "no thank you" to Fiat's overtures. But elsewhere, like in the United States and Germany, state intervention shuffled the cards in the deck. France and Germany later announced "special measures" in October to fund or prop up their national auto industries. At the start of 2009 the French would lend Peugeot and Renault nearly $8 billion.

The executives at Fiat were under no illusions that the Italian government would extend them the sort of emergency credit that the U.S. Congress had eventually approved to stimulate the world's largest economy. Italy's Economy Minister, Giulio Tremonti, was dead set on keeping the country's public spending under control. From his perch in Rome atop the world's third-largest pile of debt, Tremonti knew his country was at risk of seeing its interest payments balloon out of control if financial markets lost faith in Italy's ability to toe the fiscal line. As Europe's credit markets started to freeze up in August 2007, he had realized he was likely to inherit an economic crisis when the center-right would probably win national elections in 2008. He was right on both counts, and later managed to convince Prime Minister Silvio Berlusconi not to go overboard on promises like tax cuts during the his reelection campaign.

As Christmas approached, Sergio and a tiny handful of key confidants were in the homestretch on talks with Chrysler. John was constantly in the loop. Both Sergio and John gave press interviews hinting that the company was in talks for a partnership.

"Fiat is going to play a role in auto consolidation," John Elkann told Italian business daily *Il Sole-24 Ore* on November 30.

Asked if he would be willing to dilute his stake as majority shareholder to do that, John said that "the important thing is that it's a good marriage."[28]

The Fiat-Chrysler deal memorandum was signed on December 29, just in time to get the $4 billion in Bush-era funding. Talks leaked out on January 19, 2009. From then on, Fiat would be talking to the U.S. Treasury in addition to Chrysler and Cerberus—and one other stakeholder that started to look important: a union called the United Auto Workers.

■ ■ ■

On a freezing, gray February day a few months later, an unlikely group gathered for a meeting at the Ritz-Carlton Hotel in Dearborn, Michigan, the Detroit suburb that was the birthplace of Henry Ford and home to the Ford Motor Company. Sergio Marchionne and Alfredo Altavilla had traveled from Turin to the American Midwest for a meeting to get better acquainted with Ron Gettelfinger, president of the United Auto Workers, and the head of the union's Chrysler department, General Holiefield.

Gettelfinger and Holiefield were a good negotiating team. Ron had a slight build, wore a clipped mustache, and never had a hair out of place. Holiefield was a tall, wide man with a manner as expansive as his physique. Both had started their days on the shop floor and become union organizers early on.

Formal talks with the Treasury's auto task force hadn't started yet, but the Fiat team was already looking for ways to build momentum for the deal, and courting the union certainly couldn't hurt, given the union's support of the new administration. If the union would come around to the view that the Fiat-Chrysler partnership was the only way to keep the company from going bust, maybe it would throw its weight behind Fiat when it came time for talks to start at the Treasury.

In early January, when the U.S. Treasury released $4 billion of TARP money to help Chrysler stay afloat, Alfredo Altavilla had realized that Fiat's main counterparty from there on out was going to be Obama's auto task force, not Cerberus and not Nardelli.

"You need to deal with *us* now," task force member Ron Bloom told Altavilla in another phone call in early January.

So there they all were in Dearborn. When Henry Ford had grown up in Dearborn at the end of the nineteenth century, it was a tiny farming town along the sleepy Rouge River. Downtown Dearborn was dreary but, unlike downtown Detroit itself, had not turned derelict. A diner called Jim's Place, where patrons tucked into a heaping portion of meatloaf or Polish sausage for just a few dollars more than a *latte grande* now costs at Starbucks, sat next to an Arab grocery store, a small storefront offering tax and immigration services, and a white-tiled hamburger joint straight out of an Edward Hopper painting.

LaSorda and Nardelli were also there. The plush hotel, a nondescript modern building with stripes of glass windows running down its stone façade, was a stone's throw from the Ford headquarters, but there was little risk of getting spotted by anyone other than a busload of tourists coming to visit The Henry Ford, a sprawling museum and miniature American town that had been the Model T inventor's monument to himself and to the American dream.

Gettelfinger came to the meeting well prepared about Marchionne's track record at resurrecting Fiat.

"Look, our interest is in preserving jobs at Chrysler," Gettelfinger told Marchionne. "We understand your plan. We understand we will have to give up something. Let's have the discussion as soon as possible."

All the same, Altavilla came away from the meeting believing that negotiations with the union would not be a slam dunk. Gettelfinger still considered them a bidder, and not a real counterparty.

Marchionne, for his part, held back from talking too much about his plans for Chrysler, given that months of negotiations still lay ahead. The atmosphere, at this point, was relaxed and congenial.

"How many 300Cs are you going to buy, General, if we take this thing over?" Marchionne asked Holiefield jokingly.

"Just one," the towering Holiefield boomed.

"Nah, you better buy two or three," Marchionne countered.

I like this guy's style, Holiefield thought.

■ ■ ■

One of President Obama's first decisions in office had been bold and very controversial: to extend taxpayer-financed loans to General Motors and Chrysler, overseen by a task force. The two carmakers had submitted viability plans, as required under the terms of the Bush-era loan, on February 17. Both were deeply disappointing to Steve Rattner, who was a lead adviser to the task force. General Motors' management seemed to be living in a fantasy where the American icon was still the greatest car company on earth. Chrysler's plan was more realistic, but was still far from enough.[29] The task force's early impression was that GM, with huge changes, could survive because of its size. Chrysler's prospects were shakier, and to the task force Fiat looked like its only hope.[30]

The first few meetings between Fiat and the Treasury's task force had ended with a sense of disappointment on both sides. The Fiat people, for their part, felt that the folks at Treasury didn't understand what they were proposing. And the Treasury team was worried about giving away Chrysler. Both sides were frustrated.

At one of the first meetings, Fiat's small team had prepared a brief document outlining the value of its technology and the points of the deal. Marchionne went through it, starting out by illustrating his track record with Fiat's turnaround from 2004, and how he had pried $2 billion out of General Motors in a divorce settlement that everyone had said was impossible. He outlined his vision for brutal consolidation in the global auto industry.

Fiat and Chrysler needed each other because they were each too small to survive. Fiat and Chrysler were a perfect fit, he said.[31] Fiat was present in European and Latin American markets where Chrysler wasn't, and Chrysler's U.S. market share was appealing for Fiat. Together they could do the research they needed to build the small, fuel-efficient cars of the future, he said. Chrysler particularly needed Fiat so that it could have a small car that met the Corporate Average Fuel Economy (CAFE) standards enacted over the past two years.[32]

Andrew Horrocks then started to talk about the Fiat–Chrysler deal's financial structure. Fiat would get a 35 percent stake for free. But without Fiat, it would cost Chrysler $8 billion to develop the four new platforms, two new engines, and two new transmissions that Chrysler needed to be competitive. The Fiat–Chrysler alliance would save Chrysler from spending $4 billion to $5 billion to develop those technologies and would result in it having them two years sooner.

Rattner and Bloom quickly homed in on the topic of cash—specifically, that Fiat wasn't putting any in. Both men were unhappy with Fiat's reluctance to invest even a symbolic sum in the company, although cash mattered more to Rattner than it did to Bloom. From Rattner's point of view, coming from the world of private equity, a cashless deal made no sense at all. He wanted to avoid Fiat taking what on Wall Street is called a "free option"—coming in, taking a look around, not seeing what it liked, and then simply walking away a few months down the line. The other issue, of course, was the value perspective. What if the 35 percent turned out to be worth a lot?

"I don't think there's a deal here," Rattner told Ron and another task force member, Harry Wilson, when they got back to his office after one of the early meetings.[33]

Rattner thought the meeting went badly, but Bloom, a seasoned negotiator, took a more sanguine view. The deal negotiated between Fiat and Chrysler was logical from the two companies' point of view, Bloom thought, and he was satisfied that Chrysler had beaten the bushes of the entire global auto industry trying to flush out a buyer or a partner. Fiat was the only one at the table. Chrysler had done its homework. Bloom knew, however, that when governments intervene in an economy they do things differently from corporations. Bloom saw what his task was: he had to take this deal and make it work for the U.S. taxpayer by making Fiat abide by some very strict promises.

Bloom realized he had a very important card to play. Marchionne clearly wanted this deal badly. He might not have "skin in the game," as Rattner said, but he had something equally important: his reputation was on the line.

At that point, the task force was still divided about whether it was worthwhile saving Chrysler. Rattner cast the deciding vote in favor of the bailout. Obama himself made the final decision in favor of the Fiat-Chrysler deal in the middle of March.

On March 25, Sergio Marchionne, Alfredo Altavilla, Andrew Horrocks, and a few others strode up the steps of the U.S. Treasury for another meeting with Rattner and Bloom. The meeting began promptly at 10 A.M., around a long table in the Treasury's Diplomatic Room, a place carefully decorated to impress visitors with perfectly chosen period furniture reflecting the building's late-nineteenth-century architecture. Marchionne, as usual, wore a dark sweater and slacks. He had grown to like the simplicity of feeling comfortable, and especially liked traveling without luggage. He kept the sweaters everywhere he went.

Bloom's role in restructuring the steel industry had given him a much-needed perspective at the task force. After a stint on Wall Street, he had gone to work for the United Steelworkers union in 1996, when the former industrial titans had become bogged down in legacy costs they could no longer afford. He had seen with his own eyes what groups of stakeholders in supposedly dying industries can achieve if they come together to make a new business model in order to survive.

The meeting quickly turned into a ping-pong match among Rattner, Bloom, and Marchionne.

"We are sympathetic to the fact that you want to protect Fiat," Bloom said in his soft voice, trying to ease the conversation forward.

"I am sympathetic to the fact you are asking me for money, but I am not paying a dime," Marchionne countered.

Rattner interceded, mentioning that the U.S. taxpayer was putting up the capital that Chrysler would need to keep going forward. Could Fiat not make a symbolic payment, based on some sort of earnings multiple? Plus, the 35 percent stake was a little . . . much.

Rattner returned to the topic of price again and again. His arguments couldn't sway Marchionne, who fielded questions without using the long PowerPoint presentations his fellow auto executives at General Motors depended on.

"This thing is broken," he said. "The only thing you can do with it is dismantle it, and sell off the cars in the lot at a discount. There is one person who can fix it, and he is telling you now 'I am not paying cash.' I can fix it, but it is unfair to pay."

"You and Fiat have zero skin in the game," observed Rattner. The suggestion made the Fiat team bristle.

"I don't want to talk about 'skin in the game,'" said Marchionne. "I have plenty of it. We are contributing Fiat's technology. And me and my people are going to move over to Detroit and pour our lifeblood into this company."

Despite the back-and-forth, the talks were making progress. During a cigarette break in the stairwell with his small group of advisers, Marchionne said he thought they were inching toward a deal. He had grown increasingly certain as the weeks went by that he could fix Chrysler, even though he seemed to be one of the few people in the universe who held that view. His own advisers and a lot of the executives at Fiat thought he should leave Chrysler for dead. He could see it in their faces at meetings. To them it looked reckless, but to him it wasn't because he could actually *see* how it would work. What he saw, as he dug deeply into Chrysler's books, walked its halls, and talked to its people was what he could do with the company if he could rip it up and start over like he did at Fiat—especially since Chrysler would be in better shape than Fiat had been if it went through a speedy bankruptcy.

Bloom interjected, at that point, that Fiat was "getting great value" by getting access to the U.S. market with Chrysler. Bloom was already familiar with Fiat's plan and had been in touch with Altavilla since after Christmas, but Marchionne wasn't going to budge.

"Do you think this thing is going to turn into Cinderella by itself?" he asked.

Fiat was the task force's only choice between Chrysler staying in business and a bankruptcy.

■ ■ ■

By the time of that March 25 meeting, Bloom had taken some time to mull over the Fiat-Chrysler deal and had come to a few conclusions.

The first was that the "we're giving away the store" issue was actually fairly simple to address. Bloom had gotten comfortable with the idea that Fiat's technology could be assigned a workable value for deal-making purposes. Sure, it was unusual. But what is Microsoft but a bunch of intellectual property, he reflected. There was no question in his mind that car designs, patents, engines, and technology were worth an awful lot to Chrysler.

The main challenge, in his view, was to come up with an agreement that would somehow force Fiat to share its technology and not do a Daimler, when the German auto giant dragged its feet about platform and engine sharing for fear of tarnishing its brand. To be fair, there were also managerial and cultural problems that had dogged DaimlerChrysler. Bloom had to satisfy himself that the Fiat crew would be different, that they were not just seeking to annex Chrysler like Daimler had, but would be trying in good faith to share technology and integrate the two companies.

As far as the "skin in the game" argument went, Ron was prepared to take a calculated risk that Marchionne, his board, and Fiat's main shareholder, John Elkann, were "all in." They were all convinced that Fiat needed to become a global car company and would do anything to see that happen. If they were forced to go back to Turin empty-handed, or worse yet after a hugely public failure, it would be a disaster for them.

Bloom could also see that Marchionne was a relational, and not a transactional, negotiator. A transactional negotiator looks to get the best deal immediately because the buyer and seller will have no future relationship. Deals on Wall Street are almost always transactional, and the bankers who do them are proud of that fact.

Relationship-based negotiators realize that life is long, and in Bloom's view, Marchionne fell into that camp. He knew that at Chrysler he would be entering into relationships with the U.S. government, with the autoworkers, and with the Detroit community. Marchionne knew, in Bloom's assessment, that if he negotiated an unfair deal or tried to take advantage it would come back to haunt him.

Ron Bloom was not the only one who had had some time to think. The Fiat team had, too. The two sides, at the March 25 meeting, were both prepared to be flexible. Both really wanted a deal.

"We are prepared in due course to pay for a 16 percent stake in Chrysler that will bring us up to a controlling stake," Altavilla said. Fiat had a caveat, though. It was prepared to pay market price, but with a cap of a multiple of Fiat's earnings and share price. Otherwise, Fiat's shareholder interest would be diluted.

Rattner and Bloom showed that they were open to a cashless deal, but needed some parameters to achieve "skin in the game" as a concept. The two sides came up with a formula that made both happy: Fiat would get a 20 percent stake initially, and would be able to go up to

35 percent step-by-step as Fiat achieved certain milestones, like sell a car that hit gas mileage of 40 miles per gallon. The Fiat team found it acceptable because the milestones were things it had planned to do anyway.

The Treasury asked for a market-based pricing mechanism for Fiat to take its stake up from 35 percent to 51 percent, as well as the condition it repaid the Treasury before it did so. The repayment condition was critical.

After the meeting, Bloom called Horrocks aside.[34] He asked the sandy-haired young banker if he thought Marchionne would have a problem with the union's retirement trust having a sizable equity stake in Chrysler.

"As long as we get management control and a majority of the board, I don't think it would be a problem for Sergio," he replied.[35]

■ ■ ■

On March 30, 2009, at 11 A.M., U.S. President Barack Obama strode up to a podium in the Grand Foyer of the White House and gave a speech that would change the U.S. auto industry forever.

Obama's administration had stumbled badly in February, when Treasury Secretary Tim Geithner's desperately awaited bank bailout plan was ridiculed for being too vague. Today, just over a month later, Obama could not afford another misstep.

Television crews from CNBC, Fox, and the three networks had mounted their bulky cameras in the huge foyer that is the White House's official entrance, on a raised platform set up behind the rows of chairs reserved for the press. The cameramen were now massed behind the line of cameras, making small talk while they waited. Then they snapped to work as the President strode into the hall and took his place at the podium, flanked on his right by Geithner.

Obama paused for the photographers before he started speaking, and the clattering whirr of snapping shutters drowned out any remaining small talk as the press corps waited for the President to start. The camera noise was nerve-wracking, like grasshoppers on a muggy summer's day. If Obama was nervous, he didn't show it. He conveyed seriousness, but also hope. The flailing auto industry was an emotional issue for voters, even if they didn't work directly for a car company. In November, the heads of Chrysler, General Motors, and Ford had flown to Washington, D.C., by corporate jet to seek $25 billion in bailout money in a trip that had produced one of the most outrageous moments of the financial crisis—sort of a billboard for corporate arrogance. It made people mad. At the same time, voters felt a soft spot for Detroit. Most people had never been to Wall Street, and even Tim Geithner and Larry Summers might have a hard time explaining what a derivative was. But almost everyone has driven an American car.

Slowly, calmly, Obama laid out his plan. "More than one in ten people in Michigan is out of work," he began. "That's more than in any other state."

Chrysler and General Motors had flunked the test to get more money. They were near collapse. Obama recited a damning litany of failure, and gave a bleak assessment of the industry's future. General Motors' Rick Wagoner back in December blamed the weak economy for GM's troubles, but Obama contradicted him. The car industry's problems were the fault of a "failure of leadership year after year, of problems papered over and tough choices kicked down the road," Obama said.

"We've reached the end of that road," he stated.

GM and Chrysler's recovery plans didn't go far enough, the President continued. And they weren't moving fast enough. The President said he would give the companies more time to come up with a viable plan, which would require sacrifices from all stakeholders.

GM could rise again, he said. But Chrysler's situation "was more challenging," Obama continued, his cool delivery making his words seem almost surreal. "Chrysler needs a partner to remain viable," he said. In order to get the $6 billion it was asking for, Chrysler must partner with Fiat, which would transfer its "cutting-edge technology" to Chrysler, and build fuel-efficient cars "right here in the United States." If it did not come to an agreement with Fiat, its only alternative was bankruptcy. The companies were given 30 days and capital to continue operating during that time.

In a jarring reflection of the crisis, Obama spent several minutes explaining to viewers what sort of bankruptcy plans he envisioned, and that the U.S. government would stand behind the warranties of the two automakers should they go into bankruptcy.

"I can't promise there won't be more difficulty to come," Obama said, as he made an emotional appeal to people working in the auto industry. "I will fight for you."

■ ■ ■

Rattner was "a little awed at what we had unleashed."[36] Much was riding on this speech, in which the President announced that the government was giving General Motors and Chrysler $22 billion more in loans they needed to stave off collapse. The young President had sailed through his inauguration in January with flying colors, but now the euphoria was starting to fade and the drumbeat of economic news had been grimly, relentlessly bad. The auto bailout was controversial.

President Obama's deadline gave Team Auto just one month to line up all of Chrysler's eight stakeholders in favor of the Fiat deal or enter liquidation, when the company would be shut down and sold off, piece by piece. It was like trying to land eight planes on an aircraft carrier on the high seas during a storm, all at once.

By backing Fiat, Obama gave Marchionne and his team an incredible negotiating advantage. They were the only pure volunteers at the table. Everyone else, including the UAW, was stuck there by force. Marchionne was the only person who could threaten to leave, along with his team. He would make that threat, many times.

At the same time, however, Obama had given the task force a powerful stick to prod the stakeholders into what was politely called "shared sacrifice." The President had basically told the banks and the UAW that it was Fiat or nothing. Everyone around the table would have to give up something, or else Chrysler would go bust. It was already bust, really.

Without the taxpayer loans, Chrysler would be forced to shut down. The company's assembly lines would stop. Its workers would put down their tools and go home, jobless. Chrysler's headquarters in Auburn Hills, the second-largest building in the United States after the Pentagon, would become a ghost town as its engineers, designers, technicians, secretaries, and other staff departed for good. Chrysler's

Jefferson North Assembly Plant (JNAP) on Conner Street in Detroit, the proud manufacturer of the Jeep Grand Cherokee, would become a shell. Another abandoned industrial relic would be added to Detroit's collection of derelict buildings, testimony to the United States' waning industrial might and a stinging indictment of failure—unless, of course, the city or someone else paid to have it pulled down so no one would have to look at it. Then, at best, the former factory would become another Detroit vacant lot.

Marchionne was a crack negotiator, and the stakes were high. Fiat's survival was at stake, as was his professional reputation. On April 2, a few days after Obama's speech, the task force called a big meeting with Chrysler's creditors, led by JPMorgan's Jimmy Lee, as well as Marchionne, his bankers, executives from Chrysler, and the UAW. The dynamics of the deal had changed. At the meeting, Chrysler's executives were now sidelined. Although they were present at meetings, the main actors were now Fiat, the UAW, and Chrysler's creditors.

Marchionne and Nardelli, from that point on, clashed frequently on Chrysler's business plan. Nardelli wanted to minimize the amount of financing Chrysler needed, whereas Marchionne wanted to create the best possible conditions for Chrysler's turnaround. The differences in market and profit forecasts would become a huge source of friction between the two men.[37] But at the base of it was that Nardelli felt Marchionne was riding high on all of Nardelli's own hard work, while Marchionne thought Nardelli hadn't been in it for the long haul.

At the meeting, Chrysler's bank and other creditors were informed that the union's health care trust, the Voluntary Employee Beneficiary Association (VEBA), would be offered 55 percent of the company in lieu of the $5 billion Chrysler owed workers. The banks, which were owed about $7 billion, were offered $1 billion, which is what they would have received in a fire sale if Chrysler went bankrupt.[38] Jimmy Lee angrily rejected the proposal, and threatened to have the bank's CEO, Jamie Dimon, call President Obama.[39] He did not seem to have realized soon enough that he was now holding all the low cards.

The next negotiating session a few days later was at the Chrysler-UAW training center in Detroit, a white six-story building on East Jefferson Avenue—what was once a major Detroit thoroughfare. Like all Detroit's main streets, it was far too wide for the traffic that used it, since it had been built during a more prosperous era. East Jefferson wasn't blighted with the boarded-up homes and business like other big streets. Instead, it was dotted with vacant lots, car dealerships, and the occasional small strip mall. The Detroit skyline dominated by the round towers of the Renaissance Center poked up from the flat Midwestern horizon.

The friendly atmosphere of the earlier meetings that winter between Fiat executives and their UAW counterparts had created a reservoir of goodwill, but it would soon evaporate. As the meeting got started, UBS banker Andrew Horrocks read out a long list of new ways that Fiat wanted to save money from Chrysler's UAW contract.[40]

General Holiefield was so stunned at the new set of demands that his first thought was simply: "Wow." Chrysler and Fiat had already spent a lot of time—much of it at Auburn Hills in a conference room across from the HR department's offices—combing through the UAW contract looking for ways to save money. But it hadn't been enough. The massive man whose speeches were usually as long as he was tall was momentarily speechless.

Fiat was trying to drive a hard bargain. One of its suggestions, which made General Holiefield's skin crawl, had been to gradually replace hourly workers with permanent temporary employees.

"I would have to take my family and leave town if we agreed to that," Holiefield said later.

The "wow" factor quickly wore off as Holiefield realized that the list was a good thing. The list's very existence, and the fact he was sitting there in the room that day, meant that a possibility of life after death existed for Chrysler. He aimed to grab it. He recovered his composure and launched into a recitation about his many years at Chrysler to give Gettelfinger time to take stock of the situation and line up his ducks.

Marchionne, when he took the floor, explained his view that the union had to shake off its idea of worker entitlement and reconquer a set of rights based on economic performance. Entitlement, in Marchionne's view, was no longer an issue at this point. The whole idea of wealth distribution made no sense if there was no wealth to distribute. But the assertion that workers needed to accept "a culture of poverty" instead of insisting on entitlements irritated Gettelfinger. It sounded like a self-righteous lecture.

Ron Gettelfinger and the UAW had made what it viewed as big concessions in 2007, when it created the VEBA, a fund that covered health care payments for union retirees with about 70 cents to every dollar it was owed by the automakers. The fund was financed by payments from the auto companies, capped at a fixed amount, and administered by an independent board with minority union representation. While the fund had advantages for both parties—it let the Big Three take health care liability off their books, even as it protected the union's health care plan from any future bankruptcy—it was unpopular with union members and had been a hard sell for Gettelfinger.[41]

After all these concessions, Gettelfinger's reward, in his view, had been to see a stream of different executives coming back to ask for more. The more he gave, the more he was asked for. It was like feeding an alligator that was always hungry.

Marchionne and Gettelfinger, because of their very different personalities, had a tough time connecting. Bloom, who understood and appreciated both men, stepped in to smooth over the rough edges. Despite both sides' posturing, both wanted a deal. And Bloom knew it.

There was one thing, though, that Fiat and the UAW did agree on. It was one of those Japan-inspired "continual improvement" waste-elimination and quality-control systems that Holiefield had seen many a time before. Most of them never took root in the factory, mainly because management didn't get committed. But Fiat was different. Marchionne was swearing by World Class Manufacturing, or WCM. It broke down the union's rigid job classification system with its strict hierarchy and boundaries about who could do what. Right now in Chrysler plants, if something went wrong on the line, the line had to be stopped until the right person could be found to come and fix it. WCM did away with that, creating two advantages: it got rid of an excessive cost structure, and it created efficiency.

"I have to have it," Marchionne told Gettelfinger and Holiefield.

World Class Manufacturing seemed to be different, Holiefield had thought as he looked over the manual that Marchionne had brought. It had a culture attached to it that workers could buy into. It looked empowering. Holiefield knew Chrysler wouldn't survive if it didn't improve the quality of its products.

"If this is what you want, you can have it," Holiefield said. "I will give it to you without a fight."

Marchionne's goal overall was to have as few constraints as possible in his ability to operate Chrysler when it came out of bankruptcy. He wanted to save Chrysler, take it public, pay everyone back, and move on. In order to do that, he used every tactic in his negotiating playbook, from charm to bullying to threats to caustic outbursts of a torrent of swearwords.

He needed the unions to become a partner. Gettelfinger would have to budge from his position of "we already gave" to come around to the position of dealing with the fact that Chrysler was bust.

At a meeting at the Treasury a few days later on April 10, one of the first breakthroughs for the deal happened. Ron Bloom succeeded in convincing Gettelfinger that the union would do better for Chrysler employees by accepting a stake in the company with Fiat rather than digging in its heels and fighting for scraps in a liquidation. Giving Chrysler's unions a big chunk of the company had been "a huge point of controversy" between Rattner and Bloom, a person present at the talks recalled.

"You don't have the authority to do that," Rattner told Bloom.

"Well, you go negotiate it then," Bloom retorted.

Bloom had to work hard to get the two sides to come together, and at one point that day, the talks broke down. When the agreement was finalized at the end of a grueling day, Andrew Horrocks reached across the table to shake Gettelfinger's hand. The union leader refused.[42]

"The new contract marked the end of seventy years of steady, virtually uninterrupted UAW gains," wrote Paul Ingrassia in *Crash Course*, his 2010 book about the collapse of the U.S. auto industry.[43]

Later, critics of the auto bailout would say that the unions received more favorable treatment than Chrysler's creditors, who lost money.

■ ■ ■

It was clear to the task force that Marchionne was going to run the new Chrysler. He was the one with the vision and the know-how. But the task force did not think that Chrysler's current management could not stay on. The task force never fired Nardelli or asked him to leave.

Obama and his task force had taken a huge risk on Chrysler. For now, Chrysler would not join the long list of vanished U.S. automakers. Its factories would be spared the fate of Packard, Fisher Body, Ford's Highland Park plant, and Hudson, the shells of which dot Detroit's landscape as casualties of a relentless war for profit. The smallest of the Big Three, which had already survived one brush with death and had come roaring back with government help under Lee Iacocca in the 1980s, was given another chance.

The task force had no guarantee Chrysler would survive, even with the government cash, Fiat's managerial expertise, and its small car technology. After all, Germany's Daimler-Benz had been unable to make Chrysler profitable during their nine-year marriage. The negative dynamics of the U.S. auto market—with the Big Three forced to rely on discounts to move their product—guaranteed that. Chrysler's previous owners had been overly dependent on big cars and trucks. And legacy costs for employee health care and pensions had weighed on Chrysler's bottom line. Now it was up to Fiat, and to Chrysler's employees, to grab the opportunity to do what Daimler-Benz and Cerberus had never been able to.

At the same time, GM decided to put Opel up for sale in April 2009. Marchionne swooped in to snap up the German automaker and add it to Fiat-Chrysler. Fiat's management was much keener about Opel than it had been about Chrysler, especially the executives who ran Fiat Auto. The experience with the Opel Corsa and Grande Punto, which shared a platform that had been developed by Fiat and GM during their partnership, had been a positive one. The engineers at the two companies knew each other. There would be plenty of synergies. But the deal never got done. The German government opted for a different buyer, and GM eventually decided to hold on to Opel.

■ ■ ■

At 5 A.M. on April 30, 2008, in Washington, D.C., Alfredo Altavilla and others watched Marchionne sign an agreement taking 20 percent of Chrysler. Then the pair and a few others flew to New York, where Sergio had to attend a board meeting at UBS's headquarters in midtown Manhattan.

Five minutes before President Obama's speech to announce the task force's decision came on the air at 12 noon, Marchionne ducked out of the boardroom and joined Altavilla, Riccardo Mulone, Andrew Horrocks, Phil Gramm, and a few others who had gathered to watch.

"I am pleased to announce that Chrysler and Fiat have formed a partnership that has a strong chance of success," Obama said, adding that it would save more than 30,000 jobs at Chrysler. "Every dime of taxpayer money will be repaid before Fiat can take control of Chrysler."

Obama lauded Chrysler's management, including Bob Nardelli, and its unions for making the deal possible. He wagged his finger at a group of hedge funds that "decided to hold out for the unjustified prospect of a taxpayer-funded bailout."

The president was "supporting Chrysler's plan" to use bankruptcy to "clear away its remaining obligations." He ended on an upbeat note that would later become a sort of mantra at Chrysler that summer after it came out of bankruptcy.

"We have made great progress," he said. "We can make great American cars."

To Marchionne, it all seemed sort of surreal.

"Sergio, best of luck," Phil Gramm, a former U.S. senator who worked with UBS as vice president of investment banking, said in his thick Texas accent after Obama had stopped speaking.

Altavilla was speechless, struck dumb by a sense of pride and accomplishment. Sergio Marchionne patted him on the back, and shook a few hands. Then, overcome with emotion, he turned quickly and left the room.

# Chapter 14

# The Spirit of Ubuntu: I See You

On August 8, 2007, Chrysler's newly appointed CEO, Bob Nardelli, flipped a huge switch set up outside the automaker's 15-story glass tower, which had been decorated with a banner running down it proclaiming "Get Ready for the Next 100 Years."

"The new Chrysler is open for business!" Tom LaSorda shouted, who was acting as master of ceremonies. Red fireworks soared from the roof of the building above the company's Pentastar logo, and employees watching on the lawn applauded and shouted.[1]

Less than two years later, Chrysler employees gathered in the four-story glass-topped atrium of the carmaker's gargantuan Tech Center for a similar sort of event. Another new leader was addressing them—this time, it was Fiat CEO Sergio Marchionne, to make his first speech as Chrysler chief. Yet the tone of the two events could not have been more different.

In 2007, Chrysler employees had been treated to the spectacle of barefoot acrobats rappelling down the glass face of the Chrysler tower, in a party atmosphere that celebrated what everyone hoped would be a new start.

In the summer of 2009, the mood was different. Chrysler had just come out of bankruptcy. The United States was still in the grip of an economic crisis. There was no party. The show was simply Sergio Marchionne, at a podium, wearing a black polo shirt with the Jeep, Dodge, and Chrysler logos on it, standing next to a blue car. Employees ringed the balconies of the atrium's floors, peering down from above, as if they were watching a promotional event at a shopping mall.

If some of the Chrysler employees who had gathered to listen to Marchionne's speech were a bit skeptical about this latest newcomer and his promises, they were entitled to be. Fiat was the third owner to take control of the company. Daimler-Benz AG's "merger of equals" just over 10 years ago was supposed to redesign the auto industry. DaimlerChrysler Motors Company, as the company had been renamed in 1998, never lived up to its promise as either a merger of equals or a unit of Daimler with Mercedes-Benz. The next owner, Cerberus Capital Management, took over in August 2007, just in time for the financial crisis to hit. Chrysler's experience being part of a German automaker had hurt its pride; its experience of being owned by a Wall Street private equity fund had resulted in thousands of job losses. All in all, it had been a rough ride.

The atrium was deadly quiet. All focus was on Marchionne.

"It's not often in business or in life that you get a second chance," he began, starting the speech on a somber note. "We have to live up to the expectations of those who made sacrifices on our behalf." He was referring to the U.S. taxpayers who had lent Chrysler a total of $11.2 billion to continue running.

He warned that the next year would be "one of the most difficult I have seen in my life," and called on employees to be "open-minded and unhindered in our thinking." He urged them to take on a leadership role in working with Chrysler's just-named management team, many of whom were there listening, as was General Holiefield, the United Auto Workers official who had frequently locked horns with Marchionne in Washington, D.C., during tense moments during talks at the U.S. Treasury.

Today, Holiefield was beaming. He was a second-generation Chrysler employee who had been at Chrysler for 38 years. "Marchionne is really connecting," he thought.

"The good news here is that we're starting from a much improved position," Marchionne continued, shifting into a more positive tone as he laid out his road map. At the top of his list of things to do was flattening the organization, "which may be a bit intimidating at first," he noted.

"We're going to create a very lean and fast moving organization," he said. Second, Chrysler would improve the quality of its cars. And third, "we're going to set our objectives and attack them." Chrysler would have a fully defined product portfolio in 90 days, he said, "from the smallest world-class subcompact cars to the largest hybrid Ram pickups."

As he listened standing next to General Holiefield, Pietro Gorlier, a Turin native and longtime Fiat manager, chuckled to himself that he knew a thing or two about Marchionne's "very lean and fast moving organization." He had arrived in Auburn Hills with Sergio three days ago for what was supposed to be a short trip, and should have already left by now. Instead he had found himself on the phone with his wife earlier that day telling her he didn't know when he could come back to Turin, because Sergio had picked him to run Mopar, Chrysler's parts and accessories arm.

Gorlier prided himself on his "just the facts" approach to his job. He was a details-oriented person who could get downright picky when he needed to. His trim little beard and neat glasses underlined his state of mind. But he let himself get emotional about Fiat, because he had worked there for 20 years and his father had been there for nearly 40 years before him. And he was letting himself get carried away again right now. Chrysler touched that emotional chord in him, too. The expertise, the passion, the huge Tech Center that housed everything needed to design a car under one roof . . . you can't find it everywhere.

Gorlier was one of the few Italians who came over from Turin to run Chrysler. Marchionne's 25-member management team unveiled that day had only three Italians on it. Of the remaining 22, all were from Chrysler. By contrast, DaimlerChrysler's board ended up having nine Germans and four Americans.[2]

Mike Manley, the sales executive who had helped work on the Fiat-Chrysler deal at the Treasury, looked at the faces of people around him as Marchionne continued talking. Manley had just been named to Marchionne's management team, too, as head of Jeep. People were concentrating intensely and were clearly interested, he could tell. That was only natural. Chrysler employees had just lived through a traumatic time. Many had been given an opportunity to leave, and many had taken it. The ones standing on the balconies of the atrium today were the ones who had stayed.

Manley was struck by the humility of the speech, and by Marchionne's clear desire to communicate that the employees were the most cherished part of the company. This was the third time Manley had watched a new owner come in and talk about what should be done at the company. What made Marchionne's speech different was that it emphasized the importance of people, he thought.

Joe Veltri, who, like Mike Manley, had been at Chrysler a long time, also looked up at the faces peering down from the balconies. Joe could see from their expressions that people were engaged. The speech was honest. Marchionne wasn't beating around the bush, sugarcoating, going all squishy, making promises, or saying it would be easy, Joe realized. "We used to be a small company that could compete against some pretty big lions in a tough market, because we had passionate leadership. Maybe we'll have that again now," he thought.

Ralph Gilles, the designer of the Chrysler 300, was also standing on the group floor looking at Sergio that day. The level of concentration was so intense you could almost hear people's thoughts whirring. He thought, "People are hanging on his every word because our livelihoods rest on his vision. Is this guy in it for us? For himself? For the company?" The more he listened, the more it seemed to Ralph that maybe Sergio was really excited about fixing the company once and for all. "But I'm not sure this guy is really a car guy," Ralph thought.

Marchionne ended his speech with one of his favorite riffs about the importance of working in a group.

"The era of the Great Man, of a greater-than-life individual who, working alone, cures all the ills of an organization, is dead," he said.

The task of rebuilding Chrysler must be approached as a group and in "the spirit of ubuntu," which is a part of a longer Zulu expression from sub-Saharan Africa. In this environment, the greeting for "hello" literally means "I see you."

"I see you. I am glad you are here," Marchionne concluded.

The idea of teamwork in the auto industry, or any industry, is nothing new. Japanese manufacturer Toyota developed its Toyota Way with an emphasis on teamwork in its factories to achieve manufacturing excellence. In the 1980s, a generation of General Motors managers devoured the work of W. Edwards Deming, a management expert who urged senior executives to transfer decision-making power to the ranks of middle managers and factory workers. At a leadership conference at a resort in Traverse City, Michigan, back in 1988, GM's prickly chairman, Roger Smith, stunned the group of 900 managers assembled to talk about "people power" by actually pulling off his brown cardigan sweater and handing it to a younger underling who had complained of a chill in the room.[3] But in GM's case, such one-off displays did little to change a deeply entrenched top-down culture.

After Marchionne's speech, the event broke up and people went back to work.

"Everyone was pretty happy, but a lot of people were saying, 'Well, here's another person who has arrived to pick the last bit of meat off the bones,'" recalled a former employee.

■ ■ ■

Three days later, Chrysler's new management team convened for their first weekend-long meeting. Weekend meetings were the new normal. The group met in a conference room on the fourth floor, off Marchionne's new office in the so-called banana wing of the huge complex.

Marchionne's decision to abandon the lofty regions of the curved glass tower's top floor reinforced the "we're in this together" message of his speech, and went a long way in a short time toward changing perceptions about him among Chrysler's rank and file.

Previous managers had taken up residence on the 15th floor, in an imposing executive area created by Lee Iacocca and reflecting his grandiose style. A glass door opens off the elevator area onto a long black-granite-clad foyer dominated by a life-size painting of the company founder, Walter P. Chrysler. Luxurious leather couches and thick oriental rugs beckon. At the far end looms the 35-foot-tall Pentastar window that tops the building, dominating the cathedral-like space, which has a pointed roof like the Pentastar itself. The window looks out on the flat expanse of Midwestern prairie beyond. The CEO's office was just to the right of the glass star, and his top three executives had the other corner offices.

Marchionne had already decided during prebankruptcy meetings with Nardelli that he wasn't going to work in the tower. But he knew he couldn't be on one of the floors with the brands. So he opted for the engineers. Marchionne moved his office down to the fourth floor in the Tech Center, where he would be a short walk away from the people who actually make and sell Chrysler cars, instead of cloistered in a tower. This is no small issue in such a big building.

At over five million square feet, the Chrysler Technical Center is a tad smaller than the Pentagon but larger than Tokyo's Narita airport (though with less choice of food). Employees can use a barbershop, a cafeteria, and a store selling food, drinks, candy bars, and Chrysler-branded T-shirts and hats. The long corridors are color coded to help people find their way around, and topped with dome-shaped skylights that send light down the four floors below, to where the technical staff sometimes moves around by golf cart.

Marchionne assembled his new group around a U-shaped table in a large, anonymous conference room numbered 4E. An ashtray was clearly visible near Marchionne's place at the head of the table. He welcomed his new team and then got down to work.

He knew he had to duplicate his playbook from Fiat, and do it fast. Luckily he didn't need to meander through the park looking for the park bench, because he had already been through it before.

Chrysler's failure was due to three main reasons: poor management by Daimler and Cerberus, rigid labor costs and health care costs, and unappealing cars. Marchionne had to fix all three. The labor issues had been dealt with, for now, during talks at the U.S. Treasury that led to the landmark agreement with the UAW.

He moved to fix Chrysler's management on his first day as CEO, introducing the flat, interdependent management matrix he knew was necessary for Chrysler to reinvent itself. Its old management structure had a chairman, a chief executive, and three vice chairmen. The new group was 25 people, reporting directly to him. Most of them had been in the second, third, or even fourth tier of management. From now on, they would be expected to come to the weekend meetings with all the information necessary to make snap decisions. They were not accustomed to it.

"He was a dictator, but in a good way," recalled a member of the management team. "He couldn't have done it by consensus. It had to be done in an aggressive way."

Marchionne had spent many hours over the previous few months with Bob Nardelli and Tom LaSorda going through the candidates to decide who would work best for his new team. He spent a lot of time on it so he could come out of the gate quickly, but would soon discover that he didn't get the people completely right.

"Not all of you will be here in six months," he told the group. "Things are going to change. Once I get to know you and figure out who you are, what your strengths and weaknesses are, and whether or not you align with where we are going . . . I am sorry but that is just how it is."

The new management organization reflected the group's four brands: Jeep, Chrysler, Dodge, and Mopar. The company's commercial, industrial, manufacturing, and corporate functions were organized in support of the brands. Each brand manager was responsible for the profit and loss of his or her brand. According to one insider, each brand was deeply damaged by years of muddled thinking, me-too products, poor quality, underinvestment, and neglect.

Marchionne appointed Peter Fong to run Chrysler; he had previously been in a much smaller job as head of the Mid-Atlantic Business Center. Mike Manley was tapped to run Jeep, moving over from running international sales and global product planning. Mike Accavitti was elevated from Dodge brand marketing manager to running all of Dodge. Pietro Gorlier moved over from Fiat to run parts division Mopar.

Head of sales Steve Landry was reorganized out of a job, illustrating the impact of the new flat Chrysler. Landry had had seven direct reports, and in Marchionne's new organization, with 25 people reporting to him, Landry's reports would now be under Marchionne. Chief Financial Officer Ron Kolka and top engineer Frank Klegon were two other key Chrysler people not asked to stay on, along with Tom LaSorda and Bob Nardelli.

Each newly minted brand manager was also given additional responsibilities. Peter Fong (Chrysler) was also responsible for global sales. Mike Manley (Jeep) was also head of product planning. Mike Accavitti (Dodge) was also head of global marketing. Pietro Gorlier (Mopar) was also in charge of customer care. So the flat management team was somewhat of a misnomer; it was actually more like a matrix. The clever part of this organization was that it made each manager beholden to the others for their success. They were forced to work together. Accavitti would not have the luxury to simply focus on making his own Dodge brand look good; in his second role as head of marketing, he had to service the other three brands as well. The three brand managers needed to go to him on their ad campaigns, and he needed to make sure they got what they needed.

"If you try to go rogue, the other three will kill you" was how Fred Diaz, who was later made head of the Ram truck brand, put it.

Jim Press stayed on as Marchionne's deputy for the time being, as he looked for another job.

On the industrial side, a handful of people now reported directly to Marchionne. Ralph Gilles was confirmed as head of design, and now reported to Marchionne directly, instead of to engineering. Doug Betts continued to lead quality and Scott Garberding stayed put at the procurement office. Scott Kunselman was promoted to head of product engineering.

The agenda for that first meeting was about product, of which there was very little. Talk focused on what was in the pipeline, what the company needed, and how the brands were stacking up. It was pretty clear that the level of frustration was high and that morale was low. At the same time, Marchionne was deluged with a wave of pent-up desire for new products. Talk revolved around what to do with the Sebring, its unloved midpriced sedan, and whether Chrysler needed a new large family car. It didn't have a viable compact car to compete with the Ford Focus, the Hyundai Elantra, or the Toyota Corolla. It needed a car that did 40 miles per gallon, urgently.

The group got right down to work. They had to come up with a product plan in 90 days, and Chrysler did not have a lot of product in the pipeline. There was a new Jeep Grand Cherokee, and that was about it until mid-2011 at the earliest. The company somehow had to survive with the cash it had until it could get its new models to market.

With a new team in place, the group had to move quickly to attack bad practices: cash incentives paid to customers to entice them to buy cars. And channel stuffing, or the industry jargon for building too many cars and then pressuring dealers to give discounts or even using strong-arm tactics to take more cars than they could easily sell. All of these bad management practices were deeply rooted at Chrysler, but Marchionne knew in his gut that he had a good chance of fixing the company. Where did this conviction come from? Detroit has seen many strategic visionaries come and go. Ten years earlier at Chrysler, CEO Bob Eaton had grappled with the same problems that Marchionne still faced today: the auto industry's overcapacity, Chrysler's lack of global reach, its dependence on gas guzzlers, breakneck technological change, and fierce competition. Eaton's strategy was for Chrysler to seek a partner. Halfway across the globe, Jurgen Schrempp at German industrial giant Daimler AG had come to the same conclusion, and the result was an automotive partnership that was heralded as the first of a new, global era. Like Lee Iacocca before him, Schrempp envisioned a colossus spanning the United States, Europe, and Asia.

Schrempp, like Marchionne, was also a charismatic visionary who could think one or two or three steps ahead of everyone else. His weakness was in delegating the execution of his vision. Marchionne's unusual ability is that he can see what actually needs to be done, and then cajoles and goads his flat management structure of dozens of direct reports in weekend meetings to achieve the goal. He won't let up until it's done. He doesn't take "no" for an answer, and there are no excuses.

"Marchionne doesn't let go," said UBS analyst Philippe Houchois. "That's what his strength is. He is good at strategy *and* at execution."

On a practical note, Marchionne had 45 days before he needed to pay any of his vendors. The company was paid two days after a car was sold, and it paid the vendor after 45 days. So Chrysler wasn't bleeding cash like Fiat had been when he took over and the automaker was losing millions of euros each day. He had a tidy little pile from the U.S. Treasury to tide him over. If he was careful, he could make it last.

■ ■ ■

Weaning Chrysler off of car discounts was difficult. It was probably the worst business practice in Detroit. Ironically, it was Chrysler that had pioneered the practice of "money on the hood" rebates under former chairman Lynn Townsend back in 1974, in the wake of the first oil crisis.

"Buy a car, get a check!" urged baseball star Joe Garagiola in a Chrysler ad that ran during the 1975 Super Bowl. Chrysler's former chairman and CEO, Lee Iacocca, made the rebate a common industry practice in the 1980s.

For many members of Marchionne's new team, the memory of the Jeep Commander still smarted. Launched in the summer of 2005 when Chrysler was still part of Daimler, the seven-passenger vehicle was a prime example of all that had gone wrong at the company. Daimler skimped on the investment that would have turned it into a high-end vehicle like the Mercedes-Benz G-Class SUV. And the platform wasn't big enough to make the vehicle truly roomy. The Commander was simply not well executed from either a styling or a product planning point of view.

Auto sales started to dip at the end of 2005, and the Big Three reacted as they always did: by offering discounts. By October, Chrysler's discounts were the industry's highest at $3,075 per vehicle, compared to $618 per vehicle at Honda.[4] Chrysler was also offering free gas and a longer warranty. But despite the discounts, with rising gas prices, by early 2006 the Commanders started piling up on dealer lots, parking lots, and anywhere else Chrysler could think of storing them. But cutting production, which would have seemed to be the commonsense solution, was a nonstarter. Market share was king in Detroit, and Chrysler didn't want to fall behind its rivals to become the number four automaker in market share that year. So instead, Chrysler started offering huge rebates on the vehicles, and twisted the arms of its dealer network to take them, where they sat on lots, unsold. Others were sold cheaply to rental and corporate fleets. By the end of the first six months of 2006, more than 650,000 cars sat on dealer lots.[5] Dealer relations, not surprisingly, grew sour.

Chrysler was not the only Detroit automaker to overproduce, but it was the worst offender.[6] Its status as the smallest of the Big Three kept it running to catch up. Like all Detroit manufacturers, Chrysler manufactured unsold cars as a way to keep inventory on hand when the factories were shut down for model changeovers that took place in the summer. Under Lynn Townsend in the 1970s, however, the practice got out of control at Chrysler. The cars were parked around Detroit in rented areas, including the former Michigan State Fairgrounds, at times even for months during winter.[7] Not surprisingly, dealers soon realized they could pick up inventory from what Chrysler executives referred to euphemistically as "the sales bank" at dirt-cheap prices, instead of ordering the cars up front. Chrysler barely survived the oil crisis and managed to limp along until Iacocca took over in late 1978. One of Iacocca's first actions was to put a stop to the sales bank.[8] (The sales bank reappeared, in a way, during the Daimler era. Its bungling of the Commander, as well as the excess Dodge Rams and Jeep Cherokees that crammed parking lots in 2006, contributed to Daimler AG's decision to sell the company.)

Chrysler, Ford, and General Motors for most of the past decade had kept factories running at well beyond demand, making more cars than consumers would buy and then pushing them on to dealers, who in turn sold them for discounted prices. This practice, in part, was created by rigid union contracts, since autoworkers still got paid if they sat idle. The carmakers were seeking volume at the expense of profit margin, and it nearly drove two of them into bankruptcy. As an outsider, Marchionne stood a better chance of breaking this negative cycle than longtime Motor City executives.

If there was any time that automakers could try to kick their rebate habit, it was in mid-2009, when the U.S. government stepped in to offer cash payments to buyers. All of Detroit's Big Three grabbed the chance.

In addition to using rebates, Chrysler also became dependent on another bad practice: fleet sales. Its fleet sales had been running at just over 30 percent of total sales for 2006, 2007, and 2008. It continued to rely on fleet sales in 2010, when they accounted for 36 percent of sales, because it had little choice. While fleet sales can be an important source of revenue for carmakers, the fact that about one-third of Chrysler's vehicles were to fleets was not an encouraging statistic.[9] Fleet sales are not as egregiously bad as a sales bank. The cars, after all, do get sold. They kept factories running at a time when it would have been expensive to close them. They help massage quarterly numbers. But the practice is corrosive because it slowly erodes the value of a car. Carmakers are doubly penalized by sales to rental fleets; they lose margin on the initial sale, and they also agree to buy the cars back after a certain number of years at a set price.

Marchionne didn't care about market share. He cared about unit sales, and his goal was to sell 1.4 million cars in the United States. He was prepared to let Chrysler's market share shrink until it found a more natural level, and was ready to take the flak involved in doing it.[10] The idea of cutting back on incentives was hard for some at Chrysler to get used to. But Ford and GM were cutting back on them, too.

"Anything which would have violated the rule about not going back to the old ways of wholesaling cars out, I would have gone after your throat," Marchionne said much later. "Because I know how we got there."

On August 1, 2009, Marchionne's management team gathered as usual in conference room 4E in Chrysler's Tech Center. The talk soon turned to car incentives. Chrysler's sales had plummeted over the summer. A few days earlier, Chrysler brand chief and head of sales Peter Fong had come up with a plan to duplicate the government's $4,500 "cash for clunkers" rebate. The government cash payments had been successful at getting people into showrooms.[11] Now, besides the government's payment, Chrysler would offer up to $4,500 of its own to people who didn't qualify for the "cash for clunkers" program. Fong started to present the plan at the meeting.

Marchionne and Nardelli had argued about incentives for an entire day during the bailout talks at the Treasury, because Marchionne wanted a lower figure for incentives in Chrysler's business plan than Nardelli thought was realistic.[12]

In June, Marchionne had started pushing Chrysler to review its discounting strategy to be more targeted on models and geography. Indeed, restoring "pricing discipline," another way of saying "phasing out incentives," was a key part of Marchionne's plan to bring Chrysler back to profit.

"The fight for market share and no profit is going to devastate this industry further," Marchionne warned on a conference call to talk about Fiat's second quarter results in July. "My expectation is we will see discounting levels drop significantly over the next 12 months."[13]

Fong appeared to underestimate Marchionne's aversion to incentives, or simply didn't realize that the new Chrysler CEO could be explosive when crossed on something he believed was important. After Marchionne listened to Fong talk about the plan, he went ballistic.[14] Fong was subjected to a long tirade on incentives as fellow members of the management team could do little but look on. Gone was the jovial CEO who sometimes started meetings by saying, "Good morning, children," and asked if anyone had a joke to tell.

Doubling the discount amounted to "giving away margin," he yelled, furious. Plus, the plan came at a time when Chrysler's inventory was already shrinking. The next day, Chrysler announced that it would no longer offer the $4,500 rebate. Instead, it would vary the size of the discount depending on the model and brand.

Offering deep discounts was just one of the bad habits Chrysler was struggling to break. Its muddled thinking on brands also had to go. Jeep was unique, so that was the easy part. The company had too many similar vehicles chasing the same customer, like the Chrysler Town & Country minivan and the Dodge Grand Caravan. The bankruptcy gave Chrysler the chance to get rid of 789 underperforming dealerships and move to a format where all the three brands were sold at the remaining "stores," as they are called in Detroit jargon. As a result, the overlapping me-too products had to be eliminated, saving the company money up front in development, and hopefully leading to better sales of existing models.

Both the Chrysler and the Dodge brands were a problem. Dodge was too unfocused. It was racing, trucks, small cars, minivans, you name it. The company's Chrysler brand had both a quality problem *and* an image problem. Its 300 model was a hit, but the Sebring was seen as one of the blandest car models in the market. The Sebring was sort of Exhibit A for the challenges the company faced with its model lineup. Just like Hollywood had straight-to-DVD films, the Sebring was almost a straight-to-fleet car.

Detroit's three automakers routinely relied on rental and corporate fleet sales to round out their revenues. In 1996, when Ford's Taurus risked being overtaken by the Toyota Camry as America's best-selling car, Ford protected its five-year stint as leader by increasing Taurus sales to Hertz, which it owned at the time.[15] But it was Chrysler that had become the most dependent on fleet sales. From September 2006 to February 2007, a total of 48.5 percent of its Chrysler-brand cars were sold to rental, commercial, and government fleets. This was not surprising, though, considering the overbuilding that had gone on in 2006.

Marchionne and the new Chrysler had to pull the company out of its dependence on rebates and fleet sales by making better cars. The start of this process was a rethink on brands. As the larger of the two car brands, Chrysler, the group decided, had the potential for being an aspirational brand. Dodge was racing, muscle cars, and the mass-market, all-American brand. So how did Ram trucks fit in? They lagged Ford and GM, but the brand had potential. It was perceived as a quality product. Marchionne wanted to spin Ram out into a separate brand and make it a strong competitor, nipping at the heels of Ford and GM, with its own identity and its own ad campaigns.

As the management team dove into the customer data during their weekend discussions on brand identity, it became increasingly clear to the group that the Dodge car and Ram truck brands had more potential to grow if they were separate. Discussion on a name could last for hours. And sometimes the management team did role playing, with one member of the group acting as the customer. Other times, Marchionne would take a contrarian point of view to stimulate discussion.

Marchionne started to look for a replacement for Accavitti sometime over the summer, as his plan to split Dodge and Ram took shape. For Ram, his eye fell on Fred Diaz, a tall, blue-eyed, square-jawed Texas native, whom he had met for a one-on-one interview earlier that summer as part of his new routine. Marchionne had poked and probed Diaz for his views on how he thought his business center was being run. Diaz had spent his entire professional life at Chrysler, but little of it was in Detroit. Like Fong, Diaz was head of a 14-state business center in Denver, Colorado, in charge of sales, marketing, dealer relations network, service, and parts. Elevating him to the management team would be a huge jump in responsibility, but he had a deep understanding of the people who bought Ram trucks as well as a sincere love of the product. Marchionne seemed to be looking for people who knew the product and were able to work well with others, were team players, and were not wedded to the old way of doing things at the company.

On October 5, Chrysler dropped a bombshell: a significant reshuffle of responsibilities of a management team just appointed only a few months earlier. Dodge and Ram were being split into two different brands. Ralph Gilles was promoted to running Dodge in addition to his duties as design chief. Fred Diaz would take on the new Ram division. Olivier Francois, the French-born head of Fiat's Lancia brand, would leave Turin for Auburn Hills to add Chrysler to his duties. Marketing, advertising, and brand development responsibility were shifted over to him from Accavitti's replacement, Gilles. Mike Manley remained in place at Jeep, and was now in charge of international distribution. Production was assigned to Joe Veltri, who joined the management team.

Peter Fong was leaving "for personal reasons," and Accavitti was leaving to "pursue other interests," Chrysler said.

The shakeup caused a stir, and was perceived by many onlookers as a sign that Chrysler was floundering. The move raised questions about the focus of the company's business plan as it tried to rebuild, noted the *Los Angeles Times* on October 6.

"It's not one or two analysts that are confused by this move," the *Los Angeles Times* quoted IHS analyst Rebecca Lindland as saying. "The entire industry is scratching its head on this one."[16]

The management churn is a good example of how Marchionne works. He aims to give his team authority to make decisions and mistakes. But Fong's dismissal was more than just an execution error in strategy or a disagreement with the boss about incentives, or about a chief executive losing his temper in a pressure-cooker environment. It went right to the heart of how the management team worked together. If one member was dissonant, not in sync with the new direction, and working singly to undo what the rest of the team had agreed on, that person would no longer integrate well into the team. When that started to happen, tensions rose. And it was up to Marchionne to fix it.

By elevating Diaz, Gilles, and Francois, Marchionne was making a huge roll of the dice. Francois had done a good job at Lancia and had demonstrated a deft ability at coming up with eye-catching ads and promotional schemes. But there was little to suggest that a Frenchman could connect with U.S. customers for Chrysler cars. Diaz, for his part, was being promoted to do a high-profile job that a lot of commentators thought was controversial. Was it wise to give an untested manager such a delicate task? Gilles was already something of a star inside Chrysler and beyond for having styled the Chrysler 300, but it was "unclear how much he knows about running a business, and Fiat has set up the new brand structures so that each one is run almost as an independent company," noted *IHS Global Insight*.[17]

All three executives turned out to be strong members of Marchionne's team. Francois was able to conjure up a luxurious vision for Chrysler that—interestingly—drew on Chrysler's design heritage even as it tapped into Detroit's gritty urban present. Olivier's vision would morph from using the tagline "Imported from Detroit" at the Los Angeles Auto Show in late 2010 to a Super Bowl video with the hip-hop star driving a Chrysler 200 through a dark Detroit that turned into a signature moment in Chrysler's turnaround.

Diaz, for his part, proved to be a sure hand at Ram and had good relations with dealers, which was useful at a time when Chrysler had little product. It was probably Gilles who had the biggest learning curve at Dodge, in terms of both product and job description. Not only did he have to learn the ropes on the business side, but he would also have to inject some new energy into the Dodge brand.

And, last but not least, it was Gilles who would later have the responsibility for one of Chrysler's most high-profile, high-risk projects: designing the new 40-mile-per-gallon compact that Chrysler needed to bring to market by January 2012 as part of its deal with the U.S. Treasury. Chrysler had never been known for its small cars. Gilles's design prowess was in racy cars like the Avenger or the eye-catching 300. Chrysler's future viability in the U.S. market depended on it becoming a player in cars and not just trucks. And the partnership with Fiat was built on the assumption that Chrysler would be capable of using Fiat's small car platforms to build something that U.S. buyers would love.

He couldn't afford to get it wrong.

■ ■ ■

On June 29, 2009, workers at the Trenton South Engine Plant (TSEP) in Trenton, Michigan, returned to their jobs at the sparkling-clean two-year-old factory. Trenton South's sleek modern entrance, with its plants and glassed-in cafeteria, could almost be mistaken for a fitness center or a community college.

Plant manager Donald DeKeyser and some of his other managers walked the factory floor that morning, welcoming people back to work. Later that morning, Don invited all the staff and factory workers into the plant's conference room to see a video of workers returning to their jobs and to celebrate with cake and coffee.

"People were happy to be back," he recalled.

Something had changed at Chrysler besides ownership while they had been away. While the UAW, Fiat executives, and Obama's auto task force were hammering out details of the rescue in an ornate meeting room at the Treasury in Washington, D.C., a tiny group of Fiat executives had already started crisscrossing the Midwestern United States, Canada, and Mexico to visit Chrysler's factories in what they called Operation Condor, or a total overhaul of the way work was carried out on the shop floor. Fiat's manufacturing system, World Class Manufacturing (WCM), was part of the agreement with the unions and the U.S. Treasury. It had to be ready to roll out as soon as the ink was dry on the bankruptcy procedure in June. With the company living on borrowed cash from U.S. taxpayers, every single day was precious.

On the far side of the room, Don DeKeyser and Al Coopland, who was leading the WCM drive, had hung up a huge "commitment banner" with the TSEP logo on it, where workers could sign up for the new program. And they did. The union had already backed it, since WCM was part of Chrysler's bankruptcy agreement.

World Class Manufacturing was adopted by Fiat in 2005. Boiled down to its essence, it squeezes out waste by improving efficiency starting with a detailed audit of a worker's every move. It sort of cherry-picks the best of the Japanese "continuous improvement" systems.

It has two main strengths. First, it uses team leaders on the shop floor to involve workers in reengineering their own work processes. Second, it gives workers and management a way to put a dollar figure on each kind of waste, helping to set priority about which areas to tackle first. That helps implementation, because people start to see results and are encouraged to continue. Other similar systems are often abandoned because either workers don't buy in or the systems are so complicated that management loses interest.

Don and his management team also announced a contest for workers and staff to design a new logo for the plant. The winner's logo would be used throughout the plant. Trenton South was slated to make the new Pentastar engine in March of next year that would be powering the new Jeep Grand Cherokee, a key seller for Chrysler and one of the company's few all-new vehicle launches next year. Don had a lot on his plate.

Some of Trenton South's workers were already familiar with World Class Manufacturing. Al Coopland had started holding WCM training during two-week courses back in February. The last two days of the courses called for shop workers to tear down and rebuild an engine made out of Legos, in order to apply what they had learned. Salaried employees and management also took part.

"At first they thought it was kind of dumb," Al recalled. "But by the second day, they were really enthusiastic. Some of them had never seen how the engine parts all fit together."

One of the first changes to a plant that adopts WCM is that it gets cleaned up, because dirt hides waste. A dark floor hides an oil leak, which means something may not be functioning. A burned-out lamp hides waste. Old parts no longer in use lying around create clutter, which cuts down on efficiency. Trenton South was a new plant, so it was already sparkling.

Another big change in a WCM plant is that progress is measured on WCM boards in the lobby or on the shop floor. For example, a board on the shop floor at Trenton South is devoted to solving a problem about how to get the number of parts in a plastic box delivered in smaller lots so the operator doesn't need to pick through so many. Also, if a worker detects a problem in a vehicle, the production line must be stopped immediately. Under the old way, the vehicle would be produced and then repaired afterward.[18]

The overall WCM system is complex, with 20 "pillars" of up to seven steps each. To complete a pillar is a long process, requiring audits of workplace safety, productivity, organization, and quality.

"A lot of the principles are the same as in prior programs," said toolmaker Teresa Horn to the *Detroit News* in 2010. "The difference is it's a complete buy-in from management at all levels, to workers on the floor."[19]

■ ■ ■

Five months after Chrysler emerged from bankruptcy, it threw open its doors for hundreds of people who packed into the Chrysler Tech Center's design wing on November 4, 2009. The Dome, as it's called, is a huge room where executives come to critique new models. Outside Chrysler's headquarters stood an army of Ram trucks, Chrysler mini-vans, Dodge muscle cars, and a little light blue Fiat 500. Inside, Bruce Springsteen and other musicians picked by Marchionne played for guests as they found their seats in the cavernous space, which is designed to be big enough for executives to view new car models from a distance. Detroit auto designers have been using a version of the Dome since the late 1920s, when a man named Harley Earl set up a design studio for General Motors in the days of Alfred Sloan. Earl's original design dome sits atop a downtown Detroit skyscraper that now houses the College for Creative Studies, one of the top automotive design schools in the country.

The crowd of 450 journalists, financial analysts, shareholders, and local bigwigs had come that day to hear Marchionne and his management team lay out a five-year plan, just like it had back in Balocco with Fiat in 2004. This time, John Elkann was there, along with his cousins Andrea Agnelli and Alessandro Nasi. Just a few years earlier, DaimlerChrysler executives had held presentations to private equity funds Cerberus and Blackstone in the same room as they scrambled to sell the company.

Marchionne entered the room in a blaze of lights from TV cameras. He began his presentation on a humorous note.

"I feel like Zsa Zsa Gabor's fifth husband. I know what I am supposed to do, but I don't know if I can make it interesting," he said, lifting the line from Al Gore (whose photo popped up on the huge screen behind the podium).

Chrysler was better off than most people thought, he continued. It had stopped burning cash, for one example. It now had $5.7 billion on hand, compared to $4 billion in June. It would break even by 2011, Marchionne vowed, and would pay back the U.S. and Canadian governments by 2014. And by 2014, at the end of the five-year plan, its operating profit would be more than $5 billion. That's more than it ever did in the Daimler years.

The plan had been prepared in top secret, and Chrysler's information technology (IT) department had blocked off the live video stream with a firewall so that employees couldn't watch it and leak it to the outside world. (Marchionne gave them their own presentation the next day.)

Managers had rehearsed and rehearsed their presentations over and over again to get them right. The exact verbiage of each presentation had been reviewed and approved by Marchionne. Ralph Gilles's overview of the new Dodge had the honor of being the first brand out of the gate, which was fitting, because little had been said by the company about Dodge after its split with Ram trucks into two brands.

Ralph flipped through slides of an elderly man with red sunglasses on, a surfer, a tattooed young mom with her family, and a group of groovy-looking young people.

"Every car that we have will have a soul," he said.[20]

Fred Diaz was up next. He had been head of Ram for only a few months, and the company's decision to split the two brands had provoked howls of indignation and derision in the blogosphere. Ralph's presentation showed just how different the two brands were to become.

Whereas Ralph's slides showed young people having fun, Fred was all about work, hunting, and fishing—and included a photo of his two children in cowboy hats! He began with a quote from John Wayne: "Courage is being scared to death—and saddling up anyways."

The seven-hour marathon soon grew tedious for many in the crowd. John McElroy, the host of *Autoline*'s half-hour weekly webcast, was spotted playing computer solitaire.

"This is a lot of fluff," IHS analyst John Wolkonowicz decided sometime before lunch.[21]

The lunch break featured Italian food from Piedmont, which in Italy is seen as among the best in the country. Mike Jackson, the CEO of AutoNation, the nation's largest publicly owned auto dealer, passed the time sending e-mails back and forth to friends and colleagues, making snide remarks about how boring the presentation was.

Marchionne's financial targets made Jackson sit up, however. They were bold, and went beyond anything that had happened at Chrysler since the days of Lee Iacocca. Analysts were used to that from Marchionne. The real shocker was the promise to do 16 model refreshes in 14 months, to tweak the entire lineup, and to do it by December 31 of next year. It was unheard-of.

After the presentation, Jackson called his office, buoyed by what he'd heard. He was convinced that the plan was resilient enough to make it through the market's ups and downs, and decided to consider opening some new Chrysler dealerships.

"It's a green light," he said on his cell phone. "We're in."[22]

Jackson was not alone. The presentation also impressed John Elkann. He had been convinced from day one that the deal made sense in terms of structure and business logic. But he hadn't quite seen how it would all fit together until then. Possibly only Sergio had really understood all the moving parts.

Up until then, the deal had still been in the realm of "a great idea." Sergio had kept John up to date, day in and day out, on his progress at Chrysler. But the presentation made it all seem real and possible.

After the presentation, Chrysler would go underground again while it was working, and its dealer base wouldn't get to see as much as a photo until September 2010, when the dealers convened in Orlando for their annual conference. Until then, they would simply have to trust.

For some Chrysler employees, the November 4 event was an early turning point in the company's recovery.

"That's when people inside the company started to get the idea that Marchionne was real, and he wasn't just coming in to take the best stuff and split," a former employee said.

# Chapter 15

# Sixteen Models in 14 Months

W hen U.S. House Speaker Nancy Pelosi and a delegation of politicians toured the Detroit Auto Show at Cobo Hall on January 11, 2010, Sergio Marchionne showed them around the stand in full-on car salesman mode. He had little choice. The company was running on taxpayer's money, and after six months, despite all the targets it had presented the previous November, Chrysler had little to show for it. Yet the billions of dollars that the government had pledged to Chrysler and General Motors was "money well spent," he told Pelosi.[1]

With no new Chrysler product on view, Marchionne steered Pelosi over to a cherry-red Ferrari.

"This is part of the technology know-how of the group," he said.

Marchionne's decision to cram the Chrysler stand with Fiats, Lancias, and Ferraris drove home a key point: Chrysler might not have new cars to show off until the Jeep Grand Cherokee launch in mid-May, but Fiat was a committed partner that will make good on its promise to share technology. Mercedes-Benz would never have showed its luxury sedans alongside a Dodge. But Marchionne had no problem hopping from a Dodge Challenger SRT-8 muscle car to a Ferrari.

Nor did he have any problem with telling journalists the company would skip its usual press conference that year.

In the past, Chrysler had pulled off some of the most outrageous publicity stunts ever held at the Detroit show—quite a feat for an industry enamored of its own hype. For the Jeep Wrangler's 2006 launch, crowds watched as the fire-red Jeep drove off the stand, through the carpeted hallways of the Cobo Hall convention center, and then right through a plate-glass window out into the street (detonated by mini-explosives, in a stunt copied from a 1992 Jeep launch). The drive ended with the vehicle climbing up a "mountain" set up outside the convention hall and a triumphant Tom LaSorda popping out and doing a "we did it" celebratory fist pump.

Fist pumps were hardly appropriate this year, for "a town where arrogance and denial sowed the weakness that almost destroyed two-thirds of the American-owned auto industry in the past 12 months," the *Detroit News* noted. "Fresh, results oriented thinking is fashionable; so is having the guts to reject traditional Detroit ways."[2]

Chrysler's low profile at the Detroit auto show that year was for another, more practical reason. When he arrived in Auburn Hills in June, Marchionne had ordered the press office to put a gag order on all of his executives. They all had to be "mute as fish," one person recalled. The automotive press hadn't exactly greeted Fiat with open arms. And the bailout itself was controversial. Marchionne was aware that there were a lot of people out there who were waiting to pick apart any promise that he and his team made, any deadlines missed, overpromising, and underdelivering—the old Detroit way. So the smartest thing to do, in his view, was to simply not give them the chance. Everyone— including Chrysler's dealers—would simply have to wait until the company was ready to put the proof onstage.

The skepticism was justified. After all, if Daimler-Benz hadn't turned Chrysler around, how could the Italians from Turin ever have a chance? And Chrysler was lagging behind the other U.S. automakers in coming out of its slump, calling its survival into question. Chrysler's sales had plummeted to under a million vehicles in 2009, its lowest since 1962. Would it be able to survive on its current cash with such an anemic model lineup?

Some commentators were not so sure it would.

"Chrysler has an uphill battle," Edmunds Inc. analyst Jessica Caldwell told the *Los Angeles Times* in its report from the show. "It's hard to see how they will make it through the next 12 to 18 months with the product selection they have."[3]

Marchionne might have skipped the usual press conference, but he held forth at the stand in a huge, freewheeling press scrum—something that would soon become a familiar occurrence at any auto event. Chrysler would be able to survive its product drought on the $5 billion to $6 billion it had on hand, Marchionne told the automotive press smashed up against him, with a swarm of tape recorders in his face, because its model revamps and refreshes would attract buyers in 2010, and so would its ad campaigns. The interiors, especially, were going to get an overhaul.

Plus, if Chrysler used its cash "with discipline," it would be able to break even if it sold 1.1 million cars in the United States, he said, and an additional 500,000 in international markets. That would require a 20 percent growth from global 2009 sales. If the economy recovered in 2010, it shouldn't be too hard for Chrysler to ride it out. After all, that 20 percent increase would be from the low base of a depressed 2009.

The idea that Chrysler could coast through 2010 on government cash and a bunch of gussied-up old models was outrageous. Marchionne needed to keep the lights on and the plants running until the new models were ready, and that's exactly what he aimed to do. Some of Chrysler's past problems, like high health care costs, rigid labor contracts, inefficient dealers, and overreliance on rebates, were alleviated by going through bankruptcy. General Motors was able to take out $4,000 to $5,000 of costs per car because of the bankruptcy, for example, according to the Center for Automotive Research. Demand for new cars had been supported by the government's Car Allowance Rebate System, or "cash for clunkers," in 2009. But that meant Chrysler's competitors enjoyed those same advantages, too.

Chrysler, Ford, and General Motors started 2010 with the lowest supply of vehicles in stock since 1992—a sign that maybe they would leave the days of making too many cars behind them. All three had closed plants and slashed excess capacity during the crisis. Assembly line capacity had fallen to a 20-year low in 2009.

But the success or failure of the venture would hinge on how quickly and how closely Marchionne could merge the day-to-day operations of the Fiat and Chrysler automakers. Both were roughly the same size, although Fiat was a bit larger; Fiat would end the year with 56.2 billion euros ($75.8 billion) in sales for 2010, compared to Chrysler's $41.9 billion. And Fiat had more or less triple the number of Chrysler's 52,000 employees. But the two companies were perfectly compatible in terms of models and markets—each had what the other one lacked.

Keeping the lights on while refreshing Chrysler's tired model lineup was the first step toward the ultimate goal. The two companies could survive only if they became one.

■ ■ ■

To the world at large, Chrysler had gone "underground," to use Marchionne's expression. But behind the scenes, activity was frenetic as employees up and down the entire organization worked long hours to meet tight deadlines. The Dodge team was fired up. When Ralph Gilles tried to describe the difference between the 2010 models and the newer 2011 batch to his new ad agency, he summed it up by saying "It looks like somebody gives a shit." The battle cry "Give a Shit" soon appeared on a poster in the managment team's meeting room.

And nowhere was this activity more frenetic than at the Jefferson North Assembly Plant (JNAP), where the Jeep Grand Cherokee was to be unveiled in mid-May. The unveiling would be the first look at Chrysler's rebirth.

More importantly, Chrysler was retooling all of its plants, one by one, to be more productive and efficient by introducing Fiat's World Class Manufacturing. The company planned to invest about $155 million on WCM. If Chrysler wanted to start making money on small cars, which have small profit margins, it needed to hone its manufacturing efficiency to a very sharp point. It needed to squeeze waste from its factories, drop by drop. Plus, to merge Fiat and Chrysler into one company, their plants all had to be operating in the same way, measuring results in the same way, making cars the same way, and using the same rule books.

An older plant, like Jefferson North, suffered from a lot of the same ills that Stefan Ketter, Fiat's manufacturing chief, recalled from his early days at Fiat back in 2005, when the company was struggling to stay afloat. A thoughtful man with a slightly bemused air, Ketter had spent his career at BMW, Audi, and Volkswagen before joining Fiat at its nadir.

Ketter, a German born in Brazil, took a tour of Chrysler's manufacturing plants in Michigan, Ohio, Illinois, and Canada in 2009, and what he saw surprised him for a company that had once been a partner of Mercedes-Benz. "It was totally cash-out," he recalled. "There had been no investment there for years."

Jefferson North is one of the last automobile manufacturing plants located within Detroit city limits. It stands next to the shuttered Thyssen Krupp Budd Plant, formerly Budd Wheel, which in happier days had assembled the body of the iconic two-seat Ford Thunderbird. The old Budd plant has been closed since 2007, and its huge stamping presses had been broken down into pieces and sold off to manufacturers in Mexico, India, and Brazil by some of the same autoworkers who had recently lost jobs elsewhere.[4]

Opposite Jefferson North is a shuttered Lincoln Continental plant, with the company's logo running down the smokestack in faded white paint. The plant's parking lot, in the dark days of DaimlerChrysler, had been used by Chrysler to park unsold cars. The only sign of life nearby, apart from the Jefferson plant, was Steve's Produce Plus, "the People's Market," which had a cheerful hand-painted sign of President Obama's face on it with the slogan "Time for Change."

The JNAP factory was dark and dirty because of neglect. As recently as April 2009, a "DaimlerChrysler" sign had still stood outside. Car factories these days are not the loud, clanging, smelly, or dangerous places they were as recently as the 1970s. In most parts of the plant, the loudest noise is the clatter of empty overhead trolleys going by as they return to the start of the line to pick up another part, and the only smell, usually, is the smell of fresh rubber. Cars snake by on the assembly lines at a slow pace, and workers stand with baskets of parts next to them and affix them as the cars go by. Much of the assembly is done by machine.

But what looks simple to the eye—workers guiding a little crane bearing a car windshield as it gets lowered onto the vehicle—is devilishly complicated to organize. Just the right number of parts must be on hand. Workers must not be forced to stoop or walk too far. Sections of the car all need to arrive at the right place at the right time.

The plant shut down for three weeks in the summer of 2009 and again in the fall to retool to build the new Jeep Grand Cherokee. Ketter told Marchionne he thought the company should pour a lot of support into the plant.

"We decided that everyone should come in and help clean up the place," Ketter recalled. "We had found old equipment that hadn't been used in 20 years."

Jefferson North plant manager Pat Walsh grabbed the chance for his staff to come in for WCM training during the plant shutdown. "We never did that before," Pat recalled. "We had up to 25 coaches from Fiat. This plant was a stepping-stone for the company on the road to what it wanted to become."

One of the coaches, Giuseppe della Ragione, a rotund, English-speaking southerner with a quick smile and a friendly manner, arrived in September from Fiat's factory near Naples for what was originally intended to be a three-week trip. He stayed for 11 weeks—long enough to learn Detroit slang (filtered through an Italian accent from Naples). For two and a half hours each morning, he taught Jefferson North's workers the ins and outs of WCM in a training course, and then spent the rest of the day on the shop floor side by side with JNAP workers. The desire for change was palpable, he noticed right away.

"At first they looked at me a bit strange," he recalled. "But after a few days they were coming to us once they understood they could work better with less effort."

That's because Giuseppe was there to share WCM best practices—developed through trial and error and endless study across Fiat's car, tractor, and construction equipment plants worldwide—with people at JNAP, be it in logistics, maintenance, carts, automatic guided vehicles, inventory management, or whatever.

He also noticed that the factory had very few standardized rules. Each workshop was a little different from the next, also reflected by the fact that there were coffee machines and microwave ovens scattered around the plant.

Giuseppe, or Pino for short (Italian for "Joe"), was one of about 20 people from Fiat at any given time in the United States working on the WCM rollout during that period, although the number at times rose to hundreds at JNAP alone.

The take-up of WCM at Chrysler's plants in the United States went a lot more quickly than it had in Italy back in 2005, when Ketter had first arrived.

"The nice thing about working with Americans was that they were open to adopting this system," recalled Luciano Massone, who has worked for Fiat since the days of its first talks with Chrysler back in the time of Gianni Agnelli and Lee Iacocca. "We have had much more problems in Italy, honestly. The willingness to improve is a must."

Chrysler workers, understandably, were rooting for the company's comeback. But so were a lot of other people in the Detroit area. Massone was once offered a free meal at a highway sandwich shop near Auburn Hills—and free cake, too—when the owner discovered he was from Fiat.

"She wouldn't let me go until she had taken our pictures," he said.

He and his team would be repeatedly welcomed by words of encouragement as they came through the security checks at the Detroit airport well into 2010.

"When I came through immigration, at the end of 2010, and I told them I was coming to work at Chrysler, the guard said 'Great! Do a good job!'" recalled Massimo Simone, a logistics expert.

General Holiefield latched onto WCM because of the way it gets workers involved in improving the production process, thus also improving quality, which was one of Chrysler's weak points in the market. But what he didn't realize—and perhaps no one did—was that the system would give Chrysler another huge benefit as well: speed. With Fiat and Chrysler plant workers and managers all reading from the same page, the transfer of technology from Italy to the United States was much faster. It meant that a factory could switch over to a more popular vehicle much more quickly, which was important to break the old Detroit cycle of overproduction.

For Chrysler, every day counted.

■ ■ ■

On May 21, Marchionne drove a brand-new Jeep Grand Cherokee onto a makeshift stage at Jefferson North with Michigan Governor

Jennifer Granholm in the passenger seat, as UAW vice president General Holiefield looked on. Marchionne took the stage to a standing ovation—even before he announced that the plant would be adding a second shift with 1,080 more workers.[5] The new workers were paid less than the old ones, but at least they had jobs. General Holiefield kissed the hood of the Jeep.

It was the first new model Chrysler had launched since bankruptcy almost a year before, and Chrysler really needed a boost. Its market share had fallen in 2009 to 8.9 percent, down two percentage points, as it cut back on incentives on the old models in its showrooms. It had just a handful of new models coming out to draw buyers back into showrooms. With the new Jeep, and by adding the second shift at the revamped plant, Chrysler was telling the world it was on the way back. Of course, the real test of Chrysler's recovery would be a successful small car, as well as whether it would resist the temptation to return to its sales bank days and overproduce an unpopular model.

In the meantime, the new Jeep Grand Cherokee gave the company a much-needed shot in the arm. What surprised Mike Manley, an intense Brit whom Marchionne had plucked from running Chrysler's dealer network to take over Jeep, was the speed with which the new Jeep came together. By flattening out the management team and bringing all the decision makers into the same room every weekend for the better part of the year, Marchionne had created a pressure-cooker environment where his executives ripped apart old processes and ideas and made them quicker.

"Everyone at the company carried around an imaginary time line about what it takes to do a vehicle," he recalled later. "It's amazing. The whole product development process completely was turned on its head."

The new car was two inches longer and three inches wider than the old one, but had 11 percent better fuel economy. And the interiors were more luxurious, with softer plastics and stitching on the leather seats.

The launch was delayed by a few weeks to make sure the new vehicle was perfect, particularly from a quality and manufacturing standpoint. Management convened many times at the Jefferson North plant for vehicle reviews as the days ticked down to launch. They pored over the car to make sure that various gaps and fits both inside and outside were all exact.

Despite the slight delay, the whole process came together much more quickly than before because existing Fiat quality processes were transplanted from Fiat factories directly to the JNAP through World Class Manufacturing.

The new Jeep rollout caught Barack Obama's attention as well, because on July 30, the U.S. President visited Jefferson North and GM's Hamtramck plant, where he test-drove a Chevy Volt, to talk up the encouraging results of his administration's $60 billion bailout.

Hundreds of people lined Connor Avenue in front of the Jefferson North plant to watch Obama's huge motorcade roll by. One held up a sign saying "UAW thanks you."[6]

Obama, in his shirtsleeves, and Marchionne, in his usual black sweater, toured the plant for about 20 minutes wearing safety glasses, stopping to chat with workers on the line. One young woman, wearing a T-shirt saying "Dreams Come True," with Obama and Martin Luther King Jr. on it, got a presidential hug.[7]

Obama gave a barnstorming speech that was interrupted again and again by laughter and applause. Still, he had to acknowledge that his own auto task force had been deeply divided about whether to save Chrysler or to walk away, and in the end the decision had come down to the President himself.

"Look, this was a hard decision," he said in a speech at the plant. "I didn't want government to get into the auto business. I've got enough to do."

The crowd laughed.

Not everyone was amused. The word *bailout* had become toxic. Many Americans remained wary about big government, as the Tea Party's strong showing in the midterm elections in November of that year would show.

"President Obama's visit to Detroit is nothing more than a public relations pit stop," said Republican National Committee spokesman Ryan Tronovitch. "The Michigan auto industry still has a long way to go, and President Obama's tax, borrow, and spend policies will only prolong Detroit's recovery."

From halfway around the world, Fiat worker Giuseppe della Ragione watched Obama's speech on television and felt a glow of pride when he thought about his 11 weeks at Jefferson North.

"I felt like I was part of it," he said. "I felt I had taken part."

■ ■ ■

Chrysler celebrated the one-year anniversary exit from bankruptcy on June 10, 2010, with a huge barbeque at its Auburn Hills headquarters. It was Marchionne's idea. He had given barbeques before, at Fiat in Italy, with steaks, potatoes, and beer that he had brought back from Canada and asked the chef at the restaurant on top of the Lingotto to cook up for his team.

But this time it would be on a bigger scale. Everyone from the entire company could come. There were no speeches and no corporate rhetoric. All of the cars, trucks, and tractors were on display; everything from a CNH combine with a wheel taller than a grown man to a Maserati and a Ferrari.

This was not just any barbeque. Sergio Marchionne and his brand managers donned aprons and served the hot dogs, hamburgers, and veggie burgers themselves. Each apron was the same color as the manager's brand. Pietro Gorlier at Mopar had a dark blue one. Laura Soave, the Fiat brand chief who was the latest addition to the team, had a white one for Fiat. Ralph Gilles had a black one for Dodge, and Mike Manley had a green one for Jeep. Anyone who was not a brand manager had a black apron with the Chrysler logo on it. The entire Chrysler management team was there.

As the day got started, the huge lawn at Auburn Hills slowly filled with people. Each person got a black T-shirt with a Mark Twain saying picked by Marchionne printed on it: "Plan for the Future, Because That's Where You Will Spend the Rest of Your Life."

Pretty much every employee wanted to be served by the boss and take a picture with him.

"Hey, come on over here, there's no line," Laura Soave called out to the people standing waiting to be served, but no one took her up on it. It was better to wait for an hour and meet Marchionne. The lunch took four hours, and he didn't want to leave until they were done. For desert there was gelato and espresso.

"It was kind of like what you would throw in your own backyard," recalled Ralph Gilles.

■ ■ ■

Chrysler's employees earned themselves the right to relax during a summer picnic and bask in the success of the Jeep Grand Cherokee unveiling.

But the partnership's success or failure would be judged not on the new Grand Cherokee, but on another car code named the Dodge PF that had been in development since the last quarter of 2009. Fiat had promised a 40 miles per gallon car to the Treasury as part of its deal to scoop up Chrysler for free, and could up its stake 5 percent more after it delivered it. It was this car that would be the true test of the partnership, since it would be the first one to be developed by Chrysler from a Fiat-owned platform.

The new compact benefited from the outset from the knowledge Fiat brought to Chrysler about ways of speeding up its development process, cutting a year from its development time. Speed is a key competitive advantage in the auto business, because it means new products can get into the market more quickly and (hopefully) take sales away from competitors.

This speedier development process was the result of two main things. One was the quick decision making of the flat, matrixed management team. The other was the way Fiat moved all the development functions along at the same time. Previously, designing, engineering, producing, and marketing a new car at Chrysler were conducted like a relay race. One team finished its job, and then handed over the project to the next.

At Fiat, it was more like a sprint. Each team did its job at the same time, and development was tightly coordinated in regular meetings.

The new compact also benefited from cost savings by being based on a Fiat-owned platform and by using a 1.4-liter or 2.4-liter Fiat engine and a dual-clutch six-speed automatic transmission. Normally, it costs about $1 billion to develop a new car from scratch, and takes about two years. In the case of the Dodge PF, Chrysler saved $300 million on the development costs.

The process started by looking at Chrysler's product portfolio. It was clear that the company was missing a C-segment car—a compact sedan. It's the biggest segment in the United States, selling about two million units each year. Every carmaker had a car in that segment, except for Chrysler.

Fiat's platform had been designed to be flexible, so it was easy to widen it for the U.S. market, where cars need to be roomier to sell. The 10 centimeters more in width also helped incorporate that all-important feature, the cup holder. (Italian cars do not have them; in the United States, they are a must-have.) The platform also needed to be adapted to meet different U.S. safety standards.

The real point of discussion came down to brand. Should the new car be a Chrysler or a Dodge? Both brands would have huge competition from other compact cars: Chrysler with Lexus, Cadillac, Lincoln, and others, which were all now making smaller cars. And of course if it were a Dodge it would compete with Hyundai, Ford, Toyota, and the rest.

The old Chrysler would probably have decided to do both. Each brand manager would have clamored for his own me-too version. Dealers, too, who operated stand-alone stores selling only Dodge, say, or only Chrysler, would have put pressure on the company to have a minivan or a sedan to sell in their showrooms. If Dodge had no minivan in its lineup, the company would be under pressure from Dodge dealers wanting to sell one. Or a Chrysler-only dealer could sell just a PT Cruiser, a Town & Country, and a 300, leading the dealer to complain that the product line wasn't "broad enough."[8]

Chrysler had been trying since 2007 to reorganize its dealer network and eliminate single-brand stores. The bankruptcy achieved that goal in the space of a few months, giving the company a chance to weed out weak-selling models.

Overlapping models require more marketing spending, as well. Now, cars from all the company's brands—except Fiat—were shown on the same showroom floors. There was no more me-too product overlap. The answer: go with the mass-market Dodge for the compact, since that type of car is the largest market segment, whereas Chrysler's focus is on being positioned as a premium brand. The trick was the imbue the car with the "young" Dodge spirit while moving it away from the racing feel of the Challenger and the Charger. It had to be fresh and current, without being staid.

The process moved quickly. At the new Chrysler, brand CEOs were leading the charge. Ralph Gilles at Dodge and Olivier Francois at Chrysler were involved from the very start in conception and design. Before, the development process at Chrysler was started by less senior members of the team, and the brand CEOs were brought in nearer to the end. Now, since the brand CEOs are part of development from day one, any issues or problems are dealt with up front and right away. As a result, the whole process is quicker, smoother, and surer.

Some of this decision making took place in "small circle" groups, where Marchionne, production chief Joe Veltri, and others met early on in development, gathering in the same conference room in the banana wing where the bigger management meetings were held. These small circle meetings were where Marchionne talked about facets ranging from industrializing the new car to positioning it in the market, the sales process, and how the new vehicle will fit into the whole portfolio. They are 30,000-feet sessions, big-picture overviews used by product and commercial teams as a basis for developing ideas and plans.

Out of those meetings, a few key ideas became clear.

The new small car had to appeal to as many people as possible, both young and less young, yet still not be bland or predictable. It had to compete with the Honda Civic, the Ford Focus, and the Chevrolet Cruze. What's more, Chrysler hadn't had a successful entry in the so-called C segment for years, so the car would be examined under the microscope by a critical auto press. Last but not least, the company needed it fast.

In the third quarter of 2009, designer Ralph Gilles started sketching. It wasn't an easy task, especially for a designer whose hand almost automatically drew the likes of the sexy Viper or style trailblazers like the Chrysler 300. After all, the car was a huge test for the logic underpinning the transatlantic partnership. Fiat would be sharing its small-car platform with Chrysler to make the U.S. automaker competitive in a segment where it was not. If the car flopped, people would shake their heads and say, "I told you so." It would be a high-profile failure.

Chrysler was saving on development costs by adapting the Fiat platform, but the car itself would be all new, as well as wider than the Alfa Romeo Giulietta hatchback, its forerunner.

Even before any of Ralph's sketches were made, a lot of thought went into what the new Chrysler considered the most important element of the Dodge style to be. Early on, the management team decided that Dodge's drag strip racing heritage would have to be set aside for this car. The car could have sporty elements, but it was going to have to sit at the heart of the market. Gas mileage was also a key starting point. And Ralph was looking for a way to get young people to buy the new Dodge as their first car, without turning off older buyers who were coming back to the segment after their kids had grown up.

Marchionne was looking for two main things: the car had to be recognizable as a Dodge, and it had to look fresh, current, and relevant.

"Just don't have any preconceptions about what this car should be," he told Ralph.

Early on, Ralph and the "triumvirate"—the three main people working on the project (the vehicle engineer, the brand manager, and the lead product planner)—hit on a sure way to make the car different. The interiors, instead of being either just black, gray, or brown, could be customized in dozens of different color combinations. This would be complicated, but Fiat had come up with a way of managing the complexity back when it developed the Fiat 500. That knowledge could be transferred to Chrysler if the team was willing. Which it was. The huge array of colors would certainly make it more interesting for potential buyers. They decided to go with the idea. In the old Chrysler, it would have been too complicated. Only a Ram model had offered such interior customization. The new Chrysler did not shrink from complexity.

After months of looking at sketches, a small group of people gathered in the Dome to look at a foam mock-up of the new car in a so-called soak session. Sergio Marchionne, production chief Joe Velti, Dodge brand head Ralph Gilles, and a few other executives used these soak session to generate unhindered feedback between the people who were in charge of designing and manufacturing the car. These small meetings were vital to getting unhindered feedback from the people who would be in charge of designing and manufacturing the car.

This was different from the old Chrysler, where maybe just the designer and the brand head would look at a car. The advantage of having a bigger group of people in on the process so early on was that the engineer and manufacturing chief could immediately give feedback about any problems that could come up, like, say, the car won't fit in the plant, it doesn't have enough safety features, or some other problem that would make it impossible to execute.

While all this was going on, the car was already being worked on by teams of people looking at how its platform could be manufactured. In the past, these processes would have taken place after the styling. Now, they ran on a parallel track. Moreover, since Chrysler and Fiat factories both used World Class Manufacturing, it was easy to adapt the Fiat platform into production at Chrysler.

Finally, the car would be reviewed by the product committee, which would include people responsible for design, manufacturing, supply chain management, purchasing, engineering, product planning, and the brands. The new Chrysler product committee was more inclusive than the way it had been done before bankruptcy.

After that, a prototype was built and sent to a consumer-testing clinic in the spring of 2010. These clinics were used by automobile makers to test consumer reactions to a new car. An outside agency organized them in a hotel in a large city, lining up a bunch of competitors' cars alongside the new entry. The tests were blind, in the sense that the brand badges (hood ornaments and other identifiers) of all the cars were covered.

Gilles, Marchionne, Veltri, and the rest of the team were relieved to see that consumers didn't have any major complaints; the overall package was well received. The problem, at that point, was that Chrysler still hadn't decided whether its new entry would be a Chrysler or a Dodge. They decided to go with a Dodge.

Still, the team continued to tinker, going back to the clinic three times. On the fourth try, it came out right. Research pointed out to Ralph and the rest of the team was that compact car buyers don't want something overdesigned, so the goal became to create an understated car that relied on pleasing proportions rather than fussy details, enabling it to stay current for years.

"Left to our own devices, we would have gone crazy," he said. "But we stuck to the data. We needed a more restrained car."

All the same, he gave the car wraparound taillights like the Charger, as well as a flying buttress in the back and a slightly aggressive front end. The trademark Dodge crosshair grille has been squeezed down to an almost unrecognizable size, replaced by a more discreet double-stripe Dodge logo.

Though the car was designed from the platform up for an American buyer, Chrysler tapped into huge amounts of Fiat engineering know-how. While the outside is sleek, the interior can be highly personalized like the Fiat 500 in terms of color and trim. The insert on the door, for example, can come in a contrasting color, or be the same as the rest of the interior. Or take the car's hood cut—the line where the hood meets the rest of the body. In manufacturing terms, it's a tricky line to get right, and cheaper cars often hide it. But a clean, visible hood cut communicates quality. Italian engineers had figured out how to achieve a crisp hood cut at a low cost, and the method was easily transferred to Chrysler's factories through World Class Manufacturing.

The design studio used to be a fortress. Now it had opened up its doors to other parts of the company, to the benefit of everyone.

■ ■ ■

It had been more than a year since Chrysler had exited bankruptcy, and the moment finally arrived to show dealers what Marchionne and his team had achieved so far.

On the morning of September 14, 2010, Fred Diaz, who doubled as Chrysler's head of national sales as well as being CEO of the Ram truck brand, met Sergio Marchionne as his driver pulled up at Rosen Shingle Creek hotel in Orlando, Florida. It was Chrysler's first meeting with dealers in two years, and the management team had been preparing for the event for weeks.

"How are you doing, Chief?" the friendly, Texas-born Diaz said, making small talk as he accompanied Sergio up to his room so he could get ready.

"Miserable, Fred," Marchionne replied. "I'm exhausted. My computer blew up on the plane. I lost everything. I had to write my speech all over again." Indeed, a bleary-eyed Marchionne, who had been traveling back and forth between Detroit and Turin on Fiat's rented company jet for months, looked even more tired and rumpled than usual.

The Orlando Dealer Announcement Show was not the sort of event where an executive would want to wing it with an impromptu speech or after a sleepless night, especially the CEO of a nearly failed automaker that was living on government aid and hadn't had a strong new model—apart from the Grand Cherokee—for years.

Nearly all of Chrysler's 2,314 U.S. dealers and their spouses, plus dealers from Canada and Mexico—almost 5,000 people—had come to the Orange County Convention Center that day to see the new vehicle lineup and hear Marchionne speak for the first time. The company's credibility was on the line. Its dealer base was skeptical. Three years before, they had been wooed at a glitzy event hosted by car buff Jay Leno, who cracked, "What a thrill it is to do a Chrysler event where I don't have to speak German."[9]

Jim Press and Bob Nardelli had stood before Chrysler's dealer body in Las Vegas back in 2007 and promised all sorts of changes: better quality, no more special bonuses to high-volume dealers, fewer incentives, and end to channel stuffing, or making too many cars and then relying on incentives to move them off lots. But those things never happened. Some dealers still bore grudges, and were rightly suspicious of this new, unproven team from Italy.

"Last time we did this was a meeting in Las Vegas—guys named Press and Nardelli, and they came off terrific. Two years later, they were selling us down the road. Even if these guys come off terrific, there's still a healing process," David Kelleher, a member of the Chrysler National Dealer Council, told *Automotive News* just a few days before the event.[10]

Bill Golling was one such dealer. He was a little bit more in the loop about what was going on at Chrysler since his dealership was in Bloomfield Hills outside Detroit, where most of the auto executives live. Golling's dealership had been founded by his father, who had served in World War II and gone to college at Hillsdale, Michigan, on the GI Bill. The elder Golling had started to work at Chrysler back in 1956, and then set up his own Chrysler dealership in 1983.

Bill Golling's dealership is an automotive cathedral that employs 120 people. The smell of fresh new rubber and the sound of classical music greet potential buyers as they walk in. Black-and-white photos of the Dodge brothers hang high up on one wall, looking out over the display of shiny new Ram trucks, sporty Dodges, and Chrysler sedans. In the middle of it all sits an antique Jeep that Bill found somewhere out West and had restored, in memory of his father. The unheated vehicle with windshield wipers that must be swiped back and forth by hand is a stark contrast to the gleaming Jeep Cherokees across the room.

Bill thought that Marchionne's promise to revamp 16 models in 14 months was simply impossible. It couldn't be done. It was simply against the rules of common sense.

This time around, there were no stars like Jay Leno or Sean Connery, who hosted a dealer event during the Daimler years. Instead, the tall, square-jawed, and baby-blue-eyed Fred Diaz took the stage, welcoming the dealers with a short speech about how the company had gone to hell and back. One by one, each brand manager for Chrysler, Jeep, Dodge, and Fiat took the stage and unveiled the redesigned models the company had worked so hard on.

Gone was the Chrysler Sebring, replaced by a redesigned, reengineered, and renamed Chrysler 200. Cerberus had given up on plans to do a midcycle face-lift on this tired model. Chrysler engineers had worked hard to fix the noisy ride and upgrade the interior. The renaming had been decided in an hour, after a test-drive. It had driven like a different car.

Golling was impressed by the new Chrysler 200. It looked to him like a competitive entry in a difficult segment, dominated by the Toyota Camry, the Honda Accord, and the Ford Fusion. Now, at least, he would have a contender.

Chrysler also put a lot of effort into improving the interior and ride of the Town & Country. Both the 200 and the minivan displayed Chrysler's new winged logo.

At Dodge, the Durango SUV and the Charger were the two vehicles that got the biggest makeover. The Jeep vehicles (Grand Cherokee, Compass, Patriot, and Wrangler) were, in a way, less of a surprise.

Last but not least, Laura Soave, the latest addition to the management team, unveiled the Fiat 500. In some ways, her job was the toughest, because of Fiat's "Fix It Again Tony" reputation. Her presentation video was a hilarious send-up of Italo-American media stereotypes from "Goodfellas" to "The Sopranos." She could tell from the nervous laughter it made some in the audience uncomfortable at first. But when Joe Pesci said "forgettabouddit" and "the tua yuz," people cracked up.

Marchionne's team was fired up, and had been for months. They wanted to demonstrate that they could deliver. Marchionne wrapped up the morning's presentation in a speech that addressed the dealers' concerns head-on.

"I do not want you to think that I am suffering any illusions or delusions about the context within which we are collectively operating," he said, referring to "our past, our misses, our failures to deliver onto customer expectations."

The heart of his speech, which quoted from everyone from Machiavelli to Charles Dickens, to Albert Einstein, and to Lyndon Johnson, was an appeal to dealers to "exchange a promise for a promise."

"The leadership team and I promise to deliver all the products we have shown today and to execute the development plans highlighted before me . . . in exchange for your commitment to deliver our growth objectives," he said. "Simple, straight, and uncomplicated. I want to be able to leave this meeting tomorrow with the certainty of knowing that we have a deal."

He wrapped up with an unexpected teaser. As he ended his speech, a new Dodge Viper, "in selected dealers in 2012," rolled out onto the stage.

The speech was met by a standing ovation. Golling came away from the speech impressed with the "promise for a promise" idea. The company seemed to be knocking itself out to do the right thing, he thought.

"When you're looking at that much change in such a short time—everything from styling to suppliers to manufacturing—it's simply a huge undertaking," he said.

■ ■ ■

The next step for Chrysler was to get buyers back into showrooms to consider brands that had long been seen as lagging in quality. In order to do that, the company took a risk on a Super Bowl ad that paid off by becoming one of the year's most talked-about commercials.

On Saturday, April 16, 2011, Olivier Francois, Chrysler CEO and chief marketing officer for all Chrysler brands, arrived at the Chrysler Tech Center for a meeting with Sergio Marchionne unshaven, wearing jeans, and looking like he'd been up all night. Which he had.

"Olivier, where have you been last night?" Marchionne asked him jokingly. "And by the way, with whom?"

"I have been out all night, and I come directly to the office," said Olivier excitedly in French-accented English. "I have been up all night with seven wonderful big black ladies, and I love them all!"

When Marchionne asked to know more, Olivier popped a DVD of Selected of God, a Detroit church choir, singing an extended version of Eminem's "Lose Yourself" to images picked out by Olivier.

He spoke excitedly about how the images showed what Detroit means to him. Selected of God would perform live during the Chrysler press conference at the New York Auto Show on April 20.

The story of how a Frenchman became mixed up with a Detroit choir says a lot about how the new Chrysler works, and about how Marchionne picks his team and sets it loose. The choir had appeared a few months earlier in the $9 million Super Bowl ad that aired February 6, 2011, featuring Eminem driving a Chrysler 200 through dark, gritty Detroit, immediately becoming one of the key touchstones about the Motor City's road to recovery The fact that Eminem was driving what had until only recently been called a Sebring, one of Detroit's worst cars, only made the story more interesting.

Months later, Olivier was still tinkering around with the music and the concept.

Unlike the rest of Chrysler's management team, Olivier could easily have been a fish out of water in Detroit. The Paris-born executive started his automotive career at Citroën, and hopped to Fiat at 2005. Long interested in the arts, he had fretted before his first interviews with Marchionne that the Fiat CEO would discover he had written a book of poetry and would be turned off by it. Not only had Marchionne discovered it, he was intrigued. As head of Lancia, Olivier showed a deft touch for eye-catching advertising that Marchionne encouraged.

Instead of being a handicap, Olivier's foreignness turned out to be his calling card. As early as the LA Auto Show in November 2010, he was tapping into the Detroit heritage and came up with the "Imported from Detroit" tagline for the presentation of the new 200.

A couple of days after the LA show, Chrysler's commercial committee gathered in their usual conference room at the Chrysler Tech Center for one of their Sunday meetings. The commercial committee is where the top-level managers reporting directly to Marchionne meet to make decisions about how to sell cars.

Olivier pitched a bold idea for a new ad: he wanted to use the slogan "Imported from Detroit." He showed the script—written by Wieden + Kennedy, Chrysler's new ad agency—to Marchionne, who liked the words.

Olivier played a music-only version of "Lose Yourself," Eminem's theme song from his 2002 film *Eight Mile*. As the music played, he talked to Marchionne about the movie's powerful message of hard work and redemption. Marchionne was struck by the power of the song and of the idea, but he was cautious about the risk. The company needed to be careful. Such an emotional commercial could easily turn out to be embarrassingly cheesy.

"I think the chances of you being able to hit the right target are incredibly slim," he said to Olivier. "What are you going to show with this?"

"Images of Detroit, and of the car," said Olivier. "Pure Detroit. Gritty. Authentic."

"I get it," Marchionne said. "Keep playing with it. Keep it moving. Come back and share it with the rest of the commercial committee as soon as you can. You need to get their reaction."

Marchionne was concerned about the risk of using images of Detroit to talk about the city's heritage and history of making cars. Paradoxically, using Detroit to talk about Detroit is rare in the advertising industry. The city, in parts, is brutally ugly. There are old abandoned ruins of factories of failed auto companies like Packard that have never been pulled down, and each city block is either dotted with boarded-up houses or scarred by vacant lots.

And Detroit's image for manufacturing quality, in recent years, has taken a beating at the hands of the Japanese and the Germans.

"This idea has come up for Chrysler, Chevrolet, and Pontiac a handful of times in the last 20 years," Gary Topolewski, an independent creative director who has worked on Chrysler, Jeep, Dodge, and other brands, told *Advertising Age*. "But it always got shot down by executives who have worked in Detroit their whole lives, fearing it wouldn't play on the coasts."[11]

At the same time, though, Marchionne's instincts had proven right back in 2007 when Fiat launched the 500 with an ad that unabashedly aimed for the heart and soul of every Italian and hit the bull's-eye, big. The 500 had to embody the renaissance of Fiat by reaching for its roots, and showing that the 500 was a car that brought Italians back to their shared experiences of an earlier, happier age of economic plenty. The risk was high, but it had paid off with a big reward. Marchionne, working with Luca de Meo and Giovanni Perosino, had gone over the 500 commercial hundreds of times, crafting and polishing the text. They had repeatedly watched an iconic Apple ad from 1984. He had shown the 500 ad, as well as the Apple ad from 1984, to his team at Chrysler.

At this point, Olivier asked Wieden+Kennedy to come up with a so-called rip video—a collection of stock images with a voice-over from the agency for internal use—to show the commercial committee. On December 12, 2010, a Sunday, they showed it to the assembled group at Auburn Hills, along with two people from Wieden+Kennedy who had flown in from Portland, Oregon. The agency, convinced that Eminem's music would be impossible to get, used the White Stripes' "Seven Nation Army" as a soundtrack instead.

In early January, a version of "Lose Yourself" was played live at the Chrysler presentation at the Detroit Auto Show.

The Super Bowl had come into play at this point. Olivier needed Marchionne's backing. Olivier pitched the group for an hour.

"There is only one music," he said. "It has to be Eminem."

The commercial committee was divided. Half loved it, and half hated it.

"Detroit is not that popular," said one manager. "And this ad—it looks like a threat."

Others got tears in their eyes.

Chrysler management was also divided on the idea of using Eminem's music, because in the view of some it was too controversial. Others thought that the rapper's history and success gave him credibility.

Using Detroit in the commercial was important because the human side of the story had gotten lost in the political punching match about bailouts, many people at the meeting felt. Good commercials create connections with viewers. Chrysler had a big story to tell about its comeback, and about the human experience of what people had been living through. It had a chance to make a huge connection with people. But if they tried to do it too early, its story would fall on deaf ears. And if they did it too late, it would be old news. The timing had to be just right, Marchionne said.

Marchionne decided to take the risk.

"Go for it—go for Eminem's music," he said.

"Great," Olivier thought to himself. "I have just sold the fur of the bear before I killed it" (a French expression).

Olivier spent all Sunday trying to get in touch with someone who could connect him with Eminem, who—along with catalog co-owner

Joel Martin—had turned down over 100 requests to use the song in ads. On Monday evening, Olivier drove over to Martin's Ferndale office without an appointment and simply waited for him to turn up.

"He's a maniac," Martin said, referring to Francois. "The whole thing had a surreal quality to it . . . this French guy and all this, he was telling us about loving Detroit and how important [Eminem] is to the city."[12]

The risk and hard work paid off. The ad was one of the most popular of the Super Bowl, endlessly talked about and Googled, and by August 2011 had drawn 12 million viewers on YouTube. The NBC Nightly News did a feature. The commercial, called "Born of Fire," won five awards at the Cannes advertising festival in June 2011.

On the day of the Super Bowl, Mopar CEO Pietro Gorlier was at a reception for about 600 Chrysler dealers during a National Automobile Dealers Association (NADA) event at the Drake Hotel in San Francisco's General Square. The dealers knew that Chrysler had planned some sort of new ad, but didn't have any inkling it would include Eminem.

When it aired, the room fell silent. And then, a blast of energy.

"I remember people coming up and grabbing me and saying how great it was," Gorlier recalled. "People were just yelling and screaming." The next day, as he was flying out, he met a group of General Motors executives at the airport.

"You did something absolutely great," one told him.

■ ■ ■

On the morning of May 24, 2011, U.S. Vice President Joseph Biden called Sergio Marchionne to congratulate Chrysler on having achieved the milestone of repaying its $5.9 billion debt to the U.S. Treasury. Biden also called Bob King, president of the UAW, and Frances Soehartono, a worker at Jefferson North. A White House photo that day shows Biden sitting at a glossy wooden desk, its well-polished surface reflecting the green trees outside his window, as he told Frances it was thanks to workers like her that the company had come back from the brink.[13]

Chrysler's turnaround was happening faster than anyone had predicted back in June 2009. Sergio Marchionne, his management team, Chrysler's employees, and its hourly workers had all delivered on the promise Sergio had made to the U.S. Treasury back in those difficult sessions with President Obama's task force. Chrysler had paid back the loan.

More importantly, Chrysler and Fiat were on the way to becoming one company spanning two continents. In a few months' time, Marchionne would name a single management team responsible for shared car platforms, parts, and engines of vehicles ranging from the Alfa Romeo–based Dodge compact car to a pricey made-in-Detroit Maserati SUV to the biggest, baddest of Ram trucks.

Fiat Chairman John Elkann was in Washington, D.C., that day, attending an event at the Brookings Institution, an independent think tank where he was a member. He also made a round of visits in the U.S. capital, a series of courtesy calls on the day of Chrysler's payback that reflected John's role as a key shareholder of the one-day-to-be merged transatlantic automaker. Later that day, Sergio would stop over in Washington from Detroit, and together they would fly back to Italy.

Up until payback day, Fiat had been a sort of caretaker of Chrysler on behalf of the company's stakeholders, including U.S. taxpayers and Chrysler's workers. But that morning, when the funds were wired to the Treasury and Fiat increased its stake to 46 percent, the company—and John—took on a new role as largest shareholder. By the end of the year, Fiat planned to hold 58.5 percent of Chrysler.

After the merger, the Agnelli family's stake would be diluted. Instead of 30 percent of Fiat, like it had now, the family would own about 22 percent of the new, bigger company. This was something that had never happened before. To John, it was an acceptable price to pay for making Fiat into a global auto player. It was the only way he could hope to stay in the top tier of car companies.

But something else happened that day, too, that everyone had overlooked. This methodical young man had succeeded in doing what his flamboyant grandfather Gianni had set out to do but had never been able to achieve—find the right partnership for Fiat that would guarantee its survival into the next century. It was finally on track to succeed in becoming a global company. At the same time, John also managed to fulfill the wishes of Gianni's brother Umberto, who had quite rightly insisted over the years that the family should reduce its exposure to the ups and downs of the auto industry and put its money to work more profitably elsewhere.

By steering Fiat and Chrysler into eventually becoming one company, John had simultaneously achieved both Gianni's and Umberto's lifelong goals.

# Epilogue

When Sergio Marchionne told Sterling Heights workers on payback day, May 24, 2011, that they were at "the end of the beginning," he was right. The U.S. Treasury committed a total of $12.5 billion to Chrysler, $4 billion during the Bush administration and $8.5 billion during the current presidency (including an undrawn $2.1 billion). Chrysler had returned to profit, and paid back loans to the United States and Canadian governments. The combined Fiat-Chrysler—under a single management team from the end of July 2011—had become the world's sixth-largest automaker in 2010. That was the "beginning" part, but for Fiat-Chrysler to meet its target of making a combined six million cars in 2014 much still remains to be done.

First, improving quality is proving to take longer than the company expected. In July 2011, Dodge scored encouragingly well on J.D. Power's annual survey of customer satisfaction. Its large, sportier Charger, midsize Challenger, and the Durango were praised in the influential survey. But *Consumer Reports* in August 2011 was a big disappointment at Chrysler. The magazine tested eight Chrysler models for that issue: the Chrysler 200, the Dodge Avenger and Charger sedans, the Chrysler Town & Country minivan, and four SUVs (Dodge Durango, Dodge Journey, Jeep Compass, and Jeep Patriot). The Durango and Charger had improved the most, the magazine found, and the Town & Country had improved significantly. But the magazine was "not impressed" with the 200, Avenger, Compass, Journey, or Patriot.

"Despite some improvement, they are still mediocre over all, scoring near the bottom of their respective categories and too low to be recommended," explained *Consumer Reports*.

Second, Chrysler's lineup is still overly dependent on big gas guzzlers like the Ram truck, the Durango SUV, and the Jeep Grand Cherokee. In addition to having poor fuel mileage, these vehicles usually sell for over $25,000. Chrysler needs a smaller car to attract buyers concerned with fuel mileage and with price. That won't start to change until the new Dodge compact comes to market in early 2012. Based on an Alfa Romeo architecture, or underpinnings, the Dodge will be the basis of five other vehicles for the Chrysler lineup in the coming years. The company also plans to launch it in China. The Dodge compact will be built in Belvidere, Illinois, with a Fiat small engine built in Dundee.

The new Fiat 500 looks set to miss its initial sales target of 50,000 cars in North America, however. As of August 2011, Chrysler has sold about 8,000. Fiat's market strategy seems right for the car, and it has received rave reviews and tons of press coverage, so that could change. Sales may be behind target because of the decision to sell the car in newly opened Fiat dealerships. Fiat wanted to have 130 dealerships up and running by the first quarter, but only a dozen or so were open by then.[1] Plans to launch Alfa Romero in the U.S. are running behind schedule.

As Chrysler focuses on creating a more competitive model lineup, its management challenge is to merge the two companies into one. In order for that to happen, Fiat will have to buy the stake in the company held by the United Auto Workers' Voluntary Employee Beneficiary Association (VEBA) health care trust. The VEBA trust owns 42 percent of Chrysler and has a board seat. In exchange for government funding, the UAW agreed to exchange an almost $8 billion obligation in health care payments for Chrysler's 150,000 retired workers for an unsecured note and stock worth $4.6 billion in the new Chrysler. Originally the plan was that the VEBA trust would cash in its Chrysler stock when the automaker sold shares in an initial public offering (IPO) on the stock exchange. The offering, originally seen in 2011, now is unlikely to happen until 2013.

More recently, Marchionne has said he is willing to consider buying the VEBA stake outright, but not if it puts Fiat's credit rating at risk. Fiat has an option to buy up to 40 percent of the VEBA trust's stake in Chrysler anytime between July 1, 2012, and June 30, 2016. Prior to an IPO, the price is calculated on a multiple of Chrysler's last four quarterly reports of earnings before interest, taxes, depreciation, and amortization (EBITDA) less industrial net debt. The EBITDA multiple is not to exceed Fiat's.

Even when Chrysler and Fiat eventually merge, the issue of where the combined company will be headquartered has turned into a political flashpoint in Italy. In the years since Fiat's turnaround, Marchionne has gone from being a national hero to the target of bitter criticism due to a perception that he plans to move Fiat to the United States or that the Fiat-Chrysler combination is a so-called reverse merger with Chrysler swallowing up Fiat. His attempts to introduce more flexibility into Fiat's labor contracts in 2010 have been met with a howl of outrage and a falling-out with Italy's largest union, the CGIL. Marchionne's public appearances in Italy are still occasions for noisy press scrums. The questioning is increasingly pointed, and at times borders on hostile.

In the first quarter of 2011, for the first time since 2004, the Big Three Detroit automakers all turned a profit. The fundamentals of the car industry, for now, seem to have changed because of the Chrysler and General Motors bankruptcies. Yet it remains to be seen whether U.S. automakers will refrain from returning to past practices of deep discounting, overproduction, channel stuffing, and plumping up their numbers with fleet sales as the economy worsened towards the end of 2011.

The final question revolves around whether the auto industry will need another round of consolidation to weed out weak players and overcapacity. The Chrysler and GM bankruptcies has gone a long way to rightsize those two players' costs in relation to market conditions, but European consolidation is still a work in progress. Whatever happens, Fiat and Chrysler are in a much better position now to survive than they were before Chrysler's bankruptcy.

■ ■ ■

For the Agnelli family, the Fiat-Chrysler partnership shows that the dynasty's involvement with the auto industry will continue. It also underlines the incredible resilience of both the Agnelli family and family capitalism as an economic model.

While "family business is often family drama," as the Agnelli saga shows, family firms have some distinct advantages. Family ties make for a strong commitment to the company. Family names can be a salable asset for the customer or indeed even the firm, as author David Landes points out in *Dynasties: Fortunes and Misfortunes of the World's Great Family Businesses*. But the main thing that makes family firms strong is the same reason they are criticized: it's the ability to make decisions behind closed doors.

"Shady dealings are certainly not limited to family firms—managerial enterprises are equally ruthless in their avoidance of regulations," writes Landes. "But family firms get away with more."[2]

Carmaking families are often forced to bring in outside managers to deal with the business because of its technical and financial complexity, and the Agnellis have been no exception to this rule. The Agnellis have been fortunate to find excellent managers three times—Vittorio Valletta shortly after the company's founding, Cesare Romiti in its heyday, and Sergio Marchionne, who now has the drive and vision to take the company forward into the global marketplace.

Marchionne and John Elkann have a working relationship based on trust, shared vision, respect for each other's competence, and constant communication. John has already made a mark as the family leader with several rapid decisions. One of his first big challenges, in June 2006, after taking on a managerial role at the family holding company IFIL, was to deal with a match-fixing scandal at Juventus, the Agnelli-owned soccer team. The team had been an Italian champion, and the scandal resulted in it getting kicked out of the premier league, Serie A. John took public responsibility for what he called "reprehensible" behavior and replaced the entire board, in order to make a clean sweep and send a strong signal that the team had turned a page in its history. He also changed the team management's corporate governance, giving the board more say over investments and strategy.

He was also quick to grab an opportunity offered by the financial crisis in September 2008 to merge IFI and IFIL, a move that markets had been requesting for years, and renamed the merged company Exor. In the meantime, he has been refocusing the company's portfolio.

In January 2010, John moved forward with plans that had been discussed for years, splitting the Fiat Group into two. Fiat Powertrain

Technologies, agricultural equipment maker Case New Holland, and truck unit Iveco were spun off from the auto business to create a new company called Fiat Industrial.

He reorganized the family foundation, Fondazione Giovanni Agnelli, in 2008 to focus on education. The foundation offers a free MBA for 28 engineering graduates, and is now in its third year.

Before the economic recession of 2008, family-owned companies had fallen out of fashion with investors because of concerns that performance could take a backseat to what could be called dynastic considerations, and that corporate governance could be less than transparent. The inherent conservatism of family owners—who would be perhaps keener to save jobs and protect social standing than to take a risk on expanding in a new market—has often been criticized as a brake on growth. But the devastating consequences of the unfettered risk taking practiced on Wall Street leading up to the financial crisis has silenced those critics.

■ ■ ■

How had the Agnelli family managed to transform a fate that had seemed destined to end like a Greek tragedy, with death, destruction, and loss, into a story of renewal, seized opportunities, and second chances?

At a more basic level, how has the dynasty managed to stay influential as it moved into its second century, instead of fading into genteel irrelevance like so many family business dynasties before it? The answer clearly goes beyond a desire for money, since the family could have been far richer had it sold Fiat Auto to DaimlerChrysler when it had a chance to do so back in 2000, when the German-American colossus was ready to put $10 billion to $12 billion on the plate. Nor was the answer to be found in a thirst for power, since the Agnellis plan to scale back their stake in the merged Fiat-Chrysler to less than what it was in Fiat.

The picture that emerges shows that despite the ever-greater domination of publicly traded companies in today's economy, the elemental forces driving the family company can, at times, translate into a business advantage.

The Agnelli clan has stayed true to its Piedmont roots, shaped by centuries of rule by the militaristic House of Savoy: get on with things, do your duty, and don't make a big fuss about it. Play by the rules, but don't hesitate to grab unorthodox opportunities when survival or even strategic gain is at stake. Above all, be courageous and don't run from battle. John has added his own international perspective to the mix, updating the family tradition for the more transparent and global business climate.

Of course, no one in the family took to a public podium to explain its playbook for survival. John never opened himself to public scrutiny with his views about the dynasty's ability to hold on to the company that a former cavalry officer named Giovanni Agnelli and his fellow car lovers founded back in 1899. In business, it's never a good idea to give your competitors too much insight. John has had plenty of time to reflect on his family heritage—and mistakes—since joining Fiat's board in 1997. Like any person groomed for a powerful position, and perhaps because of his cultural background or his own sensibility, he steers clear of discussing such potentially emotional issues in public.

But he doesn't need to, really. The family's actions speak louder than speeches ever could, and its story has provided some clues about the source of the dynasty's resilience.

■ ■ ■

In the last few days of his life, Gianni Agnelli received a visit at home, where he was dying of cancer, from Gianluigi Gabetti, who had been Gianni's closest financial adviser for more than 30 years.

"Is there anything else I can do for you, or that needs attention?" Gabetti asked Agnelli, who was in a wheelchair.

No, Gianni replied. Everything that needed to be done had been taken care of, for now.

At that point Gianni did something unexpected. He leaned over to where Gianluigi was sitting, took Gianluigi's hand, brought it briefly to his cheek, and held it there for just an instant. Then he backed his wheelchair away, waved good-bye, and left the room.

# Notes

*A note on sourcing:*

To gather the material I needed for this book, I conducted over 150 interviews of Agnelli family members, Fiat executives past and present, members of Chrysler's management team, Fiat and Chrysler advisers, and former members of President Obama's auto task force. My experience of covering Fiat began in the 1990s, and many of those articles formed the basis for my assumptions when I began this project. I also drew on the *Wall Street Journal's* coverage of Fiat and Chrysler. As part of my research, I consulted over 90 books in English and Italian; read dozens of magazine and newspaper articles; burrowed into archives in Milan, Turin, and Rome; and leafed through hundreds of pages of court and police files.

I received the cooperation of Fiat and Chrysler in my telling of this story, but it is not an authorized account. Many of the people I interviewed asked to remain anonymous because of their past or current connections to Fiat or to the Agnelli family. Scenes reconstructed in this book were done on the basis of events recounted to me by direct participants in my own reporting, or firsthand accounts and interviews with those present published by reputable news organizations.

The accounts of Giovanni Agnelli and the founding of Fiat were based on historic archives and firsthand witnesses, because Agnelli himself was not inclined to record his thoughts or actions. Much of the material on Virginia Agnelli came from police records.

People I interviewed at Fiat and Chrysler were Sergio Marchionne, Alfredo Altavilla, Joe Veltri, Andrea Formica, Harald Wester, Stefan Ketter, Luciano Massone, Lorenzo Ramaciotti, Roberto Giolito, Eugenio Razelli, Lodovico D'Entreves, Fred Diaz, Mike Manley, Laura Soave, Ralph Gilles, Olivier Francois, and John Elkann. Unfortunately, former managers of General Motors and most of those at Chrysler declined to be interviewed for this book, as did Margherita Agnelli.

## Prologue

1. Lee Iacocca and William Novak, *Iacocca: An Autobiography* (New York: Bantam Books, 1984), 295.

2. Brad Wernle and Luca Ciferri, "Chrysler Mulls RWD Mid-Sized Replacement," *Automotive News*, June 22, 2009.

3. Bradford Wernle, "Chrysler 200 Takes the Brand's Sales Lead in May," *Automotive News*, June 6, 2011.

4. Brent Snavely, "Chrysler Pays Up, More Work Ahead," *Detroit Free Press*, May 25, 2001.

5. Chrysler video.

## Chapter 1    The Scattered Pieces

1. Aldo Cazzullo, "Io e Mio Nonno," *Corriere della Sera*, January 24, 2008.

2. Marcello Sorgi, "Agnelli: Al Rilancio della Fiat Serve Anche il Supporto del Sistema Paese," *La Stampa*, March 1, 2003.

3. Paolo Griseri, Massimo Novelli, and Marco Travaglio, *Processo Alla Fiat* (Rome: Editori Riuniti, 2007), 27.

4. Enzo Biagi, *Il Signor Fiat* (Milan: Rizzoli Editore, 1976), 24.

5. Sorgi, "Agnelli: Al Rilancio."

6. John Tagliabue, "Gianni Agnelli, Fiat Patriarch and a Force in Italy, Dies at 81," *New York Times*, January 25, 2003.

7. Cinzia Sasso, "La Sfida di Margherita," *La Repubblica*, September 8, 2007.

8. Moncalvo, Gigi. *I Lupi e Gli Agnelli* (Florence: Valecchi, 2009), 147.

9. Carlo Di Turchetti, "La Agnelli & C. Vale 1.3 Miliardi," *Il Mondo*, April 1, 2002.

10. M. Zat, "Umberto Agnelli, Rafforzano l'Attività Tradizionale con le Nuove Tecnologie," *La Stampa*, March 31, 2001.

11. "Agnelli-Fresco, Momento Triste, Perdita Irriperabile," AGI, January 24, 2003.

12. Maria Teresa Martinengo, "E' Stata Donna Marella ... ," *La Stampa*, January 26, 2003.

13. A RAI broadcast, 10:30 a.m.–12 p.m., RAI-1, January 26, 2003.

14. Marcello Sorgi, *Il Secolo Dell'Avvocato* (Milan: Skira, 2008), 30.

15. "A Society Transformed by Industry," *Time*, January 17, 1969.

16. Sergio Marchionne, "Fiat's Extreme Makeover," *Harvard Business Review*, December 2008.

17. Alessandra Farkas, "Io, Mia Madre e Le Donne," *Corriere Della Sera*, June 8, 2007.

18. "Agnelli Family Member Leaves Intensive Care Ward Following Drug Overdose," Associated Press, October 14, 2005.

## Chapter 2   A Dynasty Is Born

1. Carlo Biscaretti di Ruffia, *I Cinquant'anni della Fiat* (Milan: Arnoldo Mondadori Editore, 1951), 31.

2. Rosario Lavorgna, "Rievocazione della Prima Corsa per Veicoli Disputata in Italia nel 1895," www.lostato.it, April 27, 2011.

3. Enzo Biagi, "Il Caso," RAI-1, February 2, 1988 (television program).

4. Biscaretti di Ruffia, *I Cinquant'Anni della Fiat*, 33.

5. Gaetano Natale, *Giolitti e gli Italiani* (Milan: Garzanti, 1949), 397.

6. Biscaretti di Ruffia, *I Cinquant'Anni della Fiat*, 34.

7. Ibid., 41.

8. Valerio Castronovo, *Giovanni Agnelli* (Turin: UTET, 1971), 9.

9. Biscaretti di Ruffia, *I Cinquant'Anni della Fiat*, 41.

10. Valerio Castronovo, *Fiat: Una Storia del Capitalismo Italiano* (Milan: Rizzoli, 2005), 8.

11. Biscaretti di Ruffia, *I Cinquant'Anni della Fiat*, 47.

12. Ibid., 44.

13. Castronovo, *Fiat*, 5.

14. Ibid., 7.

15. Castronovo, *Giovanni Agnelli*, 11–12.

16. Alessandro Genero, from Archivio Storico Fiat.

17. Ibid.

18. Ibid.

19. Castronovo, *Giovanni Agnelli*, 15.

20. Giancarlo Galli, *Gli Agnelli, il Tramonto di una Dinastia* (Milan: Arnoldo Mondadori Editore, 1997), 35.

21. Ibid.

22. Gianni Oliva, *I Savoia* (Milan: Arnoldo Mondadori Editore, 1999), 301.

23. Ibid., 171.

24. Christopher Hibbert, *The House of Medici, Its Rise and Fall* (London: Allen Lane, 1974), 69.

25. John Julius Norwich, *A History of Venice* (London: Allen Lane, 1982), 412.

26. Guided tour of Chambery.

27. www.palazzomadamatorino.it/pagina4.php?id_pagina=625; Pier Cesare Morero, "Mille Anni di Storia," www.comune.villarperosa.to.it/index.php/storia/1000-anni-di-storia.html.

28. Castronovo, *Fiat*, 3.

29. *Gianni Agnelli* (Milan: Rizzoli, 2007), 28 (collection of Agnelli's quotes and sayings).

30. Ibid.

31. Castronovo, *Giovanni Agnelli*, 3.

32. Castronovo, *Fiat*, 3–4.

33. Italo Pietra, *I Tre Agnelli* (Milan: Garzanti, 1985), 22.

34. *L'Italia, Veneto: Touring Club Italiano* (Milan: Touring Editore, 2005), 156.

35. Biscaretti di Ruffia, *I Cinquant'Anni della Fiat*, 25.

36. Ibid., 26.

37. Ibid., 26.

38. Pietra, *I Tre Agnelli*, 23.

39. Silvio Pozzani, *Giovanni Agnelli, Primo Industriale dell'Automobile* (Milan: Nuova Mercurio, 1962), 16.

40. Ibid., 23.

41. Marie-France Pochna, *Agnelli, L'Irresistibile* (Milan: Sperling & Kupfer, 1990), 31.

42. Peter Collier and David Horowitz, *The Fords, an American Epic* (San Francisco: Encounter Books, 1987), 28.

43. www.tplex.org/2_fordcars.html.

44. Collier and Horowitz, *The Fords*, 34.

45. www.tplex.org/2_earlyyears.html.

46. Pietra, *I Tre Agnelli*, 38.

47. Collier and Horowitz, *The Fords*, 42.

48. Castronovo, *Fiat*, 354.

49. Lorenzo Gianotti, *Gli Operai Fiat Hanno Cento Anni* (Rome: Editori Riuniti, 1999), 18.

50. Riccardo Felicioli, *Fiat: 1899–1999* (Milan: Automobilia, 1999), 32.

51. Ibid., 34.

52. Giorgio Candeloro, *Storia dell'Italia Moderna*, vol. 8 (Milan: Giangiacomo Feltrinelli Editore, 1978), 75.

53. R. J. B. Bosworth, *Mussolini's Italy: Life under the Dictatorship* (London: Allen Lane, 2005), 69.

54. Agnelli speech to board, September 29, 1920 (from Fiat archive).

55. Paolo Spriano, *L'Occupazione delle Fabriche* (Turin: Giulio Einaudi Editore, 1962), 55.

56. Ibid., 64.

57. Ibid., 65.

58. Ibid., 67.

59. Ibid., 95.

60. Paolo Spriano, *Storia del Partito Comunista*, vol. 1 (Turin: Giulio Einaudi Editore, 1967), 79.

61. Ibid., 79.

62. Paolo Spriano, *L'Occupazione delle Fabriche, Settembre, 1920* (Turin: Giulio Einaudi Editore, 1964), 146.

63. Cesare Maria De Vecchi di Val Cismon, *Quadrumviro Scomodo* (Milan: Mursia, 1984), 31.

64. Castronovo, *Giovanni Agnelli*, 275.

65. Eric Hobsbawm, *The Age of Extremes: A History of the World, 1914–1991* (New York, Pantheon, 1995), 119.

66. De Vecchi di Val Cismon, *Quadrumviro Scomodo*, 104.

67. Lorenzo Gianotti, *Gli Operai della Fiat Hanno Cent'Anni* (Rome: Editori Riuniti, 1999), 31.

68. "Foreign News: Cessation of Competition," *Time*, July 14, 1930.

69. Galli, *Gli Agnelli*, 87.

70. Felice Guarneri, *Battaglie Economiche Tra le Due Guerre*, vol. 1 (Milan: Garzanti, 1953), 56–59.

71. Piero Melograni, *Gli Industriali e Mussolini* (Milan: Longanesi & C., 1972), 75–77.

72. Pochna, *Agnelli, L'Irresistibile*, 55.

73. Ibid., 46–47.

74. Ibid., 89.

75. David Landes, *Dynasties: Fortunes and Misfortunes of the World's Great Family Businesses* (New York: Viking, 2006), 163.

76. Edmondo Schmidt, *Torino, Aprile 1945* (Turin: Centro Studi Piemontesi, 1978), 32.

77. Ibid., 33.

78. Edmondo Schmidt, *Il Caso Schmidt, Da Berlino a Regina Coeli* (Turin: Centro Studi Piemontesi, 2010), 18–19.

79. Ibid., 7.

80. Ibid., 8.

81. Valletta's trial documentation.

82. Castronovo, *Fiat*, 363.

83. Gianni Oliva, *I Vinti e i Liberati* (Milan: Arnoldo Mondadori Editori, 1994), 457.

84. From historical archive of Italian Resistance in Turin.

85. Castronovo, *Fiat*, 339.

86. Galli, *Gli Agnelli*, 102.

87. Piero Bairati, *Vittorio Valletta* (Turin: UTET, 1983), 140.

88. Valetta memo, August 15, 1945.

89. Valletta memo, May 12, 1945.

90. Castronovo, *Fiat*, 346.

91. Bairati, *Vittorio Valletta*, 121.

92. Enzo Biagi, television interview, February 23, 1988, RAI-1.

93. Galli, *Gli Agnelli*, 104.

## Chapter 3    From Salad to Skinny-Dipping

1. Jane Campbell, "Memorie della Principessa di San Faustino," *Omnibus*, April 9, 1938.

2. Enzo Biagi, "Il Caso," RAI-1, February 2, 1988 (television interview with Susanna Agnelli).

3. "Milestones, July 4, 1938," *Time*, July 4, 1938.

4. Campbell, "Memorie."

5. Ibid.

6. Ibid.

7. Ibid.

8. Ibid.

9. Judith Suther, *A House of Her Own: Kay Sage, Solitary Surrealist* (Lincoln: University of Nebraska Press, 1997), 40.

10. Campbell, "Memorie."

11. Marina Ripa di Meana and Gabriella Mecucci, *Virginia Agnelli, Madre e Farfalla* (Argelato: Minerva Edizioni, 2010), 30.

12. Ibid., 31.

13. Gianni Oliva, *I Savoia* (Milan: Arnoldo Mondadoi Editore, 1999), 12.

14. Ripa di Meana and Mecucci, *Virginia Agnelli*, 35.

15. Archivio dello Stato, Rome.

16. Ibid.

17. Biagi, "Il Caso," RAI-1, February 2, 1988.

18. Susanna Agnelli, *Vestivamo alla Marinara* (Milan: Arnoldo Mondadori Editore, 1975), 59.

19. Ripa di Meana and Mecucci, *Virginia Agnelli*, 110.

20. Agnelli, *Vestivamo alla Marinara*, 30.

21. Ibid., 39.

22. "L'Inchiesta sulla Morte dell' Avv. Agnelli," *Corriere della Sera,* July 19, 1935.

23. Agnelli, *Vestivamo alla Marinara*, 42.

24. Ibid., 43.

25. Ibid., 43.

26. Ripa di Meana and Mecucci, *Virginia Agnelli*, 136.

27. Frederika Randall, "Curzio Malaparte: A Dandy in Hell," *Wall Street Journal*, August 28, 1988.

28. The Esoteric Curiosa, "The Formidable Princess Jane," http://theesoteric curiosa.blogspot.com/2010/12/formidable-princess-jane-americas-own .html, December 29, 2010.

29. Agnelli, *Vestivamo alla Marinara*, 45.

30. Enzo Biagi, *Il Signor Fiat* (Milan: Rizzoli Editore, 1976), 44.

31. Archivio dello Stato, Rome.

32. Biagi, *Il Signor Fiat*, 44.

33. Agnelli, *Vestivamo alla Marinara*, 1975. Suni, page 52.

34. Archivio dello Stato, Rome.

35. Agnelli, *Vestivamo alla Marinara*, 53.

36. Ibid.

37. Archivio dello Stato, Rome.

38. Archivio dello Stato, Rome, letter to Rome on December 20 from Turin chief of police.

39. Agnelli, *Vestivamo alla Marinara*, 56.

40. Archivio dello Stato, Rome.

41. Agnelli, *Vestivamo alla Marinara*, 62.

42. Ibid., 66.

43. Ibid., 69.

44. Marie-France Pochna, *Agnelli, L'Irresistibile* (Milan: Sperling & Kupfer, 1990), 111–112.

45. Ibid., 113.

46. Eugen Dollmann, *Roma Nazista* (Milan: Longanesi Editore, 1949), 273.

47. Robert Katz, *Roma Citta Aperta* (Milan: Il Saggiatore, 2009), 328.

48. Dollmann, *Roma Nazista*, 273.

49. Robert Katz, *The Battle for Rome: The Germans, the Allies, the Partisans, and the Pope, September 1943–June 1944* (New York: Simon & Schuster, 2003), 290.

50. Giorgio Angelozzi Gariboldi, *Pio XII, Hitler e Mussolini: Il Vaticano Tra Le Dittature* (Milan: Mursia, 1988), 250.

51. Ibid., 250.

52. Ibid., 253.

53. Ibid., 253.

54. Ibid., 253.

55. James Srodes, *Allen Dulles, Master of Spies* (Washington, DC: Regnery, 1999), 343.

56. Valerio Castronovo, *Fiat: Una Storia del Capitalismo Italiano* (Milan: Rizzoli, 2005), 320.

57. "Le Maestranze Fiat Chiedono il Consiglio di Gestione," *La Nuova Stampa*, September 19, 1945.

58. Richard Breitman and Norman Goda, *U.S. Intelligence and the Nazis* (Washington, DC: National Archive Trust Fund Board, 2004), 319.

59. Srodes, *Allen Dulles*, 348.

## Chapter 4   Gianni Agnelli, King of a Republic

1. Alexander Stille, *The Sack of Rome* (New York: Penguin Press, 2006), 133–134.

2. Valerio Castronovo, *Gianni Agnelli, Una Certa Idea dell'Europa e dell'America* (Turin: Giulio Einaudi Editore, 2005), xvii.

3. Nicola Caracciolo, "Agnelli," *La Grande Storia*, RAI-3, December 30, 1999, aired at 8:30 P.M.

4. Giorgio Galli, *La Storia della DC* (Rome: Laterza, 1978), 61.

5. Pierre Milza, *Storia d'Italia, dalla Preistoria ai Giorni Nostri* (Milan: Casa Editrice Corbaccio, 2006), 853.

6. *Time*, "A Society Transformed by Industry," January 17, 1969.

7. John Tagliabue, "Giovanni Agnelli, Fiat Patriarch, Dies at 81," *New York Times*, January 25, 2003.

8. Lally Weymouth, "On the Razor's Edge: A Portrait of Gianni Agnelli," *Esquire*, June 1978.

9. Arrigo Levi, *Intervista sul Capitalismo Moderno* (Rome: Editori Laterza, 1983), 7.

10. Giovanni Minoli, "Interview with Gianni Agnelli," *Mixer*, RAI-2, March 1, 1984.

11. Christopher Ogden, *Life of the Party: The Biography of Pamela Digby Churchill Hayward Harriman* (Boston: Little, Brown, 1994), 206.

12. Ibid., 219.

13. Wayne Francis and Jon Clarke, "Chateau Putin," *Daily Mirror*, August 31, 2001.

14. Sally Bedell Smith, *Reflected Glory: The Life of Pamela Churchill Harriman* (New York: Touchstone, 1996), 153.

15. Ibid., 153.

16. Ibid., 153.

17. Ogden, *Life of the Party*, 221.

18. Ibid., 227.

19. Ibid., 223.

20. Bedell Smith, *Reflected Glory*, 160.

21. Ogden, *Life of the Party*, 229.

22. *Esquire*, June 1978.

23. Alan Friedman, *Agnelli and the Network of Italian Power* (London: Harrap, 1988), 49.

24. Bedell Smith, *Reflected Glory*, 162.

25. Rena Sanderson, *Hemingway's Italy* (Baton Rouge: Louisiana State University Press, 2006), 28.

26. Arthur Schlesinger, *Jacqueline Kennedy: Historic Conversations on Life with John F. Kennedy*, (New York: Hyperion, 2011), 219.

27. Marco Ferrante, *Casa Agnelli* (Milan: Arnoldo Mondadori Editore, 2007), 36.

28. Bedell Smith, Sally. *Grace and Power: The Private World of the Kennedy White House* (New York: Random House, 2004), 287–290.

29. "Kennedys Begin Vacation," *Chicago Daily News*, August 9, 1962.

30. Ibid.

31. "Mrs. Kennedy Slips Away to Visit a Sidewalk Café," *Chicago Daily News*, August 13, 1962.

32. Kitty Kelley, *Jackie Oh!* (New York: Ballantine Books, 1978), 58.

33. Edward Klein, *Farewell Jackie: A Portrait of Her Final Days* (New York: Viking Penguin, 2004), 151.

34. Bedell Smith, *Grace and Power*, 287–290.

35. Liz Thomas, "Explosive Jackie O Tapes Reveal How She Believed Lyndon B Johnson Killed JFK, Had An Affair With a Movie Star," *The Daily Mail*, August 8, 2011.

36. Liz Smith, "An Off-the-Cuff Talk with Fiat Tycoon," *The Record*, September 12, 1991.

37. Enzo Biagi, *Il Signor Fiat* (Milan: Rizzoli, 1976), 81.

38. Giancarlo Galli, *Gli Agnelli: Tramonto di Una Dinastia* (Milan: Arnoldo Mondadori Editore, 1997), xiv.

39. Biagi, *Il Signor Fiat*, 84.

40. Arrigo Levi, *Intervista sul Capitalismo Moderno* (Rome: Editori Laterza, 1983), 161.

41. Marie-France Pochna, *Agnelli, L'Irresistibile* (Milan: Sperling & Kupfer, 1990), 263.

42. Ibid., 264.

43. Steven Hahn, *A Nation under Our Feet: Black Political Struggles in the Rural South from Slavery to the Great Migration* (Cambridge, MA: Belknap Press/Harvard University Press, 2003), 465.

44. Ibid.

45. Ibid.

46. Levi, *Intervista sul Capitalismo Moderno*, 10.

47. Paul Ginsbourg, *A History of Contemporary Italy, 1943–1980* (London: Penguin, 1990), 35.

48. Galli, *La Storia della DC*, 308.

49. Friedman, *Agnelli and the Network*, 68–69.

50. Ibid., 80.

51. Lally Weymouth, "On the Razor's Edge: A Portrait of Gianni Agnelli," *Esquire*, June 20, 1978.

52. Ginsbourg, *History of Contemporary Italy*, 384.

53. Giampaolo Pansa, *Quest'Anni alla Fiat* (Milan: RCS Rizzoli Libri, 1988), 95.

54. "Quatto Colpi alla Nuca," *La Stampa*, September 21, 1979.

55. Pansa, *Quest'Anni alla Fiat*, 95.

56. Ibid., 97.

57. Friedman, *Agnelli and the Network*, 85.

58. Pansa, *Quest'Anni alla Fiat*, 115.

59. Jennifer Clark, "Focus: Fiat and General Motors Forge Alliance," Reuters, March 13, 2000.

60. Paul Ingrassia, *Crash Course: The American Automobile Industry's Road to Bankruptcy and Bailout—and Beyond* (New York: Random House, 2010), 151.

61. Ibid.

62. Deborah Ball, "Fiat and GM Launch Alliance but Fail to Tackle Overcapacity," *Wall Street Journal*, March 14, 2000.

63. Marcello Sorgi, "Questo E' il Commonwealth dell'Auto," *La Stampa*, March 14, 2000.

64. Ibid.

65. Jennifer Clark, "Agnelli Dynasty on the Wane in Italy's New Economy," *National Post*, March 14, 2000.

**Chapter 5   A Lament like a River**

1. Gianni Minoli, "Edoardo Agnelli—L'Ultimo Volo," *La Storia Siamo Noi*, RAI-2, September 23, 2010, 11:30 P.M.

2. Renato Rizzo, "La Morte di Edoardo Agnelli sul Greto della Stura," *La Stampa*, November 16, 2000.

3. Tollway records in police report.

4. Police report.

5. Police report.

6. Minoli, "Edoardo Agnelli."

7. Luigi Offeddu, "Viveva Sempre Più Appartato con la Sua Grande Passione, una Canzone di Armstrong," *Corriere della Sera*, November 16, 2000.

8. Police report.

9. Ibid.

10. Ibid.

11. Marco Ferrante, *Casa Agnelli* (Milan: Arnoldo Mondadori Editori, 2007), 133.

12. http://marcobava.tk.

13. Minoli, "Edoardo Agnelli."

14. Aldo Cazzullo, "Io e Mio Nonno, Le Prove Coraggio e i Film a Parigi," *Corriere della Sera*, January 28, 2008.

15. Marco Bernardini, *Edoardo, Senza Corona . . . Senza Scorta* (Turin: Spoon River, 2003), 59.

16. Sergio Bocconi, "Sensibile, Inquieto, Curioso, Colto, Fragile," *Corriere della Sera*, November 16, 2000.

17. Giovanni Piperno, *Il Pezzo Mancante* (film produced by Cinecittà Luce and released June 17, 2011).

18. Minoli, "Edoardo Agnelli."

19. Bocconi, "Sensibile, Inquieto."

20. Giovanni Piperno, *Il Pezzo Mancante*.

21. Letters on Marco Bava website (www.marcobava.eu).

22. Letter on Marco Bava website dated November 16, 1993 (www.marcobava.eu).

23. Alan Friedman, "Fiat's Crown Prince Takes Aim at Old Guard," *International Herald Tribune*, April 9, 1996.

24. Interview with Franscesco Profumo, Dean of Turin Politecnico.

25. Nicola Caracciolo, "Agnelli," *La Grande Storia*, RAI-3, aired December 30, 1999 at 8:30 P.M.

26. "Face Value: Dynasty Calls," *Economist*, May 10, 2008.

27. Aldo Cazzullo, "Io e Mio Nonno, Le Prove Coraggio e i film a Parigi," *Corriere della Sera*, January 24, 2008.

28. Ibid.

29. Minoli, "Edoardo Agnelli."

30. Salvatore Tropea, "Fiat, Vince la Continuità," *La Repubblica*, December 19, 1997.

31. Raffaella Polato and Giacomo Ferrari, "Fiat, l'Avvocato Chiama John Elkann," *Corriere della Sera*, December 19, 1997.

32. Minoli, "Edoardo Agnelli."

33. Salvatore Tropea, "Edoardo Agnelli Sfida il Padre Sulla Nomina di Iachi in Fiat," *La Repubblica*, January 16, 1998.

34. Minoli, "Edoardo Agnelli."

35. Vera Schiavazzi, "Il Delfino Dell'Avvocato E' Già Nella New Economy," *La Repubblica*, December 16, 2000.

36. Gianni Oliva, *I Savoia* (Milan: Arnoldo Mondadori Editore, 1998), 13.

37. Ibid., 15.

## Chapter 6 Only One Person Rules at a Time

1. "Agnelli, Ancora un Abbraccio Tra Famiglia e Torino," ANSA, February 23, 2003.

2. Gigi Moncalvo, *I Lupi & Gli Agnelli* (Florence: Vallecchi, 2009), 151.

3. Mark Seal, "The Woman Who Wanted the Secrets," *Vanity Fair*, August 2008.

4. Ibid.

5. Text of letter from Agnelli dated July 17, 1996.

6. Moncalvo, *I Lupi*, 160.

7. Ibid., 162.

8. Emanuele Gamna, *M: L'Importanza di Chiarmarsi Agnelli* (Milan: Milano Finanza, 2011), 93, 112.

9. Ibid., 205.

10. Paolo Griseri, Massimo Novelli, and Marco Travaglio, *Processo Alla Fiat* (Rome: Nuova Iniziativa Editoriale, 1997), 126–156.

11. Raffaella Polato, "Gabetti Riapre il Caso Agnelli," *Corriere della Sera*, December 4, 2008.

12. Ibid.

13. Moncalvo, *I Lupi*, 162.

14. Marigia Mangano, "Patti e Donazioni per Blindare Dicembre," *Il Sole-24 Ore*, July 29, 2007.

15. Seal, "Woman Who Wanted Secrets."

16. Moncalvo, *I Lupi*, 163.

17. Marie-France Pochna, *Agnelli, L'Irresistibile* (Milan: Sperling & Kupfer, 1990), 381.

18. Ibid., 381–382.

19. Moncalvo, *I Lupi*, 26.

20. Pochna, *Agnelli, L'Irresistibile*, 384.

21. Moncalvo, *I Lupi*, 32.

22. Ibid., 35.

23. Maria Latella, "Io, un Agnelli Lontano dei Riflettori," *Corriere della Sera*, September 8, 1997.

24. "Fiat—John Elkann; Margherita Agnelli," ANSA, December 18, 1997.

25. Gamna, *M: L'Importanza*, 175.

26. Ibid., 179.

27. Ibid., 182.

28. Ibid., 182.

29. Ibid., 184.

30. Ibid., 197.

31. Ibid., 207.

32. Ibid., 214–215.

33. Ibid., 311.

34. Published copy of pact in court documents.

35. Gamna, *M: L'Importanza*, 214.

36. Ibid., 222.

37. Moncalvo, *I Lupi*, 235.

## Chapter 7   The Wedding of the Year

1. Antonella Piperno, "Unioni Eccellenti: Il Matrimonio di John Elkann e Lavinia Borromeo," *Panorama*, August 27, 2004.

2. Aldo Cazzullo, "Vi Svelo Quando John, Lapo e io . . . ," *Io Donna*, March 10, 2010.

3. Luciano Regolo, "Lavinia e John Elkann, Nozze di Pace," *Chi*, September 15, 2004.

4. Maria Combi, "La Ceremonia Riservata, Poi una Grande Festa sull'Isola Bella le Nozze di Elkann-Borromeo," *La Stampa*, September 5, 2004.

5. Ibid.

6. Regolo, "Lavinia e John Elkann."

7. Combi, "La Ceremonia Riservata."

8. Regolo, "Lavinia e John Elkann."

9. Maria Volpe, "Anche uno Splendido Sole," *Corriere della Sera*, September 5, 2004.

10. Combi, "La Ceremonia Riservata."

11. Regolo, "Lavinia e John Elkann."

12. Ibid.

13. Ibid.

14. Gabriel Kahn, "Agnelli Heir Files Lawsuit against Dad's Consiglieri," *Wall Street Journal*, May 31, 2007.

15. Mario Gerevini, "La Verità di Marella e Gabetti, 'Agnelli Gestiva da Solo i Suoi Beni,'" *Corriere della Sera*, August 27, 2009.

16. Jennifer Clark and Milena Vercellino, "Agnelli Lawsuit on Estate Dismissed," *Wall Street Journal*, March 18, 2010.

## Chapter 8 Unfixable Fiat

1. Giuseppe Oddo, "Fiat, Summit con Banche e IFI," *Il Sole-24 Ore*, May 26, 2002.

2. Jennifer Clark, "Fiat's Top Three Creditors Meet to Discuss Co's Health," Dow Jones Newswires, May 25, 2002.

3. Oddo, "Fiat, Summit con Banche e IFI."

4. "Last Chance Saloon—Troubled Fiat," *Economist,* May 2, 2002.

5. Alessandra Galloni and Marcus Walker, "Banker Seeks to Loosen Mediobanca's Grip over Italian Finance," *Wall Street Journal*, July 22, 2003.

6. Luca Ciferri, "Umberto Gets His Wish—Cantarella Is Gone," *Automotive News Europe*, June 17, 2002.

7. Alexander Stille, *The Sack of Rome* (New York: Penguin, 2006), 33.

8. Michael Bergmeijer, "Fiat's 1990 Earnings May Fall Short of Early Forecasts Due to Weak 2nd Half," *Wall Street Journal*, January 21, 1991.

9. Exor trial documents.

10. Franco Bechis, "Berlusconi Mette Paletii a Italauto," *MF*, October 15, 2002.

11. Deborah Ball, "It Takes Two to Retool Fiat," *Wall Street Journal*, March 17, 2000.

12. Giuseppe Volpato, *Fiat Group Automobiles: Un'Araba Fenice nell'Industria Automobilistica* (Bologna: Il Mulino, 2008), 81.

13. Ibid., 30.

14. Luke Baker with Jennifer Clark, "Update: Italy Court Finds Ex-Fiat Chief Guilty," Reuters, October 19, 2000.

15. Volpato, *Fiat Group Automobiles*, 75.

16. Enrico Manoja, "Domenica sera a Villa Frescot il Benservito dell'Avvocato," *La Repubblica*, December 10, 2002.

17. Ibid.

18. Robert Cox, "Fixing Fiat," *Institutional Investor*, May 1, 2003.

19. Manoja, "Domenica."

20. Ibid.

21. Exor trial court documents, IFIL document.

22. Paolo Panerai, "Orsi & Tori," *Milano Finanza*, December 14, 2002.

23. Jennifer Clark, "Fiat's Fresco Says Management Shakeup an Error—Report," Dow Jones Newswires, December 11, 2002.

24. Luca Ciferri, "Fiat Platform Strategy Remains Fragmented: Problems at Saab Haven't Helped Italian Automaker as It Searches for Synergies with Partner General Motors," *Automotive News Europe*, June 30, 2003.

25. Ibid.

26. Ibid.

**Chapter 9    Running on Empty**

1. Paola Antonelli and Steven Guarnaccia, *Achille Castiglioni* (Mantua: Corraini Editore, 2001).

2. Gail Edmondson, "Fiat: Running on Empty," *BusinessWeek*, May 13, 2002.

3. Alessia Cruciani, "Fiat Ora si Lascia Tentare dalla Moda," *Gazzetta dello Sport*, December 18, 2003.

4. Alessandra Galloni, "Fiat's New Recovery Plan Calls for Plant Closings, Fresh Capital," *Wall Street Journal*, June 27, 2003.

5. Francesca Delogu, "Con Lapo Elkann Nasce la Felpa Vintage Fiat," *MF Fashion*, December 18, 2003.

6. Paul and Anita Lienert, "Innovative Concepts Steal the Limelight," *Detroit News*, March 10, 2004.

7. Piero Di Bianco, "Oggi a Ginevra Periodica Incontro di Verifica con L'alleato USA," *La Stampa*, March 4, 2004.

8. www.caroftheyear.org/previous-winners/2004_1/coty.

9. Luca Ciferri, "Outsider Shakes Up Fiat, Brings Other Outsiders on Board to Help," *Automotive News*, December 2003.

10. Yaroslav Trofimov, "Pirelli Will Split Division into Two Separate Units," *Wall Street Journal*, December 29, 2000.

11. Alessandra Galloni, "Fiat Unveils New Recovery Plan," *Wall Street Journal*, June 27, 2003.

12. *Umberto Agnelli, Verso Le XXI Secolo, Parole e Immagini* (Turin: Editrice La Stampa, 2009), 203.

13. Mario Rosso, "Fiat, Sconfitta Annunciata," *Corriere della Sera*, March 10, 2003.

14. Christian Plumb, "Fiat Workers Fear Future After Agnelli Dies," Reuters, May 28, 2004.

15. Pierluigi Bonora, "Torino Saluta il Dottore al Centro Storico Fiat," *Il Giornale*, May 29, 2004.

16. "Domani Lutto Cittadino a Torino," AGI, May 28, 2004.

17. "Un Cuscino di Peonie Bianche sulla Bara," AGI, May 29, 2004.

18. Christian Plumb and Illario Polleschi, "Thousands Pay Last Respects to Fiat's Agnelli," Reuters, May 29, 2004.

19. Raffaella Polato, "Allegra e i Suoi Figli, un Saluto per Tutti," *Corriere della Sera*, May 30, 2004.

20. "Agnelli, Camera Ardente, Tanti i Vip, Anche la Juve," Reuters, May 29, 2004.

21. Ibid.

22. Salvatore Tropea, "Montezemolo Scelta Mediatica, Ero Io il Capo Azienda Giusto," *La Repubblica*, June 3, 2004.

23. "Anno Zero," RAI-3, May 14, 2009.

**Chapter 10   You Deal with It, and You Move On**

1. Gianni Oliva, *Foibe* (Milan: Arnoldo Mondadori Editore, 2002), 50.

2. Ibid., 33.

3. www.arcipelagoadriatico.it/sommario.php?id=00042&sel=INTERVISTE& mese=09&anno=2007.

4. Ibid.

5. Oliva, *Foibe*, 55.

6. Ibid., 59.

7. Ibid., 61.

8. Ibid., 62.

9. Ibid., 17.

10. Marco Gregoretti, *L'Uomo dal Maglione Nero* (Milan: Milano Finanza, 2009), 13.

11. Ibid., 37.

12. Speaking to Mario Calabresi at the Turin Book Fair, May 16, 2009.

13. Massimo Ciavolella and Amilcare Iannucci, eds. *Quaderni di Italianistica*, vol. 2, no. 1 (Toronto: Canadian Society for Italian Studies, 1981).

14. Andrea Malan, "Sergio? Il Miglior Negoziatore," *Il Sole-24 Ore*, May 3, 2009.

15. Lawson Mardon press statement, November 15, 1993.

16. Margaret Studer, "A-L Promotes Marchionne, Fueling Rise in Share Price," *Wall Street Journal*, November 6, 1996.

17. Peter Nielsen, "Alusuisse Reorganizes, but No Spinoff," Reuters, July 4, 1997.

18. "Alusuisse Seen Staying Independent—Analysts," Reuters, March 10, 1998.

19. Charles Fleming and Margaret Studer, "Algroup's CEO Takes a Back Seat— For Now," *Wall Street Journal*, August 23, 1999.

20. Parris Kellermann, "Algroup Succeeds with Merger after Failure," *Globe and Mail*, August 12, 1999.

21. Fleming and Studer, "Algroup's CEO."

22. "Kingmakers Decided on Top Jobs in Aluminum Merger," Reuters, August 11, 1999.

23. John Tagliabue, "Alcan Revises Its Blueprint for Giant Aluminum Merger," *New York Times*, April 14, 2000.

24. Luca de Meo, *Da Zero a 500* (Venice: Marsilio Editore, 2010), 46.

25. Eric Reguly, "Fiat Gets a Marchionne Makeover," *Globe and Mail*, July 21, 2007.

26. Clara Ferreira-Marques, "Fiat's Auto Unit Shakes Up Management Structure," Reuters, September 1, 2004.

27. Walter Bennis, *Organizing Genius: The Secrets of Creative Collaboration* (London: Nicolas Brealey, 1997), 43.

28. Luca Ciferri, "Marchionne Helps Demel Fix Fiat Auto; Group CEO Takes Sales and Dealers; A Role for Leach?" *Automotive News*, November 29, 2004.

29. Nestore Morosini, "Ferrari, il Centro per la Ricerca Disegnato da Fuskas," *Corriere della Sera*, June 24, 2004.

### Chapter 11    Sergio Marchionne's Two-Billion-Dollar Bet

1. Vito Racanelli, "European Trader: Fiat Test-Drives a New CEO," *Barron's*, July 26, 2004.

2. Conference call transcript.

3. Gabriel Kahn, "Fiat Turnaround Hits Bump—CEO Insists Option to Sell Car Business to GM Remains 'Valid,'" *Wall Street Journal*, July 27, 2004.

4. "Q2 Fiat SpA Earnings Presentation & Conference Call," *Fair Disclosure Wire*, July 26, 2004.

5. Serena Saitto, "Detroit Suburb Beckons Fiat Executives with $1,595 Sandals," *Bloomberg News*, June 8, 2009.

6. Lee Hawkins Jr., "GM to Take $1 Billion in Quarterly Charges," *Wall Street Journal*, January 19, 2005.

7. David Pearson, "GM Says European Car-Making Overcapacity Will Be Cut," Dow Jones Newswires, September 22, 2004.

8. Jane Barrett, "Fiat CEO Says Won't Delay GM Put Option," Reuters, September 21, 2004.

9. Marco Gregoretti, *Il Uomo del Maglione Nero* (Milan: Milano Finanza, 2009), 17.

### Chapter 12    A Completely Different Beast

1. Press reports.

2. Fiat press release, July 22, 2005.

3. Exor trial documents.

4. Gianluigi Gabetti, in a television interview on May 14, 2009, "Anno Zero," RAI-3.

5. Ibid.

6. Ibid.

7. Ettore Boffano and Paolo Griseri, "Tutti i Documenti dell'Affare IFIL-Exor," *La Repubblica,* June 13, 2007.

8. E-mails in Exor trial file.

9. Documents in Exor trial file.

10. Rosario Dimito, "Fiat, No Delle Banche a Lehman," *MF,* April 27, 2005.

11. Raffaella Polato, "Gabetti: Gli Agnelli Resteranno Soci di Riferimento Fiat," *Corriere della Sera,* April 28, 2005.

12. Document in Exor trial file.

13. Ibid.

14. Ibid.

15. Ibid.

16. Ibid.

17. Ibid.

18. Ibid.

19. Ibid.

20. Ibid.

21. "Still in the Driving Seat: How the Agnelli Family Retained Control of Fiat," *Economist,* October 13, 2005.

22. Kenneth Maxwell, "Italian Regulator Fines IFIL over Fiat Share Deal," *Wall Street Journal Europe*, February 14, 2007.

23. Mo.Ma, "Grande Stevens, Così Fiat si è Salvata," *Il Sole-24 Ore,* October 7, 2005.

24. "IFIL-Exor: Gabetti, un Incidente di Mestiere," ANSA, November 14, 2007.

25. Luca de Meo, *Da Zero a 500* (Venice: Marsilio Editore, 2010), 67.

26. Aldo Grasso, "La Nuova Cinquecento e l'Unità d'Italia," *Corriere della Sera,* July 6, 2007.

27. "Fiat 500: Sul Tetto del Lingotto Anteprime per Prodi," ANSA, July 4, 2007.

28. "Fiat, Prodi: I Hope They Sell Many Many of Them," AP.Com, July 4, 2007.

29. "Fiat 500: Damiani, E' Stata La Mia Prima Macchina," ANSA, July 4, 2007.

30. Emanuela Minucci, "500 Day Personaggi," *La Stampa*, July 6, 2007.

31. "Fiat 500: Uno Show Tra Tecnologia e Realtà," AGI, July 5, 2007.

32. De Meo, *Da Zero*, 69.

33. "Fiat 500: Montezemolo a Fina Festa, Sospiro di Sollievo," *AGI*, July 5, 2007.

## Chapter 13 Skin in the Game

1. Daniel Roth, "The Most Dangerous Deal in America," *Portfolio*, September 2007.

2. Ibid.

3. "Sen. Christopher J. Dodd Holds a Hearing on the U.S. Auto Industry," *CQ Transcriptions*, December 4, 2008.

4. Steven Rattner, *Overhaul: An Insider's Account of the Obama Administration's Rescue of the Auto Industry* (New York: Houghton Mifflin Harcourt, 2010), 30.

5. Ibid., 31.

6. Ibid., 31.

7. Ibid., 31.

8. Ibid., 31.

9. Ibid., 5.

10. Ryan Lizza, "Inside the Crisis: Larry Summers and the White House Economic Team," *New Yorker*, October 12, 2009.

11. Ibid.

12. "Sen. Christopher J. Dodd Holds a Hearing on the U.S. Auto Industry," *CQ Transcriptions,* December 4, 2008.

13. Ibid.

14. Ibid.

15. Viability plan on Chrysler website (www.chryslerllc.com).

16. Tom Walsh, "Through It All, LaSorda Stays True to Auto Roots," *Detroit Free Press*, December 20, 2009.

17. Chrysler bankruptcy filing.

18. Ibid.

19. Ibid.

20. Geoff Colvin, "Nardelli's Downfall: It's All about the Stock," *Fortune*, January 3, 2007.

21. Katie Merx, "Stock Falls to $9.98: Dire Outlook Sends GM Shares to 54-Year Low," *Detroit Free Press*, July 3, 2008.

22. Chrysler bankruptcy filing.

23. Ibid.

24. Rattner, *Overhaul*, 26.

25. Neal Boudette and John Stoll, "Chrysler Faces Massive Cuts in a GM Deal," *Wall Street Journal*, October 31, 2008.

26. Jeff Bennett, "Cerberus to Restart Talks After GM Merger Stalls," Dow Jones Newswires, November 7, 2008.

27. Giancarlo Galli, *Gli Agnelli, il Tramonto di una Dinastia* (Milan: Arnoldo Mondadori Editore, 1997), 246.

28. Paolo Madron, "Fiat, Squadra Che Vince Non Si Cambia," *Il Sole-24 Ore*, November 30, 2008.

29. Rattner, *Overhaul*, 86.

30. Ibid., 91.

31. Jennifer Clark, "Focus: Fiat and General Motors Forge Alliance," Reuters, March 13, 2000.

32. Chrysler bankruptcy filing.

33. Rattner, *Overhaul*, 93.

34. Ingrassia, *Crash Course*, 249.

35. Ibid., 250.

36. Rattner, *Overhaul*, 139.

37. Ibid., 156.

38. Ibid., 149.

39. Ibid., 150.

40. Ibid., 143.

41. Ingrassia, *Crash Course*, 201.

42. Rattner, *Overhaul*, 156.

43. Ingrassia, *Crash Course*, 252.

## Chapter 14    The Spirit of Ubuntu: I See You

1. Corporate video.

2. Bill Vlasic and Bradley Stertz, *Taken for a Ride: How Daimler-Benz Drove Off with Chrysler* (New York: HarperCollins, 2000), 352.

3. Paul Ingrassia and Joseph B. White, *Comeback: The Fall and Rise of the American Automobile Industry* (New York: Touchstone, 1994), 176.

4. Dee-Ann Durbin, "Chrysler Announces New Incentives in Detroit Price War," Associated Press, November 18, 2005.

5. Matthias Krust, "Chrysler Lowers 2006 Sales Outlook," Dow Jones Newswires, September 28, 2006.

6. Amy Wilson, "No More Push: How Detroit Stopped Overproducing," *Automotive News*, February 8, 2010.

7. David Halberstam, *The Reckoning* (New York: Avon Books, 1986), 555.

8. Ibid., 563.

9. Chrysler Securities and Exchange Commission (SEC) filing, February 25, 2011.

10. Amy Wilson, "No More Push: How Detroit Stopped Overproducing," *Automotive News*, February 8, 2010.

11. Kate Linebaugh, "Chrysler Mulls Changing Incentive Plan to Double Government Rebate—Sources," *Wall Street Journal*, August 1, 2009.

12. Steven Rattner, *Overhaul: An Insider's Account of the Obama Administration's Rescue of the Auto Industry* (New York: Houghton Mifflin Harcourt, 2010), 157.

13. Kate Linebaugh and Stacy Meichtry, "More Losses Ahead for Chrysler: Fiat Chief Sees Red Ink in Short Term but Aims to Ready U.S. Car Maker for Offering," *Wall Street Journal*, July 23, 2009.

14. Kate Linebaugh and Jeff Bennett, "Marchionne Upends Chrysler's Ways— CEO Decries Detroit's 'Fanatical' Focus on Market Share; Deep Discounts Are Out," *Wall Street Journal*, January 12, 2010.

15. Frank Williams, "The Big 2.5's Fleet Sales Fiasco," Truth about Cars, April 25, 2007, www.thetruthaboutcars.com.

16. Ken Bensinger, "Chrysler Dumps 2 Execs, Splits Dodge Brand," *Los Angeles Times*, October 6, 2009.

17. Aaron Bragman, "Two Chrysler Brand Chiefs Resign, Dodge Officially Splits Up," *IHS Global Insight Daily Analysis*, October 6, 2009.

18. Alisa Priddle, "Chrysler Builds Cars the Fiat Way," *Detroit News*, June 10, 2010.

19. Ibid.

20. Shawn Langlois, "Rebuilding Chrysler," *Chicago Tribune*, November 15, 2009.

21. Greg Gardener, "AutoNation Chief Backs Chrysler Plan," *Detroit Free Press*, November 6, 2009.

22. Ibid.

**Chapter 15   Sixteen Models in 14 Months**

1. Grace Macaluso, "Money Well Spent; Chrysler CEO Says Investments Will Pay Off," *Windsor Star*, January 12, 2010.

2. Daniel Howes, "Marchionne Steers New Course for Chrysler," *Detroit News*, January 13, 2010.

3. Jerry Hirsch, "A Plan to Remake Chrysler by Fiat," *Los Angeles Times*, January 12, 2010.

4. Paul Clements, "Dismantling Detroit," *New York Times*, September 28, 2007.

5. Alisa Priddle, "Chrysler Adds 1,100 Jobs to Build New Cherokee," *Detroit News*, May 22, 2010.

6. David Shepardson, "Obama Touts Detroit Autoworkers," *Detroit News*, July 31, 2010.

7. Ibid.

8. Bradford Wernle, "Chrysler Becomes Rent a Car King: Nearly Half of Brand's Sales Are to Fleets," *Automotive News*, April 23, 2007.

9. Dave Guilford, "Chrysler Presses On in New Direction," *Automotive News*, October 15, 2007.

10. Bradford Wernle, "Chrysler Dealers Flock to Meet Marchionne, at Last," *Automotive News*, September 13, 2010.

11. David Kiley, "How Chrysler Chief Olivier Francois Is Selling Detroit," *Advertising Age*, February 21, 2011.

12. Ibid.

13. U.S. Federal News Service, readout of Biden's speech, May 24, 2011.

## Epilogue

1. Tim Huggins, "Chrysler Adds Fiat 500 Times Sqaure Drive-in as Sales Set to Miss Target," *Bloomberg News*, August 12, 2011.

2. David Landes, *Dynasties: Fortunes and Misfortunes of the World's Great Family Businesses* (New York: Viking, 2006).

# Acknowledgments

O
ne of my earliest memories of Italy was watching Gianni Agnelli at a gala dinner in the mid-1980s, gliding through the crowd with the effortless and graceful ease of a powerful yacht. I was captivated, and slightly flustered by the sensation. Years later, at the end of 2007, as I hunched over a computer screen helping edit a story about Fiat's amazing recovery, I realized what a whacking good story it all was. "I should write a book about it," I thought. The process of turning a series of impressions or desires into a shelf-ready editorial product has been the result of family, friends, colleagues, and acquaintances each committing random or serial acts of kindness. I am deeply grateful to every last one of them.

At Dow Jones & Company, my professional home for the past 10 years, I would like to thank Marcus Wright, Gren Manuel, and Robert Thompson for having generously granted me a year's absence from a very busy news bureau. Their unwavering commitment to hard-headed newsgathering and storytelling has been an inspiration to me again and again. Art Mooradian sorted through the Italian paperwork my leave entailed with his usual good humor.

A heartfelt thank-you goes to my bureau chief, Alessandra Galloni, and my comrades in arms in Milan and Rome for their forbearance every time they looked at my empty desk while I was away on leave: Christopher Emsden, Sabrina Cohen, Liam Moloney, Giada Zampano, Gilles Castonguay, and Stacy Meichtry. Their pithy and pointed opinions on this tale were and are a continual source of amazement and stimulation. My colleagues at the *Wall Street Journal* in Detroit, Jeff Bennett and Neal Boudette, weighed in with auto industry intelligence, help, and encouragement.

My agent, Jane Dystel, and her partner, Miriam Goderich, at Dystel & Goderich Literary Management, took my hastily cobbled-together book proposal and helped me turn it into a commercial prospect, and then guided me through the manuscript process with expert hands. At John Wiley & Sons, my editor, Debra Englander, made the decision to fast-track the manuscript through production when Chrysler's turnaround came out of the gate faster than anyone had imagined. Developmental editor Emilie Herman toiled endlessly to polish, prune, primp, and prod my mass of text into a fine-looking manuscript, for which I am grateful. Production editor Vincent Nordhaus pushed the manuscript through production at a speed that would give Chrysler a run for their money. Vicki Satlow at Vicki Satlow Literary Agency in Milan deserves a special mention for her early advice on my first attempt at a book proposal.

I had covered Fiat off and on for years as an Italy-based correspondent, but trying to navigate the highways and back alleys of "planet Fiat" was another matter entirely. A huge thank-you goes to Richard Gadeselli at Fiat and Gualberto Ranieri at Chrysler for their endless patience in replying to all questions big and small, and for organizing my many visits to offices, museums, and factories, as well as sharing their insights and knowledge of the company with me. Likewise for the Exor press office—which, in keeping with its Turinese upbringing, has asked me not to mention individuals by name.

When it came time to start my research, interviews would often end with the subject shaking his or her head and saying to me, "Ah, but to understand that, you need to understand *Turin*." Each Italian city is almost a world unto itself, with its own food, dialect, patron saints, and lore, and the clueless foreigner doesn't really stand a chance.

Little did they know I had a secret weapon: Milena Vercellino, a bilingual Italian journalist who grew up in Turin before setting out for the United States and London. Not only did Milena prove invaluable at tracking down the material I needed to write large portions of this book, but she also conducted many interviews, did fact-checking, and helped with photos. Last but not least, she was able to translate my vague and increasingly panicked ramblings about "more color" or "more documents" into coherent and actionable requests.

A key guide to unlocking the secrets of Turin was Marco Bava, who generously shared his invaluable knowledge of the ins and outs of the Agnelli empire with me.

I am eternally grateful to Massimo Novelli, journalist at *La Repubblica* and prolific author, most recently of *La Cambiale dei Mille*, who opened the door to his office whenever I was in town, which was often. He shared obscure books, tidbits of knowledge, sources, observations, and many a good meal with me.

Journalist Sofia Celeste in Rome expertly navigated what I imagined to be the dusty corridors of the Archivio di Stato to hunt out Mussolini-era records tracking the Agnelli family comings and goings of that period. She also provided hand-holding at certain key junctions that shall remain between us.

Being a first-time author is, at times, like being at sea without a compass. I could not have put together my book without Deborah Ball at the *Wall Street Journal*, the author of *House of Versace: The Untold Story of Genius, Murder and Survival*, who tirelessly gave me advice throughout the proposal, writing, and editing period. No one could ask for a better friend, literary mentor, and colleague. I am grateful to two more authors who shared their experience with me: former *Wall Street Journal* colleague Teri Agins, who wrote *The End of Fashion: How Marketing Changed the Clothing Business Forever*, and Sara Gay Forden, a dear friend and an inspiration in more ways than one, whose *House of Gucci: A Sensational Story of Murder, Madness, Glamour and Greed* sat on my desk close at hand throughout, and who was unstinting with tips and advice.

If a first-time author is at sea without a compass, my safe harbor was the Foreign Press Club, or Stampa Estera, where Betti Grassi's dedication, hard work, and smiling face were a constant source of comfort to me when deadlines loomed. Many thanks to Dominique Muret, Michael

Day, Emily Backus, Betta Povoledo, Eric Sylvers, and the all the rest of the *stranieri* there who welcomed me into the fold. I couldn't have asked for a more congenial place to tap away in peace. Computer wizard Davide Mandelli helped me coax my laptop into speaking English to me instead of Italian and performed many other wonders besides.

My research took me to New York, Detroit, and Washington, D.C., as well as to Switzerland, France, Rome, and Turin. I shamelessly took advantage of the hospitality of friends for as long as they would put up with me. I would like to thank Jacqueline Daldin; Constance Klein; Sara Forden (also for her editing); Jon Clark, his wife, and the "bump"; Colleen Barry; Giovanna Camozzi; and Gene Rizzo for their encouragement and generosity. Many thanks also to Gérard Charpin at the Chambery Tourist Office for organizing my visit to Chambery, and my guide, Isabelle Lafay.

I relied on the expertise of many Italian or Italy-based journalists whose work helped me understand Italy, the Agnellis, and Fiat. Paolo Panerai, Luca Ciferri, Marco Ferrante, Gabriella Mecucci, Marie-France Pochna, William Ward, Gian Luca Pellegrini, Mario Gerevini, Stefano Caratelli, Gabriele La Monica, Alessandro Mocenni, Noris Morano, and Fiat historian Valeria Castronovo gave me insights in print and in person I could never have gleaned on my own. In Detroit, I found the knowledge of Alicia Priddle and Christina Rogers to be essential in putting together the pieces of the puzzle. Rhonda Welsh at Detroit's College for Creative Studies gave me a peek at a piece of Detroit history that helped shape my understanding of the city.

In Milan, Mauro Chiabrando was a lifesaver for his help in locating out-of-print books, as was Paola Marinoni at the Biblioteca Sormanni. Pierpaolo Righero at the Archivio e Centro Storico Fiat patiently helped us retrieve many a document, as did Mariapina di Simone at the Archivio di Stato. Matteo Noja at the Biblioteca di Via Senato went out of his way to be both courteous and helpful.

I had always read that the creative process is a selfish and solitary one, and now I know that to be true. I can add, at this point, that the process is also extremely unfair. Friends and family who have shared the burden of a self-absorbed author rattling on about research and writing do not get to bow in the limelight. But nothing of true value is ever accomplished alone. My deepest thanks therefore go to my sister Melissa Clark Nielsen, for giving me the push (kick?) I needed to get started; my brother Jon Clark for his patience, humor, and expert advice; and my mother, Marilyn Clark, for teaching me the value of hard work and the rewards of optimism, and for reading me all those bedtime stories. And of course my dear father, John Clark, whose kindness and lively intellect are greatly missed by all who knew him.

My warmest thanks also to my husband Dino's family—Gemma, Maria, Antonella, and Riccardo—for all their encouragement, advice, and unflagging interest in this project. Finally, my husband Dino has been an ideal companion in life, love, and work, offering every sort of help and guidance imaginable, usually even before I realized I would need it. Without him, this book would not exist.

# About the Author

JENNIFER CLARK for 10 years until 2010 was the Italian Bureau Chief for Dow Jones & Company, which covers all aspects of Italian business, politics, and finance for the *Wall Street Journal*, the WSJ.com website, and Dow Jones Newswires. Prior to working at Dow Jones, Clark was a banking reporter at Reuters in Milan, and documented Silvio Berlusconi's entry into politics at Bloomberg News in the early part of the 1990s. From 1988 to 1993, she was bureau chief at *Variety*, the U.S. entertainment weekly, covering the Rome-based film and television industries.

# Index

347